SAM HOUSTON

SAM HOUSTON

The Life and Times of
the Liberator of Texas,
an Authentic American Hero

by JOHN HOYT WILLIAMS

First Promontory Press edition published in 1998.

Promontory Press
A division of BBS Publishing Corporation
386 Park Avenue South
New York, NY 10016

Promontory Press is a registered trademark of BBS Publishing Corporation.

Published by arrangement with Simon & Schuster, Inc.

Designed by Karolina Harris.

Library of Congress Catalog Card Number: 97-77431
ISBN: 0-88394-100-7

Photo credits:
1, 3-19: C. Barker Texas History Center,
University of Texas at Austin
2: The Bettmann Archive

Printed in the United States of America.

ACKNOWLEDGMENTS

It is both my obligation and my pleasure to give credit to the people who were helpful to me in the preparation of this book, people sprinkled liberally from Austin, Texas, to London, England. They are too many to name. For thoroughly professional courtesy and help I am indebted to the staffs of the Eugene C. Barker Texas History Center at Austin, the South Carolina Historical Society at Charleston, the Lilly Library at Bloomington, Indiana, the British Museum and Public Record Office, London, and the patient and savvy ladies of the Inter-Library Loan Department of my own Indiana State University. These dozens of people were all that a scholar might wish. My thanks are also due to the American Philosophical Society and the Indiana State University Research Committee for financial support for this research endeavor. There are disparate individuals who also proferred help that facilitated the writing of this book, and I must single out John Slate of the University of Texas, Robert Gottlieb, and my editor, Bob Bender, in New York, Jordan Laffoday, of Mount Pleasant, South Carolina and Clyde Weaver of Landrum, South Carolina. My family eased my burdens in a thousand ways, and to them I owe perhaps the greatest debt; my wife Martha, daughter Elisabeth and son Owen, all, in their very different manners, inspired me with their wit, grace and charm. I thank them deeply.

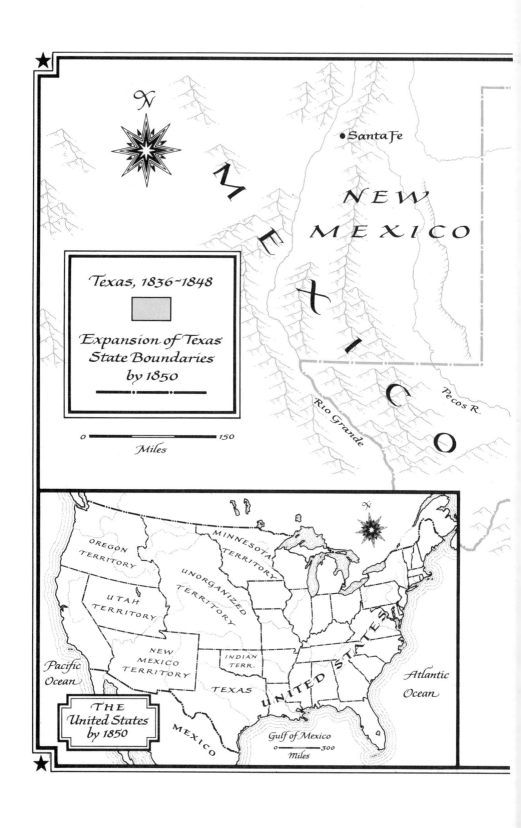

N

•Santa Fe

NEW MEXICO

Texas, 1836~1848

Expansion of Texas
State Boundaries
by 1850

0 ———— 150
Miles

Rio Grande

Pecos R.

N

OREGON TERRITORY

MINNESOTA TERRITORY

UNORGANIZED TERRITORY

UTAH TERRITORY

NEW MEXICO TERRITORY

INDIAN TERR.

TEXAS

UNITED STATES

Pacific Ocean

Atlantic Ocean

THE
United States
by 1850

MEXICO

Gulf of Mexico

0 ——— 300
Miles

For my daughter, Elisabeth

CONTENTS

INTRODUCTION

In the swirling, roiling smoke of that April 21, 1836, battle, Sam Houston, riding before his screaming men, sword glistening in his hand, reeled in his saddle, his breath torn from him by pain. A Mexican musket ball had shattered his right leg just above the ankle, smashing bone, tearing cartilage and pushing pieces of torn boot leather deep into the mangled flesh. Somehow he stayed in the saddle and within minutes knew that the day was won, as his sprinting Texians cleared the Mexican barricade, shooting, stabbing and clubbing, and drove the enemy before them disorganized and almost helpless with fear. Only after the victory did he allow himself, dazed and weak, to be lowered from his horse and taken back to camp. Before the sun set less than two hours later, he knew that his defeat of General Antonio López de Santa Anna, the legendary "Napoleon of the West," had been total, and that he had saved Texas. A new era dawned.

Sam Houston before the Battle of San Jacinto had served his state, his nation and his province well. He had been almost mortally wounded in the War of 1812, a lieutenant in the Regular Army of the United States, an Indian agent, a district attorney, a militia major general, a congressman, a governor, and a signer of the Texas Declaration of Independence and commander of its rebel army. His latest wound healed, he would go on to be twice president of the independent Republic of Texas, a member of that nation's Congress, a United States senator for thirteen years, a strong contender for the White House, and again a governor, his last tenure cut short by the Civil War he had predicted and striven mightily to prevent. Throughout most of his adult life he was also a visionary, schemer and expansionist, who fairly lusted to conquer Mexico, and at times Central America and Cuba as well.

Sam Houston's life was an exciting one, but it had its share of failures. One marriage early soured and discarded, a fruitful second union produced eight children but could not keep him at home or involved. He excited thousands with his visions of conquest to the south, yet usually confounded them with vacillation and doubt. While he rallied hundreds of thousands with his quest for the presidency, the outcome was similarly disenchanting.

If, as is sometimes claimed, a man is known by the enemies he makes, Sam Houston was indeed famous, for arrayed against him at various times was a veritable pantheon of famous Americans: John C. Calhoun, John Quincy Adams, Martin Van Buren and Jefferson Davis among them. Had Houston accepted dueling invitations, he would have had little free time for public service. An egotist, he had a negative talent for generating anger and criticism, and even his hour of triumph at San Jacinto produced a long-lasting debate in which almost half of the officers present accused him of indecision and even cowardice.

Sam Houston chopped his way roughly through the underbrush of life, leaving behind a wide trail of detritus. Few confidants were privy to his true thoughts and plans, and he viciously assailed those who attempted to guess at them. President of Texas, he might have been president of the United States, yet he threw away his chances for the White House as he cast aside opportunities for which he had labored to conquer Mexico. He appeared to many to be a man for all occasions, but he was not. A flawed giant, he often stepped onto the stage and froze.

The duality of the man is what most drew me to Sam Houston years ago. It appeared that he had been contradiction incarnate. Even the victory at San Jacinto, which guaranteed him a prominent place in American history, generated a tidal wave of vicious character assassination by men who had shared that triumph. Was Sam Houston a prototypical all-American hero, or was he instead a carefully packaged illusion of no real substance, a "Sham" Houston? While we might not ever be fully satisfied that we "know" Sam Houston, I believe that this biography dispels some of the myths enveloping the man while clarifying the major achievements and failures that made him such a prominent American.

J. H. W.

ONE

Sam Houston and His America

Virginia, first of England's thirteen mainland colonies, was, with more than four hundred thousand inhabitants, the most populous state in the infant American Union in 1793, the year Sam Houston was born. The Old Dominion was to provide the United States with its first president, its third (Thomas Jefferson), fourth (James Madison) and fifth (James Monroe). Virginian leadership was to guide the nation from George Washington's first inaugural in 1789 until Monroe relinquished office in 1825, but Virginia gave the emerging nation far more than four legendary chief executives. It bestowed upon the wider United States intermittent streams of its restless sons and daughters, including men like Stephen F. Austin and Sam Houston, men who were to restructure one nation and create another.

America was young and turbulent at the time of Houston's birth. Two days after that event, on March 4, 1793, George Washington was reinaugurated, charged with guiding a nation of fifteen states and some four million souls, of whom perhaps seven hundred thousand were held in bondage. Most Americans clustered near the coast, as if clinging to the security of the Atlantic shelf and its umbilical cord to the Old World. That same 1793, just as many were coming to believe that the institution of slavery was fast becoming an embarrassing, uneconomical anachronism, Connecticut Yankee inventor Eli Whitney perfected his cotton gin, thereby presenting his nation with, in many ways, its greatest single historic pivot point.

Cotton, a minor commodity grown locally for homespun, within twenty years of Whitney's invention was America's largest crop and most lucrative export. It would sustain the mighty textile industries of Britain and France and create clothing mills in isolated New England villages, ushering in the American industrial revolution.

An ungluttable market demanded high-grade American cotton, and production would increase exponentially as the decades swept by, spawning vast plantations that made Mount Vernon and Monticello appear quaint country farms. Those opulent plantations would arise as if by magic where forest, delta and virgin savannah had soothed Indian eyes in 1793. The cotton boom touched off an astonishingly rapid internal migration as hundreds of thousands loosened their grip on the Atlantic shelf and slid farther and farther west and south. And, as they did, they casually, often brutally, uprooted all obstacles in their fortune-seeking paths, including the Eastern Indian. By 1817 many of them, including the "Five Civilized Nations"—Cherokee, Chickasaw, Choctaw, Creek and Seminole—were being wrenched from their ancestral lands in the Southern states and moved west under pressure, bribe and threat. The stubborn but outnumbered Seminoles began their First Seminole War that year, resisting the rising white tide. The blood shed then only hinted at what was to come two decades later.

In 1830, Congress passed the Removal Act with President Andrew Jackson's benign assent. Under the terms of that act all organized tribes east of the Mississippi River were to be deposited in the vast Indian Territory in the west. This, the "Trail of Tears," virtually destroyed the Cherokee, Choctaw and other Eastern tribes, while opening millions of acres in the South to almost overnight settlement by whites. The Seminoles again resisted, fading back into Florida's potential cotton lands, and the unusually brutal Second Seminole War erupted in 1835. That "low-intensity conflict" ended inconclusively in 1842, at a cost to the cotton-manic United States of some fifteen hundred lives and a staggering twenty million dollars. But northern Florida was opened to plantation agriculture, and that is what the war had been about.

Former vice-president Aaron Burr and General James Wilkinson, who may have been on Spain's payroll, would be disgraced in 1806 by their conspiracy to forge their own "empire" in the Old Southwest, and President James Madison annexed west Florida in 1810 with the transparent logic that it was an organic—if overlooked—part of the Louisiana Territory acquired in 1803. The census that year revealed 7,239,881 Americans, including a doubling of the nation's slave community in a single decade due to the expanding cotton belt, despite the 1808 abolition of the Atlantic slave trade. In 1819 the Florida peninsula was ceded by Spain to the United States, after General Andrew Jackson had seized it the previous year, and in 1821, Stephen F. Austin founded San Felipe de Austin, the first Anglo-American colony in the Spanish (soon Mexican) province of Texas.

Two years later President James Monroe issued his famous Doctrine, a warning to European nations to neither settle nor attempt to conquer, or reconquer, any portion of the Western Hemisphere. The message was clear: America for the Americans. In Mexico City, Lima and Buenos Aires, however, there was speculation about just *which* Americans Monroe meant. President Andrew Jackson, a Tennessee planter, offered to purchase Texas in 1829, but was stingingly rebuffed, while his vice-president, John C. Calhoun, attempted in 1832 to take South Carolina out of the Union in the "Nullification Crisis," largely because federal tariffs were crippling the South's cotton exports. Cotton and the institution of slavery had turned ardently nationalistic Calhoun into the premier spokesman for Southern rights. In 1835, Anglos in Texas rebelled against Mexico City and declared independence, because of a Mexican government pledge to enforce an earlier prohibition of slavery. Even at this early juncture in Texas history, slavery was essential to the economy, for most of the Anglo settlers had migrated there from the American South, and cotton plantations had become the economic mainstay of the province. And, while in one of his last acts as president, Andrew Jackson in 1837 recognized the Republic of Texas, bitter controversy on the issue of slavery prevented Congress from calling for its annexation as a state.

Eli Whitney in 1793 had unwittingly laid the foundation for American expansion and the creation of a true Southern slaveocracy, and his invention had vast social and demographic impact. The Atlantic slave trade was illegally reborn, and the number of blacks in the United States grew dramatically, nine-tenths of them slaves for life; chattel. While the United States Congress prohibited the seaborne slave trade under British pressure in 1808, that trade greatly increased in volume, with Spanish Cuba the conveniently located clearinghouse. In fact, the number of slaves on the island called the "Pearl of the Antilles" more than doubled between 1810 and 1840, in large part to meet the needs of plantations in the American South and the new Republic of Texas,[1] which were trying to satisfy the world's insatiable demand for American cotton. Natural increase could not provide enough field hands. As the number of slaves soared so too did fear of slave rebellion (Latin America offered a number of grisly examples); slave codes in the South became ever more draconian, and manumission increasingly difficult. In 1822, Denmark Vesey and thirty-four slaves were executed at Charleston for plotting insurrection, and the 1831 Nat Turner revolt in Virginia killed some sixty whites before it was crushed. These incidents merely hardened Southern resolve to further tighten the system. That Vesey was a free black intensified Southern hostility to manumission.

The Southern elite was riding a tiger and was uncomfortably aware of it, and in the 1840s and 1850s there evolved—stimulated by growing abolitionist sentiment and general criticism in the North—a distinctly Southern, sectional culture. The slave trade continued, and the 1860 census showed 31,443,321 Americans, of whom just under four million were slaves. While none of this could have been limned while Eli Whitney was tinkering, 1793 had indeed been a fateful year.

"A man of moderate fortune."

SAM HOUSTON

In 1793, Samuel Houston and his wife, Elizabeth Paxton Houston, lived with their four sons in hilly, wooded Rockbridge County, just east of the village of Lexington, Virginia. On March 2, two days before George Washington pronounced his second oath as president, robust Sam Houston came squalling into their world. Comfortably middle class, the Houstons lived in bucolic tranquility with a few slaves and some livestock on a large farm, the very image of Thomas Jefferson's ideal "yeoman farmer." Samuel and Elizabeth were both descended from British immigrants who had arrived in Virginia in the 1730s, well after the finest tidewater lands had been claimed, but, industrious folk, they had scratched out a respectable existence in the rugged Piedmont.

"My father was a man of moderate fortune," wrote Sam Houston later, "a man of powerful frame," who had served with distinction as a captain in Morgan's famous Rifle Brigade under Washington in the Revolution.[2] Following the war he became an officer in the Virginia militia, and by 1793 held the rank of colonel and regional brigade inspector. Often traveling to inspect local militia units, Samuel was absent from his family a great deal while young Sam was growing. In Virginia, wrote a wandering British adventurer, "Almost every person of the better class is at least a colonel, and every tavern-keeper is at least a major. Occasionally a few kaptains are met with amongst the stage-drivers, but such an animal as a *lewtenant* only exists on the muster-roll of the militia." Samuel Houston, clearly, was of "the better class."[3]

In his later life Sam almost never mentioned his father, and it seems clear that the Colonel had little influence upon his fifth son, for good or ill. Strikingly, from his teen years, young Sam took pains to distinguish himself from his father, pointedly using the name "Sam" instead of Samuel and completely rejecting the suffix "junior," or "II." Yet he would name his own first-born Sam, and at times refer to him as "Sam Jr."

If his father had little discernible influence on Sam, neither did his mother, Elizabeth. In later life Sam gave three of his children the first names of their grandparents, but none carried Elizabeth's, save as a middle name. His mother, so often alone, was a hard-driving, hard-working woman, who for several years left toddler Sam in the care of a family slave, the nurse, Peggy.[4] After he joined the army in 1813, Sam had virtually nothing to do with his mother, even while he was governor of Tennessee. Although she lived until 1831, he rarely corresponded with or visited her. Neither did she make any efforts to stay in touch with him.[5]

In a revealing letter to his fiancée Margaret Lea written in 1839—one of the exceedingly rare extant letters mentioning Elizabeth—he wrote self-pityingly: "Thy *Mother* lives to guard thy path & direct thy step. *Mine* is gone—long since gone—not a feature of her countenance, not a tone of her voice can be recalled."[6] He admits amnesia concerning his own mother (dead but eight years), and cannot even bring himself to use the word "mother," referring instead to Elizabeth only as *"Mine."* In his commissioned 1855 campaign biography, designed to persuade voters that he was presidential timber, Elizabeth appears in only a few scattered allusions.[7]

Reading Houston's lifelong correspondence one might easily conclude that he had been an orphan, and, indeed, he purposefully fostered that conclusion. He was wont to write of Andrew Jackson in terms of filial piety, often specifically noting that the childless General and his wife Rachel had "adopted" him.[8] Also, he felt—at least until 1840—strong familial bonds with the Cherokees. He regularly referred to Chief John Jolly as "father," and in Indian Territory in 1830 he was legally made a Cherokee citizen, citing "the letter of adoption" as proof.[9]

He was also estranged from his five brothers and three sisters. Only a handful of Houston's letters (none written after 1841) appear to contain any reference to a sibling, and none seems to mention a brother. In September 1824, in a letter to fellow congressman and future president James Buchanan, he noted that his travel plans had been disrupted due to "the indispositions of some of my family," but that vague reference might have been to the family of cousin John Houston.[10] Not long after their marriage, he wrote to Margaret Lea of the death of a brother-in-law: "My sister Mary is left in very comfortable circumstances, and the family all well . . . the connexions are all very anxious for us to visit them."* But, he continued, "My Dear, I can not say when that will be the case." There is no record of any such visit to Sam's "connexions."[11] One biographer, discussing Houston's first marriage, quotes cousin Emily Drennen as saying that he would not discuss his separation from Eliza "to any one not even his brother," the only epistolary indication that he had a male sibling.[12]

If Sam was alienated from parents and siblings, he did have close relations with some members of the extended Houston family. In fact, both the Houstons and the Paxtons (Sam's maternal relations) constituted "large extended clans," numbering in the hundreds.[13] One influential clan member, the Reverend Samuel Houston, who also lived in

---

* The spelling, grammar and punctuation of the era have been left as in the original documents here and in the quotations throughout.

Rockbridge County, is thought to have had significant, albeit not religious, influence on young Sam. The Reverend Houston was described as "a Classics scholar," a truly rare bird in those rustic surroundings. His books and stories entranced the Houston boy, who was to evince a lifelong love of *The Iliad* and other classics of Greece and Rome.[14]

The extremely warm and open relationships with cousins John Houston and, to a lesser degree, Robert McEwen stand in very stark contrast to his disaffection from his immediate family. John and his wife Gertrude had many children, and their family became Sam's. Houston's surviving correspondence with John is marked by strong, forthright emotions, expressions of endearment, personal gossip, and ideas and news he shared with no one else. He kept in close contact with cousin John even while a despairing exile in Indian Territory.

John and Gertrude's first child, Mary, was Sam's goddaughter and favorite, and from 1826, in letters fairly gushing with emotion, he referred to her as "My beloved daughter," often postscripting letters to John with "Kiss my child."[15] In one 1828 letter he thanked John for naming his new son Sam and agreed to stand as godfather for him the following spring.

The one other personal influence that touched Houston deeply and helped mold him was that of his "adoptive" father, patron, mentor and idol, fellow Tennesseean Andrew Jackson. The parallels in their lives defy probability theory.

Neither man really knew his father. Houston's, so often absent, died when he was twelve, Jackson's before he was born. Both had mothers described as strong and brave, rather than in motherly, feminine terms. Both learned early to feign rage and passion and showed almost preternatural self-control. Neither enjoyed a formal education, and both were touchy on the subject. Contemporary literature and the liberal arts were anathema to both. Despite cursory educations, both briefly taught school. Both became attorneys, yet neither practiced law on a regular basis, using it instead as an entree to politics. The two married fanatically religious women, but themselves joined the church only late in life. Both were slandered because of divorces of questionable legality. Both at times were political outcasts in Tennessee. Jackson and Houston entered the army while young and owed much of their political prominence to battlefield prowess, and both were protégés of powerful Tennessee political bosses. Each won one of the two battles in United

States history with the smallest losses against a supposedly superior enemy (New Orleans and San Jacinto). They both had been elected to judgeships in Tennessee and elected major generals of Tennessee militia, a political stepping-stone in that state. Both men had been young Tennessee congressmen. Each helped draw up a state constitution. Both served multiple terms as United States senators. Each man resigned a prominent political position for potential obscurity, with no explanation (Jackson as senator in 1797, Houston as governor in 1829). Each helped organize a state's first Masonic lodge, and remained an active Mason. Both were shot and carried bullets in their bodies that caused them agony for the rest of their lives. Both men envisioned and worked for United States expansion at Mexico's expense and were involved in conspiracies to usurp foreign lands. They shared an arrogant defensiveness about their controversial military careers. Both men were bitter enemies (Jackson after 1829) of South Carolina's influential and acerbic John C. Calhoun.[16]

Jackson was, between 1814 and his death in 1845, a strong father figure for Sam Houston, who often stayed at his home, the Hermitage, and constantly sought his advice, help and counsel.

===

"First as plow-boy, my school-mate, bedfellow,
and co-store-boy."

SAMUEL D. MORGAN, 1878

Sam Houston's life, growing up in rustic Rockbridge County among an expanding family (one brother and three sisters followed his birth), was unremarkable. He only occasionally entered a schoolhouse. Without hyperbole, he would write his son Sam in 1860 that "If I had only enjoyed an education of one year, I would have been happy," but his sketchy formal learning was somewhat supplemented by 1803 by reading and rereading *The Iliad* and a handful of other classics, which stoked the fires of his imagination.[17]

Sam Houston's Virginia years, 1793–1806, were fraught with danger for the United States, for in addition to the lessened but still real Indian threat on its frontiers, there were serious external menaces and ominous internal rumblings as well. The Wars of the French Revolution, which phased into the Napoleonic Wars by 1800, pitted Britain and its allies against France and its supporters in a shifting kaleidoscope of conflict. Washington's 1796 farewell address pointedly warned of the risk of foreign "entanglements," and the following year saw the outbreak of the "Quasi-War" with France (1797–1800), which threatened to embroil the young republic in the bubbling European caldron. Congress in 1798 passed the Alien and Sedition Acts in response, and many saw those acts as threats to American liberty. If all this were not enough, the first years of the new century saw saber-rattling Emperor Napoleon acquire the vast Louisiana Territory—a Europe-sized domain that blocked American westward expansion at the Mississippi River—and a "low-level conflict" between the United States and the pirate satrapies of North Africa (the Barbary Wars), which was to sputter on for many years.

Then, as Indian depredations (in part instigated by the British) reached crescendo pitch along the Canadian border and as far south as Tennessee, the United States nonchalantly acquired the Louisiana Territory, more than doubling the nation's size, and in 1805–1806 former vice-president Aaron Burr—with considerable support, including help from militia general Andrew Jackson—began organizing his still enigmatic filibuster, whose aim was to commandeer the southern portion of the Louisiana Territory and perhaps Texas as well. Burr had invested heavily in lands on the frontier, but his plot to forge a new nation was discovered. In 1806 the prominent politician was arrested, tried for treason and acquitted. All the while, the slide to war with Great Britain was gathering unstoppable momentum.[18]

It was in this uncertain and tense milieu that Sam Houston grew, a big fellow even in 1806 in the first year of his teens. The external threats and their internal reverberations were the air he breathed, and they kept his father almost constantly in motion in his militia capacity. With a minuscule regular army, a ready militia was the linchpin of American defense, and public order as well.

In September 1806, on one of his routine inspection trips, Colonel Houston fell ill, and died at Dennis Callighan's tavern on the Old Kentucky Road.[19] Elizabeth had regarded her husband as "an improvident visionary," for he had made unwise investments and even riskier loans. The Colonel, in fact, had been on the verge of selling their farm to pay off outstanding debts, and now she felt she had no choice but to do so herself, determining to guide her brood westward and establish a new life with whatever money remained. This was a difficult move, but she did have five adult or teenage sons to help her, so she sold the farm, most of the livestock, furniture and some slaves, paid her debts and squirreled away what she could in the family strongbox.[20]

When the Houstons headed west to Tennessee, they participated in an American epic, joining a stream of restless, hungry, visionary people seeking new lives on a raw frontier. Unlike many, however, the Houstons were hardly destitute. Elizabeth carried some $3,600 with her, a very respectable sum for that era, and she led two huge Conestoga wagons piled dangerously high with necessities, nine children and at least five slaves.[21] Elizabeth was nearly fifty, but she was undaunted by the prospect of a new life. Land was cheap on the frontier, and there was unlimited opportunity for those willing to work.

In the spring of 1807, just weeks before a naval clash with Britain caused war fever to sweep the United States, the Houston caravan halted near Maryville, Tennessee, a dispersed hamlet of perhaps forty "blockhouse families," for in 1807 much of Tennessee was still a dangerous frontier. As one authority has noted: "The presence of the Indians and the danger they constituted shaped in very large measure" life in the Tennessee wilderness.[22] The most numerous of Tennessee's Indians were the proud and warlike Cherokees, of whom it was remarked, "They never bowed to any other creature, they were not even willing to nod." The year Sam Houston was born more than a thousand warriors had razed Knoxville and threatened other settlements as well.[23] Even Nashville, founded by Captain John Donelson in 1779 and described as "a town as tough and raw as a fresh-cut hide" years later, remained an armed and vigilant camp.[24]

At Maryville, seat of Blount County in central Tennessee, Elizabeth negotiated the purchase of 419 "prime" acres, the boys knocked together a house and a farm was slowly sculpted out of the wilderness. Not, however, thanks to much effort from young Sam, for, as he later admitted, he was not "ept" at farming.

As in Virginia, Sam rarely darkened a school doorway, attending only for a few months in 1808. But as before, the young man spent hours reading and rereading Alexander's Pope's noble translation of *The Iliad* and other classical literature.[25] Instead of doing his chores, he would wander away in the forest, usually with a book, sometimes disappearing for hours, or even days.

It was probably in 1808 that Elizabeth reorganized the family's assets. The farm was prospering and she purchased part interest in the Maryville general store, sending her unindustrious fifth son there to learn clerking. She also divided the family resources, both liquid and real, into shares, one for herself and one for each child. The ratio soon changed, however, for her eldest son, Paxton, died in early 1809, and daughter Isabelle soon followed, thanks to the paucity of medical care on the Tennessee frontier. Now each share was one-eighth of the family wealth.[26]

Sam, it turned out, was no more "ept" at clerking than he had been at farming. The fact is that he hated his humdrum existence and dreamed of individual heroism, honor and excitement as they existed in *The Iliad*. Still, he tried to uphold his end of the family bargain, and while doing so met and clerked with the younger Samuel D. Morgan and his future close friend, Willoughby Williams. Morgan, who for years tagged along with Sam, wrote decades later that he had known the victor of San Jacinto "first as plow-boy, my school-mate, bedfellow, and co-store-boy."[27]

Despite his sporadic efforts Sam's absenteeism soon caused serious familial disharmony, and one day he simply disappeared into the forest and made his way across the Tennessee River. After a week, the family began scouting around, but no one knew the runaway's whereabouts. Then, weeks later, Elizabeth heard from two white poachers who had been hunting on Cherokee tribal lands that a lad of his description was living at the confluence of the Tennessee and Hiwasee rivers, with a Cherokee band led by Oo-Loo-Te-Ka.[28]

Sam had encountered the Cherokees on earlier wanderings and found their way of life congenial. Most Cherokees were then enjoying a hiatus of peace with their white neighbors, fruit of a series of "perpetual" treaties recently signed. With these Indians Sam found *The Iliad* come alive: the warrior society of brave, chivalric individuals, living by their wits off the land and moving on when—and only when—they willed.[29]

He had deserted a rough-hewn, emergent white middle-class society on an evolving frontier, a society where "to kill an Indian was a public-spirited act, to swindle one, an exercise of common sense," but to befriend one, almost beyond comprehension.[30] Yet this was the path Sam had chosen, and his brothers John and James found him among Oo-Loo-Te-Ka's band, on an island in the Tennessee River, supposedly, according to Marquis James's ideal account, reposing in the shade of a tree perusing *The Iliad*.[31]

The brothers did not change Sam's mind, and he remained with the Cherokees while his brothers trudged back to Maryville. Sixteen-year-old Sam had found new brothers who, unlike those of his blood, accepted him without question or demand. Nor did he question or make demands of them. Despite their warlike history, the Cherokees (and the other Civilized Tribes) were known for their hospitality. Indeed, not only had they welcomed many a white such as Sam over the years, they had biologically absorbed thousands of strangers, white and red.

The Cherokees were largely sedentary, settled in major portions of the Carolinas, Georgia and Tennessee. They had a very sophisticated social structure, and while for the men "war is their principal study and their greatest ambition," Cherokee women played a highly respected role. Divorce was common, women were accorded many rights, and while the man constructed the conjugal house, it belonged not to him, but to his wife.[32]

In the eighteenth century many Highland Scots had entered Cherokee territory via the commercial entrepôt of Charleston, and they not only dominated the tribe's trade, but married into it as well. In fact, like subchief John Rogers and Alexander McGillivray, many chiefs of the Civilized Tribes were Scottish, or their mixed-blood offspring.[33] Thirteen of the nineteen Cherokee war leaders with General Jackson at the Battle of Horseshoe Bend in 1814 were "half-bloods."[34] Despite their propensity for the warpath, the Cherokees were accomplished farmers, some operating on a commercial scale as planters with African slaves. When they were forced to migrate to Indian Territory, they brought their slaves with them and created new plantations, much as did the white settlers. So "Southern" were they in this regard that Cherokee regiments fought under legendary Ben McCulloch and other Southern generals during the Civil War.[35]

Ravaged by smallpox in the 1790s and threatened by white migration, the Cherokees had flexed their warlike muscles frequently enough to impress both the United States and individual states to negotiate treaties recognizing their "perpetual" rights to tens of millions of acres of land east of the Mississippi. Cherokee delegations had visited and put their cases to every president from Washington to Andrew Jackson.[36]

But, although they were numerous, prosperous and warlike, the Cherokees could not halt the roiling tide of white settlers. Hence, in the first years of the century some bands agreed with state and federal governments to cede their treaty lands in exchange for new tracts across the Mississippi River in Arkansas Territory, as Indian Territory was then known. There, supposedly beyond the juggernaut of white expansion, they would live in peace and receive promised government indemnities.[37] By 1806, some fifteen hundred Cherokees had trekked westward, and by the time Sam Houston joined Oo-Loo-Te-Ka's band, perhaps a thousand more had followed.

"The moulding period of life."

SAM HOUSTON, 1848 (?)

Accepted like the Scottish traders before him, Houston settled in comfortably with the Cherokees, adopting their language and their ways, and Oo-Loo-Te-Ka, who also used the name John Jolly, took him under his wing. Houston was soon close friends with John and James Rogers, who taught him woodlore, hunting, stealth and tribal customs. Sons of Jolly's brother-in-law, headman Captain John Rogers ("Hellfire Jack," a Scottish trader), they were soon the admiring white teenager's "brothers."[38]

After about a year with the Cherokees, Sam suddenly appeared unannounced at Maryville. His clothes hung about him in tatters, and he had simply come back to renew his wardrobe and purchase a few gifts for his Indian family.[39] He had certainly not returned to Maryville to stay. In mid-September, freshly attired, he gave the first evidence of a serious propensity for alcohol acquired among the Cherokees. In company with John Cusack, an older man, Sam got thoroughly drunk at a local watering hole, disturbed the peace mightily and disrupted a drill

session of the Mounted Gunmen, the Blount County militia unit of
which Cusack was captain. Refusing to stop flailing loudly and atonally
at the militiamen's big drum, Sam and his friend also resisted efforts to
restrain them, and were jailed on charges of "abusing their sheriff."[40]
Houston was fined five dollars (which he did not have), while Cusack
(it was not his first offense) was mulcted double that sum.[41] Both fines
were remitted at the next sitting of the court, but by then the nonchalant young man was back in Cherokee country.

For almost exactly a year, from the autumn of 1809 to the first hard
frosts of 1810, Sam Houston again melded into Jolly's band, later fondly
recalling that "my early life among the Indians was a necessary portion
of that wonderful training that fitted me for my destiny."[42] In that year,
and the next, with the "Children of the Great Spirit," Sam underwent
what he later described as "the moulding period of life." He left no
other record of this period, and it remains but vaguely known, but called
by the Cherokees the "Raven," he felt master of his destiny.[43]

A brief return to Maryville in the late autumn of 1810 proved both
uninteresting and unfruitful and he soon returned to his Indian "family," where he remained, except for brief visits to Maryville, until the
spring of 1812. On some of those visits, Sam clerked at a store owned
by a Mr. Sheffy, where Willoughby Williams also worked. As Williams
later explained, Sam could always find a job, for "the Indian trade being
much valued, his services were highly appreciated from the fact that he
spoke with fluency the Cherokee language."[44] But, as soon as he had a
few dollars, he was off to the forests again.

While at Jolly's camp he must have learned of the arrival of the chief
Tecumseh, great leader of the restive Shawnee, far to the north. Supported by the British in Canada, Tecumseh was a dedicated foe of
Anglo-American expansion. He and his brother, "The Prophet," had
forged a mighty coalition of tribes in the North, and they sought to do
the same in the South, where the "prophetic movement" was spreading
among the Five Civilized Tribes, especially the Creeks, many of whom
were of Shawnee descent.[45] Certain that the United States and Britain
would go to war, Tecumseh was determined to set the entire American
frontier aflame, for this might well be the last time the Indians could
count on having white (British) allies.

Most of the Civilized Tribes' chiefs naively believed that their treaties with the Americans were valid and perpetual, and it was only

among the Creeks that the charismatic Shawnee found widespread support. Even they were so badly split that for them the War of 1812 was destined to be a civil war.[46] The Creek war faction was led by William Weatherford, also known as Red Eagle, a man but one-eighth Creek. Son of a Scots trader and a quarter-breed half-sister of Alexander McGillivray, he was perhaps the most influential white among the tribes. Those who followed Weatherford painted their war clubs crimson, and would be known across the frontier as the dreaded "Red Sticks." When they learned that Britain and the United States had begun their prophesied war, the Red Sticks immediately initiated their own conflict.[47]

Though he knew of Tecumseh's sanguinary mission, Houston probably discounted it. The nonchalant reaction of the Cherokees lulled him, and he left no written mention of the famous and ill-fated visitor from the north.

"We now shot them like dogs."

DAVY CROCKETT, 1835

Back in Maryville in the fateful spring of 1812, just before Congress reluctantly declared war on Britain, Sam Houston cast about for a way to make money in a manner less tedious than clerking or farming. He had to work, for in the preceding two years he had accumulated bills of over a hundred dollars at various general stores. His credit had dried up, and dunning clerks had explained to him that imprisonment for debt, while illogical, was still common in Tennessee.[48] With a stunning display of ego, which would be one of his hallmarks, the untutored young man announced in late April that he, Master Sam Houston, would open the doors of a new Maryville school! He did so in May, in a rickety cabin outside town, charging what at the time was a rather stiff fee: eight dollars per term, payable one-third each in cash, corn and local homespun.[49] That he was successful indicates the dearth of educational establishments in the area. He soon had twenty students enrolled in the May through September term, which, he was happy to calculate, worked out to $53.20 in hard coin, and whatever he could sell the corn and cloth for. Strapping Sam, with less than a year (in bits and pieces) of formal education, was now headmaster, reciting *The Iliad* to students of wildly varying age, wearing "a hunting shirt of flowered calico."[50]

The term passed unremarkably, and Sam, now at last a member of Maryville "society," "his prodigious charm and strapping good looks" making him generally popular, decided to return to school himself late in the year.[51] His debts paid off, he enrolled in nearby Porter Academy, later claiming that he felt it necessary to master the art of mathematics so that he could apply for a commission in the army, as had his older brother Robert.[52]

Not only had war been declared, but William Weatherford and a thousand or more "Red Sticks" had perpetrated a number of grisly frontier depredations, culminating in the infamous Fort Mims Massacre in Alabama in August 1813. This atrocity, the killing of more than five hundred Indians and whites hiding in the fort, in addition to its small garrison, shocked and outraged the entire nation.[53] Davy Crockett recalled that the Red Sticks had killed "as a butcher would in a slaughter pen," with a frenzy climaxed by a hideous mutilation of the dead.[54]

Despite his patriotic zeal and stated intention of obtaining a commission, the nineteen-year-old Houston failed to master "ciphering," and deciding that school expenses represented money down a rat-hole, he withdrew from the academy after a few fruitless months. He had made up his mind to join the army, commission or no, lest the war end without him.[55]

On March 1, 1813, a day before turning twenty, Sam Houston joined the United States Army as a private. A recruiting party for the new Thirty-ninth Infantry Regiment had come to Maryville, "with music, a banner, and some well-dressed sergeants," and the young men of Blount County were swept away by their tales of heroism.[56] Since he was not yet twenty-one, he needed his mother's permission to enlist, and by some accounts she presented him with a musket as well.[57] Willoughby Williams, later sheriff of Nashville, was present that day as Sam, Samuel D. Morgan, and thirty-seven others took the token dollar from the drumhead.[58] While his brothers "scorned Sam for joining the army as a common soldier,"[59] most sources agree that neighbors, friends and possibly some family members appealed to President Madison to commission him as an officer.[60]

Although recruited into the Thirty-ninth Infantry, Sam and his friends were sent to Knoxville for training with the Seventh Infantry Regiment, where after a month he was made a drill sergeant.[61] This is not surprising, for the quality of recruits in this era was appalling. Official army surveys of the period reveal that 42 percent of all recruits were illiterate, most were sickly and their average height was five feet eight inches.[62] In such an army, a classics-spouting, brawny former schoolmaster standing six feet, five inches, was a prize catch.

In July 1813, Sam was commissioned ensign—then the lowest officer rank—and transferred to the Thirty-ninth Infantry. That small (360-man) regiment, in which Houston was a platoon leader, was commanded by the hulking, harsh-voiced Tennessee Colonel Thomas Hart Benton, later governor of Missouri and a powerful senator. Benton, who kept an eye on the young ensign, regarded him highly, as he would throughout his career, and would later serve with him in the Senate.

The colonel, however, was no friend of General Andrew Jackson. Possessed of "an ego twice the size of his physique," Benton had taken an instant dislike to the general[63] and at the time was recovering from a tavern brawl during which his brother, Jesse, had almost killed the future president. Jesse Benton had shot Jackson while allegedly trying to save Thomas's life. As one of Benton's biographers has pointed out, "shooting Nashville's hero was no step on the pathway to fame and fortune," yet Benton was destined to achieve both against the odds.[64]

In February 1814 the Thirty-ninth Infantry was sent into the field to join General Jackson, who was on extended campaign against Weatherford and his Red Sticks. Jackson, a man of considerable if erratic political and military experience, had been in eclipse, tainted by peripheral involvement in the Aaron Burr imbroglio. The United States government had adamantly refused him a command early in the war, although he was Tennessee's ranking militia general, but Governor William Blount, a political ally, named Jackson major general of United States volunteers on his own authority in 1813—a move of dubious legality—with soon-to-be governor William "Billy" Carroll as his brigade inspector and young Thomas Hart Benton his chief aide-de-camp.[65] The governor then instructed Jackson to raise an army and chastise the Red Sticks, whose depredations had not stopped at Fort Mims.

In late 1813, while Houston was training, Jackson had set out on his own warpath, putting one column of his army under General John Coffee. A series of pitched battles were fought against the Red Sticks, and once Jackson's army was almost destroyed by the messianic warriors, whose black-faced shamans had assured final victory. Red and white warriors died in windrows at Talladega, Enotachopco, Emuckfaw and, on November 3, at the Creek village of Tallushatchee, where General Coffee and his rabid frontier volunteers obliterated a thousand Indians, most of them women and children. Davy Crockett, just becoming a frontier legend, was an eager participant, later writing that during the frenzied fighting a squaw killed an officer, "and his death so enraged us all" that "we now shot them like dogs" and completely razed the village.[66]

It was a ghastly war of no quarter, often pitting red against red, for Jackson used both Creek and Cherokee scouts and troops, including three of the Rogers boys, Houston's friends James, John and William (the last would briefly command Houston's son's regiment at Shiloh, in 1862). While the Cherokee Council had voted neutrality, most leaders of the Civilized Tribes feared that siding with the British would bring down utter disaster upon their heads, voiding all the treaties so laboriously negotiated with the Americans. To attract Cherokee recruits Jackson wisely commissioned some as officers and paid all Cherokee volunteers at the same rate as whites. A thousand or more Cherokees had chosen to enlist with Jackson. Chewing their corn-mush rations, they rode off to war, all wearing white men's clothing, supplemented with two white feathers and a squirrel's tail adorning their hats to distinguish them from the enemy. Superb scouts and warriors, they served Jackson better than he was to serve them.[67]

What Jackson most needed in early 1814, and what he had been badgering the War Department for, was disciplined Regular Army troops. Orders finally reached the Thirty-ninth Infantry on February 1, and the next day its ranks eagerly filed south to rendezvous with the general at Fort Strother. Sam Houston, newly promoted third lieutenant, led one company.

"That arm he had given to his country."

FRANCIS SCOTT KEY, 1832

Colonel Benton, Jackson's chief aide-de-camp, but obviously out of favor, admitted that "my life is in danger" because of the tavern brawl, and turned the Thirty-ninth Infantry over to aspiring Tennessee politician Lieutenant Colonel John Williams. That gentleman, instead of Benton, would have the honor of leading it in its baptism of fire. An officer in the Regular Army, Williams had campaigned with some success against the Creeks and Seminoles in northern Florida before replacing Benton in command of the Thirty-ninth. For reasons unclear, Williams developed a visceral dislike for Third Lieutenant Houston, a dislike that was to grow into a full-blown feud following the war.[68]

The regiment, its small band playing, strode smartly into rude Fort Strother on February 6, finding Jackson eager to take the field. When his scouts finally reported that a large force of Red Sticks was busily fortifying a peninsula jutting into the Tallapoosa River at Horseshoe Bend, fifty-five miles to the south, the general immediately put his army in motion. He was determined to end the Creek uprising once and for all, and led his ebullient volunteers and regulars, "with tobacco in their jaws and gunpowder in their pouches," toward what he hoped would be the final confrontation.[69] With the general, who was still weak from Benton's almost mortal gunshot, marched more than two thousand whites and more than five hundred Cherokee and Creek warriors.

When Jackson's army reached Horseshoe Bend in the morning of March 26, its spirits soared. Although protected by formidable fortifications, the Red Sticks had unwittingly doomed themselves. Some thousand warriors and a few hundred women and children had constructed a very stout rampart across the peninsula, protecting themselves from the foe, but also sealing themselves off from possible escape. Three tiers of thick pine logs, rising more than head high, reminded one of the side of an immense man-of-war, and loopholes cut through the logs completed the illusion. Within this barricade were some three hundred acres of tangled underbrush, stands of timber and shallow ravines.

While he parleyed with the Red Sticks and convinced them to evacuate their women and children, Jackson sent veteran Indian fighter
General Coffee and a strong force of white and red volunteers across
the river to fire on parts of the peninsula and block the river route of
escape. Then, at ten-thirty on March 26, Jackson's two small cannon
began to hammer with no visible result the loopholed breastworks.
While cannon balls and even less effective musketry hailed against the
absorptive pine logs, drawing the Red Sticks' attention without depleting their ranks, two hundred or so of Coffee's men, mostly Cherokees,
reached the peninsula by canoe, sneaked stealthily through the brush
and set fire to the enemy camp.[70]

When, two hours later, Jackson saw thick, greasy smoke from the
burning Creek camp in the warriors' rear, he ordered a frontal assault
on the now-distracted Red Sticks. The Thirty-ninth's regulars sprinted
forward in the vanguard, charging through a withering fire from the
scores of loopholes. They hit the barricade like a wave, some thrusting
bayoneted muskets through the firing ports, some shooting into them
blind, others leaping upon the works. The first man to scale the barricade was Houston's superior, fellow Tennessean Major Lemuel Montgomery, but within seconds his head was blown off by a close-range
musket shot. Undeterred, Lieutenant Houston and a handful of his
men followed and, swinging his sword in great arcs, the young giant
leaped within the works among the Red Sticks, soon joined by dozens
of other regulars.[71]

Almost as soon as he hit the ground, Houston was felled, hit high on
the inside of his left thigh, an inch from the groin, by a wickedly barbed
arrow. He collapsed to the damp soil in frightful pain as the hand-to-
hand fight swirled viciously around him. Slowly, the combat receded
down the peninsula as more of Jackson's men spilled over the breastworks, while Sam Houston attempted to wrench the long arrow from
his thigh. Achieving nothing save new levels of pain, he cajoled a passing fellow officer to pull the arrow out. At first he too failed, but "with
a desperate effort he drew forth the arrow, tearing the flesh as it came,"
to produce a cavernous wound and a great spout of blood.[72]

Pressing a cloth to the gaping cavity Houston somehow made his way
through the tangled bodies, and with the din of battle ringing in his
ears dragged himself across the rampart in a torrential cloudburst to
find the regimental surgeon. That overworked, underequipped individ-

ual inspected the massive, probably fatal, wound and merely plugged it with rags to control the bleeding, laying the young officer down among the other casualties.[73] Later, with the sound of battle receding and muted, General Jackson rode by to console the wounded, stopping to talk briefly with many of them, including Houston—probably their first contact.[74]

The Red Sticks, falling in heaps in blind, close-quarter combat, were slowly squeezed into one corner of the peninsula. Those few who attempted to swim to safety were picked off by marksmen, red and white. But still their dark-visaged shamans danced and chanted to their failing god, while the remaining warriors grimly fought on. By four in the afternoon, only one pocket of strong resistance remained.

A hundred or more Red Sticks had retreated to a position under the river bluffs, a strongpoint that could only be approached through a ravinelike passage. Attackers would be channeled into the Indians' clear field of fire. Jackson's men contented themselves with harmless, harassing musketry, but the general craved to settle the issue before nightfall and called for volunteers to storm the redoubt. Several half-hearted probes were quickly driven back by storms of gunfire, but still Jackson harangued his men for yet another effort.

Spectral Sam Houston, one trouser leg cut away, waxen, limping grotesquely and spattered with blood, hauled himself to the voice of his general and beyond. Grabbing a musket from the ground, he rasped out "Charge," and hobbled toward the Red Stick bastion at the head of a few reluctant men. Hundreds of others, including Jackson, looked on with frank admiration. Some forty yards from the barricade, the advancing soldiers were met with a roar of musketry, and Houston spun wildly and crashed to the ground. He had been hit simultaneously by two musket balls. One shattered his upper right arm, while the other smashed into his right shoulder a few inches higher.[75]

Semiconscious, Houston barely felt himself being carried back to what passed for an aid station and laid upon a dirty blanket on the open ground. After a glance, the surgeon all but wrote him off, removing only the plainly visible ball in his arm and not even bothering to probe for the one embedded deep in his shoulder amidst ragged bone chips.[76] Houston later recalled of the experience that "The surgeon said it was unnecessary to torture me, since I could not survive till the morning . . . it was the darkest night of my life."[77]

It was probably fortunate that scant medical attention was paid to the "dying" officer. Had the surgeons worked to save him, the first thing they would have done was amputate his right arm. That and digging around in his massive shoulder wound for the other bullet would have almost certainly killed the young man through combined loss of blood and shock.[78]

As it was, the surgeons left him alone and, while his right arm was never the same, neither was it crippled. In 1832, Houston's defense attorney, Francis Scott Key, would make much of that wound. He would righteously intone that "He had once indeed an arm fit to execute the strong impulses of a brave heart—but that arm he had given to his country."[79] In any case, it was the thigh wound that was to cause Houston true misery. While bone chips would work their way painfully from his shoulder for years,[80] the gaping arrow wound never fully healed, and suppurated constantly.[81] Houston's closest personal friend in later years, physician Ashbel Smith, wrote five decades later that "the wound remained a running sore to his grave."[82] That it was forty-nine years after his first battle that he went to his grave is truly astonishing.

"My blood boiled."

SAM HOUSTON, 1814

As Houston lay semiconscious among the other wounded, the unbreachable Red Stick fallback position was finally destroyed by fire arrows, and the last screaming warriors were flushed out in the open and cut down. The battle was over, and the general—upon whom Houston had made a fateful impression that day—ordered a body count. The tally was unusually precise, for the tip of each Red Stick's nose was cut off, brought to headquarters, and enumerated. In all, 917 nose tips were collected, but the Creeks' losses were even higher, for scores had been picked off in the river, their bodies swept away.[83] Some 300 prisoners, all but four of them women and children, had been taken. It was a devastating defeat for the Red Sticks, and although Weatherford had not himself been present, the battle ended the Creek uprising. This was to have great significance, for when the British landed an army on the Gulf coast seven months later to threaten New Orleans, there were no Indian allies to support them. This permitted Jackson to concentrate his slender resources to win the resounding victory at New Orleans in January 1815.[84]

The victors' losses were not negligible. That night, Jackson learned that 47 of his soldiers and 23 Indian auxiliaries were dead, and 159 more soldiers and 47 Cherokees and Creeks wounded.

While some of his rustic volunteers cut patches of skin from the fallen enemy to fashion into reins and tobacco pouches, Jackson ordered his dead wrapped in shrouds, weighted and thrown into the river and had his officers ready their men to march at first light for Fort Strother.[85] Houston and the other severely wounded were sent to Fort Williams, some sixty miles to the northwest. As Jackson's army marched from Horseshoe Bend it gratuitously laid waste to all Creek villages, livestock, orchards, fields, peopled by both Red Stick and friendly, an object lesson to Indians who might contemplate raising their war clubs against Americans in the future.[86]

Weatherford later surrendered to Jackson, was pardoned and became a prosperous Alabama farmer.[87] In August the general forced a treaty on a council of thirty-five Creek chiefs (only two of whom had been Red Sticks), by which they ceded fully twenty-three million acres to the United States. As one of his biographers put it, "Jackson converted the Creek civil war into an enormous land grab."[88] No friend of the Indian, Jackson, on this one issue, differed (radically) from Sam Houston, who would defend the Indian throughout most of his career.

The general's Cherokee allies fared little better than the Creeks. Jackson and the United States government failed to reward the tribe for its important role in the Creek War. In fact, as the victors wended their way slowly back to Fort Strother, they acted as if all Indians were enemies, looting Cherokee villages as gleefully as Creek, with Davy Crockett and others stealing hogs from peaceful Cherokee farmers along the way.[89]

Sam Houston knew nothing of this, of course. He spent several fever-bathed weeks at Fort Williams, and then, on sick leave and still feeble, he set out for the nation's capital. En route he stopped off at Maryville in early May, "suffering the extremest agony" from his still open wounds.[90] He spent several weeks at his mother's home, receiving friends, including Willoughby Williams, who found his friend "greatly emaciated" and weak as a baby, his wounds running sores, and his condition complicated by measles. The convalescent Houston did not seem long for this world.[91]

Although still in miserable physical condition, the now popular Maryville hero slowly made his way north to Washington, arriving there in October, just two months after a British army had burned most of the town to the ground. He later recalled staring at the rubble of the capital, his anger overwhelming: "My blood boiled."[92] It was while he was in the smoldering capital that he learned of his promotion to second lieutenant, effective May 20, 1814, largely on the strength of Andrew Jackson's official reports of Houston's conspicuous bravery.[93] The young man's star was in the ascendant—as was Jackson's—and in the future he would be a force to be reckoned with in rebuilt Washington.

T W O

Some Sam Houston Contretemps

"He is a fine young man and in my opinion merits to
be noticed."

CONGRESSMAN JOHN RHEA, 1815

Second Lieutenant Sam Houston spent the last months of 1814 in
rubble-strewn Washington, assigned to the Army Quartermaster Department. Even before traveling to the capital he had been on light
active duty as an army wagonmaster.[1] He also visited New York, where
that autumn the world's first steamship, *Demologos*, was noisily
launched before a crowd of the unbelieving. Like most Americans he
also learned about the Hartford Convention, convened in mid-December and considered treasonous by many because it took place during
hostilities. At this meeting, delegates from New England aired grievances against the federal government, the first major expression of
states' rights.

With the Battle of New Orleans (fought after the peace treaty had
been signed) a crushing British defeat in January, the War of 1812 was
over. Most Americans were relieved, but not Sam Houston, for with
peace erupting the army was to be trimmed back to its minuscule frontier strength, and many units, including the Thirty-ninth Infantry,
would be demobilized. Houston, a hero, did not want to leave the
service and hazard obscurity.

Following his victory, Andrew Jackson, despite lingering rumors of
his connection with Aaron Burr, was appointed commanding general of

the Southern Division of the army, covering more than half of the
nation. He made Nashville his headquarters, and operated from his
own plantation home, the ever-expanding Hermitage, just outside
town.[2] There, he monitored both military matters and state political
intrigues.

Houston doubtless wrote the general, as he did so many others, pleading for retention in the service. The day before his twenty-second birthday he informed Secretary of War James Monroe of his wish to remain
in uniform: "I have given proofs of my Valour & fidelity in the cause of
Liberty and in return I carry honorable scars," which should be re-
warded by the government.[3] He also wrote Tennessee congressman
John Rhea, putting his case more strongly, noting that his wounds
"rendered [me] unfit for other business" than soldiering. In a somewhat
contradictory postscript he added that "my wound is nearly healed &
my health entirely recovered," so that he was again fit for duty. Impressed by Houston's case, if not his logic, Rhea recommended him to
the War Department: "He is a fine young man and in my opinion merits
to be noticed and continued in the army."[4]

Large wheels, however, revolve slowly, and having heard nothing
almost two months later, the now dejected lieutenant wrote a friend
that "It is very probable that I will be disbanded." He was sufficiently
cheerful at the same time to jokingly add that "I will not court any of
the Dear Girles before I make a fortune."[5] Since there was absolutely
no chance of making even a modest "fortune" in the army, he may have
had some other plans.

But, within days, Andrew Jackson smiled on the young Tennessean.
While officers of the disbanded regiments—including Benton and John
Williams—were dismissed or retired with cursory thanks, Houston was
informed by the War Department, to his immense pleasure, that he
would be retained and transferred to the First Infantry, then barracked
at New Orleans.[6] In short order he was on his way, tarrying briefly in
Tennessee, where he paid his respects at the Hermitage and stopped
off to see his family and friends. In his bags went a small library: *The
Iliad,* the Bible, *Pilgrim's Progress,* various works of Shakespeare, *Robinson Crusoe, The Vicar of Wakefield* and several volumes of poetry.[7]
Later in life he would deride poetry as "frivolity," but at this time he
both read and wrote it.

Houston arrived in sweltering, fever-swept New Orleans in the early summer of 1815, in time to witness the first steamboat ascend the Mississippi, harbinger of profound economic change for the nation's interior. But his shoulder wound almost incapacitated him, and that summer surgeons operated to remove the misshapen musket ball buried deep inside.[8] For all their cutting, however, the doctors could extract only fragments, and they recommended that Houston travel to New York, where he could find better surgical care. The army granted him a furlough, and he traveled north with as much dispatch as his weakness permitted. In the late summer, surgeons in New York successfully extracted what was left of the musket ball and some large bone chips, and Houston was granted indefinite medical leave.[9]

Stopping again at Maryville for several weeks while recuperating, Houston socialized often with cousins John Houston and Robert McEwen and their mutual friends, and the various "Dear Girles" of the county. In fact, it appears from the few letters he wrote at this time that he became quite smitten with a certain "Miss M——," and was at least vaguely contemplating marriage.[10] Lacking his "fortune," however, he could hardly take such a step, and, with his health basically restored by late 1815, he received orders to return to active duty. And what duty it was! At the general's personal request, he was posted to Jackson's staff at the Hermitage, with every prospect of future promotion.

Jackson was as much politician as soldier (he had already served in both houses of Congress), and in tranquil 1816 he was building his power base from the capacious veranda and study of the Hermitage, his eye fixed firmly on the White House. His staff consisted more of a circle of political protégés than a board of military experts, and was, in embryonic form, the famed "Tennessee Junto," or political machine, which existed to boost his aspirations for the presidency. Jackson supported the ambitions of his staff as well, and those men would all become influential in politics and diplomacy, using their influence to help their mentor. When Houston arrived at Nashville early in the year, he joined a staff that included Andrew Jackson Donelson, Jackson's ward and a future politician-diplomat; James Gadsden, South Carolina politician, future diplomat and presidential hopeful; John H. Eaton, future secretary of war, governor of Florida, and center of bitter scandal; John and Samuel Overton, future arbiters of Tennessee politics, and Robert Butler.[11] To these were added frequent visitors to the Hermitage such as

Governor Joseph McMinn, Billy Carroll (soon to be governor) and a swarm of Tennessee politicians and hopefuls. If a man wished to be "known" in Tennessee politics, the Hermitage was the place to be.

But, while Houston certainly had a prized post, he also had his problems. When he arrived at Nashville to take up his new duties, he felt constrained to write the secretary of war about "My former Col. [John] Williams." According to the lieutenant, "He has ever been inimical to me, since I have joined the Regiment he has written letters to officers calculated to prejudice them against me." He possessed some of those slanderous letters, and "can assure you that I can substantiate" the story.[12]

What caused this enmity is unknown, but it would be long and grievous. It would have been crippling to the young officer but for his powerful patron, the master of the Hermitage, who defended his protégé, at times viciously. Williams was no lightweight. A decorated war hero, he was elected in 1815 to the United States Senate, and was frenetically building a state political machine, with the help of such movers and shakers as Colonel Andrew Erwin. Williams's budding machine was a direct challenge to Jackson's primacy in the state, and Houston's identification with the general deepened Williams's antipathy toward him. As Jackson complained at the time, "Col. Williams . . . is the enemy of every highminded honourable man," and a dangerous enemy at that.[13]

Despite the brouhaha with Williams, Houston's Nashville service was another "moulding" experience. He not only participated in fervent political discussions on the plantation veranda and discussed national and state affairs, he did the same at the Nashville Inn where he roomed, the political vortex of the state. In the inn's public rooms and private suites, militia officers and politicians (often one and the same) gathered to toss a pot or two in the evenings, and Lieutenant Houston was an attentive player in those heady festivities. In addition to deluging himself with "Demon Rum," he became well-acquainted with such political animals as future presidents James K. Polk and James Buchanan, future influential Texans such as merchant Adolphus Sterne, John and William Wharton, Charles F. M. and William Noland, and many others who were to have a major impact on the United States, Texas and his future life. Nashville was on the road west, a major frontier stopover, a clearinghouse for news, gossip and rumors, and the Nashville

Inn was a key venue. It was a highly charged atmosphere, and Houston swam happily in its fast currents of opinion and information. He also joined the Cumberland Masonic Lodge, which Jackson had founded, and to no one's surprise soon "won" promotion to first lieutenant, which carried with it the decent salary of thirty dollars a month and considerable allowances.[14]

"The friendly disposition of the United States
towards us."

CHEROKEE DELEGATION, 1817

While Lieutenant Houston was learning the fine arts of politics and sustained tippling, his friends the Cherokees were undergoing a troubling transition. In 1816, some Tennessee Cherokee chiefs had agreed to a treaty by which they ceded 1.3 million acres of land to the state in return for lands beyond the Mississippi and cash annuities. As was all too common, the chiefs had been plied with good whiskey and bad bribes.[15] Most of their warriors repudiated the treaty, for in Cherokee lore the west (as a direction) signified death and defeat. Jackson and Governor McMinn, both of whom were involved in land speculation and were callous toward the Indians, were behind the treaty and hoped to profit from it, but now the majority of the Cherokees involved, including John Jolly, were having second thoughts.[16]

At Jackson's suggestion, Houston applied for temporary posting as subagent for the Eastern Cherokees. The general knew of Houston's life with the Indians and that they trusted him, and he counted on his protégé to convince the Cherokees to honor the treaty. Whether Houston realized that he was being cynically used or not, he took the better-paying job when the War Department approved his application.[17] He believed that the move west would in the long run be beneficial, for it would remove his Indian friends from the growing strains and potential violence of being surrounded by increasing numbers of land-hungry white settlers. He was appointed on October 21, 1817, and while on leave from the army would receive the subagent's considerable salary of one thousand dollars (he later claimed it was fifteen hundred dollars) per annum and travel expenses.[18] Donning buckskins and homespun, the "Raven" set out for John Jolly's lodge, which he reached in late November.[19]

At Jolly's camp, he was as persuasive as his mentor had hoped, convincing the chief that the government would rigorously honor all the terms of a basically equitable treaty, and Jolly agreed to fulfill his part of the pact. Houston did not want his friends bamboozled or further swindled and agreed to personally lead a delegation of Eastern Cherokees to Washington to treat with the highest officials face to face.

The Cherokee delegation had to leave for the capital without him, however, for he was felled by malaria. He remained in Tennessee, writing the War Department numerous letters and reports, many condemning the perfidy of other agents, while he anxiously waited to get well enough to travel. In one letter he informed the department that with the "advice" of Governor McMinn, he had distributed government blankets to all Cherokees willing to move west, in the *"belief* that the measure will be approved by the Executive." It was, for it was a small price to pay.[20]

While the subagent was recuperating the Cherokee delegation had a series of interviews with the new secretary of war, South Carolinian John C. Calhoun, whose charge included the Indian Bureau. They realistically demanded that he put in writing his interpretation of what was due them under the terms of the treaty "to show our people on our return to our Nation the friendly disposition of the United States towards us."[21] Though ruffled, he did so, for it too was a small price to pay. Calhoun, while no staunch defender of the Indian, was an honest man, and he thoroughly expected the treaty to be honored. A month later, in January 1818, as Houston was at last preparing to join his delegation in Washington, Governor McMinn wrote Calhoun to introduce the subagent, highly commending his work with the Cherokees.[22]

Calhoun, a planter-politician of compulsive dynamism, was a jingoistic nationalist. He several times seriously considered a presidential bid and would serve both John Quincy Adams and Jackson as vice-president before becoming the architect of the new states' rights. A tall, cadaverous, aristocratic man, he was one of the keenest political thinkers of nineteenth-century America. He was also an asp-tongued political gladiator who had mixed emotions about Andrew Jackson. At the moment the secretary had his hands full, for the First Seminole War had broken out, demanding his attention both as secretary of war and as chief of Indian Affairs. In fact, he had already sounded out subagent Houston concerning recruitment of Cherokees to fight the Seminoles.[23]

Meanwhile, in January, as his delegation was seeking assurances from the white man's bureaucracy, John Jolly led his band of Cherokees west to Arkansas Territory; 341 men, women and children. Houston had ensured that they were properly supplied, providing blankets, kettles, traps and other gear, and for each of the 109 warriors, a new, government-issue musket.[24] As Jolly trekked west, Houston finally reached Washington, joining the somewhat bored Cherokee delegation at Brown's Indian Queen Hotel,* where such delegations were usually quartered at government expense.[25] Within days the emaciated subagent was granted an interview with the harried secretary of war, but rashly appeared in his office dressed in full Cherokee regalia; breechclout, blanket and feathers.[26] Calhoun, a gentleman of formal bearing, was outraged. He had expected a subagent, "an officer and a gentleman," but instead found himself face to face with the "Raven." He was not amused that a government official would materialize at a formal interview dressed as a "savage," and after a brutal reprimand he abruptly ended the meeting.

In an interview with President Monroe a few days later, a suitably garbed and subdued subagent pleaded the Cherokees' case for equitable treatment, but already forces were converging against him. In early February he was summoned to Calhoun's office and presented with a list of charges against him. Houston was stunned. Among the more serious accusations (made by agents he had denounced for corruption) was that as subagent he had smuggled slaves onto Indian lands. Calhoun also asked him outright if he had, as charged, sold whiskey to the Cherokees, and raised the question put by others whether he had somehow "prevented a Cherokee force from marching to the relief" of army units fighting the Seminoles. The latter charge was successfully answered in a nine-page letter on February 24,[27] but the others Houston took angrily to the president, believing that the hand of Senator Williams could be seen behind the affair, a hand attempting to ruin his reputation and General Jackson's as well.

Monroe and Calhoun investigated all charges against the young sub-

---

* Sometimes referred to as Brown's Indian Hotel, and later, simply as Brown's Hotel.

agent thoroughly and expeditiously. On the last day of February they completely exonerated him. No matter his pique, Calhoun was in no man's "pocket," and had come to see that the accusations were merely a crude smear campaign.[28]

Houston, however, felt humiliated and badly treated. On March 1, 1818, a day before his twenty-fifth birthday, he wrote a brief note to General David Parker at the War Department: "Sir, you will please accept this as my resignation to take effect from this date."[29] He resigned from the army (and, apparently, the subagency at the same time, a move he was later to regret) five years to the day after picking a dollar from the drumhead.[30] General Jackson was dismayed, but he would keep an eye on this brash youngster who had made such a distinct impression on him on the battlefield and on the Hermitage veranda.

"Houston is better qualified for the station than any man of his age."

ANDREW JACKSON, 1819

In the spring of 1818, jobless, prospectless and staggering under "a load of debt," Houston turned his back on Washington and struck out for Nashville. The future loomed dark, but a contemporary noted of him that he was "a man commissioned for leadership by God,"[31] and he knew it.

Stopping over in Maryville, Houston sold his eighth share in the family assets to his brother James, but still could not cancel all his debts,[32] and in Nashville, he was forced to sell most of his personal possessions to meet daily expenses. But sometime in the summer his back pay as subagent reached him, and that $645.60 permitted him to begin the study of law.[33] That money, however, was not all he felt the government owed him, and he initiated a series of claims destined to further clog bureaucratic arteries for many frustrating years.

In Nashville, freed from the immediate necessity of working for a living, Houston studied law under Judge James Trimble, a distant relative. He studied hard, often late into the night, and he played hard, usually at his old haunt, the Nashville Inn. He also found time to join the city's dramatic club, of which Jackson and John Eaton were members, and appeared in several stage plays, once realistically portraying a habitual drunkard. He also joined the Tennessee Antiquarian Society, the state's first learned institution. Despite these demands on his time, he was frequently at the Hermitage. There, to his relief, he was treated as a son by Andrew and Rachel Jackson. Rachel, a dour, overweight woman, whose constantly lit pipe was her "solace," was childless, and evinced a deep maternal interest in Houston (and some of her husband's other protégés), and the ambience at the Jackson plantation was distinctly familial.[34]

Law came easily to Houston, and from the start he approached it less as a career goal than as a rung on the ladder to the lofty heights of politics. "I grasped the great principles of the science, and they were fixed in my mind forever," he later wrote with a touch of ego, and Judge Trimble was no doubt impressed that his student was able to compress what was normally an eighteen-month course of study and apprenticeship into six. He easily passed the bar examination in December.[35]

Since his successful examination coincided with expenditure of his last dollars, lawyer Houston cast about for a convenient place to hang his shingle. He settled on tiny Lebanon, some thirty miles east of Nashville. The town needed a lawyer (actually, he functioned more as a notary), he desperately craved income and Isaac Halladay, a local merchant, was willing to stake him for lawbooks and rent him an office for a nominal fee.[36]

The new attorney swiftly built a respectable practice in Lebanon, where for the most part he was occupied with minor civil and criminal cases, the day-to-day mechanics of a litigious society. He was popular, outgoing and social, and his booming voice and towering form were effective in court. He traveled often to Nashville and to the Hermitage, of course, for politics had already become the fuel that powered him. Jackson was absent on campaign in the Seminole War in this period, and in a controversial "interpretation" of his vague orders, invaded Spanish Florida, precipitating a major diplomatic flap. This curious filibuster was part of a larger vision, for to the secretary of war he unblushingly expounded: "add another Regt. and one frigate and I will insure you Cuba in a few days."[37] Though the general was absent, many of his protégés and political allies still gathered at the Hermitage to discuss politics and the other great issues of the day and thrill to news of Jackson's exploits.

In early 1819 Governor McMinn, almost certainly at Jackson's request, appointed Houston adjutant general of the state militia, a part-time post carrying the rank of colonel, tremendous prestige and political entree. Colonel Houston's "work" as adjutant general was minimal; an occasional report to the governor or secretary of war on the number of militiamen available for potential duty.[38]

It was not only militia reports Houston sent to the War Department, for he maintained an acerbic correspondence with Calhoun and his assistants as well. His major—and rather doubtful—claim was for back pay as first lieutenant, from October 21, 1817, to the date of his resignation the following March 1. Calhoun felt constrained to explain, as if to a child, that he had already been paid once for that period, as subagent, and no one could be paid by the government twice for the same services. Houston considered that his lieutenancy was in force while he worked as subagent, and the secretary labored mightily to convince him of the contrary. Sam Houston rejected those labors bitterly. In his words, he was "mortified at the treatment I have received from my Government," and he blamed both Calhoun and the shadowy Senator Williams. The latter, he believed, was still spreading rumors about him, including one that he was being sued by the government. The design was to tarnish his reputation, jeopardize his credit and perhaps even cripple his legal practice.[39]

Jackson sprang to the defense of his protégé. He used his influence liberally, writing Calhoun on several occasions, and at least once sending Colonel James Gadsden of his staff to hand-deliver a letter that reminded the secretary (his future vice-president)* that Houston, "though poor is one of those noble-minded fellows" who should be treated with consideration.[40] Finally, the iron-willed Calhoun gave in. He wrote Jackson (not Houston) that he had "re-examined the claim of Houston for pay," and had at last approved it.[41] That cheered Houston immensely, for he felt that he had been once more investigated and exonerated. However, the angry secretary was to gore him once more.

---

* Jackson and Calhoun, political allies of convenience, later had the most bitter of falling-outs when the former learned a dozen years after the event that the latter, as secretary of war, had argued to President Monroe that Jackson should be censured— or worse—for his unauthorized invasion of Florida in 1818.

Instead of sending the back pay ($170.09) to a branch of the Bank of the United States, the draft was made on a Nashville bank. Like most local banks this one discounted the government draft (27 percent in this case), and Houston fired back intemperately: "I can see no reason for the conduct pursued by you . . . unless it is that I am the same man against whom you conceived so strong a prejudice in 1818." This was just one more insult, he shrilled, and "your reiteration shall not be disregarded." In language that might have provoked a duel, he made a blunt accusation: "your personal bad treatment, your official injustice . . . was to oblige a Senator [Williams]—secure his interest and crush a Sub-Agent . . . all this Will I remember as a man."[42] Houston got what he wanted, and Calhoun sent a new draft to a government bank. The hand of Andrew Jackson in this can be felt, if not seen. There were other minor claims stemming from Houston's service, and they too were eventually resolved in his favor, but he had made a lifelong political enemy pursuing them.[43]

While Houston's claims were being pressed in 1819, John Rogers paid him a visit in Tennessee. Things were unsettling in Arkansas Territory, and the Cherokees there had many grievances. Not the least of these was a sporadic war with the Osage Indians, on whose lands the Eastern Cherokees had been settled. The Osages had never been party to the Cherokee–United States treaty, and considered the Red Man from the East as trespasser. Rogers, speaking for John Jolly, begged Houston to seek another appointment as subagent and come west to put things straight.[44]

Convinced, Colonel Houston turned as always to the gaunt figure at the Hermitage, and the general wrote Calhoun in September: "I have recommended him to accept the appointment of Agent . . . Houston is better qualified for this station than any man of his age." More to the point for Jackson, "he can draw to the Arkansas in a few years the whole strength of the Cherokee Nation, now on the East of the Mississippi River." The land speculator also promised that Houston "can and will govern them," despite what Senator Williams might have said in "hidden underhanded slander."[45] This message produced the expected results and Houston's appointment was duly approved, but by the time the paperwork was done, his delicate political antennae had detected something more promising. He rejected the post, later disingenuously asserting that he did so because subagent salaries had been slashed.[46]

He had learned that a political door wide enough for his sizeable ambitions was about to swing open. Under the guidance of Governor McMinn (and Jackson), he campaigned for the attorney generalship (district attorneyship) of Davidson County, and in October handily won it.[47] The seat of Davidson County was Nashville, the state's political caldron, so of course the post was more alluring than an Indian agency. Ironically, he would later urge former governor McMinn himself to accept a subagency, stressing the "philosophical," cleansing effect of life on the frontier: "There we can examine ourselves in the abstract— and draw conclusions, unbiased by passion."[48] Houston would fade to the frontier himself in 1829, but not to indulge in philosophy.

"Vagabonds and people of bad customs."

HADEN EDWARDS, 1824

Back in Nashville, Sam Houston re-entered Jackson's widening political circle, and was once more carousing in the riotous Nashville Inn, but the mundane work of attorney general neither appealed to him nor provided suitable financial rewards. At this juncture he was becoming fond of flashy, almost garish clothes, and his tab at the inn was awesome.[49] Hence, after having used the attorney generalship to maximize its political potential, he quietly resigned after a year and returned to private practice, this time with his office located in Nashville.

In the autumn of 1821, as he was again dunning the secretary of war, his fellow officers elected him major general of Tennessee's Southern Militia Division, a command earlier used by Andrew Jackson as a political springboard.[50] The young man who seven years earlier had left home a private was now a major general.

Within a year Jackson, always hovering in Houston's background, confided to James Gadsden that he expected the militia general to soon successfully run for Congress.[51] As a member of the now fully functioning "Tennessee Junto," it was Houston's destiny, for the Junto largely existed to promote Jackson's presidential aspirations, and it could best do that from positions of state and national influence. With the support of Jackson, the Junto, and current governor Billy Carroll, how could Houston lose?[52]

As he groomed himself for greater things, Houston, like most Americans, began to hear more and more about Texas. That vast and all but empty land had been a major topic of conversation for years, and the 1819 Adams-Onís Treaty added the spice of controversy to that conversation. Spain's cession of the Florida peninsula to the United States was universally popular in the United States, but the treaty clause forbidding United States interference with Texas was not. Governed loosely from distant Mexico City, underpopulated Texas was the border province of the huge Spanish viceroyalty of New Spain that most attracted Americans. The treaty defined the border between the United States and Texas at the Sabine River, but Andrew Jackson and other expansionists (including John Melish, famous American cartographer) raged. They accused Secretary of State John Quincy Adams of signing away land already American by virtue of the Louisiana Purchase, the precise boundaries of which had never been delineated. "Manifest Destiny" was becoming a potent political slogan.

Texas was already newsworthy for its raucous political turbulence, much of which was sparked by Anglo outsiders. Although crisscrossed by legendary *conquistadores* in the sixteenth century and implanted with a few settlements as early as 1680, the province of "Tejas" had for more than a century remained a somnolent backwater. Lacking gold, silver and other alluring sources of wealth, and with an embarrassment of perpetually hostile Comanches and Apaches, Texas remained poor and underpopulated, its settled population less than three thousand Spanish-speaking *Tejanos*.

As early as 1800, Belfast-born Philip Nolan entered Texas from French Louisiana with a band of armed men to stir up what local Spanish officials considered trouble. He had been in and out of Texas, trading or stealing horses, and the first reasonably accurate maps of the province, which he drew, were widely disseminated. He was finally arrested by Spanish troops and summarily shot, becoming to some a martyr.[53] Three years later, the Louisiana Purchase placed land-hungry Americans on the Texas border, and the Purchase's ambiguous boundaries sparked strong American interest in Texas. Acquisition of Louisiana in its turn had led to the Aaron Burr conspiracy, with its cast of hundreds of filibusters; a conspiracy that involved Texas. To Nolan, to

the Burr conspirators, and to many others, Texas was an enticingly ripe
fruit, connected to distant Mexico City by only the most slender of
vines. Many—including Jackson—felt the same about Cuba, another
vulnerable appendage of a withering imperial power.

Next to excite the American public and keep the Texas question alive
were the tragic adventures of Dr. James Long, who with his wife Jane
(considered the "Mother of Texas" because she gave birth to the first
known American child there, on Galveston Island) entered Texas in
1818 or 1819, after serving as a surgeon with Jackson's army in the
First Seminole War. At the same time, John Melish published his
influential *Information and Advice to Emigrants to the United States,*
whose maps indicated that much of Texas lay inside the Louisiana
Territory.[54] Long built a mud fort on Galveston Island and then trekked
inland with a sizeable band of armed freebooters. He apparently expected to eject the Spanish from Texas with the aid of Mexican radicals
seeking independence. Mexico's revolutionary wars had erupted in
1810, were crushed and then ignited anew, ebbing and flowing until
independence was at last gained in 1821. Mexico was in chaos, and
Long counted upon Tejano support. But, after a desultory "campaign,"
which was well-covered by United States newspapers, the Spanish captured Long and most of his men. The surgeon was executed in 1821,
generating front-page news in the United States.[55]

Also, scattered bands of Cherokees had made their way into Texas as
early as 1816, many settling in the area of Nacogdoches, near the
United States border, and according to some accounts, Houston, as
subagent, had given some thought to sending Jolly's band there instead
of to Arkansas Territory.[56] Thomas Hart Benton, sporadically in contact
with Houston, was himself fixated on Texas and American expansion
there since 1818, and in letters shared his ideas with his erstwhile
subordinate.[57]

In 1822 "General" Houston and two friends purchased shares in the
Texas Association of Tennessee. This was one of many speculative
companies that sprang up after Moses Austin negotiated his "empresario" colonization contract with Spain (his son, Stephen, had the contract approved by independent Mexico after Moses's death*). Land

---

* Moses had negotiated a colonization contract in 1820 with Spanish authorities in
New Spain. It called for his settling three hundred families of American emigrants on

speculation, and in many cases the dream of emigration and settlement, led people to buy shares in such companies. The Texas Association of Tennessee's secretary was a Nashville politico on the outs with the Junto, John Erwin, whose father Andrew was a political ally of John Williams.[58] At least as late as 1827 Houston and one of his friends, Dr. John Shelby, were still stockholders.[59]

Then, returning Texas to the front burner of public opinion in the United States, came the eccentric Edwards brothers, who had pledged to Mexico that in return for a huge land grant they would prevent "vagabonds and people of bad customs" from entering Texas.[60] In reality, they were to do the opposite, and their bizarre "Fredonia Rebellion" of 1826–1827 was daily newspaper copy in the United States. Houston was well aware of this "upheaval" not only because of his investments, but also because Nashville friends, John and William Wharton, were at least peripherally involved in it. The Whartons, dedicated drinking buddies, were in and out of Nashville and Texas in the 1820s.[61] No matter how alluring, however, Texas was for the future. As far as Sam Houston was concerned, politics was now.

In 1823, prestige high, money in the bank from his solid law practice, and smiled upon by Jackson and Billy Carroll,* Houston announced for the congressional seat of Tennessee's Ninth District. Essentially unopposed, he was duly elected in August, and Jackson was elected to the Senate in a contest against incumbent John Williams. The two rode off together to Washington that fall, to get one general elected president and the other general politically seasoned.[62]

---

a two-hundred-thousand-acre tract of land near San Antonio de Bexar. He himself would receive a very considerable portion of good land for his own use. Moses died, however, in 1821, the year Mexico became independent of Spain, and his son Stephen Fuller Austin, born in Virginia the same year as Sam Houston, renegotiated Moses's empresario grant with the new authorities and began the laborious settlement process.

* Carroll, a linchpin of the state Jackson organization, was a successful Nashville businessman and politician, who had served Jackson during the Creek War, and had coolly commanded a brigade at the Battle of New Orleans. A charismatic but "folksy" politician, he parlayed his war service and closeness to Jackson into an unprecedented six terms as governor of Tennessee.

"He was only notable for his want of integrity."

EDMUND RUFFIN, 1857

In Washington the freshman representative performed, one biographer has noted, "strictly [as] Jackson's liege man" and stalking horse.[63] His voting record mirrored that of his mentor,[64] who was focused on the 1824 presidential campaign. Before long he, like Jackson, became a habitué of Major O'Neale's "Sociable Tavern," and did much of his politicking with toddy glass in hand.[65] O'Neale's was to Washington in this epoch what the Nashville Inn was in Tennessee—a political drinking club. High-proof potables and pungent political deals were consumed and consummated there daily. In that tavern Houston is said to have grown infatuated with vivacious Peggy O'Neale (the future Mrs. John Eaton), the tavernkeeper's lusty daughter.[66] Eaton was to marry this lady of rumored immorality within weeks of Houston's first nuptials, and both weddings would produce more scandal than bliss.

Houston was hardly overworked in the House and easily found time to have a hand in writing campaign pamphlets touting Jackson (who, ironically, was seated uneasily in the Senate next to Thomas Hart Benton of Missouri) and his presidential bid. In January of 1824, Congressman Houston gave his first speech in the House, fittingly in support of Greek independence, lacing his rhetoric with images drawn from *The Iliad.*[67] When Congress recessed, he returned to his Nashville law practice and friends, who by now included three future presidents; Jackson, James K. Polk* and Buchanan, a Pennsylvania congressman he had befriended in Washington.

The 1824 campaign was the first national dogfight, with resplendent personalities, swollen egos, vitriolic verbiage, underhanded deals, and for the first time, four strong candidates, partly because no true na-

---

* Polk, who had emigrated to Tennessee from North Carolina, served in the state legislature 1823–1825, before going on to replace Houston in Congress, where he served for fourteen years. He was governor of Tennessee 1839–1841, and president, 1845–1849. Like Houston a habitué of the Hermitage and Nashville Inn, Polk supported Jackson and his policies with fervor.

tional parties yet existed. The contenders were: Jackson; John Quincy Adams, son of second president John Adams, Bostonian, aloof, abolitionist, a man of towering temper; William Crawford, Georgia politician, former secretary of war and treasury and perennial presidential hopeful; and Henry Clay, gifted orator, attorney for Aaron Burr, duelist, and self-styled spokesman for the Upper South. John C. Calhoun, unannounced contender, was coyly waiting in the wings. When no candidate received a clear majority of electoral votes (Jackson had 99, Adams 84, Crawford 41, and Clay 37), the political bargainers swarmed to garner the support of Crawford and Clay for either one of the front-runners. Positions of influence and perhaps even money were offered, and biographer Llerena Friend asserts that Houston was told to give Clay "anything he pleased" for swinging his votes to Jackson.[68] It is known that he negotiated with the Ohio and Pennsylvania delegations to the House, saying that if they supported Jackson, "their man" (Clay) could have any position he desired in the new administration.[69] As a Georgia politician would later snipe, "He was only notable for his want of integrity." Clay, however, was listening to another siren, and steered his political craft toward the haven quietly offered by the Bostonian.

On February 9, 1825, John Quincy Adams was elected sixth president of the United States by the House despite Houston's efforts, and the Jackson camp hypocritically howled foul when the president-elect named Henry Clay his secretary of state, a position seen as springboard to the White House. Amidst all the smoke of the presidential infighting, John C. Calhoun had wafted easily into the vice-presidency. Houston's old nemesis had simply settled back and watched with mild interest to see just who "his" president would be. The disappointed Jacksonians, screeching "corrupt bargain," began their 1828 campaign in 1825, and from this vast anti-Adams, anti-"fraud" coalition would evolve the Democratic party.

> "I dislike even the appearance of being a candidate
> in opposition."
>
> JAMES K. POLK, 1824

In Congress, Houston was known as an "internal improvements" man, especially in regard to public works he wanted his colleagues to fund in the Western states. He voted consistently for such projects as the National Road, aid to turnpikes and canals, and a more liberal policy for the sale of federal lands. He also probably helped pen more pro-Jackson literature, including the 1825 campaign biography, *A Civil and Military History of Andrew Jackson, by an American Army Officer.* John Eaton, who had been in the Senate since he left Jackson's staff in 1817, collaborated.[70]

He also found time for romance. At age thirty-two he was one of the capital's most eligible bachelors, and his letters reveal that he was casting about seriously for a helpmate. He met and was briefly stricken by Mary Parke Custis, Martha Washington's granddaughter (who would later marry Robert E. Lee), and wrote her some rather cloying poems,[71] but it was the mysterious "Miss M——" from South Carolina who almost became Mrs. Houston. He wrote a friend early in 1825 that "for my *single* self I do not know yet the sweets of matrimony, but in March or April next I will."[72]

He had met the object of his romantic attentions while in tiny, inland Cheraw, South Carolina, conducting some handsomely paid legal business between House sessions.[73] He fully planned to propose marriage in the spring of 1825. However, as he wrote cousin John (now in Washington) on April 20 from South Carolina, his plans had unraveled. Already, "some of my friends at home wish me to run for Governor," he confided, and he also admitted fretting that he was not yet a man of property. So, he informed his cousin, "I felt bound in honor to let Miss M—— know all these facts, and she concluded to defer matters until fall." He lamented that while he found "no difficulty in my way in So. Carolina," he was embarrassed that he lacked "a house for the reception of Madam, when I would bring her home," and "no relations in 200 miles of this place where she could stay." So he decamped for Tennessee, "with a promise to return next fall."[74] This was the last he would write of his beloved "Miss M——" from Cheraw.

Politics had become Houston's true passion. When he announced that he would seek re-election to the House, a surprised friend, aspiring politician James K. Polk, apologetically wrote him that he had just announced his own candidacy for Houston's seat. Polk had assumed that his friend was about to move to the governor's mansion. "The deed has been done," Polk confessed, deploring that "I dislike even the appearance of being a candidate in opposition to you."[75]

In the event, Polk withdrew when he realized that Houston's re-election was sanctioned by the Carroll machine. As a member of Jackson's Junto, and a tireless campaigner for the general, he knew his time would come, and in fact, when Houston left the House, Polk was his agreed-upon replacement.[76] Houston was easily re-elected, content to try for the governorship as soon as he, Jackson and Carroll felt he was ready for it.

The year 1826 was tumultuous for Houston, and in the House he continued to plug the Jackson line, opposing American representation at the Inter-American Panama conference called by South American "Liberator" Simón Bolívar,[77] who sought to weld the new Spanish-speaking republics into a semblance of political and diplomatic unity. Only reluctantly, he had decided to invite "observers" from both Europe and the United States, but these, pointedly, would have no vote, and would not be signatories of any treaties. The conference was to fail to achieve any of the Liberator's desired goals. In a long speech on the issue Houston waxed proud, like his isolationist mentor, that "Hitherto we have been pursuing a national policy," and had rightly "evinced a disinclination to entangle ourselves with alliances . . . we stand unshackled from all connexions with the nations of the Earth." He was chagrined that President Adams named two observers to go to Panama, but as it turned out, one died en route, and the other arrived after the conference had ended. A few weeks after Houston's speech, Jackson congratulated him for his level-headed approach to foreign policy, claiming nonsensically that American participation in the Panama conference "may lead to war."[78]

A short while later Jackson asked Houston to use his influence to ensure the admission of Junius Sonders and Sam Overton (son of political ally John) to West Point. The congressman was then on the military academy's "Board of Visitors," and he did use his official position as requested, just as Calhoun had for young Jefferson Davis two years before.[79] The general also stroked the younger man's ego; "I was very pleased with your course" on the Panama issue, noting that Rachel had herself been "very pleased" by Houston's New Year's gift. He also assured Houston that "Every thing as regards yourself is moving on in this quarter smoothly." He could bank on being Tennessee's next governor.[80]

Things, however, were about to become very rough in Tennessee for Sam Houston. The Nashville postmaster had resigned, and President Adams had nominated John Erwin (of the Texas Association of Tennessee), an anti-Jackson man, to fill the post. Houston was furious and wrote that the president should withdraw his nomination. He advised Adams almost libelously that "Mr Erwin is not a man of fair and upright moral character—he does not pay his debts tho all believe him able to do so." And, he continued, "He was detected, by three respectable members of the State Legislature, eavesdropping at the window of a Gentleman of Character to whom he was politically opposed at a very late hour of the night."[81] Such charges (based upon hearsay) could get a man shot in Tennessee.

Erwin, who became postmaster in spite of Houston's protests, soon learned of his "slander." A son-in-law of the powerful Henry Clay, Erwin challenged Houston to a duel—but not with him personally. Instead, the congressman was asked to shoot it out with accomplished duelist John Smith. He refused the call, on the grounds that Smith was not a Tennessean. A relative of John Williams wrote to Clay at this time, gloating that "it appears the General *has backed out,* in other words refused to fight."[82] This, however, was not the case, and following brokered negotiations Houston agreed to meet William A. White on September 22. They would trade shots on the Tennessee-Kentucky state line, to confuse jurisdiction should there be legal complications. The choice of weapons went to the challenged, and Houston opted for pistols at fifteen paces.[83]

For a week before the duel Sam Houston practiced with his new dueling pistol, sometimes under the guidance of Andrew Jackson, himself no stranger to dueling. There, on the senator's plantation, gunshots disturbed the slaves working in the field as the young man honed a new skill under the eyes of his patron. Finally, on the appointed day the duel took place, and when the two large puffballs of gunsmoke cleared, White was screaming on the ground, a bullet in his groin. White survived, but Houston admitted that it had been a sorry affair, painful to him as well. In the future he would firmly reject scores of challenges. The state of Kentucky brought legal actions against the congressman, but he simply ignored them.[84] He could not, however, evade an investigation by the Cumberland Masonic Lodge. Its members were upset by Houston's slandering Erwin, a fellow member, and his dueling with White, also a Mason. Powerful politico or not, he was suspended from the lodge for a year.[85]

While in Congress Houston was active on the Board of Visitors for West Point, a supervisory committee that periodically inspected the military academy and its cadets. Though destined to be a harsh critic of the "elite" academy in the future, he was quite supportive of it in the House. He was also impressed, as he later wrote, by one of its brightest cadets, Virginian Robert E. Lee, whom he met and interviewed in 1826, and with whom he would have a crucial correspondence on the eve of the Civil War.[86]

"He does not possess talents of the highest order."

JULIA ANN CONNER, 1827

Despite the Erwin and Masonic tangles, Houston, whose term expired in March of 1827, was confidently gearing up for the gubernatorial campaign. Unknown to him, Billy Carroll had doubts. He wrote of a potential opponent of Houston that he was "a grade superior in talents to Houston," who was, in Carroll's appreciation, "excessively vain."[87] Despite his reservations, at Jackson's urging Carroll was willing to support Houston, with the understanding that the younger man would serve for one term only, after which he would turn the reins of the state back to "Billy." Houston's drinking cohort Polk, who had been tapped by Jackson and the Carroll machine to fill Houston's seat in the House, received a letter late in the year reviewing the upcoming elections; "a contest already so well settled that little if anything need be said about it. Evrybody knows that Houston will be elected." [88] Indeed, it was common knowledge in the state that no viable opponent could be found for "Jackson's man."

In Tennessee in the spring of 1827 to campaign, Houston boarded again at the Nashville Inn, and while there conversed with William Wharton. Just returned from a visit to Texas, Wharton spoke of the Fredonia Rebellion and the reasons for its failure, and waxed eloquent about the endless opportunities across the Sabine. Houston's interest was aroused by what he heard of the restless Mexican province in which he still had an investment. [89]

That summer Houston was elected governor of Tennessee, but hardly with the expected ease. The Williams machine was far from lifeless, and, as the election approached, it gained fresh vigor. The Williams candidate for governor was Newt Cannon, and in a nasty campaign, he garnered 44 percent of the vote. Williams himself was elected to the state Senate, and Davy Crockett defeated a "Jackson man" in a congressional race, while John Bell defeated Jackson's old friend Felix Grundy and remained in the Senate, serving with John Eaton, who was at this time acting as Jackson's Washington campaign manager. [90] The 1827 elections had been something of a draw for Jackson's people, and the state was hardly solidly behind the general on the eve of his presidential bid. Still, the thirty-four-year-old governor-elect, sporting clothes "equal to the rococo tastes of his generation," [91] emerged proudly from the Nashville Inn to an active social life.

On September 21, Julia Ann Conner, a traveler from South Carolina, witnessed a "great parade" in Houston's honor. She had heard much of him; that he was "the most popular man in the State," and "his rapid & almost unparalleled rise is sufficient evidence of the fact." But Miss Conner had some sharp-eyed comments to jot in her travel journal. She observed after first meeting the governor-elect that "I beheld not the God-like grace I had been led to expect but [merely] a figure of herculean proportions."

After chatting with Houston a few days later, she scrawled that she "could not discern that superiority . . . which has gained him such universal popularity . . . as he does not possess talents of the highest order." She admitted that he was "graceful," yet "I cannot agree with the general opinion relative to his beauty." He was extremely "polite & attentive which cannot fail to render him popular," yet she found him somewhat shallow and far too ingratiating, and wrote of the constant stream of compliments that flowed from his lips. Unfortunately, too many people took his flattery at face value and "often forget the *truth* of a graceful compliment & seldom question it. Experience has taught him that they compose the majority." In other words, Miss Conner saw Sam Houston as a manipulative and deliberate charmer.[92]

On October 1, 1827, Houston was inaugurated governor in the large Nashville First Baptist Church. In his inaugural address that heady day he informed the overflow crowd of well-wishers that while he was governor of a *state*, "One of my obligations is to support the Constitution of the United States," for only by doing so could he provide for the common good. Through good times and bad, he would always mightily endeavor to do exactly that.

THREE

Sam Houston on the Pendulum

"There are some no doubt that would like to
see you killed."

ROBERT ALLEN, 1825

Tennessee governor Sam Houston automatically became a national figure when Andrew Jackson was elected president in 1828. His "program" focused, as it had in Congress, on stimulating the state's
economic development, and creating a primary school system financed
by the sale of the state's considerable patrimony of land.[1] The years of
his governorship were years of smug contentment in Tennessee and,
indeed, in the rest of the nation. Houston did nothing to rock the boat
with either his mentor or his constituents. He even put his sympathy
for the Indians on hold. In this atmosphere of uneventfulness (though
jarring changes were gestating), the publication of James Fenimore
Cooper's *The Prairie* in 1827 was a major event, fittingly focused upon
the American interior. Americans were drifting away from the coasts,
discovering the vast land, and themselves in the process. Houston's
inaugural year also marked the beginning of the nation's gaudiest party,
as New Orleans hosted its first Mardi Gras, a symbol of this self-
contentedness.

Houston's elevation and the first Mardi Gras offer a certain symmetry, for the United States was a nation on a gigantic toot, what W. J.
Rorabaugh, in his study, *The Alcoholic Republic,* has termed "the great
alcoholic binge of the early nineteenth century."[2] The first thirty years

of the century saw the greatest per capita consumption of spirits in United States history, and by 1830 the average American was lustily quaffing an astounding five gallons of whiskey, or its equivalent. Since many abstained and many more were too young to tipple, the real figure for adults, especially males, must have been horrifying.[3] In this vast bacchanal Sam Houston was a legendary reveler.

Sam Houston was not the only prominent American in this epoch to frequently drink himself into roaring, garrulous inebriation. Even the "God-like" orator Daniel Webster was commonly "so drunk on the floor of the Senate that he could not articulate his mother tongue."[4] Nor would Monroe's vice-president, Daniel D. Tompkins, have noticed. A contemporary wrote of the Senate president that "He was several times so drunk in the chair that he could [only] with difficulty put the question." Andrew Jackson's own first inaugural reception, held at the White House, was a notorious drunken brawl, with "several thousand dollars in smashed china."[5]

So heavy was the boozing that distilled spirits became the third-leading industrial product of the United States, and excessive drinking was so common that local temperance societies were formed by the hundreds to combat it. The National Temperance Society was founded in 1826, and the Mormon church, created in the following decade, embraced abstention as a matter of doctrine.[6]

It was through the whiskey glass that Houston observed the world around him, and saw and articulated his growing dreams of empire. Living in the Nashville Inn, where whiskey was blended with politics, may well have contributed to his grandiose visions. Even Charlestonian Conner, who stayed at the Nashville Inn herself, marveled at the "many toasts" she saw imbibed there.[7]

In 1828, the year of Jackson's victory at the polls, Houston's attention was again briefly drawn to Texas and its possibilities. William Wharton returned from yet another sojourn there and regaled the governor with tales of a rich, restive and underpopulated province, which was attracting thousands of Americans. Texas certainly held an allure for the governor, but he was again distracted and captivated by the "Dear Girles." He had not truly made his "fortune" yet but he was clearly on his way.

Since 1824 Houston had been a frequent house guest of Robert Allen of Gallatin, Tennessee. Allen and his brother John had been officers with Jackson during the War of 1812, and had met young Sam while on campaign against the Creeks in 1814, and at the Hermitage on many occasions since. Their friendship continued over the years, and from 1819 to 1827 Robert served as a congressman, two of his terms alongside the future governor.[8]

John Allen, an imperious planter and horsebreeder of high repute in Tennessee, lived in "a stately mansion" on the bluffs of the Cumberland River, some twenty miles northeast of Nashville, and Houston, at times in company with Jackson or members of the Junto, was wont to visit him and attend the almost weekly races.[9] On one of those visits in 1824 he first met Eliza, who at almost fifteen was the eldest of John's progeny. A slender blonde, Eliza was already an excellent horsewoman, and her vivacious charm and equestrian skill made a deep impression on Houston.

In the summer of 1825, Robert Allen wrote Houston a curious missive, apologizing for being as yet unable to repay a hundred dollars the congressman had loaned him. "Can't you come up [to Gallatin] and spend a week?" he inquired, nonchalantly noting that "there are some no doubt that would like to see you killed." Such men were, however, not to be taken seriously, for they were cowards: "Nobody doubts Sam Houston's bravery, many his discretion."* This was fully a year before Houston's scrape with John Erwin reached the serious stage, and Allen's use of the word "discretion," in the context of the times, hints strongly at his bachelor friend's womanizing. No matter the threats, Houston returned to Allen's home often.

Over the years his attraction to Eliza grew, and the allure of an alliance with the powerful Allen clan was surely not absent from his calculations.[10] His eye was trained on Eliza with the full approbation of her parents. The match—no matter the difference in age—would be a good one for both parties. The Allens were of the genteel "Old Tennessee" elite, a family well-connected in politics, social circles and the planter economy, and Andrew Jackson's most promising protégé was obviously destined for greatness. It appeared to be an auspicious pairing. So, quite naturally, a "low-intensity" courtship of Eliza continued, and as governor, the suitor was in Tennessee full-time, permitting him the luxury of watching his nearby bride-to-be blossom.

* Robert Allen to Houston, June 23, 1825, E.C.B. 3N199.

"He will lay about Nashville, neglict his friends just
enough to get himself beaten."

ARCHIBALD YELL, 1828

In 1828, Houston made two fateful decisions. He would marry and he would seek re-election—in that order. Announcing that he would strive for another two-year term as governor meant breaking his agreement with Billy Carroll, who thought it his turn to move into the governor's mansion. Houston's move was politically dangerous, a tolerable risk only because of his confidence in his popularity and in Andrew Jackson's unqualified support. Carroll had made his own candidacy known early in 1828, and Houston's decision would mean open political warfare. Though he refrained from publicly promoting himself until after his marriage, he did not hide his desire to run again from his friends. As early as March 1828, Archibald Yell wrote Congressman Polk that "Houston is getting along about as you would imagine. He will lay about Nashville, neglect his friends just enough to get himself beaten desasently [*disastrously?*] at the next election . . . some exertion *should* be used by him to sustain himself, though he has great confidence in himself. But if he has to pull against Billy Carroll," he had better get his campaign under way![11] After all, there was such a thing—even in Tennessee—as having too much faith in Andrew Jackson's coattails. Yet the confident Houston did indeed "lay about Nashville," save for regular excursions to Gallatin.

In November he wrote gleefully to cousin John that "I am not married but it may be the case in a few weeks." This was an odd bit of news indeed, for no engagement had yet been announced.[12] It might have appeared "indecent haste" on his part, since in polite society engagements were commonly a year or more long.

It soon seemed, however, that his marriage plans had gone awry. Early in December, in a letter to Tennessee congressman John Marable, he hinted of serious problems in his affair of the heart. "I have as usual had 'a small blow up,' " he wrote; "What the devil is the matter with the gals I can't say but there has been hell to pay."[13] He did not elaborate, but his relationship with Eliza was obviously less than tranquil.

It had indeed been a "small blow up," for just a few weeks later, in Gallatin, the governor and Eliza exchanged rings and formally announced their engagement, causing much benign excitement in the state—and enhancing Houston's chances of re-election. Their wedding, scheduled a mere month later, would be the social affair of the season, but it also set gossips' tongues moving like windmills.[14] Surely something was amiss.

"Not pretty, but dignified."

ANON.

Eliza, now eighteen, was, in the words of a relative, "not pretty, but dignified, graceful and queenly in her appearance."[15] She had apparently been courted by other hopefuls, but had rejected their intentions, for reasons perhaps not "of the heart."[16] One of the most recurrent themes in the literature dealing with Houston and Eliza is that he had a rival for her affections. The anonymous M.B.H. wrote that she was really enamored of a certain "William T.," but that her parents—"two more ambitious people never lived"—were adamantly opposed to the young man and championed Houston.[17] Many others agree, including Balie Payton, who knew Eliza well,[18] and most later biographers.[19]

At any event, the impending nuptials hugely pleased Andrew Jackson and his wife, whose wedding present was Rachel's own prized sterling silver flatware, a fitting gift of a "mother" to her son,[20] and strong testimony of the bond between Houston and the Jacksons. On the surface everything appeared happy, but one rock jutted in the road. Rachel Jackson, grossly overweight and long in poor health, died in late December, never to wear the beautiful gown she had had made for her husband's inaugural ball. Houston, chief pallbearer at Jackson's request, carried her coffin grief-stricken to the grave, on a gloomy Christmas Eve.[21] Rachel's death cast a pall over the impending wedding, but it did not delay it.

The ceremony took place in the mansion of Eliza's father on January 22, 1829.[22] It was a candlelight service presided over by the Reverend William Hume, and scores of distinguished guests were present; "a cavalcade worthy of a monarch," according to one report.[23] The groom appeared, in the words of one witness, "the figure of elegance in a black suit of velvet, topped by a Spanish cloak lined with scarlet satin." Houston would not mute his taste in clothes even for his marriage.[24]

The newlyweds spent their marriage night in John Allen's capacious home—in separate rooms—and departed the next day, forced by a severe storm to overnight at the home of the Robert Martins, on the Nashville Road.[25] There, it has been claimed, Eliza unexpectedly and explosively told Mrs. Martin "that she hated her husband."[26]

Yet others soon described the Houstons as "an affectionate couple."[27] In their relationship, paradoxes abound. When they left the Martins' they spent a few days with Robert McEwen and his family and then settled into rooms at the Nashville Inn, probably on January 26.[28]

It would seem that relations between the newlyweds deteriorated immediately, and probably for a variety of reasons. One reason, logic suggests, was the Nashville Inn itself. It was routinely clogged with Houston's drinking buddies and fellow political hacks and, given his strong proclivities for spirits and the fact that he was furtively campaigning, it is hard not to picture him caught up in the boozy political maelstrom. The inn may have provided a rude awakening for the sheltered young plantation girl.

On January 30, the now married and respectable governor announced that he would stand for re-election, and a bitter campaign against an angry Billy Carroll commenced.[29] This further detracted from Eliza's marital bliss, for his re-election effort took an increasingly large proportion of the governor's time.

"She was cold to me, & I thought did not love me."

SAM HOUSTON, 1829

Eliza packed her bags and abandoned the inn and her husband on April 9, less than three months after exchanging marriage vows, and fled back to her stunned family.[30] Despite her shattering flight, Houston somehow retained sufficient aplomb to publicly debate Carroll at Cockrell's Springs on April 11. Willoughby Williams, now sheriff of Davidson County, was present and recalled that Houston appeared in fine fettle, betraying no sign of emotional turmoil.[31] He probably yet hoped to win Eliza back. He must have, for he was experienced enough a politician to realize that there would be no chance of election or re-election to any public office in Tennessee if he could not win her—and respectability—back.

Surprisingly accurate gossip about the governor's marital problems was rife even before Eliza bolted. Jackson, for one, was pessimistic. As early as April 2 he was aware of Houston's domestic crisis, writing in a postscript to a letter about another scandal that "I have this moment heard a rumor of poor Houston's disgrace. My God, is the man *mad?*"[32] The president immediately grasped what a separation or divorce would mean for Houston's carefully nurtured political career. The crisis, then, did not come out of the blue, for Jackson learned of it a full week before Eliza's flight, and from a third party. More intriguing, the president felt he knew enough about it to assess the blame as Houston's.

What makes this situation—especially Houston's calm April 11 debate—truly remarkable and confusing is that two days before he jousted with Billy Carroll he had written (probably while drunk) an incredible, rambling and chaotic letter to his father-in-law; a letter brimming with hints, yet empty of conclusions. This letter represents Houston's only record of his separation from Eliza:

Mr. Allen   The most unpleasant & unhappy circumstance has just taken place in the family, & one that was entirely unnecessary at this time. Whatever had been my feelings or opinions in relation to Eliza at one time, I have been satisfied & it is now unfit that anything should be averted [averred] to. Eliza will do me the justice to say that she believes I was really unhappy. That I was *satisfied & believed her virtuous*, I had assured her on last night & this morning. This should have prevented the facts ever coming to your knowledge, & that of Mrs. Allen. I would not for millions it had ever been known to you. But one human being knew anything of it from me, & that was by Eliza's consent & wish. I would have perished first, & if mortal man had dared to charge my wife or say ought against her virtue I would have slain him. That I have & do love Eliza none can doubt,—that she is the only earthly object dear to me God will witness.

The only way this matter can now be overcome will be for us all to meet as tho it had never occurred, & this will keep the world, as it should ever be, ignorant that such thoughts ever were. Eliza stands acquitted by me. I have received her as a virtuous wife, & as such I pray God I may ever regard her, & trust I ever shall.

She was cold to me, & I thought did not love me. She owns that such was one cause of my unhappiness. You can judge how unhappy I was to think I was united to a woman that did not love me. This time is now past, & my future happiness can only exist in the assurance that Eliza & myself can be happy & that Mrs. Allen & you can forget the past,—forgive all & find your lost peace & you may rest assured that nothing on my part shall be wanting to restore it. Let me know what is to be done.

Sam Houston

9 Apr. 1829[33]

The most famous—and least clear—letter that Sam Houston ever wrote followed Eliza home and landed on the Allens like a second bombshell. Houston felt that the problem—separation—need not have occurred "at this time," implying that Eliza's flight was inappropriate, though not necessarily without reason. The very next sentence clearly indicates that he had been jealous, but since he was now "satisfied," he saw no reason to bring up the issue again. He then admitted that he had questioned his wife's virtue, but that in the past twenty-four hours had told her that he believed her faithful. Having so assured her, Houston felt that she should have remained with him, and he seems almost surprised by her flight. He testified that he loved her and that he would have killed anyone rash enough to question her virtue (as he himself had), and he asked the Allens for a calm, rational meeting in which to straighten matters out. "Eliza stands acquitted by me," which as a lawyer Houston (while sober) knew implied that a trial had taken place. He also admits to having been both judge and jury, as well as prosecutor.

The distraught husband claimed that even Eliza had confessed to being "cold" to him, and that her coldness had made him doubt her love. Then, perhaps realizing the gravity of the situation and the potentially violent reaction of the Allens, he proclaimed loudly that he could find happiness only with Eliza, leaving the actual mechanics of reunion in her father's hands. The "one human being" he had told of the problem (with Eliza's consent) never revealed what he had been told. Given the fact that someone had been informed by Eliza's "consent and wish," it was probably the Reverend Hume. Houston's letter must have caused the Allens as much consternation as their daughter's unexpected return.

We know few details of what transpired over the next several days, but the day following the debate with Carroll Houston was at Gallatin attempting to heal the rift and regain his wife. He may well have been summoned there by John Allen, and it must have been a tense meeting. He was permitted to see Eliza briefly in her father's parlor, but only under the unwavering gaze of an elderly aunt. The older woman recalled that Houston begged Eliza on bended knee to return with him to Nashville, and "with tears streaming down his face implored forgiveness." She refused.[34]

Anguished, Sam Houston rode back to Nashville and shut himself up in his rooms at the inn, giving himself over to self-pity and liberal doses of John Barleycorn. He permitted—perhaps demanded—only two close friends to share his despondency; Sheriff Williams and Dr. John Shelby, coinvestor in Texas lands.[35] While they sat, paced and drank, news of the separation spread like gunsmoke in a battle, for the Allen family lost little time in making public that their chaste daughter had been wronged.[36]

"I am a ruined man."

SAM HOUSTON, 1829

Tennesseeans of the age were not forgiving of such embarrassment on the part of their chief executive. This was a scandal, one in which a great Tennessee family had suffered public humiliation. Houston was burned in effigy at Gallatin, and mobs in Nashville became so threatening that local militia units were called out.[37] According to Willoughby Williams, the red-eyed governor "was deeply mortified, and refused to explain this matter," even to Shelby and him in the privacy of his rooms. After a few besotted days Houston decided that his only course of action was to resign the governorship.[38] Williams and Shelby helped him burn stacks of his personal papers (which is why no correspondence between him and Eliza can be found today). As he contemplated resignation and voluntary exile, he also sought solace in religion, something unknown to him until this time of travail. He summoned the Reverend Hume to the inn, and Hume, who knew both the governor and Eliza well, remained magisterially circumspect, never divulging whatever he learned.

Hume was surprised when the hard-drinking governor asked him for baptism into the faith, and he begged time to consider the matter. After conferring with respected Presbyterian pastor Obadiah Jennings, Hume returned and icily told Houston he would not, could not, do it.[39]

On April 16, recalled Sheriff Williams, Houston arose from his writing desk and without preamble informed him that "I am a ruined man; will exile myself, and now ask you to take my resignation to the Secretary of State." Failing to dissuade the governor, Williams did his friend's bidding that same day.[40]

The resignation refers vaguely to "private afflictions," the "Vicissitude of my life," "my own misfortunes," and the like, concluding that, "overwhelmed by sudden calamities," he could no longer serve the people and the state.[41]

Houston's bridges—matrimonial and political—were burned, and one week later, on April 23, in disguise and flanked by his two friends, he left the Nashville Inn and walked nervously through the morning crowds. They were joined by a mysterious Irishman, one H. Haralson,[*] and at the Nashville levee, Houston and Haralson boarded the small southbound steamer *Red Rover* and departed for the frontier.[42]

"He is insanely jealous and suspicious."

ELIZA HOUSTON, 1829 (?)

It has been posited, most authoritatively by Dr. W. D. Haggard (Houston's physician, who later himself married a daughter of Eliza's second marriage), that the effete Eliza was repulsed from the first by the "running sore" in her husband's thigh. That might indeed have induced a certain "coldness," but it hardly seems in itself cause for separation.[43] What the curious are left with, corroborated by Houston's chaotic letter to John Allen, is the matter of his jealousy, which appears indisputable.

Congressman Balie Payton recalled fifty years after the fact that Eliza had told him that "I left General Houston because I found he was a demented man. I believed him to be crazy. He is insanely jealous and suspicious. He required me to promise not to speak to anyone, and to lock myself in my room if he was absent." He himself sometimes locked her in. Eliza further claimed less credibly that the unstable Houston was haunted by ghosts "and supernatural influences."[44]

Eliza's brother Robert, dedicated to vindicating her name publicly in rumor-swept Tennessee, published Houston's bizarre letter to their father six months after the separation and formed a committee in Nashville to "investigate" the former governor's perceived slander. The committee published its report on April 30, 1830, finding that Sam Houston "is a deluded man," who "rendered his wife unhappy by his unfounded jealousies and his repeated suspicions of her coldness and want of attachment." Eliza "has remained in a state of dejection and despondency" ever since returning home.[45] Houston later thanked the

---

[*] He might have been Hugh Anderson Haralson, Georgia lawyer, planter and later politician.

committee: "You did a noble thing in vindicating the character of Eliza." [46]

Eliza waited seven years to obtain a divorce on grounds of abandonment, while Houston waited eight. Ironically, both were remarried in 1840, she to Dr. Elmore Douglas. She died in 1862, a year earlier than her first husband, and was buried in an unmarked grave along with her secret, the greatest mystery in the life of Sam Houston. [47]

"Merciful God! Is it possible that society is to be deprived of one of its greatest . . . ?"

CHARLES F. M. NOLAND, 1829

As the former governor and Haralson worked their way west by steamers and barges that spring, Billy Carroll—again governor—gloated. "Poor Houston," he penned, "rose like a rocket and fell like a stick." [48] To Jackson, his now questionable political ally, he confided, "I have always looked upon him as a man of weak and unsettled mind . . . incapable of fully meeting a reverse of fortunes." [49] Carroll, who himself had considered Houston something of a protégé, replaced him in that role with Congressman John Bell, who would contest a presidential nomination with the exile three decades later. [50]

Carroll was incorrect about Houston's ability to confront adversity, and some people believed that what was happening was not a reverse at all, but perhaps part of a clever plan. One of these was G. W. Featherstonhaugh, a peripatetic English observer who had earlier haughtily dismissed the entire state of Tennessee as "a kind of Ultima Thule." Coping with a similar frontier primitiveness decades later, he encountered Houston in Arkansas Territory and became convinced that he was scheming to "grab" Texas from Mexico, and that his separation was merely a convenient excuse for being on the frontier. [51]

Transferring from riverboat to riverboat, most of which were crewed by scabrous frontier types ("We know not that any on board either fear God or regard man," according to one traveler), [52] Houston and his enigmatic companion drank, gambled and in general bathed in dissipation. While the exile claimed to believe that "a great destiny waited for me in the West," [53] no one who observed him at the time would have guessed it. The man destined to give the keynote speech at many a temperance conclave was now swilling whiskey "until he was physically helpless." [54]

On one boat he encountered and imbibed mightily with Jim Bowie, probably dwelling on Texas affairs. [55] Bowie, a Georgian, had moved to Texas in 1828 and married into the elite Tejano Veramendi family, and by the time Houston encountered him, was a businessman-landowner in the San Antonio area. He was a true Texas-booster, and his tales must have made their mark on the exile. [56]

Although in mufti, Houston was hardly unrecognized by those around him. Unknown to him, he was being closely observed by a number of people. On May 11, Charles F. M. Noland wrote his father William from Little Rock about meeting the former governor at that frontier hamlet. The elder Noland knew Houston well and was a major stockholder in Texas land companies, which were attempting to recruit settlers to emigrate to their lands. [57] Noland's letter presents an interesting view of the down-and-out Tennessean:

> Governor Houston arrived here three days since on his way to the Indians—Merciful God! Is it possible that society is to be deprived of one of its greatest ornaments, and the United States of one of her most valiant sons, through the dishonor and baseness of a woman? He converses cheerfully, made a great number of inquiries after you . . . He wishes to go to the Rocky Mountains, to visit that tract of Country between the mouth of the Oregon and California Bay. He came with his rifle on his shoulder. General Jackson will certainly persuade him to come back from the woods. [58]

Hardly cocooned in despair, Houston was talking—and not for the last time—of his dream of creating something on the far frontier, a dream that was to gain strength and definition over decades. The Nolands, not alone in blaming Eliza for the broken marriage, kept track of Houston through that time.

"This wretched, miserable, and ill-fated man."

DANIEL S. DONELSON, 1829

Houston's traveling companion, Haralson, not only closely observed his famous friend but opened and read his mail as well. For some time the former governor did not realize that the man sharing his adventures had been assigned by the worried president to do just that. He did, however, become aware that he was being monitored, for the same day Noland wrote his father from Little Rock, the former governor wrote Jackson that he had learned that "you have been assured that I meditated an interprize calculated to injure, or involve my Country" by leading some kind of filibuster. That was not so, he promised. Of such a rumor, he wrote, "I suppose it was intended to complete my ruin." Although "the most unhappy man living . . . a houseless unshelter'd wanderer, among the Indians," Houston denied filibustering and offered to be of service, reporting to the president on frontier and Indian affairs, and, "If I can keep peace among the Indians & between them & the *whites* I will cheerfully do it." This he would endeavor, however, only in "my *individual* capacity," and not as a government agent.[59] The only way Houston could have learned of Jackson's concern was through Haralson, who soon left his company and faded from history.

Apparently Houston was talking too often and too loudly about his "plans" and had been for some months. This was, of course, an age of American expansion, and while many Americans were splashing across the Sabine to the South, thousands of others were making the long and dangerous trek to the Northwest. There the exquisitely fertile Oregon Territory beckoned (today's states of Oregon and Washington, and a large portion of British Columbia, all of indeterminate ownership). To Noland, Houston had waxed euphoric about the Oregon Territory, and he was aware of the recent founding in Boston of the jingoistic American Society for Encouraging the Settlement of Oregon, designed to pump Americans into the territory faster than the British could build up their population there.

To others, including Daniel S. Donelson, it was Texas and Mexico that he verbally wove into empires. Donelson had first learned of what he termed Houston's "Texas vision" in March, when the governor told him that he had just sent William Wharton back to Texas "as Houston's agent to foment the revolution from Mexico, a nation in almost constant political chaos, and with a growing Anglo-American population which felt little sympathy to the government in Mexico City."[60] In June, encountering the exile on the frontier, Donelson wrote the president, warning him in no uncertain terms that "this wretched, miserable, and ill-fated man" had developed a detailed and grandiose scheme to conquer Texas and much of northern Mexico and had solicited Donelson's help. Like Featherstonhaugh, Donelson believed "that he married Miss Allen to leave her, in order to have a justification for his leaving the U. States."[61]

Donelson was not exaggerating the exile's verbal imperialism. The circumstantial evidence is too clear to ignore.[62] Houston's old regimental commander, Thomas Hart Benton, now an influential Missouri senator, communicated with him on the frontier; perhaps *because* he was on the frontier. Benton knew of Houston's Texas musings, and he wrote one letter in the summer of 1829 "for the purpose of renewing old Friendship, and to request you to call upon me freely if I can be of service to you." An outspoken expansionist who had long coveted Texas, he assured Houston that "you have too much energy to be idle" on the frontier, and he pointedly enclosed two articles he had written on the subjects of the Southwest frontier and public lands. On these interrelated subjects, he advised, "If you have ulterior views your *tongue* and *pen* should dwell incessantly" on them, for these are the "two great topics. Write to me."[63] This is an odd message to send a man in disgrace on the frontier, with no apparent chance of regaining political power; that is, unless Benton believed that his friend was considering a move to expand the already vast bounds of the United States.[64]

Jackson, then attempting through special emissary Anthony Butler to purchase Texas from Mexico, was well-informed about Houston's ramblings and was concerned. He would be so for many years, no matter his protégé's disclaimers. Far from being a participant in the alleged schemes, Jackson did everything he could to forestall and frustrate them. For years he would attempt to disassociate himself from the putative filibuster, defending himself in communications and conversations with Mexican leaders and congressional opponents such as John

Quincy Adams. Whatever Houston was up to on the frontier was politically dangerous for Andrew Jackson.

In May, political publicist and editor Duff Green sent the president a letter he had received from John Marable (with whom Houston was in frequent contact), "containing declarations of Governor Houston, late of Tennessee, that he would conquer Mexico or Texas and be worth two millions in two years." Although he professed to be shocked by such news, Jackson believed it "the mere effusions of a distempered brain." He did, however, order his secretary of war to write Governor Pope of Arkansas Territory, enclosing an abstract of Marable's worrying letter. Pope was instructed "to make diligent inquiry," and to ascertain if such an "illegal project" was indeed afoot.[65]

The president also wrote Houston himself concerning the rumors, pledging all the while that "I cannot believe you have any such chimerical, visionary scheme in view."[66] The Arkansas authorities, including Colonel Matthew Arbuckle, commander of Cantonment Gibson (the westernmost army installation), did keep their eyes and ears open, but Arbuckle, who often tippled with Houston, discovered nothing from him, drunk or sober. Nor did Governor Pope.[67]

_____

"Thy letters will reach my wigwam."

SAM HOUSTON, 1829

Whatever else he was doing, Sam Houston had reached John Jolly's camp near Cantonment Gibson about May 20, after an eleven-year absence from his "father's" wigwam. Although at least sixty-five years old, Jolly was still erect and active, living in "patriarchical simplicity and abundance."[68] He and his braves welcomed the Raven with a grand party and dance near Weber's Falls.[69] The old chief later wrote President Jackson proudly that his "son Genl. Houston or the Raven came to me," seeking shelter. It was eagerly proffered.[70]

Effortlessly, Houston melded again into the Cherokee way of life, speaking the Indian tongue and dressing as a warrior "in breech clout and turkey feathers."[71] In June he wrote his cousin John that "the world may care nothing for me, but I deserve its regard in kindest Shape . . . Write to me. Thy letters will reach my wigwam."[72]

All was not right with the Cherokees in Indian Territory, however, nor with those who had not yet moved west. The Arkansas Cherokees had been enmeshed in "impoverishing warfare" with the implacable Osages, and were at times raided by the Pawnees and Comanches as well.[73] The Cherokees, after all, were wealthy by Indian standards, and their herds of livestock, lush fields, slaves, muskets and other possessions made them prime targets for the other tribes, who, in any case, essentially lived by prairie piracy. Tiny Cantonment Gibson, the only army post inside Indian Territory, was garrisoned only by infantry, and offered scant protection to the Cherokees. Never threatened with extinction by other Indians, they were often sore-pressed by them, however, and as Houston knew, mistreated by their white "guardians" as well.

The Civilized Tribes east of the Mississippi were confronting a no less implacable, and far more powerful foe: white society. Even after thousands had migrated west and a score of treaties had divested them of millions of acres, the Eastern Indians still clung stubbornly to some thirty-three million acres, caught in a constricting vise of white demographics. Desperate, the fifty-three thousand or so civilized Indians in the East did everything they could to resist, bringing suits against both state and local governments all the way to the Supreme Court. In the latter forum they sought recognition as independent and sovereign nations.[74]

The Indians had very few friends in Washington, and even fewer in state legislatures. Jackson was himself virtually a declared enemy of the Red Man, his political stature resting more on his reputation as an Indian fighter than on the laurels won at New Orleans. As president-elect, in a typical letter, he wrote to a Georgia congressman about the Cherokee "problem" urging that the state "build a fire under them. When it gets hot enough, they'll move."[75] His influence helped drive the ugly Removal Act through Congress in 1830, effectively voiding all previous Indian treaties and mandating the expulsion of all Indians from the East.

White population pressure was by then overwhelming, voters were lighting fires under their elected representatives because they wanted access to more land, federal land prices were falling and terms becoming easier, and Indian lands constituted the "last frontier" in the eastern United States. In addition, by unfortunate coincidence, gold deposits were discovered in 1829 on Cherokee land in Georgia, at Dahlonega and other sites, touching off a gold rush of whites, who ignored tribal boundaries.[76] Congress was also tiring of scores of treaties with a congeries of tribes and subtribes, the expenses of surveying tribal lands and garrisoning potential flash points, and other Indian expenses (over three thousand dollars was spent in a matter of months on official portraits of chiefs visiting the capital), and "the hotel bills of the Indian delegations did appear exorbitant, with oysters on the half shell, gin slings, and broken furniture figured in."[77]

And so Congress in 1830 simply decided to "remove" the problem and deposit it in the trans-Mississippi. The following year John Marshall's Supreme Court crumbled the Indians' last defenses in a case known as "Cherokee Nation versus Georgia." In that decision, which was to directly affect Houston, the Court held that the Indian tribes were not sovereign states but "domestic dependent nations," at the mercy of the United States. There was precious little of that commodity in 1831.[78] In 1832 the Choctaw began their sorry mass migration west. The other tribes would follow.

Thus the Indian, East and West, was under the gun, both figuratively and literally, and in Arkansas Territory Sam Houston was an embittered witness to the tragedy.

FOUR

The Frontier

"The duty would recreate my mind."

SAM HOUSTON, 1829

Sam Houston's home among the Cherokees was only a few miles from Cantonment Gibson on the banks of the Arkansas River, a hundred miles north of the Red River frontier of Texas, near the well-worn "Texas Road." Gibson was a wretched place even by contemporary military standards, and its isolation ate away at the small infantry garrison. This "Hell hole of the Southwest" was commanded in 1829 by Colonel Matthew Arbuckle, a hard-drinking, eloquently profane bachelor, with whom Houston was soon tippling into the wee hours.[1]

The Cherokees had settled near the cantonment to take advantage of the largely illusory protection it represented. With the Texas Road carrying increasingly heavy traffic, and Pierre Auguste Chouteau's large trading post nearby, here was an island of "civilization," no matter how squalid, jutting out of a vast sea of dangerous prairie.

If Houston was steeped in despair he showed little sign of it that summer and, while often drunk, and felled for a month by a nearly fatal return bout with malaria, he worked tirelessly to arrange peace between the Cherokees and their unneighborly neighbors.[2] Those who believed that he had come west with Texas on his mind suspected that he was working to recruit the frontier tribes for his projected invasion of the Mexican state, something he may briefly have considered.

His first step was to treat with the fierce Osages, a warlike people somewhat weakened by "two generations of debauchery," which followed their fateful introduction to the white man's alcohol.[3] According to French observer-savant Alexis de Tocqueville, Houston ranked the Osages at the bottom of his order of Indian civilizations, for "they live in continually moving hordes; are almost naked, hardly use firearms at all, and know no Europeans except the fur traders."[4]

One such fur trader, and one drawn on an unusually grand scale, was Pierre Auguste Chouteau, respected by the Osages above all men. Chouteau, the aristocratic son of one of the founders of St. Louis, was a legendary frontier figure. He had been a pioneer of the lucrative Santa Fe Trail and an ally of John Jacob Astor's fur-trading empire, and was a father figure to the Osages.[5] To deal with the Osages was to deal with Chouteau, and in early June Houston went to Chouteau's trading post for what amounted to a formal audience. The two men got on well from the start, for the trader also had a strong motivation to restore peace to the frontier—warfare cost him money—and that summer Houston enthusiastically recommended Chouteau to his friend, Secretary of War John Eaton, to fill the post of Osage Indian agent.[6] Since the older man was a veritable encyclopedia of the Southwest and Texas, the two must have talked at length about events and prospects across the Red River.

On a visit to the Osages the two persuaded them to briefly bury the hatchet. Meanwhile, as he was studying a memorial the Creeks had drawn up for President Jackson, Houston learned that the Cherokees, with elements of the other Civilized Tribes, were preparing to take the offensive against the Osages. Elderly John Jolly sent the Raven to a war parley at Bayou Menard in early July as his representative to speak in his name for peace. Houston gave it his best, but failed to deter some Cherokee hotheads, who took up their spears and muskets against the Osages.[7]

In July and until he was felled by malaria in August, Houston did everything in his power to calm the frontier, reporting back to Eaton in Washington what he heard and suspected. He was, with some help from Chouteau, remarkably successful.[8] Like the charismatic fur trader, he "thrust himself into a position of leadership" amidst a congeries of tribes spread over thousands of square miles.[9]

As Houston's relationship with Chouteau deepened through mutual respect (both were superb linguists), he wrote Eaton suggesting that he appoint the two as special government emissaries to make peace on the frontier. Chouteau, "a man of fine intellect, clear, vigorous, and active —he has the best practical knowledge of Indians of any man with whom I have ever been acquainted," was a natural, according to Houston. He promised Eaton that the two could pacify the frontier in part through "the distribution of some trifling presents, and medals of the Presidents (not Mr. Adams) given to the Chiefs." Houston would be pleased to accompany Chouteau "but will not accept any compensation for my services as the duty would recreate my mind." [10] Unfortunately, he was soon bathed in malarial sweats and Chouteau was never offered an official position.

Recovering in mid-September, and in exceedingly high spirits for a supposedly dejected and disgraced outcast, Sam wrote the president that he was already finding the frontier boring. He was giving some thought to moving to thriving Natchez, Mississippi, for "I am well known to the first men of that State." He confided that he often dropped in at Gibson, "where I can obtain News Papers," and his interest in things political "is rather increased than diminished. . . . Having been so actively engaged for years past in politics, it is impossible to lose all interest in them." [11]

"A disposition to remain with us."

CHEROKEE COMMITTEE, 1829

On October 21, the Raven's petition for citizenship in the Cherokee Nation was approved by the council as a reward for his efforts on behalf of peace. A committee of three subchiefs, presided over by John Jolly, granted citizenship to the white man, who "has manifested a disposition to remain with us." The citizenship document openly admitted that the honor had been conceded in large part so that Houston would not have to "comply with certain rules and regulations" mandated by the federal government, such as licensing for outside (white) traders. Jolly and the other chiefs were content to "grant him forever all the rights, privileges and Immunities of a citizen of the Cherokee Nation . . . as if he was a native Cherokee." It was done. Houston—the Raven—could now embark on a commercial career, deftly evading the letter (and license fees) of the law.[12]

Citizenship document in his traveling bag, he almost immediately set out for Fort Smith, Arkansas, to witness the government's annuity payment, or subsidy, to the Cherokee and other tribes. This annuity (fifty thousand dollars) was to be paid in gold coin, but the Cherokee agent, sticky-fingered Major E. W. Duval, instead doled out fifty thousand dollars' worth of government "certificates of indebtedness." Always discounted in terms of cash, these government IOUs were mere pieces of paper to the Indians, and soon ended up again in white hands. Most Cherokee recipients were baldly swindled out of the pretty engraved paper, given whiskey, a pittance in cash or both. According to Cherokee citizen Sam Houston, Duval and a coterie of merchant friends made a small fortune. His immediate complaints to Eaton and Jackson made him some powerful and vocal enemies, and when he agreed to lead a Cherokee delegation to Washington to present the Indians' case and denounce Duval's chicanery, he made yet more.

"Genl. Houston is to be at the head."

ANDREW JACKSON, 1830

In the last weeks of 1829 the Raven and three subchiefs headed north to the capital. En route he wrote John Overton that "the hour of anguish has passed by." He was now ready to be more than an exile. He was impatient to take an active part in something, but did not elaborate on just what he had in mind. Overton, a powerful Tennessee politico, a business partner and staunch supporter of Jackson, and a founding member of the Junto, had been a key figure in Jackson's presidential bids. The former governor informed Overton that he was on his way to Washington, "and perhaps New York," hoping to return via Nashville, where he could "make known the object of my visit" to those cities. He was loath to put that purpose on paper because the "curious" had been opening his letters.[13] In all probability, he was planning to seek financial support for his still vague plans involving Texas.

After less than nine months in exile, Sam Houston checked into Brown's Indian Queen Hotel on January 13, 1830, with his three Cherokee "brothers." Unlike the previous time he had visited the capital, he had no official position, no military rank, no money, no job, and, in fact, rather questionable citizenship.* He even dressed in Indian garb in the capital, acting very much the Indian he sought to be. He actually went so far as to visit the White House in Indian-styled buckskins.[14] He did, however, have ideas, ideas that transcended his presentation of Indian grievances. He met with the president and Eaton, blisteringly censuring Major Duval, his subagent John F. Hamtramck, and others who were cheating the Indians—probably the first such detailed denunciations from a source credible in high-level Washington.[15]

As Houston's so-called *Autobiography* notes, while a spokesman for the Cherokees, he dressed the part; "He wore a different blanket and handsomely ornamented buckskin coat for each occasion."[16] Luckily, he did not have to deal with Vice-President Calhoun. He also did some heavy-duty whiskey-guzzling at Brown's and other Washington watering holes, renewed friendships, and as before, wagged his tongue while in his cups about various Texas schemes,[17] which invariably had him leading some sort of armed expedition.

He was also arranging other ventures he hoped would bring him fortune, if not fame. He contracted with Benjamin Hawkins, an educated Creek, to purchase 10,025 acres of land in a "desolate section of Eastern Tennessee," abutting Georgia's rich placer gold strikes. He must have found an associate willing to speculate, for he had no money.[18] This venture occupied a good deal of Houston's attention over the next years, but fortune would again elude him.

Also, Houston and New York financier John Van Fossen applied through Secretary of War Eaton to supply rations to the Cherokees in Indian Territory. The government let contract bids for the supply of

---

* Before the 1831 Supreme Court decision—if one accepted the sovereignty of the Cherokee Nation—Houston lost his United States citizenship the moment he gained status as a Cherokee citizen.

treaty-mandated basic rations, each "ration" defined as one and a quarter pounds of fresh beef or a pound of fresh pork, plus two quarts of salt for each hundred rations.[19] The War Department had opened the bidding on February 18, and Houston's name and the New Yorker's money were soon in a sealed bid on Eaton's desk.[20] Given that Houston and the secretary were longtime friends and political allies, they should have expected an outcry. But Houston and Van Fossen were counting on the political influence of New York congressman Robert S. Rose, something Houston openly mentioned in a letter to his financier partner.[21]

They did not win the contract, in part due to Eaton's sensitivity to the potential conflict of interest, but also because theirs was not the lowest bid. Also, by then a storm had appeared on the exile's ragged horizon, a storm he should have anticipated. Houston's protests concerning mistreatment of the Cherokee and other tribes had led to the summary dismissal of five agents and subagents, including Duval and Hamtramck. They and their many friends launched a smear campaign linking Houston and his friends Eaton and Jackson in an alleged conspiracy to fraudulently obtain the ration contract.[22] Though there was no proof of this, the denunciations further depreciated Eaton's stock and embarrassed the president. Rumors of fraud persisted and would for many years haunt Houston and Eaton, whom Jackson sent to Florida Territory as governor in 1832 to get him out of the way.[23]

Another and far more threatening storm cloud was towering above Sam Houston, and soon President Jackson as well. Building on the rumors that Houston had been conspiring to gouge Texas from the body politic of Mexico, Doctor Robert Mayo charged him in very specific terms with a new Texas plot. In February, Mayo had stayed on the same floor of Brown's Indian Queen Hotel as Houston, and they often chatted, at times over copious draughts. According to Mayo, the former governor explained his entire plan to him, a plan that could hardly have succeeded without the support or at least benign indifference of the president.[24] Mayo himself, he recalled, was offered a position as surgeon in the projected filibuster.[25] He professed to have been horrified, and after reflecting on Houston's scheme, he informed Jackson, so that the president, aware that the conspiracy was no longer secret, would move to stop his protégé.[26]

As finally revealed by Mayo to Jackson late in the year,* the conspiracy did have a Houstonian ring to it. With Van Fossen's finances, Houston was said to be covertly recruiting an army, which he would launch across the Mexican border into Texas in early 1831. With Indian allies he had prepared within Texas, Houston would have a substantial force, with which he would sweep Mexican troops from the province and be welcomed as a liberator by the large Anglo population of Texas.† Not only did Houston personally confide his plans to Dr. Mayo, but so too had a mysterious, loose-tongued "Mr. Hunter," also lodging at Brown's. Hunter, a frustrated man who had been expelled from West Point, was "a *bona fide* agent of the recruiting service for this district," running one of scores of recruiting stations, "along the sea-board, from New England to Georgia." Thousands had already signed up, said Hunter, and were making their way to rendezvous points in Arkansas Territory.[27] Mayo was certain that Houston had gone to live with the Cherokees "to afford a cloak" for his budding conspiracy.

Jackson learned all this from Mayo in early December and, apparently shocked, almost immediately wrote William S. Fulton, secretary of Arkansas Territory. He minced no words: "D'r Sir, it has been stated to me that an extensive expedition against Texas is organizing in the United States . . . and that Genl. Houston is to be at the head of it." Jackson admitted that he was skeptical, but since the issue was so potentially dangerous for the United States, it must be looked into. He told the secretary that recruits were allegedly gathering along the Mississippi, soon to clamber aboard steamboats already chartered, and he ordered Fulton to "keep me truly and constantly advised of any movements which may serve to justify [my] suspicions," all with "the utmost secrecy." The president, not the War Department, would reimburse Fulton for any expenses incurred in the investigation.[28]

While Fulton was searching the frontier for shady characters, Jack-

---

* Why Mayo waited until December when he knew much of the alleged plot in February or March was never made clear.

† The liberal (large) land grants available free under the empresario system, and for that matter, the ability to squat, titleless, without molestation or taxes, made Texas seem very alluring to many Americans, and they were crossing into Texas in ever-greater numbers, bound by the scantiest of allegiances to any government.

son informed envoy Anthony Butler in Mexico City of the possible Houston embarrassment, evidencing apparently genuine concern.* "There is reason to fear that a project is already on foot by adventurers from the United States, acting in concert with disaffected citizens of Mexico, to take possession of Texas and declare it an independent republic." Clearly worried, he informed Butler that if such a clandestine expedition formed up "west of the Sabine River," it would be unconstitutional for him to act to forestall it. He ordered the envoy to advise the Mexican government of what might occur and promise that he would do everything possible to avert the danger, "punishing the citizens of the United States who may be detected as forming part of the conspiracy" within the boundaries of the United States. If the conspirators reached Texas, he could do nothing, but he would exert himself to prevent that.[29] The president, still hoping to purchase Texas, and worried that the British were seeking to do the same, feared that even rumors might make Mexico intractable.[30]

Meanwhile, in Arkansas Territory, Fulton soon penned a confidential report to the White House: "I went myself to the western frontier and ascertained in person all the facts . . . getting satisfactory information from the Mississippi River at the various points, at which it would be likely that such an expedition could be prepared or fitted out." In short, he was "satisfied . . . that no organized expedition was at that time in contemplation or on foot from any point within the Territory of Arkansas against Mexico, either on the part of Genl. Houston or any other person."[31]

Although no one could prove that a filibuster was being planned, the issue refused to die, and Jackson had to reassure the Mexican government on several occasions. Indeed, during discussions in the United States a decade later concerning the annexation of Texas, Mayo and his tale resurfaced, attached firmly to the lancehead of inveterate Jackson-baiter John Quincy Adams. During a congressional investigation, Adams and his allies demanded all diplomatic and other documents relating to the Texas question. A long, nasty political slugfest ensued,

---

* Butler, originally from South Carolina, had convinced Jackson that in its weak, corrupt and chaotic condition, Mexico could be persuaded to sell Texas to the United States. That is, if the price (and the bribes) were right. Jackson then appointed him special envoy to achieve that end, authorizing him to offer up to five million dollars. Partly due to his personality, partly owing to Mexico's instability, Butler failed.

with the bitterest of political foes spewing pure acid. At one point a letter stolen from Jackson's desk surfaced, written to him by Houston in a supposedly "Masonic cypher," but this "incriminating" evidence came to naught, since no one could satisfactorily decode it.[32] Jackson denounced his antagonists ("that scamp Doctor Mayo," and "Mr. Adams is vindictive, reckless of truth"), but accusations of collusion in conspiracy dogged him until his death.[33] Adams remained convinced that "Houston was his agent for the rebellion" in Texas.[34]

> "My situation is peculiar . . . *I am a citizen of the Cherokee Nation.*"
>
> SAM HOUSTON, 1830

Disappointed at losing the ration contract and disconcerted by the continuing rumors about a Texas filibuster, Houston left Washington in early April, returning to Arkansas Territory via Nashville, where he might have been approached by the Allen family, as Marquis James alleges, and may have briefly seen Eliza.[35]

With his plans for financial gain gone awry, Houston returned to the Cherokees determined to carry out at least a semiofficial role. During the next year he sent a series of reports to Eaton and Jackson both on Indian affairs and on what he learned of Texas, mainly from William Wharton, who had purchased a large tract of Texas land in 1827, and who kept him informed on his many transits of the Texas Road.[36] Houston promised to inform the president "whether the Mexican troops have reached the borders of the U. States," a strange offer, given that Colonel Arbuckle and his paid scouts were in a far better position to do so. Perhaps he merely wanted to be "useful" to his powerful friends.[37]

In late May Houston was "home" and while helping calm a major conflict between the Osage and Delaware tribes, he married Tiana (Diana, to most whites, also known as Talahina) Rogers in a traditional Cherokee ceremony. They were soon settled at "Wigwam Neosho," on the Texas Road, not far from the "Hell hole of the Southwest." Tiana, tall, slender and beautiful, was a daughter of "Hell-Fire Jack" Rogers, a Scots trader with the Cherokee and father (by a different wife) of Houston's friends and "brothers," John, James and William.[38] Houston had known Tiana since her childhood in Tennessee, where she had married a prosperous, mixed-blood blacksmith, David Gentry, later killed in the Osage wars.[39]

The marriage, much applauded by their Cherokee friends, took place amidst raucous gaiety in her father's substantial house, and seemed on the surface to mark Houston's definitive transformation to the Raven. While his "official" biographies avoid mention of Tiana, Jeff Hamilton, his slave, later testified that everyone who knew Houston also knew about "the beautiful widow, Tiana Rogers," * and their marriage.[40]

At Wigwam Neosho, Houston—with some capital loaned by Chief Bowl—opened a modest trading post, raised livestock and drank Homeric quantities of whiskey.[41] He also set out to publicize the continuing injustices done to the Indians. In late June his first article condemning abuses by government officials appeared in the *Arkansas Gazette* under the pen name "Tah-Lohn-Tus-Ky." The *Arkansas Gazette* was an unusually influential newspaper, for its articles and news were widely reprinted in the American press.[42] He wrote five articles for the newspaper in the second half of 1830 (which drew equally blunt counterattacks) and long letters to the editors of the *Arkansas Gazette* and *Arkansas Advocate* under his own name, one defending Eaton and the ration contract.[43] Houston's articles constitute the first coherent defense of Indian rights and exposé of official corruption to be published by a major Western figure. They could not be ignored in the East, and they helped spur at least some reform in the Indian Bureau.[44]

Ironically, Houston himself was using his Cherokee citizenship to escape federal trade regulations. In July he reported to Colonel Arbuckle the arrival at his wigwam of a shipment of merchandise, which included four barrels of Monongahela Whiskey, one of corn whiskey, one of cognac, one of gin, one of rum and several of wine. These, he assured the colonel, were intended not for trade, but for his own use, "and for the accomodation of the officers of the Government," including, of course, the friendly post commander. Of the federal Indian

---

* Will Rogers was a descendant of hers, and famed Indian scout and peacemaker Jesse Chisholm a nephew.

Intercourse Laws he brashly averred that they "have no other bearing upon me or my circumstances than they would have upon any other native born Cherokee!" After all, he pronounced to the skeptical Arbuckle, "My situation is peculiar . . . *I am a citizen of the Cherokee Nation.*"[45] He enclosed a copy of his citizenship papers, and Arbuckle, though unimpressed, passed on Houston's claim for exemption from the law to the War Department, which denied it. When the exile protested, John M. Berrien, attorney general of the United States, ruled that "adopted" Indian citizens must have licenses to trade. Then came the Supreme Court decision that Indian tribes were "dependent nations," rather than sovereign, and that ended the issue. Would Sam Houston never get rich?[46]

With the issue still pending, Houston traded, raised cattle and swine and waxed modestly prosperous. But, even as he wangled a partnership with Nashville's John Drennen and some Cherokees to purchase the Grand Saline saltworks from Chouteau,[47] the volume of his drinking—already legendary—moved beyond the danger point.

"His gun was on his shoulder, two dogs at his feet."

MATTHEW FONTAINE MAURY, 1831

There among cottonwood, ash, persimmon and mulberry, Houston's "enthusiasm" chained him to bottle and keg. Bleary months slid by and their passage left despondency in their turbulent wake. The Cherokees were soon snidely referring to their white compatriot as "Oo-Tse-Tee Ar-dee-tah-Skee," or, the "Big Drunk."[48] A traveler that year complained about the scourge of drunkenness afflicting the few whites in Indian Territory. He "saw but one drunken Indian . . . but more than one drunken white man," noting that the Cherokees had a strong temperance movement. The same tribe, however, owned commercial distilleries on the frontier, and in a bizarre twist of the tale, may well have been selling the end product to Sam Houston, thus contributing to the debauchery of the white man![49] In any case, he routinely boozed until rendered insensate and his prestige among his Indian friends plummeted.

As 1830 faded into 1831 Houston's credibility faded with it, and in this woozy period he fought a ridiculous, and luckily bloodless, "duel" with a young clerk in his store over some imagined insult. Far worse, he also mindlessly struck old John Jolly while in a stuporous rage. For this, an utterly humiliated Raven was forced to make a painful public apology before the Cherokee Council. While he was not expelled or punished for this outrage, the council expressed its biting disdain for his lack of control and manners. Following his sad act of contrition he drank more frequently at the Bachelor Officers' mess at Cantonment Gibson, and less often among the Cherokees, which further alienated him from their ranks.[50] In May he was soundly defeated in his bid for election to the Cherokee Council, for its members neither needed nor wanted a "Big Drunk" within their ranks.[51]

Rebuffed, Houston decided to travel East, to check on his "gold lands" on the Tennessee-Georgia border. He was sorely disappointed that no gold had been unearthed, or at least reported to him. He set out in early June, encountering young navy officer Matthew Fontaine Maury (future "father" of the science of oceanography), a man he had as a congressman helped obtain a commission in the navy.

As Maury recalled the chance encounter, his steamer made an unscheduled stop to pick up a man signaling from the shore: "a man who stood on the upper bank waiting to embark, his gun was on his shoulder, two dogs at his feet, & he wore an old Straw hat & a hunting shirt of coarse calico."

No one recognized the man who clambered aboard, though they did find him a dramatic and imposing figure. "One thought him at most a Captain; one that he might be a General, another a Western member of Congress, perhaps even Davy Crockett." Houston went on the steamer carrying "Indian knapsacks & Buffalo skins in lieu of Trunk and Traveling Bag . . . a man of handsome & pleasing countenance . . . a figure so well proportioned that the eye would never have measured him as exceeding six feet" in height.

Not only was the enigmatic passenger physically impressive, he was a nonstop conversationalist. According to Maury, "we were much amused with his talk & continued to pass the bottle," while the newcomer expounded grandiosely on his plans for national expansion. "The

US can only hold together so long as there is an abundance of rich unoccupied wild land for settlers," was his view. Houston demanded the entire vast Oregon Territory for the United States, "and by God, gentlemen," said he, striking the table, "if they don't do it & if I can get some capitalists to join me, I would easily collect 2 or 300 Volunteers on the Western frontiers & I would proceed to establish a Colony myself at the mouth of the Columbia . . . there I would build a fort & establish a Government—I should get plenty of settlers, & from our great distance we could & would maintain an independence of any power on earth." * It no doubt struck the nationalist in Maury that Houston did not mention joining the Union in this scheme, but merely "independence." Just what would be his role in an independent Oregon? This he did not elaborate upon, but Oregon might be easier fruit to pick than Texas, and more legal as well, given the 1818 joint occupation treaty.

Perhaps to lend a shred of credibility to his drunken musings, Houston offhandedly let it drop that he had just made some three thousand or four thousand dollars' profit trading with the Indians. He was, he insinuated, a man of means, not some lunatic frontier vagabond. The young naval officer, sipping his whiskey and listening, was not entirely convinced. The man and his tale made him, like Alexis de Tocqueville, remark upon some of the oddities of democracy, including "the operation of universal suffrage in making such a man as Houston a Governor of a State." Maury, it should be noted, did take the time to carefully record what he heard.[52] Sam Houston continually gave Jackson cause for concern.

* Houston here (and elsewhere) displayed a fairly detailed grasp of Oregon geography. He had obviously been reading and thinking about that territory, as about Texas.

"Everything about him indicates physical and
moral energy."

ALEXIS DE TOCQUEVILLE, 1831

The visit to his "gold" lands gave Houston little reason for cheer, since not an ounce of gold had been found. He soon returned to Wigwam Neosho, whose trading post was at least a going concern, and in July he sold his interest in the Grand Saline for sixty-five hundred dollars in cash, in 1831 a princely sum.[53]

Pocketing his money, Houston soon hit the eastbound roads and rivers again, for he had learned somehow that his mother lay dying. It is not known whether he made it to her bedside before she expired, but apparently he did arrive at least in time to help bury her, probably in early September.[54]

He was poorly received in Tennessee, where he was still seen as the cause of Eliza's shame. In ill-considered defense, he paid to have an utterly bizarre broadside printed and distributed—about the same time he had his famous Caius Marius portrait painted over a background of ruined Carthage. This broadside, almost certainly inspired by distilled spirits, gave Houston's permission to *"all Scoundrels whomsoever"* to libel, slander and attack him, and "I will in *no wise* hold them responsible to me in law, or honor."[55]

His chilly reception in Tennessee was a (figuratively) sobering experience, for he learned that his credibility there was even less than among the Cherokees; hardly enough to let him harbor even distant thoughts of re-entering that state's political contests. Something dramatic was needed to save him from deepening obscurity.

Returning to Wigwam Neosho, Houston vegetated. No matter the trading post's success, a clerk he was not, nor ever had been. Probably by his own suggestion, he joined another Cherokee delegation bound for Washington, kissing bemused Tiana goodbye once again in early December.

Two days after Christmas, while changing steamers for New Orleans, he encountered the urbane and congenitally inquisitive Alexis de Tocqueville. The French savant—skeptical of democracy, but the

very best of listeners—was in the United States to learn what made
this new society work, and having heard of Sam Houston, was eager to
ask his opinions. "His figure is athletic; everything about him indicates
physical and moral energy," enthused the man who would write the
classic *Democracy in America.* "This man has an extraordinary history,"
he jotted, marveling that "the sorrows and exertions of all sorts by
which his existence has been beset have as yet left but slight trace on
his features." At the traveler's urging the Tennessean rambled at length
about the various Indian tribes and the causes for their current plight,
unblushingly admitting over drinks that "Brandy is the main cause of
the destruction of the natives of America." [56]

"Damn rascal!"

SAM HOUSTON, 1832

Houston and the Cherokee delegation moved into Brown's in early February 1832, and the next five months occupied the former governor
with two distinct but major concerns. One was a legal contretemps that
would make his name a household word, the other a business opportunity that would infect him with true "Texas fever." Whatever was
achieved on behalf of the Cherokees is not known, but Houston did a
great deal of socializing with cousin John and the surprisingly large
number of politicians (including Polk, Buchanan and Speaker of
the House Andrew Stevenson) whose friendship he had managed to
retain. [57]

A major issue in the capital at this time was the flap over the 1830
rations contract bid. Since 1832 was an election year, those opposed to
Jackson resurrected the issue in order to undermine his re-election
campaign. Houston, fresh from his wigwam, simply sidled into the eye
of a growing storm, and it promptly broke about him.

On March 31 Representative William Stanbery of Ohio gave a ven-
omous speech in the House, in which he accused Houston and Eaton
of outright corruption in the Indian rations matter. Houston soon
learned of this "slander," and had to be physically restrained by his

friend Congressman Polk from bulling his way into the House the day following the Stanbery speech.[58] Deterred, he nevertheless sent another Tennessee congressman, Cave Johnson, to hand Stanbery a note demanding that the Ohioan explain his accusations or prepare to defend his honor. Stunned and frightened, Stanbery did neither, and for days the issue festered within Houston.[59]

It might have remained merely another running sore had the partisan, anti-Jackson press not immediately reprinted Stanbery's speech, adding, as in Duff Green's *Telegraph,* more than a little editorial acid on the side.[60] Aware of the danger, but refusing to even contemplate a duel, Stanbery took to carrying a brace of pocket pistols and never went out in public without at least one friend by his side.[61]

Then, early Friday evening, April 13, while strolling with Tennessee congressman John Blair and a senator from Missouri, Houston spied Stanbery on the street. He yelled at the congressman, demanding that he explain what he had meant by his charges, and irately bore down on him. The Ohioan, frozen by fear or simply nonplussed, mutely stood his ground. As Houston, more enraged by the minute, came close, Stanbery fumbled for a pistol. Screaming out "damn rascal!" Houston slashed his stout cane across Stanbery's shoulders and commenced beating him rhythmically with the hickory stick as his victim tried to free a pistol.[62]

With Stanbery staggered under the rain of blows, Houston threw his oversized frame upon him, knocking him to the ground. The Ohioan finally freed his pistol and pulled the trigger, but it misfired, and Houston, in uncontrollable rage, continued flailing away until his two companions hauled him from the bleeding congressman.

"Severely bruised and wounded," Stanbery next day wrote Speaker of the House Stevenson (Houston's friend and fellow quaffer) that "I was waylaid in the street" by the giant Tennessean, "knocked down by a bludgeon" and badly wounded, all "for words spoken in my place in the House of Representatives." Supposedly bedridden by his injuries, he demanded the Speaker bring the issue of the assault "before the House" immediately.[63]

Although Houston had many supporters* and Stanbery comparatively few, the House surprisingly voted 145 to 25 to arrest the former

---

* James K. Polk wrote that after he had read Stanbery's speech, "my blood run so hot, that had he been present, I would have struck him myself."

congressman on April 17, the first time a private citizen was ordered arrested by the House for an attack upon one of its members "as a result of words spoken before Congress."[64]

The following day, the "prisoner" was interrogated by the House and explained that on the evening in question "he was neither seeking for, nor expecting to see the said Stanbery," and that his unpremeditated violence did not imply "contempt or breach of privilege." In a classic of understatement he did admit that when Stanbery had refused to respond to his shouted question, he became "excited."[65]

After the initial interrogatory, the House decided to try Houston, who immediately retained super-patriot Francis Scott Key, a noted defense attorney and avid Jacksonian recommended by the president. The issue, blown out of all proportion in the nation's press, hinged for the prosecution upon the question of freedom of speech on the floor of Congress, and for the defense primarily on the constitutionality of such a trial in the House, and secondarily, Stanbery's alleged "slander."[66]

Day after day the trial dragged on, Key making interminable, rather confusing speeches, proud "to stand by such a man, in such a cause." Houston was not "a man of violence and blood . . . lying in wait as an assassin," but was a patriot who had given his right arm for his nation at Horseshoe Bend. And it was Stanbery, not Key's client, who was armed and ready, "with two cocked pistols, and a dirk, and a friend" to support him. Key's most telling point revolved around the unconstitutionality of the trial. The House, he noted, had charged Sam Houston; it gathered the evidence against him; it argued the case against him, and it arrogated to itself the right to judge him. Where, asked Key, was the separation of powers guaranteed by the Constitution? Where, indeed, was simple justice?[67]

Jackson did not desert his ever-embarrassing friend and monitored events quite closely. As the trial progressed, the defendant, at Jackson's urging and with a loan from him, purchased from a modish tailor "a coat of the finest material, reaching almost to my knees, trousers in harmony in color, and the latest style in cut, with a white satin vest to match, and I was ready with a garb befitting the occasion."[68]

For almost a month arguments were heard and Houston's name and life story appeared in every newspaper in the land, his guilt or innocence bruited about on countless street corners. He became the focal point of one of the nation's first genuine "media events." For his summation—he instructed Key to stand aside—Houston for the first time donned his splendid new raiment.[69]

The night before that summation, he, Polk, Speaker Stevenson, Felix Grundy and a raft of other supporters held an all-night party at Brown's, and as Houston recalled, "the gathering became hilarious."[70] Polk, a moderate drinker, soon departed, the Speaker eventually passed out and Grundy and Houston drank through the night.[71] As Houston later admitted, "I had been very drunk" that evening, and the next morning was so painfully hung over that he couldn't keep any food down, even his first sip of coffee. After waiting a groggy hour or so, he attempted "another cup and it stuck."[72] Then, in sartorial splendor, if muddled mind, he lurched off to the House to take center stage.[73]

Houston defended himself brilliantly, picturing himself as a humble defender of "the rights of American citizens." In full-blown and largely irrelevant hyperbole, he would defend those rights, "safe and unimpaired, and transmitted as a sacred legacy from one generation to another till discord shall wreck the spheres—the grand march of time shall cease—and not one fragment of all creation be left to chafe on the bosom of eternity's waves." He also did a great deal of flag waving, recited select portions of Greek, Roman, British and American history, and averred that "Surely it cannot possibly be supposed that this court has a right to exercise powers which the Parliament of England does not claim for its members, though they are Lords and Dukes."[74] It was quite a performance, and "so appealing and eloquent that the galleries," to Stanbery's chagrin, "gave him an ovation."[75]

As the House entered a four-day debate on his guilt or innocence, Houston basked in confidence. So cocky was he that he wrote James Prentiss (with whom he was attempting to concoct Texas land deals) that "Congress can do nothing with me."[76] He had earlier written Colonel Arbuckle in the same dismissive vein about the trade regulations and had been wrong, but here he was almost correct.

By a split vote (106 to 89) the House found Houston guilty but sentenced him to a mere reprimand.* That reprimand was delivered by Houston's fellow reveler Speaker Stevenson (who managed to keep a

---

* In high irony, later in the year Congressman Stanbery would make history as the first member of Congress officially censured by that body: for insulting the Speaker of the House.

straight face), and to many it "sounded more like a commendation than reproof."[77] It nevertheless enraged the defendant, who blustered that it constituted "punishment unknown to our laws . . . inconsistent with the spirit of our institutions, and unfit to be inflicted upon a free citizen."[78]

Houston at least was a "free citizen," and he had taken full advantage of the bully forum that had been inadvertently offered him. The irate Ohioan, however, was not through and soon introduced a peculiar resolution to bar Houston from the House of Representatives forever. This was easily voted down. Twice defeated, Stanbery next brought charges of criminal assault against the cane-wielder in the city courts. That trial, far swifter and less deliberative than the House contest, concluded on June 28, with the former governor found guilty, but sentenced only to a five-hundred-dollar fine, which he was permitted years to pay off.[79] Even this token punishment offended Houston, who considered that paying the fine would be an admission of guilt. Thus he later wrote Jackson a letter in which he "prays that the *fine and costs of suit* may be remitted by *your* PARDON." The president was accommodating, scratching on the margin that "I regard this fine as excessive and therefore remit it."[80] Houston had won again.

He had essentially gotten off scot-free, and in the process had gained invaluable national exposure. He realized it, too, writing perceptively: "I was dying out and had they taken me before a justice of the peace and fined me ten dollars it would have killed me. But they gave me a national tribunal for theatre and that set me up again."[81] His recognition that it had been "theatre" is fitting, and Sam was a consummate actor.

"If we should live, our wealth must be boundless."

SAM HOUSTON, 1832

While trials, hearings and testimony were taking place, Houston was keeping other irons in the fire, the longest of which reached all the way to Texas.

Throughout the Stanbery imbroglio, the Tennessean was in constant contact with the president and was a peripheral member of Jackson's almost familial "Kitchen Cabinet." He remained an active player in politics and diplomacy and a credible advisor to his mentor. And he was also treating—rather mysteriously—with New York financier and front man for several Texas land companies James Prentiss, to whom he had been introduced by Van Fossen.[82]

As early as March 1832, the two men were in contact, and they wrote each other with such great circumspection (at times in code) that their letters could never be used against them in court. There is no question, though, that Prentiss (who had an agent, "Gen. Mason," in Texas) and his backers wanted Houston to reconnoiter, assess and purchase huge blocks of land in Texas. He for his part wanted more, and so too did many of his New York associates.[83]

By early May an agreement had been reached and an eager Houston wrote Prentiss that once his legal complications were finally settled, he would "set out for the *land of promise*" as the New Yorker's agent.[84] The following month, with Houston still enveloped in court proceedings, Prentiss anxiously wrote him that the projected land purchases had to be consummated soon, for changes were about to transform Texas. The New Yorker, like Houston himself, believed that a revolution was brewing that would lead to independence. Prentiss told the exile that his New York backers and associates had "strong hopes and expectations of the lands being in a short time worth ten or twenty times their cost."[85] Since annexation (or purchase) of Texas by the United States would be the only reason for land prices there to skyrocket thus, they must have known of a revolution in the making. Houston himself may have been the one to apprise them.

A revised agreement called for Houston to purchase all or a large portion of the immense, unsettled Leftwich Empresario Grant. He would have to negotiate with the Mexican government, and also with Stephen F. Austin and other empresarios who were seeking parts of the defunct grant for themselves. If negotiations failed, Houston was to finagle a new empresario grant. As partial payment for his services, Prentiss would transfer to Houston 53,140 "English acres" that his backers owned in another grant.[86] This agreement, like several others, was soon canceled, but Houston drew considerable cash from Prentiss for expenses, perhaps as much as eight thousand dollars.[87]

Thick and fast flew the correspondence between the two, Houston urging the New Yorker to hurry in arranging the funds, while he in turn was goaded to settle his legal difficulties in Washington. All the while the former governor was receiving reports on events in Texas from "my friend Wharton," and was anxiously preparing to head southwest to join Charles F. M. Noland, who he hoped would become his traveling companion and assistant.[88] Noland, living in Fort Smith, on the border of Indian Territory, had already invested in Texas lands like his father, and knew a great deal about the province. The scope of the latest arrangement was hinted at in a letter in which Houston informed Prentiss that Noland should be allotted fifty thousand acres "out of my share of the land, upon the *same conditions* that I am to receive it." The recompense Houston was to receive from the New Yorkers had obviously grown substantially from the 53,140 acres originally agreed upon. In the same letter he bitterly railed against "that fool Butler," Jackson's agent in Mexico, a man he saw as a bungler and perhaps even a traitor, whose activities in Mexico threatened American land speculation there.[89]

Houston wrote Noland, who had moved to Cantonment Gibson to await him, in heady, visionary terms. If Noland helped him accomplish his goals, "what ever my destiny is, yours shall be the same, so far as I may be able to make it glorious, prosperous, or happy. . . . If we should live, our wealth must be boundless," he promised the young man.[90]

However, financial snags on the New York end continued to delay Houston's departure, and he grew increasingly frustrated. In July he wrote one of Prentiss's associates: "If the project should fall thru, of sending me on to Texas, I will have to make some arrangement for going, on my own account," but if that happened, "upon my *honor,"* he promised, he would not *"take advantage* of my friends by using information derived from them, to prejudice their interests." If they could not move, he would, but not as a competitor.[91] Houston smelled both change and money on the wind, blowing north from Mexico.

Late in July Houston finally departed Washington for Nashville, en route to Texas, advising Prentiss that he would enter Mexico alone, for Noland had decided not to share in the adventure.[92] From Tennessee he again urged the New Yorker to move with dispatch, dropping a telling hint: "The people [of Texas] look to the Indians in Arkansas as auxiliaries in the event of a change; so I will pass that way, and see my *old friends,"* the Cherokees. He also noted enticingly that "I will ride to the Hermitage this evening and see the Old Chief," with whom he had unspecified business.[93] Obviously, more than land sales was involved, and Houston was prepared to move even if the New Yorkers were not.

He was, however, still in Nashville on September 11, writing Prentiss and receiving some disappointing news from the New Yorker. He fired back an angry missive of his own, terminating all agreements between them: "All considerations have certainly failed on your Part, which were held out as inducements to me," so he was off to Texas as a free agent, leaving Robert McEwan as his Tennessee contact, should Prentiss want to communicate with him.[94] No agreement between the two ever bore fruit, but as late as the spring of 1834 Houston wrote him that he was willing to serve as company agent in Texas, if a retainer's fee of two thousand dollars were made available. It was not.[95]

In any case, as Sam Houston set forth to Texas, he was an agent, for the president had accepted his offer to talk peace with, and gather information about, the Comanches of Texas, who were raiding both sides of the border. He carried west a government passport accrediting him to treat with the frontier tribes. Dated August 6, 1832, it identified him as on government business, and described him as six feet, two inches in height.[96] If Houston was bent upon prowling around the frontier and Texas, Jackson would take advantage of his presence.

Traveling with veteran boozer Elias Rector, a United States marshal, Houston made a brief stopover at Wigwam Neosho, where he bade permanent adieu to the "tall and slender" Tiana; "graceful as the bounding deer," according to one who had seen her.[97] He deeded her the wigwam and trading post, all livestock and their two slaves,[98] decamping with little save a decrepit horse. Tiana married Samuel McGrady in 1836, and died of pneumonia just two years later.[99] Years afterward she was reinterred at Fort Gibson National Cemetery, Oklahoma, her simple headstone reading "Talahina R. Wife of Gen. Sam Houston."[100]

Noland saw Houston and Rector when they passed through Gibson, and wrote his interested father that his friend was "in fine spirits—his destination—Texas."[101] The visionary tarried some before crossing the Red River in search of his destiny, for more than six weeks after Noland saw him, Houston wrote cousin John from Fort Johnson that "I am about to enter Texas . . . my habits sober." He added another chimerical note: "It is reported that my friends have announced my name as a candidate for next Governor of Tennessee . . . I do not doubt it [success], if I should run as I think I shall."[102]

At last, in early December, Sam Houston crossed his Rubicon, the Red River, and entered Texas. Perhaps fantasizing about the Tennessee governorship, he was a government agent, aspiring land agent, and, probably, a revolutionary. He had finally "G.T.T."

F I V E

The Texas Crucible

"G(one) T(o) T(exas)."

ANON.

"Spanish Texas was a remote and dangerous frontier, huge in area, vague in definition, and, to the end, meager in development."[1] Called "the land of war," northern Mexico, which had been explored in the sixteenth century by *conquistadores*, was virtually empty in 1800. The Comanche, Apache, Yaqui and other tribes made ordinary settlement impossible. Only in the eighteenth century did authorities in Mexico City begin to create a loose string of missions and their associated *presidios* (army posts) to plant small centers of civilization in the inhospitable soil of Texas. Like the local cacti, these grew slowly and blossomed sparsely.

So undeveloped was Texas that no surveyed frontier divided it from the Louisiana Territory when Jefferson acquired that Europe-sized domain. Jackson and many others complained that the commonly accepted boundaries, the Sabine and Red rivers, were inaccurate and that the true frontier lay considerably farther to the south and west.

With the adventurous exploits of Philip Nolan and Aaron Burr dictating painful lessons, Spain attempted to shore up its fragile empire through accelerated settlement of the marcher provinces of Texas, Coahuila and Sonora. Even with Madrid's prodding, however, it was a slow and costly process; people did not migrate to Texas without economic inducements and military protection. In 1819, the Adams-Onís Treaty was signed, trading the Florida peninsula for a United States pledge to keep hands off Texas.[2]

But the boundary was not properly surveyed, and well before the treaty was signed, Americans were crossing the Sabine and the Red or landing from the Gulf of Mexico. So too did many frontier entrepreneurs, such as Anthony Glass, who wrote a splendid description of early Texas, *Journal of an Indian Trader*.[3] American settlers far outnumbered the Spanish migration.[4]

Spain's motive in signing the Adams-Onís Treaty was to deflect American migrants elsewhere, including to Oregon, by transferring to the United States Spain's sixteenth-century claims to that area. Madrid —and, after independence in 1821, Mexico City—perceived Texas in *strategic* terms, as protection for the valuable portions of New Spain; the rich mining zones and population centers far to the south.

There had been little tranquility in Texas since the Nolan scare, with continuing civil disorders involving both Americans and Tejanos (Hispanic settlers of the province), such as the Bernardo Gutierrez– James McGee uprising of 1811–1812.[5] In 1819 the ante was raised at a time when Spain was seriously overextended, its armies fighting grimly to retain the remnants of its American empire: Mexico, Venezuela, Bolivia and Peru.

At this juncture, Tennesseean Dr. James Long slipped into Texas with a polyglot band some three hundred strong,* seizing Goliad and Nacogdoches and settling in. A Long supporter, Horace Bigelow, began publishing the *Texas Republican* at Nacogdoches, and called in its pages for massive American immigration, offering land "of the first quality" for a pittance. Much of Bigelow's sheet was soon reprinted in United States newspapers, including *The Nashville Clarion*.[6] Two years later Long and most of his followers were captured at Goliad and editor Bigelow fled across the Sabine. Many died in prison in Mexico City, including Dr. Long, who was executed.[7]

In the same year Dr. Long surrendered, Spain ceded Mexico to its independence movement, which had been consuming lives and property since 1810. The new government, bankrupt and facing a host of daunt-

---

* In his band were freebooters from the United States, England, Sweden, Poland, Ireland, Prussia, various German states, Scotland, Holland, France, Spain and Russia.

ing problems,* recognized its empty, beckoning north as a major asset. In the first year of independence, Mexico ratified its first empresario contract for colonizing Texas, negotiated the previous year by Spain with Connecticut visionary Moses Austin. In return for a huge tract of land, Austin would settle at least three hundred families at his own expense, each to be given its own sizeable holding from the original grant.

Moses died in 1821, before his colonization scheme was under way, but his son, Stephen Fuller Austin, assumed his contractual obligations. Austin was a plain man, slender, of average height and prematurely balding. Described as "abstemious, humorless and reticent," he was also gallant, recklessly brave, generous and dedicated to achieving his Texas dream. A "singularly reasonable man," he remained a bachelor, living with his sister Emily and her husband James F. Perry. "Texas is my mistress," he oft proclaimed.[8]

By 1824 the Old Three Hundred were busily driving boundary stakes near the village of San Felipe de Austin, on the winding Brazos River, some hundred miles from the coast. Although it was assumed that the new settlers would be from the United States, it was required that they be, or become, both Catholics and citizens of Mexico.

Coinciding with the arrival of the Old Three Hundred, Texas lost its independent statehood in 1824, being merged into the gigantic new state of Coahuila-Texas, whose capital, Saltillo, lay an inconvenient two hundred miles south of the Rio Grande. With its first national constitution Mexico was attempting to forge a streamlined, modern nation. Austin and the other Americans were unhappy with this change (and with absence of a right to trial by jury), for it diluted their political leverage. The new constitution provided no effective government for Texas and its growing American population, leaving them politically powerless. Its one major advantage for the new arrivals was that it ensured loose and ineffectual control by the Mexican authorities, who for years even neglected to collect trade taxes in Texas.

Austin's grant became the prototype for the empresario system, whose basic aim was to attract thousands of new settlers, whose pres-

* Much of Mexico's infrastructure, including its famed silver mines, had been destroyed or damaged in the years of revolutionary warfare. Banditry appeared on a massive scale (especially in the north), and Mexico was less a nation than a collection of ill-connected states whose local elites often ignored Mexico City.

ence would bolster Mexico's claim to the region. The newcomers were
to be treated so liberally that they would fight, if necessary, to retain
their privileges. The timing was perfect. In 1819 a vast financial panic,
a sort of elemental depression, swept the United States. The next year
a federal Land Act made it impossible to purchase public lands without
cash on the barrelhead, which the financial panic made more difficult
than ever. Adding to the demographic pressures, the two-decade-old
cotton boom had already led to the settlement of the best Deep South
cotton lands. Would-be planters greedily eyed coastal Texas, and
"G.T.T." was marked on hundreds of Southern cabin doors.[9]

Add to this Mexico's offer of *free* land, not land at $1.25 per acre, as
in the United States. Each successful empresario received 23,000 acres
of good land for his own use for each hundred families he could lure to
his colony. Each family in turn received two valuable tracts: a *sitio*, or
Spanish square league (4,428 acres), for ranching, and a *labor* of 177
acres of prime farmland.[10] That was a powerful incentive to emigrate,
even if it meant accepting Catholicism and draconian albeit erratically
enforced laws.

"Vagabond and ruffian types."

HADEN EDWARDS, 1824

Scores of ambitious men applied for empresario grants, dozens received
them, and a handful, including Austin, were successful, but thousands
of Americans poured into Texas independently of the system, often
scrawling "G.T.T." on their cabin doors as a mocking forwarding address. While the empresario structure was designed to channel and
regulate settlement, the real exodus into Texas was a succession of
"unorganized folk movements," impossible to predict or control.[11]

In January 1824, Virginian Haden Edwards wangled an empresario
grant in Mexico City, claiming Mexico as "my country." He pledged to
settle more than a hundred families, all of whom promised to "submit
themselves" to Mexican law. Edwards asked for a large grant near

Nacogdoches in northeastern Texas, where his colonists would serve to "impede the emigration of vagabond and ruffian types" from the United States. This was alluring to Mexico City, for "drifters and adventurers, the smugglers and speculators" of the United States were all on the march toward Texas, their first stop often Nacogdoches.[12]

By the time Haden and his brother Benjamin began to distribute land to their first colonists in early 1826, there were probably ten thousand American settlers in Texas, a figure far exceeding the Tejano population.[13] Later in the year, with scores of families settled, Haden traveled to Louisiana to ferret out more recruits, and while he was gone, Benjamin raised the flag of rebellion. With a few feisty settlers and some heavily armed adventurers, he soon drove the small Mexican garrison from Nacogdoches. Then the brothers formed a protogovernment for what they termed the independent state of Fredonia, called in vain upon the other empresarios for support, sent appeals abroad for armed "ruffians," and negotiated with nearby Indians for an alliance. To these Indians they offered virtually half of Texas, and some chiefs pledged to aid Fredonia.[14]

But in 1826–1827 most American settlers were far too content with their lot to jeopardize their privileges at the capricious call of the Edwardses. Many, in fact, like Stephen Austin, were adamantly opposed to the Fredonians, even raising a militia to help local Mexican authorities. The idea behind the empresario system appeared to be working; loyal American-Mexicans were springing to the defense of their new nation and their new property. Mexican officials quickly accepted the offers of help and most Indians, even if tempted by the Edwardses' land mirage, stayed cautious, waiting to see which way the issue would go.

Only a few recruits arrived from the United States, and the mercurial behavior of the brothers alienated many, including most of their own colonists. One of those, Alexander Horton (later Houston's aide-de-camp), refused to join the rebels. Instead, he rounded up a ragtag band of armed settlers and Indians and marched on the Edwardses' newly constructed "fort." As he recalled, the Fredonians holed up in the fort—who had expected Indian allies, not enemies—soon "threw down their arms and begged for quarter."[15] Austin's militia, together with a few companies of Mexican troops and Horton's "irregulars," swept into Nacogdoches, and the Fredonian Rebellion simply collapsed.

The Mexican government thanked Austin for his loyalty but, concerned over the upheaval, dispatched General Manuel Mier y Terán to Texas to investigate. The general was alarmed by what he found and his 1828 report caused anxiety in Mexico City. He reported that Americans already outnumbered Tejanos by more than three to one, that their loyalty was dubious at best and would become even less dependable as their numbers grew, and that many Americans entering Texas were dangerous outcasts. The general recommended strengthening Mexican garrisons, implementing a program of countermigration of Mexicans and banning further foreign immigration.[16]

Mexican authorities swiftly adopted most of Mier y Terán's recommendations. In 1830 the government formally prohibited emigration from the United States and canceled all unfulfilled empresario contracts. A forced movement of civilians and soldiers northward was begun, many of both groups criminals released from Mexican prisons. However, the countercolonization was too little, too late; the northern borders of Texas remained porous.

By 1830 only three of the twenty-four empresario contracts (seventeen of which had been granted to non-Mexicans) were considered successful—the grants of Austin, Green De Witt, and Martín de León —although several others soon would be. Austin now had four distinct colonies, with perhaps five thousand settlers. He was the best-known of the empresarios and his dynamic leadership and network of contacts gave him an advantage in recruiting new settlers. De León's much smaller colony, founded in 1824, counted perhaps three hundred families scattered around Victoria, and De Witt's 1825 grant, centered at Gonzalez, claimed about four hundred.[17] Lorenzo de Zavala, David G. Burnet and Joseph Vehlein had merged their thinly settled, struggling grants and were depending upon the Galveston Bay and Texas Land Company for people. That company was doing its best to peddle land scrip in the United States, each share entitling the bearer to 177.136 acres (a *labor*) on "the Gulph of Mexico." Despite the 1830 emigration ban, the scrip was still being marketed.[18] Even more disturbing to land speculators in the United States than that ban, however, was Mexico's abolition of slavery in 1829, which loosed howls of protest from Americans in Texas already piecing together a plantation economy. So intense was their protest that Mexico City permitted a "temporary" exemption from the law to the state of Coahuila-Texas.

Other colonies on the verge of success included the largely Irish

operation of James Power and James Hewetson, who began settling
Hibernians around San Patricio and Refugio. Later an English colony
was established by the Rio Grande, but the wandering, warlike Comanches circumscribed its growth (in reality, the nomadic Comanches long
defined the true boundaries of Texas). Ben Milam's colony, northwest
of Gonzales, also suffered from Indian depredations and was consequently retarded in its growth. Emigrants were in for a tough time
simply carving a farm or ranch from the frontier and the added and very
real danger of Comanche raids made it difficult to attract manpower
to Milam's colony. Generally, the successful colonies were on or near
the coast, the wild interior being too far from ports and too exposed to
the Comanches, comancheros and Apaches to draw any but the very
hardiest.

Despite the ban on American emigration, the tide of *Yanquis* crossing
the ungarrisoned border actually increased. The weak chain of under-
manned forts loosely encircling the American colonies could neither
protect the settlers nor contain them.[19]

"The Sabine River is a greater Savior than
Jesus Christ."

ANON., 1832

American society grew, and the *Texas Gazette* appeared in English at
San Felipe in 1829, to keep the expatriate community abreast of such
issues as abolition and a strangely anti-intellectual tariff on books.[20]
This did not disturb most Texans for, as an anonymous "Emigrant"
recorded, "a large proportion of the settlers in the country are composed
of the more unlettered parts of mankind."[21] Frederick Law Olmsted
wandering in Texas was shocked as late as 1860 that in the state capital,
"there is a very remarkable number of drinking and gambling shops,
but not one bookstore."[22]

Texas was something of a "haven for debtors and undesireables," and
would continue to be such for decades more.[23] One blasphemous Texan

put it more crudely: "The Sabine River is a greater Savior than Jesus
Christ. He only saves men when they die from going to Hell but this
river saves living men from prison" or the noose.[24] Another jaded visitor
from the effete East laconically recorded that at his boardinghouse
breakfast table "seated with me [were] four murderers who had sought
safety in this country."[25]

Life was rough and crude in "the land of war," and unscrupulous
yanqui traders were known to barter modern firearms with the Comanches for their loot. By 1830 or so, "American armaments had shifted
the balance of power to the Indians" and the warpath was well worn in
the Texas soil.[26] The San Antonio municipal government complained in
1832 that the town was threatened "with total extermination by the
new Comanche uprising."[27]

With Mexican soldiers few in number, poorly armed and trained,
horseless and presidio-bound,* the settlers themselves, American and
Tejano, had to bear most of the burden of defense,[28] fighting against
the Comanches and Apaches in the old Tejano guerrilla style, a style
that had permitted the original settlers to survive for generations. It
was a low-intensity conflict waged by small bands of horsemen engaging
in ambush, hit-and-run and, often, massacre; a sporadic warfare of
singular brutality, and few prisoners.[29] Texas was an armed camp in
the early 1830s, as it had long been, but it was now a largely American
armed camp.[30]

In 1832, American-born Texans (known generally as "Texians")
again challenged Mexican officials with arms in their hands. The irri-
tant was an attempt to collect trade taxes at a number of new *aduanas*
(customs houses).[31] Texas had blissfully escaped taxation—as it had
evaded abolition—and the new imposts rankled, especially as they coincided with a gradual buildup of Mexican garrisons.

Flash point was reached when General Antonio López de Santa Anna
launched a federalist (states' rights) revolt against President Anastasio
Bustamante's conservative, centralist regime. Santa Anna called upon
the people of all states to strike down the autocratic centralists,[32] and
Texas, like most other areas of Mexico, hastened to do so, its people
enthused by the opportunity to destroy the hated aduanas. With mini-

---

* In the United States, the Army created its first mounted regiment, the First
Regiment of Dragoons, only in 1833.

mal violence Texians took the Mexican garrisons at Velasco and Anáhuac, while from Nacogdoches two companies of Americans, in whose
ranks were Alexander Horton, Haden Edwards and Adolphus Sterne,
moved on the five-hundred-man force of Colonel José de las Piedras,
the largest garrison in Texas. "Armed with shot-guns and various other
guns as citizens used for hunting purposes," Horton and his fifty or so
companions marched on Piedras's camp just outside town and demanded his surrender. A desultory fight took place through the afternoon, and the following day Colonel Piedras surrendered to the small
band of Texians. Three militiamen and about forty Mexicans had been
killed in the clashes, and the captives were escorted to Santa Anna's
recently arrived forces by Jim Bowie, who was "passing through" on his
way to San Antonio.[33]

Thus, in August the armed Texians were—if briefly—considered
heroes by Santa Anna, whose revolt had succeeded. A new experiment
in Federalism, or "Liberalism," would soon be implemented. The Texians were also dangerously confident that one of them was worth at
least five Mexicans on the field of battle.

In this time of uncertainty Texians held their first large "Consultations" to air grievances, debate and formulate positions. These were at
first similar to New England town meetings but soon became conclaves
with elected representatives from various Texas settlements. The first
such meetings took place at San Felipe, with delegates from most areas
of Texas. Informal democracy was evolving on the coastal plains of
Texas.

"What the devil I am going to do in Texas?"

SAM HOUSTON, 1833

Such was the milieu encountered by Sam Houston as he rode into Texas
in December 1832; nervous uncertainty compounded with growing
American self-confidence. By this point there were some fifteen thousand Americans in Texas, and only about three thousand Tejanos.[34]

Houston passed through Nacogdoches, tarrying only briefly to visit with Adolphus Sterne, and continued along the Camino Real ("Royal Road") to San Felipe, where he hoped to encounter the "Father of Texas." But "Col. Austin not being there, I had not the pleasure of reporting to him in person." He headed further south and after a short visit to San Antonio, returned to San Felipe late in the month. There he was introduced to Stephen Austin and they got on well. The famous empresario was both sympathetic and generous, and on Christmas Eve Houston applied (as a "married man") for a headright in one of his colonies. Austin transferred "League No. 3" to the former governor, neither expecting nor receiving payment. While Houston later recalled presenting the Texian with "a very fine American horse," the latter in turn gave him "a small horse and some cash,"[35] actually, a substantial five hundred dollars.

His land obtained, Houston the Indian commissioner set out for the frontier to negotiate with the Comanche bands that had been raiding both sides of the Red River. While he held a few "parleys" with a handful of chiefs and did some negotiating, his report of the mission was not well received in Washington. Albert Pike, an expert on Texas and its Indians, informed the War Department that Houston had conferred only with the semitractable Southern Comanches but not the warlike northern branch.[36] Houston's report was so vague and Pike's critique so specific that the War Department disallowed the commissioner's entire expense account, some thirty-five hundred dollars.[37] Significantly, Houston did not protest this humiliating decision.

In any case, he spent little time on the Comanche frontier, for in mid-February 1833 he was in Louisiana writing a confidential report to President Jackson. In it he boasted that he had traveled widely within Texas, "as far as [San Antonio de] Bexar," gathering information that "may be calculated to forward your views, if you should entertain any, touching the acquisition of Texas." Such a move he considered "desireable by nineteen twentieths of the population." Mexico was again torn by civil strife, the new regime was incapable of governing Texas and at best "the rulers have not honesty, and the people have not *intelligence*" to do so. Misreading the situation, the Tennessean claimed that the Texians had "already beaten and expelled all the troops of Mexico from her soil," and "will not permit them to return." If the United States did not soon acquire Texas, "England will most assuredly obtain it," he warned, then assailing Jackson's envoy, Colonel Butler. He asserted that Butler was controlled by the British, rather than the American Legation in Mexico City. And, he wrote with graphic emphasis, "*I pledge myself to you that I do know his interest* is at war with a transfer of Texas to the United States." Houston then described the real and potential wealth of Texas, which he compared favorably with Western Tennessee. In an attempt to enthuse Jackson and goad him into action, he estimated that it could "sustain a population of ten millions of souls."[38]

Two months later, Houston attended a consultation at San Felipe as an elected delegate from his new town, Nacogdoches. His political, legal and military experience had given him instant standing in the community. At San Felipe, he and such men as his old friend William Wharton, Jim Bowie, and David G. Burnet, president of the meeting, drew up a *Memorial al Congreso General de los Estados Unidos Mexicanos* ("Memorandum to the General Congress of the United States of Mexico"), a long, eloquent plea for a "totally independent [of Coahuila] state, in conformity with the Federal Constitution of 1824." It was something of a warning.[39] A committee of which Houston was a member soon produced a state constitution, based on the 1780 charter of the state of Massachusetts.[40]

While the consultation failed to achieve its aims, the new Mexican government did postpone collection of customs duties in Texas and, more important, again threw open the borders of Texas to American immigrants. News of this spread quickly in the United States, and "G.T.T." was scrawled on ever more cabin doors.

Not long after the consultation, Houston's shoulder wound began to suppurate heavily, almost crippling him, and he traveled to Hot Springs, Arkansas, to take the cure. From there he wrote cousin John about his physical afflictions, adding, "You want to know 'what the Devil I am going to do in Texas'? Part I will tell you and the balance you may guess at." He went on to explain that "with two other gentlemen (who furnish the capital) I have purchased about 140,000 acres of choice land," of which he had a share himself. Further, "I own and have paid for 10,000 acres that is, I think, the most valuable land in Texas."[41] Just where he acquired the money for all of this is a mystery, and even more mysterious is the "balance" at which John was left to guess. That it had something to do with separating Texas from Mexico is clear. He also informed Secretary of War Lewis Cass in his "official" capacity as commissioner that he had reconnoitered widely in Texas and talked with Mexican officials, repeatedly assuring them that the president had no plans to grab the province, noting, with feigned surprise, "Yet they, upon reflection, supposed that there might be some covert design!"[42]

He was at this juncture again in contact with James Prentiss, yet there is no concrete indication that the New Yorker and his backers had supplied the money for Houston's land purchases.[43] He was also successfully applying for more free land, this time in Burnet's colony.[44] Just how many land grants he accumulated over the years is not clear, but his 1863 estate inventory notes dozens.

In late summer, Houston was again in Nacogdoches, plying his trade as attorney with modest success. There he spent a great deal of time with the families of Adolphus Sterne, local merchant and *alcalde* (mayor), late of the Nashville Inn, and Henry Raguet. Sterne, a Jewish Rhinelander who had immigrated to Tennessee, had moved on to Texas in 1826. A prosperous businessman and smuggler, Sterne had aided the Fredonia revolt and had narrowly escaped execution at its collapse. Nevertheless, his business interests in Nacogdoches flourished, and he held a number of important municipal posts. His wife, Eva Rosine, was a devout Catholic, as were their seven children.[45] While living with the Sternes for several months, Houston became deeply smitten by seventeen-year-old Anna Raguet, who had just returned to Texas from a fashionable school for young ladies in Philadelphia. For years, he would carry on an odd, one-sided courtship with the brilliant, beautiful Anna, whose only known commitment to the relationship was to help him learn Spanish.

Sam Houston became a Roman Catholic in 1833, "introduced into the faith by a singularly broad-minded priest" who was eager to offer such a "convenience for Americans" who made a suitable donation.[46] Eva and Adolphus Sterne, who had "converted" years before, stood as his godparents, fully aware that his "conversion" was not one of conscience. From this date, in his legal practice he used the name "Paul Sam Houston," or "Pablo Samuel Houston," on all official documents.[47] Now a Catholic, Houston was on his way to Mexican citizenship.

In the autumn, as a cholera epidemic churned inland to decimate the western tribes,[48] Houston's growing infatuation with "Miss Anna" led him to appeal to William McFarland, alcalde of the small town of Ayish, for a divorce from Eliza. The grounds he gave were length of separation and impossibility of reunion. McFarland, with dubious legality, granted the divorce, one of the first in Mexican history.[49]

<hr>

"Shut up in a small tavern, seeing nobody by day and
sitting up all night."

G. W. FEATHERSTONHAUGH, 1834

Early in 1834 Sam Houston headed for the United States on the first of two trips that would keep him away from Texas for most of the year. He tarried briefly at Cantonment Gibson and at Nashville and then visited Cincinnati, Washington, New York and several other cities, for purposes never revealed but clearly relating to the future of Texas.

It was at Gibson, probably in March, that Houston first met one of his future nemeses, Jefferson Davis. The man destined, like Houston, to become president of a separatist nation was a West Point graduate and army captain just posted to the boring and lonely frontier. In a drunken stupor, stark naked except for a filthy Indian blanket, Houston staggered into the captain's tent and passed out. The next morning the Big Drunk shrugged off a monumental hangover, gathered what dignity his disheveled appearance would permit and introduced himself to the nonplussed Davis, whimsically remarking that "the future United States Senator salutes the future President." This was prophetic as they would serve together (unharmoniously) in the Senate and Davis would indeed be president—of the Confederate States of America.

Houston then treated the bemused officer to what had become his standard soliloquy about Texas, "breaking it off from Mexico, and annexing it to the United States." His stated ambition, Davis remembered, was to first become governor of Texas, then senator, and perhaps president. If the last should come to pass, said the semicoherent Nacogdoches lawyer, he would appoint "Davis for his Secretary of War," another odd coincidence, as Houston would be both governor of Texas and its senator, and Davis secretary of war (under Franklin Pierce). Davis never forgot his introduction to the legendary Sam Houston.[50]

Jefferson Davis was not the only man to be exposed to Houston's expansionist vision in 1834. The exile hinted at it in letters to Prentiss, writing him from New York that spring that, while Texas might never become part of the United States, it would soon be free. He did not elaborate, but precisely two years and one day later he would cap the process at the Battle of San Jacinto.

Later in the year, while in Washington conferring with the president, the schemer again shared his dream with a stranger. Drinking seriously at a tavern with famed British actor Junius Brutus Booth (father of John Wilkes Booth), he outlined a grandiose plan for Texas and Mexico and exulted that he was "made to revel in the halls of the Montezumas."[51] This may have been his first enunciation of a wider vision: the conquest of all of Mexico. His intemperate boasting was a continual embarrassment for the president.

Finally, late in the year, his circuit of Northern cities completed, Houston was observed on his way back to Texas by English wanderer G. W. Featherstonhaugh, under mysterious circumstances. It was at "the little insignificant wooden village of Washington," on the Red River frontier:

> I was not desirous of remaining long at this place. General Houston was here, leading a mysterious sort of life, shut up in a small tavern, seeing nobody by day and sitting up all night . . . I had been in communication with too many persons of late, and had seen too much passing before my eyes, to be ignorant that this little place was the rendezvous where a much deeper game than faro or rouge-et-noir was playing. There were many persons at this time in the village from the States lying adjacent to the Mississippi, under the pretence of purchasing government lands but whose real object was to encourage the settlers in Texas to throw off their allegiance to the Mexican government. Many of these individuals were personally acquainted with me, they knew I was not with them . . . I perceived that the longer I staid the more they would find reason to suppose I was a spy upon their actions.

So the Englishman prudently moved quietly on.[52]

What the traveler described—save what he inferred about Houston —was what he might have found in 1834 at any border town, for a thousand Americans were now streaming into Texas each month and most were male, armed and spoiling for a fight with Mexico. Texas was alluring to many Americans and was assumed by most to be on the eve of rebellion. And so they came, driven to some degree by the same motives that had driven the Spanish conquistadores three centuries earlier: Gold (wealth, anyway), God (most Americans were anti-Catholic) and Glory (the chance to participate in an independence movement).

"The Anglos brought customs a bit grotesque."

COLONEL JUAN N. ALMONTE, 1834

While Houston was finagling, politicking and probably conspiring, the Mexican authorities were also pondering Texas. Yet another change in government policy was in the wind, a vast recentralization that would fully extend the powers of the central government into all the fractious provinces. Santa Anna had played at "liberal" rule and flirted with laissez-faire policies, but now, named president in 1833, he was determined to exercise real power and pull the nation together. Austin, who had gone to the capital to explain Texian protests, was rudely tossed into prison, for Santa Anna, never friendly toward Americans, was in no mood to grant American-dominated Texas its own government and special privileges. Austin's pleas appeared to be demands and thus by definition seditious.

Increasingly worried about events in Texas, Santa Anna dispatched his confidant, the extraordinarily astute, diplomatic, bilingual Colonel Juan Nepomuceno Almonte, to investigate. The colonel was to wander Texas, tarry at even the smallest villages, towns, missions and presidios, and observe. Just what was Texas? How important was it to Mexico? What was the mood of the English-speaking majority there? What sort of commitment need the government make to its distant dependency?

Almonte knew what he was doing and why and he carried out his assignment thoroughly. While his geopolitical conclusions were communicated directly to the president, the bulk of his report became the first "encyclopedia" of Texas, published in 1835 as the hundred-page *Noticia Estadística Sobre Tejas (Statistical News of Texas)*. Almonte's data surprised both the Mexican reading public and the government, which, for instance, had had no idea even of the size of the population of Texas.

"That interesting country," wrote the colonel, was capable of producing a cornucopia of agricultural products and manufactured goods. He expected Texas to "soon be the most flowering section of the country," and warned that, "Ultimately, Texas is the most valuable possession the country has and I hope to God that our negligence has not cost us this, so precious a part of our territory." He had strong intimations of threats from the north, and reported worriedly that "The Anglos brought customs a bit grotesque."

Noting that Austin's colonies alone were home to more than six thousand "souls," he then presented a breakdown of the three "departments" that composed Texas.

Bexar, where most of Texas's Tejanos lived, had four *municipios* * (San Antonio de Bexar, population 5,000; Goliad, 1,400; Victoria, 300; and San Patricio, 600) by 1834, an Irish colony, and a few missions, with a combined total of about 8,000 *civilizados*. There were no schools, and "not more than one priest" for the entire department, for the vicar had recently died of cholera, and another *cura* had ominously "committed suicide." About 10,000 Indians, for the most part Comanches, uneasily shared Bexar with the whites. Between the municipio of San Antonio and the Rio Grande, reported Almonte, was a huge, dangerous *despoblado,* or unpopulated zone.

Los Brazos Department embraced San Felipe (2,500), Columbia (2,100), and Matagorda (1,400), as well as Austin's and De Witt's colonies, and a new colony being established by Sterling Clack Robertson, a Nashville acquaintance of Houston's and his probable cospeculator. [53] In all, some 8,000 "civilized" people dwelt in Los Brazos, which boasted one school. Only 900 or so Indians were thought to roam the plains.

Nacogdoches, the most thickly settled department (and most American) claimed four substantial municipios: Nacogdoches (3,500), San

---

* A municipio was not only a town itself but the vast surrounding hinterland controlled by its municipal government. Theoretically, the municipio of San Antonio de Bexar (sometimes, Bejar) "controlled" an area the size of the state of Tennessee!

Augustin (2,500), Johnsburg (2,000), and Libertad (1,000), and the struggling Burnet, Zavala and Vehlein colonies. There were about 10,000 citizens in the department, three schools, some 4,500 generally peaceful Indians, and an alarming torrent of immigration.

The Texas population, according to Colonel Almonte, who was a bit on the low side, was about 26,000 "civilized" (including more than 2,000 slaves) and 15,400 Indians (a wildly inaccurate guess). No attempt was or could be made to calculate the number of Indians beyond the "Comanche Barrier" in western Texas.[54]

Almonte's report was meant to inform, to warn and to goad the government into action. It did so, but again, it was a case of too little, too late. By the time the book was on sale, another three or four thousand foreigners had entered Texas, and thousands more were in movement toward the Sabine and Red, or boarding vessels bound for Galveston. Featherstonhaugh, on the Texas frontier, predicted that Mexico would lose Texas simply because Mexico City could never govern this "race of active and intrepid men, who are hostile to her laws, religion and manners." To the Englishman "the moment for action was drawing nigh," and he was convinced that Sam Houston would be the one to seize that moment.[55]

"To establish himself under a wise and
just government."

THOMAS JEFFERSON RUSK, 1835

In the last week of 1834 Houston again crossed the Red River, and as the critical new year opened, he appeared the very soul of propriety, a simple country lawyer practicing at Nacogdoches and writing fawning letters to Anna Raguet,[56] who rarely answered.* He was relieved to

---

* For example, in 1839 he wrote her, "With so much sensibility, intellect, and reflection, you are eminently qualified to render some noble fellow the most happy of mortal beings. . . . You have nothing lacking on the score of personal charms." While Houston wrote her every chance he got for years, almost none of her (few?) letters to

learn that a double misfire had saved the life of Andrew Jackson in the first attempted assassination of an American president.[57]

Early in 1835, a letter written months before by Stephen Austin found its way into partisan print, causing a furor. The American settlers in Texas were now almost bitterly divided into "War" and "Peace" parties, the former demanding secession from Mexico now, the latter negotiations for home rule. The "Father of Texas" excoriated the "War party," which included in its ranks William Wharton and, he believed, Houston, and he accused those hotheads of flirting with disaster, causing crises with Mexico and even occasioning his own incarceration.[58] Enraged by the letter and its publication, Houston lashed out at Austin for "his public expose of his want of understanding"[59] and asserted that the empresario had "shewed the disposition of a Viper without its fangs." There was painful little unity among the colonists and Houston for one did not yet want to be identified with the radical element in Texas.

Not much is known about his activities in the first half of the year, save that he kept busy with his expanding law practice and was often called upon as a sworn witness in citizenship cases.[60] Court records show that he defended both Texian and Tejano (his Spanish was improving),[61] and that he testified concerning the good character of new arrival Thomas Jefferson Rusk, a twenty-nine-year-old Georgian "farmer and rancher." Rusk was begging permission "to establish himself under a wise and just government that offers the protection of laws beneficial to an honorable and industrious man."[62] The future Texas secretary of war and vice-president and United States senator soon belied this verbiage and became leader of the War party in Nacogdoches.

On April 21, 1835, exactly one year before the Battle of San Jacinto, Catholic Pablo Sam Houston himself swore allegiance to the United States of Mexico.[63] Santa Anna's centralization campaign made this a wise move, and a few weeks later citizen Houston was again a character witness in court, swearing that the foreigner Robert F. Millard "is a man of very good morality" eminently fit for citizenship.[64] Millard would command the regiment of Texas regulars on the field of San Jacinto.

---

him have been found, and he often chided, scolded or even begged her to answer his missives.

If there was not a great deal of activity in the spring of 1835, there was a palpable sense of anticipation, of tension, of inexorable crisis as Texians, who knew what centralism would mean for them, prepared for the worst. Austin was in Mexico arguing the Texian cause for autonomy, but he was widely known as leader of the "Peace party" dedicated to negotiations. While he dealt diplomatically with the Mexican government, rumors flapped about Texas like flushed grouse. The centralists, according to some, were about to enforce abolition. Other Texians spoke darkly of Mexican plans to expel American settlers, most expected heavy taxation where there had been none, and some predicted martial law.

And what of Sam Houston, alleged filibuster, conspirator and new Aaron Burr? He was testifying and defending, whittling (a lifelong habit), dreaming and drinking, blissfully unaware that a new literary genre, the temperance story, was becoming popular and that the Reverend Charles Giles estimated that distilled spirits were killing some fifty-six thousand Americans a year.[65]

Everyone in Texas was marking time. A cloying sense of unreality pervaded all, but still the tidal surge of emigrants continued in 1835, transforming the political and military equation by their sheer numbers. And at this moment there were not more than five hundred Mexican troops in all of Texas, split up in small garrisons at presidios and towns.

In this dreamlike spring, Santa Anna ordered a company of troops to the aduana at Anáhuac. William Barret Travis and other "patriots," fearing that this meant that taxes would soon be collected, marched angrily there in late June and forced the bewildered Mexican soldiers to surrender. Travis, an Alabaman, had moved to Texas in the late 1820s and was a militia leader of distinction and a key figure in the War party.[66] Disarmed, the Mexican soldiers marched to San Antonio, where they were soon joined by a sizeable force under General Martín Perfecto de Cos, who had just arrived in Texas. Cos, Santa Anna's brother-in-law, and a professional soldier with years of solid service, hesitated for some weeks and then made the fateful decision to send a force to Gonzales to arrest Travis and other "rebel" leaders there.[67]

Before Cos dispatched his troops to Gonzales, Stephen Austin, now seen in Mexico as a voice of moderation, was leaning toward "war" because of what he had witnessed in Mexico. He was pushed headlong into that abyss by Mexican aggression. The Mexican war schooner

Correo de México attempted to stop the *San Felipe,* an armed merchant ship on which Austin was traveling, and a ship-to-ship fight erupted. Following the exchange of a few salvos, it was the Mexican warship that surrendered. The first actual "battle" of the Texas War of Independence had been fought and Austin shed any doubts he might have had about secession.[68] He now saw it as inevitable. On September 8, he formally called upon all Texians to cast off the chains of Mexican despotism.[69] Sam Houston, for one, awaited the explosion with great expectations. In early October he had written a friend, *"War in defense of our rights, our oaths, and our Constitution is inevitable in Texas!"*[70]

In November the Second Seminole War (1835–1842) exploded, almost eclipsing events in Texas, while in December remnants of the once-proud Cherokee tribe signed away the last of its Eastern domains in the Treaty of New Echota and the most massive phase of the Trail of Tears, guideposted by Cherokee bones, would truly begin. The West that the Cherokee would set out for, however, was about to change.[71]

S I X

Texas in the Fire

"A few ragged looking Mexican troops."

MARY AUSTIN HOLLY, 1835

B_y the final month of 1835 fear was sweeping through Texas, an emotional version of its famous "Northers," but this fear was windborne from the South, from the deserts of Sonora and Coahuila. Antonio López de Santa Anna, it was rumored, was on the move, marching north with a powerful Mexican army to crush the Texians. His aim was to enforce Mexican rule, it was said, re-enshrine the Catholic faith, end slavery and crush all who dared oppose him. The "Napoleon of the West," a title earned for victories against external and internal foes,* was marching on Texas with ten thousand disciplined, well-armed troops, and under the dreaded black flag, signifying no quarter.†

One Texian, John Sowers Brooks, late of the United States Marine Corps, knew of the black flag. He scrawled in his diary his satisfaction that it whipped in the wind; "so much the better for us: we will not be burdened with prisoners."[1] But most Texians—most rational men— were hardly so flippant. Brooks was fated to be summarily executed under that pennant.

---

* In 1829 he had shown great courage in expelling a Spanish expeditionary force from the port of Tampico. This endeared him to the Mexican people, and emboldened him to overthrow a series of presidents in the next decades.

† Quite common for armies sent to quell internal rebellion.

In the late summer and early autumn of 1835, as Texians speculated and debated, Mexico's control of its border province was tenuous at best. Stephen Austin's diarist cousin Mary Austin Holly noted that this "control" amounted to "a garrison with a few ragged looking Mexican troops," found in some towns; hardly the cream of the Mexican army.[2] And Mexico City lay a long, long way to the south.[3]

Stephen Austin, too, was far to the south until late summer, hoping to avert premature violence and win time for the burgeoning separatist cause. In Mexico he had written a pamphlet, *Exposición al Público Sobre los Asuntos de Tejas (Exposition to the Public Concerning Texas)*, designed to assure the authorities that all right-minded Texians desired continued "union with the Mexican Republic." What Texians sought, and the reason for their many noisy consultations, explained the wily Austin, was not secession but autonomy. "Texas has a natural right to organize itself as a state," he explained.[4] After all, between the population centers of Coahuila and Texas lay a great despoblado, an almost impassable waste peopled only by hostile Indians and bandits. The political instability of the artificially twinned province was appalling, even by Mexican standards. During the period of the Coahuila-Texas union, 1824–1835, twenty men had served as governor! With so many governors there could be but little governing.[5] The "union" with Coahuila was clearly unworkable. Left unspoken was Austin's hope that autonomy would enhance Texas's attractiveness to yet more American immigrants.

Despite the uncertainty and potential for violence, there was an air of supreme confidence, as most Texians seemed to realize that their difficulties with Mexico would soon be resolved. Immigration into Texas, meanwhile, actually swelled, as people—mostly men—poured in from the United States and a dozen European nations. Most were armed and willing to fight for a new American Revolution. Organized companies arrived to "serve" Texas in its hour of need; one sixty-five-man company that debarked at Galveston in October was composed of men from seventeen states, England, Ireland, Scotland, Canada, Wales and Germany.[6] A company of high-spirited "New Orleans Greys" was one-third of European origin.[7] Also, hundreds of restless, bored, or idealistic military men arrived in Texas in 1835 and early 1836 to offer their experience to the cause. These men, like former Marine John Sowers Brooks and Colonel Eduard Harkort, a German artillerist, were heartily welcomed by the eager but untested Texians.[8]

Recent empresario Ben Milam was pleased that many new arrivals settled in his colony. A Kentucky-born wanderer, Milam was an early emigrant to Texas, and a close friend of David G. Burnet, whom he had met among the Comanches. He gleefully wrote a friend that at the present rate his huge land grant would be "completely settled" in a matter of months.[9] During what might have appeared as the period of Texas's greatest insecurity, the largest number of newcomers to date swarmed across the border. In November and December, an estimated two thousand settlers arrived at the mouth of the Brazos alone.[10] Daily, the raw material of nation building was being augmented, and statehood within Mexico became less alluring, especially to the new arrivals. As one authority has noted, "The American frontier had literally spilled over onto the Mexican frontier," and engulfed it.[11] By midyear, only one in ten in Texas spoke Spanish.

"The work of Liberty has begun."

SAM HOUSTON, 1835

Consultations grew more frequent and argumentative, as the War party, reinforced by aggressive new arrivals, began to dominate the discussions. At San Felipe a mass meeting wildly applauded R. M. Williamson, editor of the *Cotton Plant,* who loudly proclaimed that "Liberty or death should be our determination and let us one and all unite to protect our country from all invasion." Fittingly, his speech prominently bore the date July 4.[12]

This was the situation when General Cos ordered a column of troops to Gonzales to arrest the "agitators," including Williamson, and to remove the cannon used for defense against the Indians. The Texians had heard, meanwhile, that Santa Anna was brutally enforcing his brand of centralism in Zacatecas on his way north.[13] They also believed a rumor that Cos wished to disarm Gonzales as well, allowing only one man in ten to carry a firearm.[14]

Unwilling to disarm or allow the "agitators" to be arrested, the citizens of tiny Gonzales refused all Mexican orders and threatened and bluffed the Mexican column into retreat. As the Mexicans backed away, a call went out for help, and heavily armed mounted settlers converged on what soon became a fortified, defiant village. Over its thatched roofs rippled a crude flag bearing the motto "Come and Take It."

As volunteers crowded into Gonzales in early September a larger Mexican column materialized nearby but, when the *regulares* faced the hundreds of determined Texians "all hot for fighting," they too prudently retired.[15] By September 12, with volunteers still pouring into Gonzales, a believable army was emerging, and many favored an offensive to eject Mexican forces from Texas.[16]

At this volatile juncture Austin returned on the battered *San Felipe.* Now convinced that independence was desirable and inevitable, Austin became de facto leader of a rebellion.[17] All over Texas, Vigilance Committees and Committees of Public Safety, local quasigovernments, sprang up, and the equivalent of Minuteman units as well. On September 14, the Nacogdoches Committee, under Thomas J. Rusk, appointed Sam Houston commander of its scanty military resources. The same day, it called a mass meeting, which endorsed a Texas-wide consultation to convene at San Felipe to consider what—if any—ties Texas should maintain with Mexico.[18]

In his new military capacity, Houston called for the men of Nacogdoches to rally, for "the morning of glory is dawning upon us. The work of Liberty has begun. . . . Union and courage can achieve everything."[19] He had just been informed that a band of Texians had taken the Mexican fort and garrison at Goliad, on the San Antonio River. The pungent scent of gunpowder and victory was in the air.[20]

Events, however, soon outstripped the local committees. The men gathered at Gonzales "elected" Stephen Austin their commander, begging him to lead them against San Antonio. Although inexperienced in military affairs and weighed down with political concerns, Austin accepted the role of military *jefe.* Houston later dubiously claimed that Austin had "urged me to take the command" but that he had demurred. The exhausted* Austin then dispatched Colonels Jim Bowie and James Fannin to Gonzales to ready the forces there.[21]

---

* A relative wrote of Austin that "he was so debilitated from disease contracted in the dungeons of Mexico, that he had to be lifted into his saddle."

Sam Houston settled instead for election as commander-in-chief of the Department of Nacogdoches. Immediately, he called for volunteers to form fifty-man companies under elected officers.[22] He also offered to sell four thousand acres of his own prime land on the Red River for only twenty-five hundred dollars if the buyer could produce an immediate thousand dollars in cash, which he needed for personal expenses, among which was the purchase of a uniform from New Orleans, complete with general's stars.[23]

A mass meeting at Columbia in mid-October confusingly—given Austin's earlier election—named Houston commander of all Texian forces. The Columbia meeting then merged into the San Felipe consultation, which lasted the first two weeks of November.[24] Houston served on the select committee on Indian Relations, for the consultation correctly estimated that in a showdown with Mexico, friendship with the Indians could be the deciding factor. Also, on November 3, he was appointed to the committee to draft a "Declaration on the Causes of Texas Taking Up Arms."

The declaration was made public four days later and, in a complicated attempt to buy time, obfuscate the issue and placate uneasy Tejanos, it declared creation of a state government within Mexico, even though Houston was at the time writing that "the Independence of Texas is . . . the prize for which we battle!"[25] A provisional state government, with Henry Smith as governor, and a General Council drawn from the different departments, was hastily elected by the consultation, which then elected Houston major general of the still-to-be-formed Texas army, with headquarters at San Felipe. He in turn appointed Colonel James Fannin, one of the few West Pointers in Texas, inspector general and second in command.[26]

Meanwhile, Austin, Bowie, and the Gonzales "army" were at last moving against San Antonio, a course Houston considered rash. According to Moseley Baker, Robert Morris Coleman, Amasa Turner and other Texian officers, Houston wasted no time in criticizing this "folly." Turner recalled that the general spoke at Gonzales "to discourage the army from proceeding," but that "he was hissed down" by the fired-up volunteers.[27] He and some others attributed Houston's caution to cowardice. Houston later averred that he had been seriously ill and not up to campaigning: "I was confined at Nacogdoches all summer, and part of the fall," but this was not the case.[28]

To be sure, San Antonio appeared a tough nut to crack. The town was being prepared for defense by the experienced General Cos, and a second position, the stout Alamo, like most frontier missions, had been built to serve as a fortress when necessary. Moreover, the veteran Mexican general, reinforced, commanded as many as fourteen hundred regulares there, stiffened by more than thirty cannon. To march against such a foe without the element of surprise, and with only some three hundred ragtag militia and a few antiquated light field pieces, was indeed dangerously arrogant.[29]

Major General Houston had more important things to do than preside over what he deemed undisciplined rabble destined for disaster. As Texas's ranking officer he had to organize and coordinate the defense of an immense and vulnerable territory, and he had no time for glory seeking. But his departure from Gonzales was denounced as "abandonment" by his enemies, who wove it into their portrait of cowardice, debauchery and arrogance. Years later, Moseley Baker asked Houston, "Where were you and what was your action during this interesting and alarming period? . . . you were intoxicated the whole time."

Robert Morris Coleman, of Houston's staff, related the same damning story in his famous diatribe, *Houston Displayed: Or, Who Won the Battle of San Jacinto*, written in 1837, adding that the general became unhinged by jealousy and "attempted to blow out his brains." Amasa Turner also charged the general with abandoning his army, admitting, however, that during this critical period, "He kept sober until 8 or 9 o'clock P.M. generally." Even Houston's friend and supporter Rusk was worried about the general's drinking, writing his wife with uncharacteristic alarm that "he is very dissipated and [consequently] in very bad health."[30]

That Sam Houston tippled during the last tense months of 1835 is neither to be doubted nor to be considered remarkable. Most Texians did, and he did more than most Texians. But, leaving the men at Gonzales, though painful to his reputation, was utterly necessary to Texas. Not lightly would Houston hazard his charge, Texas, on the roll of a die.

"The enemy gave way inch by inch."

SHERWOOD Y. REAMS, 1836

The Gonzales force, a true Texas pantheon—Austin, Milam, Edward Burleson, Sr., Bowie, Fannin, "Deaf" Smith, Francis W. (Frank) Johnson, Alexander Somerville, William Wharton—was skirmishing with Mexican outposts by late November. Within a few days both the town and the adjacent Alamo were under rather porous siege. Austin was commissioned by the San Felipe consultation to travel to the United States where, wrote Houston, "his identity . . . would have more influence in [Texas's] behalf than all the men in Texas united."[31] He appointed Colonel Burleson, a North Carolinian who had migrated to one of Austin's colonies in 1830, commander in his stead.

The "fighting" was desultory, causing few casualties while depleting Texian ammunition without observable result. Burleson became dispirited and nearly broke off the siege on December 5 as the shrill Northers scythed across the flatlands, but younger officers, including Milam and Frank Johnson, bluntly refused and prevailed on him to permit an attack. Disillusionment with Burleson was demonstrated when Milam, not he, was elected by the men to lead a major assault before dawn on December 6.[32]

For five days and nights the outnumbered Texians tightened their noose around San Antonio while a handful of sharpshooters neutralized the Mexican garrison at the Alamo. In the house-to-house fighting Texians' marksmanship compensated for their many disadvantages. The Mexicans' discipline, however, held, and one Texian noted admiringly that "the enemy gave way [only] inch by inch."[33] Milam was killed leading a charge (one of only three Texians to die in this unusual campaign) and Frank Johnson, a Virginian who had served as alcalde of San Felipe, was elected to succeed him. On December 10 General Cos lost his nerve and surrendered the city.[34] By the Mexican general's own count, he had lost about three hundred killed by rebel snipers.[35] Significantly, the Alamo raised the white flag only when Cos ordered its commander to do so.

The Mexicans were disarmed and paroled after swearing to never again bear arms against Texians. The impossible had happened! A small band of untested Texians had bested a much larger force of Mexican regulars and conquered one of the largest towns in Texas. They now had a martyr in Ben Milam, an artillery park, an exaggerated disdain for Mexican soldiers, and some exceedingly arrogant, independent-minded officers who would cause Sam Houston, Texas and themselves much grief. They had ignored Houston and they had triumphed; there was now little incentive for them to adhere to any chain of command. In truth, such vainglorious men would almost doom the Texian revolution.[36]

"1,000 tomahawks well tempered"

SAM HOUSTON

While Houston was marshaling what he could of Texian fighting strength that autumn and winter, word was received that Commissioners Austin, William Wharton and Dr. Branch Archer, operating from New Orleans, had obtained a desperately needed loan, chartered five vessels to serve as privateers against Mexican shipping and recruited hundreds of footloose men. These were promised such generous bounties of public lands that Houston would find it all but impossible to enlist men in the "regular" army.[37]

Sober or not, Houston was a man in constant movement, riding through Nacogdoches, Washington-on-the-Brazos, Victoria and other towns and villages, recruiting, exhorting, chiding, sometimes damning and, in general, organizing for the wider struggle to come. Two days before the Texians took San Antonio he appointed Almanzon Huston quartermaster, under the circumstances perhaps the most difficult job of all. Huston was provided with endless lists of what the general needed for his prospective army—lead, flour, shoes, soap, tobacco, whiskey, "1,000 Butcher knives . . . 1,000 tomahawks well tempered with handeles." How Huston was to obtain all this, bereft as he was of cash and credit, was not clear.[38] Luckily for Texas, several New Orleans merchants, most notably William D. Christy, extended substantial credit.

Skeptical of informal militias, Houston officially moved on December 12 to create a regular army. With the authority of Governor Smith, he offered a cash enlistment bonus, eight hundred acres of good land, and instant Texian citizenship to all who would pledge to serve Texas under arms for two years or the duration of the conflict. Headquarters were moved to Washington-on-the-Brazos because of its more central location.[39] Yet he had difficulty competing with the commissioners' offers and never came close to his goal of signing up five thousand men.

Despite his efforts to ignore the political infighting going on at San Felipe, where the General Council was sharply factionalized, the major general was soon driven to fury by that body's meddling in military affairs. Without consulting him, the Council was appointing officers to independent commands, attempting to create a "reserve army" and separate cavalry units, and was openly discussing wild schemes to invade Mexico. For the moment, no armed Mexican troops were on Texas soil, but even the most sanguine Texas patriot knew that Santa Anna was approaching with an awesome host and reputation.

"our military power is weak, let our strength be
in our unity!"

SAM HOUSTON, 1836

The Council and the officers it appointed as virtual warlords seemed bent on preventing Houston from concentrating Texian strength to meet the coming invasion. Fannin, stationed at Goliad, was a major beneficiary of the Council, receiving the finest volunteer units entering Texas, including a "battalion" of eager Georgians, two hundred armed but semidisciplined men. These were soon followed by a fifty-man company, the "Red Rovers of Alabama," under Captain Jack Shackleford, with new muskets given direct from their state's arsenal. Also arriving at Goliad was one company of the New Orleans Greys, which included in its ranks Herman Ehrenberg, a teenaged German immigrant who kept a keen record of events and who, unlike John S. Brooks, lived through them. Houston's friend Adolphus Sterne, acting as a Texian agent at New Orleans, personally raised and equipped out of pocket another company of the Greys.[40]

To Houston's growing ire, the Council and the officers it created ignored him and instead of a Texas army abuilding, half a dozen mini-armies were in the field. While the Council was pointedly shunning the commanding general, it was constantly badgering Governor Smith to order an invasion of Mexico. On December 17 he reluctantly instructed Houston to prepare some sort of expedition to seize the town of Matamoros.[41] Horrified by such a foolhardy plan, Houston was even more outraged to learn that the Council had issued secret orders to Fannin, Johnson, Dr. Grant and others to ready their units to cross the Rio Grande. Houston warned that such employment of the best Texian units would leave the long frontier denuded and its few linchpin defensive positions, such as the Alamo, untenable.[42] His caution, however, was dismissed as want of resolve, and men of unrealistic confidence committed themselves to unrealistic goals. The revolution was already in danger and only Sam Houston seemed to realize it.[43]

As soon as he was able, Houston galloped into Goliad, where Fannin's men were readying themselves for the Matamoros expedition. In a long and impassioned speech to the assembled troops, he tried to dissuade them from the venture. One who heard the speech remembered Houston saying;

In order to win, we must act together. *United we stand, divided we fall.* I am told that you intend to take Matamoros; I praise your courage, but I will frankly confess to you, my friends, that I do not approve of your plans. . . . Since our military power is weak, let our strength be in our unity!

But his words held no magic that day. The men would not even agree to await reinforcements to give their invasion some slim chance of success. They responded that Fannin would be joined on the march by the smaller commands of Colonels Johnson and Grant, which should be reinforcement enough.[44] John S. Brooks, who also heard Houston's imploring speech, wrote his father that Fannin planned to rendezvous with some seven hundred other Texians "for the invasion of Mexico . . . commanded by Gen. Houston or Col. Fannin." However, wrote Brooks with healthy cynicism, this was hardly a true invasion, "but, primarily, to give employment to the Volunteers," who were clamoring for action.[45]

Houston similarly failed to sway Dr. Grant at Refugio and in frustration dispatched Jim Bowie and a company of volunteers to the Alamo. Bowie's orders were to strip the mission-fort of all supplies and cannon, blow it up and rejoin Houston in the field.

Once more, as at Gonzales, Sam Houston had to leave a part of what should have been his army on the eve of what he believed to be an ill-starred offensive operation. Perhaps a third of all Texian units were poised for the Matamoros folly, and thus independent of the one man specifically charged with the defense of Texas. Worse, recruitment of regular soldiers, which he saw as the key to Texian survival, was not meeting with success. "Two years or the duration" were uncongenial words, especially when officers involved in the projected invasion of Mexico were stressing that operation's potential for loot.

Had not the hoofbeats of Santa Anna's lancers soon resonated along the baked plains near the Rio Grande, Houston would probably have felt forced to lead the Matamoros expedition himself, if the troops would have accepted him. Utterly frustrated, he wrote Council member D. C. Barrett early in January that "Dissension will destroy Texas."[46] Ironically, the situation was even more chaotic than Houston knew, for Barrett himself had just received a frightening note from Henry Millard warning him to urge the government to abandon Washington-on-the-Brazos for San Felipe. The danger came not from Santa Anna, he wrote, but from disaffected, power-hungry Texian officers forming their own "mobs" and planning to arrest the government—or worse: "Rest assured that the assassination of some of you and Gen. Houston is in contemplation."[47] Houston's greatest fear—disunity—was reaching a critical stage.

Yet another problem interfered with Houston's direction of military affairs. The Council had ordered him and experienced Indian agent John Forbes to negotiate a critical treaty with the Cherokees and the other tribes, guaranteeing at least their neutrality.[48] If caught between Santa Anna's lances and Indian spears, the Texians would have little

chance of survival. Houston was a logical choice since he spoke Cherokee and knew Bowl (John Jolly had died), Big Mush and other Cherokee
leaders personally, and his title of major general, although meaningless
to most Texians, would add to his credibility. Mexican agents were
infiltrating the Indian encampments and had to be countered. Neutral-
izing the Indians meant, however, that Houston would have to absent
himself from military command for the sake of Texas and to the further
detriment of his military reputation.[49]

"Who is Dr. Grant?"

SAM HOUSTON, 1836

Sam Houston cast his dice in January, sending orders in all directions
and praying that some would be obeyed. Fannin was told to halt preparations to invade Mexico, undertake no operations at all without Houston's consent and report personally to headquarters.[50] In view of Santa
Anna's approach, the first order was obeyed; the latter two were not
and the colonel remained at Goliad awaiting events.

On January 2, while trying to decide whether to first deal with the
Indians or his own jumbled army, the general wrote D. C. Barrett that
although he was preoccupied with the anarchy that seemed to be sweeping Texas, personally at least "I am most miserably cool and sober so
you can say to all my friends, instead of egg-nog I eat toasted eggs in my
office."[51]

As Houston summoned Bowl and other chiefs to parley and prepared
to ride to Goliad to deal with Fannin face to face, he wrote Governor
Smith: "No language can express My anguish of Soul. Oh, save our
poor Country!"[52] That cry was probably prompted by news that the
fractious Council had named Colonels Fannin and Johnson independent
"military agents" responsible to no other officer. As Houston bitterly
wrote, that order "effectually supersede[d] the Commander-in-Chief in
his authority."[53] Hence Houston set out for Goliad, writing Jim Bowie
at the Alamo to raze that position so that the Mexicans could not use it

and then to march to Goliad.[54] The general later claimed that William Barret Travis, now in command of the Alamo because of his rank as a Texas Regular Army officer, soon received contrary orders from the Council, but it appears that the Alamo garrison remained behind its adobe walls because it expected Fannin to join them there.[55] He also sent Indian expert Hugh Love to Nacogdoches to explain the crisis to the Cherokees and to try to raise an auxiliary force of their warriors.

Unknown to the general as he rode into Goliad, factionalism within the provisional government had at last truly exploded. The Council on January 11 "suspended" Governor Smith and charged him with leading Texas toward what Acting Governor James Robinson termed "absolute Despotism," a vague but impressive, if unwarranted, accusation.[56]

Houston did not learn of Smith's ouster for weeks, and wrote him as governor in late January concerning growing disunity in the army. "Who is Dr. Grant?" asked the perplexed general in anger, and why should he be given an independent command and orders to invade Mexico? "I do consider the acts of the Council calculated to protract the war for years to come," he wrote, again stressing the need for a coherent chain of command.[57] Felix Huston (destined to be a divisive figure himself) concurred, writing grimly that "I see nothing before us but a long, protracted and desperate war."[58]

Little is known of Houston's visit to Goliad save that it was unpleasant. He was poorly received and his pessimism devolved into despair. He felt so little in control of the army that he considered resigning and living again with his Cherokee friends.[59] What he encountered at Goliad was an indecisive James Fannin and some four hundred zealous, directionless men. Most of the rest of the Texian army was spread incoherently in small, quasi-independent commands under Colonels Travis, Johnson, Amon King, William Ward, Richard Morris, and James Grant. Johnson, King and Grant were still committed to the Matamoros fantasy and refused to concentrate their forces under Houston's command to deal with the main threat, Santa Anna.[60]

Through force of personality rather than logic or rank, Houston persuaded Fannin to dissociate himself from the Mexican invasion. He was further buoyed by a letter from Stephen Austin in New Orleans. He advised Houston that the approach of Santa Anna "leaves us no remedy but one, which is *an immediate declaration of Independence,*" a step Houston had been advocating for some months.[61]

Again ordering destruction of the Alamo and concentration of Texian forces, Houston and his small staff headed for Washington-on-the-Brazos, where he endorsed a call for a convention in San Felipe in March to consider independence. He was mortified, however, when he learned that Nacogdoches balked at electing him one of its delegates. He was present in any case, however, for Refugio did select him.[62] Just how he was to treat with the Indians, organize the defense of all Texas and represent Refugio at a crucial convention was not clear even to him.

The situation was soon resolved, for at this critical point, with Santa Anna's battle flags almost visible on the frontier and Texian defenses in utter disarray, Sam Houston was furloughed to deal with the Indians, effective until March 1. Oddly, the furlough was signed by recently deposed governor Smith, whose authority only the general still recognized.[63] No matter the potentially explosive Indian threat, he probably should have stayed and continued his efforts to rally the army. Instead, he demanded of the chiefs a Cherokee council meeting at which he and Forbes would speak. In mid-February the two commissioners rode north.[64]

"They remained amicable throughout the struggle."

SAM HOUSTON, 1836

The mission, though undertaken at a most inauspicious moment, was a signal success. Houston and Forbes concluded a treaty with eight important Cherokee chiefs on February 23, which guaranteed the tribe's neutrality in return for a large "permanent" tract of land in northeast Texas. Houston knew that the Mexicans too had courted the Cherokees, and hence his "offer" was suitably generous. Bowl and some other chiefs had earlier traveled to Mexico City as guests of the government and had been assured of their lands and given gifts. Some had been recipients of commissions in the Mexican army; Chief Bowl was a lieutenant colonel, with a fancy official document to prove it.[65] The danger of the Cherokees' siding with Mexico was significantly lessened by the negotiation, which would, however, remain merely a piece of paper until ratified as a treaty by whatever passed for Texian government.

Probably only Houston could have obtained such a favorable treaty, and so swiftly. The general, who had no time for modesty, later wrote truthfully that he had "conciliated thirteen bands of Indians, and they remained amicable throughout the struggle of the Revolution."[66]

However, during his sojourn among the Indians, later denounced by opponents such as Moseley Baker ("You were in the East removed from danger"),[67] Texas had fallen on the hardest of times. As Houston later graphically put it, "The provisional government had become extinct; self-combustion had taken place and it was utterly consumed." He was not exaggerating. All eyes turned to San Felipe, where the convention soon to meet would simply have to save Texas.[68]

If the political situation on the eve of the convention was grim, the military scene when Houston galloped into Washington-on-the-Brazos on February 28 was funereal. The Napoleon of the West, whose military skills were never denied by Houston, was within Texas, his large army in several powerful columns prepared to confront the fragmented, unprepared and leaderless Texians. Houston's earlier orders had been ignored; there had been no concentration of troops. Fannin stubbornly clung to Goliad, which at least had a substantial stone fort; Travis had remained at the Alamo and was now under siege; Colonel King was holed up at Refugio after a frightening brush with the Mexicans; Ward was somewhere nearby and Grant, Johnson and Morris with their small units were scattered and vulnerable in the south. Only a few hundred Texians were at Gonzales, waiting to be commanded by the supposed commanding general, who himself was at Washington-on-the-Brazos. It had been decided to hold the convention there, since it was more geographically secure than San Felipe.[69]

"I am in a devil of a bad humor."

COLONEL JAMES FANNIN, 1836

In the last days of February, Frank Johnson and four of his men staggered through Fannin's lines at Goliad to tell a sobering tale. Johnson, Grant and Morris had decided against invading Mexico until Fannin could be cajoled into joining them. Grant and Morris had set off to capture wild horses to turn a profit, but were surprised by Mexican troops at Agua Dulce and all but three killed—some after surrender. Following that, Johnson himself was caught unawares at San Patricio and surrendered after a vicious firefight. The Texians were summarily executed. Johnson and his four survivors had escaped the slaughter and, eating little save cactus fruit, had reached Goliad on foot.

In the meanwhile, Santa Anna personally led about three thousand of his best troops toward San Antonio and on February 23 commenced the siege of the Alamo. As that epic confrontation between some 150 Texians—another thirty or so volunteers broke through Mexican lines after the siege had begun—and the Mexican host got under way, news reached Goliad and Washington-on-the-Brazos that Amon King and his thirty-one men had been slaughtered.

Besieged in the church at Refugio by 150 Mexicans and some Indians under General José Urrea, King's men gave a good account of themselves and the few survivors who surrendered paid the price of the black flag.[70] Thus, piecemeal, as Houston had feared, Texian defenses were being expunged, and the vacillating James Fannin now became incapable of action.

As news of the destruction of the "independent" commands drifted in on the winds like smoke from a prairie fire and the siege of the Alamo tightened, Fannin, according to one of his men, "would neither retreat nor march to the aid of San Antonio," as the garrison there and many of his own men expected.[71] Instead, he wrote a friend on February 28 that he would remain at Goliad, "hoping for the best, and prepared for the worst," adding, in stark understatement, "I am in a devil of a bad *humor*. Farewell."[72]

When the survivors of Dr. Grant's fiasco staggered in, discontent within Fannin's ranks forced him to make a decision. Oddly, he ordered the slaughter of 800 oxen to provide marching rations for the 390 of his 420 men whom he planned to force march to the relief of the Alamo some eighty miles northwest. Goliad, itself a strong position, would be held by a single company. John S. Brooks, now Fannin's aide, wrote that his colonel's plan was to sprint to San Antonio, and "cut our way through the enemy's lines, to our Friends in the fort."[73]

Fannin's scheme meant leaving Goliad's strong position and trekking across the flat plains where the Texians would be especially vulnerable to Mexican cavalry. In addition, most supplies, including such basics as shoes, were scarce at best. With no cavalry of his own, Fannin would be unable to gather intelligence on the march or screen his movement or even gain advance warning of an impending Mexican attack.

On March 19, out on the naked plains, the Fannin relief expedition encountered swarms of Mexican cavalry, part of General Urrea's two-thousand-man column, the vanguard of which soon came into sight. There, under the worst possible conditions, the Texians had their first action, a clash which left one in five of them dead or wounded. Fannin himself was all but crippled by three bullet wounds.

During a lull in the fighting, the New Orleans Greys and some others begged the colonel to authorize "a bold dash at the Mexicans" to cut their way through to freedom rather than await certain destruction. The colonel, however, pleaded with his men to await relief from some unnamed source, promising that at eight the next morning he would reconsider the situation. Dispirited, his men did their best to seek safety in their exposed position, hunkering down behind the bodies of horses, oxen, their comrades, baggage and the like, where they nervously listened to the sounds of Mexican artillery being trundled up. As dawn highlighted his precarious situation, "his reluctance to act became even more marked," remembered Ehrenberg. The Greys decided to take matters into their own hands and readied themselves for a desperate sally, but, just then, Mexican officers appeared under white flags and a parley ensued. Promised parole and transportation to New Orleans, Fannin naively ordered surrender.[74]

The colonel and his dejected, grumbling men, many of them wounded, were marched back to Goliad and bivouacked under heavy guard in the presidio courtyard. They were soon joined by Colonel Ward and the survivors of his "independent" command and some Texian civilians captured at Copano Bay.

Urrea was a loyal subordinate and well aware of Santa Anna's edict of no quarter, but he attempted to convince his leader of the wisdom of sparing the latest, and largest, batch of prisoners. Magnanimity might pave the way for Texian surrender. Santa Anna, however, was adamant that all prisoners must die and Urrea ordered Colonel José Nicolás de la Portilla to perform the grim work. The colonel divided the prisoners into three main groups, each surrounded by a heavy escort, and marched them separately away from the presidio under the pretext of taking them to the coast. It was March 27, a bright and clear Palm Sunday, and suddenly the soldiers began to fire into the groups of screaming prisoners. It was swift, unexpected and brutal; bayonets finished the wounded. Some few, like young Ehrenberg, escaped the slaughter by sheer luck. The teenager dashed away through the thick gunsmoke, "shouting 'the Republic of Texas forever!' " as bullets zinged past.[75] The young man would fight again, at San Jacinto, and later become a prominent Lutheran pastor, but few had his luck that grisly day.[76] Some escaped through Christian charity; the eighty civilians taken at Copano Bay were spared and Urrea's second-in-command, Colonel Francisco Garay, personally saved the lives of Fannin's three surgeons, including John Shackleford, because he needed their services. A few others, including Andrew Boyle, were for some reason not shot down.[77] Further, a Señora Alvarez managed to successfully plead for several more lives.[78]

The horror did not end on Goliad's rutted roads. Colonel Fannin, uniquely, was offered his life in return for kneeling in submission to Mexico but, decisive at last, he refused. As a mark of his rank he was permitted to tie a blindfold across his eyes and die seated on a chair in the courtyard.[79] Almost as an afterthought, the forty or so severely wounded prisoners, including John S. Brooks, were dragged from the noisome infirmary and shot. A stunned Joseph Field, one who was spared, later wrote Brooks's father that his grievously wounded son "had no warning of his death until the blow came that set his spirit free."[80]

The dead, estimated by Boyle at 417 (by others variously from 320 to 400), were manhandled into heaps and hastily burned. Their hideous, singed cadavers shocked and enraged Texians a month later when they were found.[81]

They were all gone now: Travis, Grant, Morris, Johnson, Ward, King and Fannin. Only Sam Houston remained. He later blamed meddling politicians for the February and March massacres, correctly noting that "Texas ought never to have lost 500 men in her revolution."[82] Had he been permitted to actually command Texian forces and had they obeyed him, they would not have been cut off and cut down piecemeal.*

Just where was the commanding general? In mid-March, between the fall of the Alamo and the Goliad massacre, he was at his Gonzales headquarters, absorbing the litany of morbid news pouring in and organizing his army of 374 "effectives" for an orderly retreat in the face of what he feared were ten thousand victorious Mexican regulars. Now was a time for prudence and unity, for only Houston was in the field and, as he later recalled in the regal third person, "He was to produce a Nation; he was to defend a people; he was to command the resources of a country, and he must give character to the Army." He would indeed do all this but it would be a very close thing.[83]

---

* However, had he commanded a unified army, Santa Anna would not have divided his, and a lopsided victory such as that of San Jacinto could not have occurred.

SEVEN

The San Jacinto Controversy

"The melancholy and philosophic Santa Anna."

FANNY CALDERÓN DE LA BARCA, 1842

Antonio López de Santa Anna, president of Mexico, commanded that nation's substantial military, more than three times as large as the U.S. Army, and led by a highly trained officer corps, including many European mercenaries. While the army he led across the barren wastes of northern Mexico (an achievement in itself) was neither as large nor as practiced as many Texians believed, it was a powerful force of more than seven thousand Mexican regulares, mostly infantry, but with highly professional cavalry and artillery elements as well. The last group, especially, numbered many German, French and Italian professional officers. So confident was Santa Anna of victory over the Texian rabble that he ordered some twenty-five hundred women and children to accompany his army, with a view to settling some of his personnel as colonists.[1]

Sam Houston never made the mistake of underestimating the short, somewhat pot-bellied "Napoleon of the West," though he did sneer at the high-flown sobriquet. Reflecting years later, the Texian admitted that "the plan of campaign gave evidence of the superior ability of Santa Anna," and had not weather, geography and some luck intervened, the outcome might well have been different.[2] In 1851 he told a rapt audience that "Santa Anna . . . was no common man; with genius and capacity for greatness, he was, and is, an illustrious man."[3] Irish-born American Fanny Calderón de la Barca, wife of the Spanish ambassador to Mexico, observed the man closely: "One would have said a philosopher, living in retirement . . . [marked by] placid sadness . . . the melancholy and philosophic Santa Anna." While she admitted that the Mexican was "ambitious of power—greedy of money—and unprincipled," he was also "altogether a more polished hero than I had expected."[4]

This was the man who set out to bring Texas to heel, neither the comic opera buffoon nor the bloodthirsty maniac so often depicted. He marched under the black flag and believed this fitting. Houston, his principal adversary, never questioned the Mexican commander's policy of no quarter.

"Houston was habitually drunk—drunk often
to beastiality."

DAVID G. BURNET, 1852

Sam Houston, his work with the Indians done, cantered into Washington-on-the-Brazos on the last day of February somewhat "broken in appearance" from travel and tension, one of scores of delegates pouring into town for the convention.[5] Two days later, the great work commenced, as Texian defenses were almost audibly collapsing. By March 17 Texas was declared independent, with a constitution and a new provisional government headed by President David G. Burnet and Vice-President Lorenzo de Zavala. The latter was not elected merely to placate the Tejano minority. Born five years before Houston into a wealthy family in the Mexican Yucatan, Zavala was superbly educated and had served in a variety of political and diplomatic posts. After a brief stint as minister of Mexico in France, he had resigned and migrated to Texas, settling near Harrisburg. From his arrival, he strongly supported the cause of Texas independence.

The Declaration of Independence was written, approved and signed in a trice, with Houston's bold signature inked prominently on the first day of independence, his forty-third birthday, March 2, 1836.[6] He was present for the first four days of the convention, while the Alamo trembled under the blows of Mexican cannon and Fannin vacillated . . . and, with exquisitely poor timing, Sam Houston went on a toot. Burnet minced no words, claiming that "Gen. Houston was habitually drunk —drunk often to beastiality, during his attendance at that Convention," a charge corroborated by a number of other key figures.[7]

He was also straightforwardly politicking in support of independence and to gain genuine control of what remained of Texian armed forces. Heavy drinker or no, the convention on March 4 officially appointed him "Commander in Chief of the Armies of the Republic of Texas." This gave Houston power over all Texian regular, volunteer and militia units.[8] There would be no more "independent" commands but instead the unity he had so long sought.[9] Armed with this unambiguous mandate and with little else, Houston prepared to go to the relief of the distant Alamo, hoping to coalesce the Texian force at Gonzales with that of Fannin. The latter was finally to receive clear instructions, dispatched as Houston, John Forbes and two aides pounded swiftly southwest. The general ordered the colonel to fall back with his artillery to Victoria on the Guadalupe River. There, Houston would join him with the Gonzales army.[10] Those orders were sent March 11, a day before Houston learned for certain of the fall of the Alamo five days earlier. One is struck that Fannin was ordered to evacuate Goliad and retreat in a direction nearly opposite that of the besieged mission. The general had obviously already written Travis off. The next day, having received reports from scouts, he wrote Captain Philip Dimmit about the fate of Travis and Bowie: "All our men are *murdered!* We must not depend on forts; the roads, and ravines suit us best."[11]

As he was leaving Washington-on-the-Brazos, Houston was authorized to establish his headquarters wherever he wished (implicit permission to retreat), organize the army as he saw fit, and "require all officers of the Army of whatever grade to report to you in person."[12] This further centralization should have assured Fannin's compliance with his orders but did not.

At Gonzales on March 11, the day he issued Fannin his long-awaited orders, the general was unpleasantly surprised to find fewer than four hundred armed Texians awaiting him, long on spirit but short on everything else. As he struggled to organize this small band and sent "spies" to gather intelligence, Mrs. Almaron Dickinson, her young daughter and one of Colonel Travis's slaves stumbled into the Gonzales camp with eyewitness news of the fall of the Alamo. She related the heroic defense, the overwhelming might of Santa Anna's army and the casual execution of the five male Texians taken alive.* She also warned that the Mexican was even then marching on Gonzales with five thousand victorious troops (a wild exaggeration).[13]

Given that shocking news, Houston decided to take to the "roads and ravines." Throwing his few cannon into the river and burning what he could not take with him—which added fuel to those who believed him defeatist—he began to retreat toward the Colorado. This was mere prudence, for the force led by Santa Anna was but one of three large Mexican columns ranging through southeast Texas. The Texian "army" filed out of camp in the guttering light of a burning Gonzales. The long retreat had begun.

"west of the Brazos was soon depopulated."

JOHN M. SWISHER, 1879

The month-long retreat known in Texas as "The Runaway Scrape" was both a military withdrawal and a folk migration, for hundreds of families from communities along the Guadalupe, San Antonio and San Marcos rivers packed what they could in panic and streamed northeast. Houston's soldiers were in the thick of the exodus, heading away from Fannin's position at Goliad and toward the Colorado, a barrier they hoped to put between them and the Mexicans.

On the second day of the retreat a dispatch rider caught up with the column carrying a note from Fannin informing the general that "I am delicately situated." Fannin had decided to remain at Goliad.[14] The position he occupied was at least as strong as the Alamo had been, and

* The wounded Davy Crockett was one of these.

he could count on more than twice as many men as Travis had had as well as twelve cannon. The colonel would defend Goliad and "assumed the responsibility of disobeying" Houston's written summons.[15] The general must have roared with rage! He had ordered the Alamo blown up and its garrison withdrawn in January but Travis and Bowie had disobeyed him and squandered the lives of their men.[16] Now it appeared that Fannin, with his vitally needed troops, would repeat the tragic error on an even larger scale.

The Texian exodus soon became a flight. Mary A. Baylor, a good friend of Provisional President Burnet, who was in the thick of the hurried migration, laconically described a typical scene:

> We passed a house with all of the doors open the table had been set all of the victuals on the table and even the chairs set up in their places on the table was a plate of biscuit a plate of potatoes fried chicken (a real nice dinner had been prepared . . .

"It was supposed," continued the punctuationless diarist, that "the owner had left in a hurry."[17] Indeed, a new despoblado had sprung into being, for most Tejanos were also in flight. Within three weeks of the Goliad slaughter, according to Captain John M. Swisher, an officer with Houston's force, "all the country west of the Brazos was depopulated."[18]

Contrarily, Sam Houston's small army was growing in size as it approached the Colorado. Local militia units, individuals in the exodus and men newly arrived in Texas joined his column, swelling its numbers to more than a thousand.[19] Unbeknownst to the general, on March 20 the government, in fear, had abandoned Washington-on-the-Brazos. Houston pleaded with what he believed was a stationary government for more men, artillery and supplies and all but begged the civil authorities to "ratify the Indian treaty," to guarantee that the Cherokees and other tribes did not take advantage of his deteriorating situation to rise up.[20]

At the same time, Houston's adjutant, Colonel George Hockley, was writing Texian secretary of war Thomas J. Rusk that "our Army is in very fine spirits," adding that "I am further directed to inform you of the pleasure he [Houston] feels in reporting the complete subordination of the troops."[21] That "complete subordination," if it ever existed, was not destined to last.

"as much fighting as you
can eat over."

SAM HOUSTON, 1836

Two days after Hockley penned his upbeat message to Rusk, Houston wrote the secretary in a radically different tenor, noting that "a constant panic existed in the lines," as well as desertions, plummeting morale and a host of other serious problems that he largely ascribed to news of the government's recent flight. "Oh, why did the cabinet leave Washington?" he wrote, claiming that in the past few days "I have found the darkest hours of my past life!"[22]

By March 25 the Texian army was on the east bank of the Colorado, where scouts brought word to the general that Mexican General Joaquín R. de Sesma, with six hundred to eight hundred men, was almost in sight. The majority of the Texians were eager to take advantage of their unaccustomed numerical superiority. Colonel Sidney Sherman, sensing Houston's caution, even offered to attack Sesma with his unit alone, but the general demurred and after four or five days confronting the nervous Mexicans, who expected the blow to fall at any moment, the retreat was resumed.[23]

Houston's decision caused open dissension. Captain Swisher noted that "much fault was found with General Houston for not giving battle to Sesma's Division on the Colorado," but granted that "there are times when it requires more courage to retreat than to stand and fight and this was the case at the Colorado."[24] Not many of Houston's officers agreed. Moseley Baker wrote the general himself that "the sentiment in the Army became universal that you were a coward."[25] Houston's future vice-president, Mirabeau B. Lamar, was equally blunt: "A petition was got up to have [Houston] broke" from command. According to Lamar, only the efforts of Colonels Hockley and William Wharton averted a coup.[26] The discontent, even among the rank and file, was only calmed by the general's promise to soon *"give you as much fighting as you can eat over."*[27] The desertion rate soared. Even Houston himself admitted that "the officers were sullen and refractory."[28]

"General Houston the wisest of the wise."

SHERWOOD Y. REAMS, 1836

Skirting Sesma's column, Houston led his grumbling Texians again northeast in what David Lavender has aptly termed a "spirit-withering retreat" toward the Brazos, which he reached on March 28 with an army considerably smaller, exhausted and in a foul temper.[29] There he learned that the government had skipped out again, this time to Harrisburg, prompting him to write Rusk: "For Heaven's sake, do not drop back again with the seat of Government! Your removal to Harrisburg has done more to increase the panic in the Country" than anything since the fall of the Alamo![30]

The Texian army was torn with contrary emotions. While many—especially the officers—doubted Houston would ever seek, or even accept, battle, the general was an inspiration for many of his men. Frederic Gaillardet wrote that the commanding general "was skilled in inspiring men with hope," and he lauded his chief for his "confidence of success, and courtesy to his soldiers."[31] In fact, his unostentatious, common touch made Houston beloved of many and even critical Swisher recalled that "he became the idol of the army and was the only man in Texas who could have kept it together." Sherwood Y. Reams simply found "General Houston the wisest of the wise."[32]

If he had a plan, the general shared it with no one. "I consulted none —I held no councils-of-war. If I err, the blame is mine" alone.[33] Ordering Captain Baker to raze San Felipe (he later denied doing so), Houston moved his dwindling force a few miles away to a thick stand of timber on Mill Creek and established a camp, dispatching scouts—led by legendary "Deaf" Smith—in all directions.[34] There he rested his men, collected supplies and gathered information, learning that Mexican forces were divided into three major and a number of smaller columns. Santa Anna was personally leading one column of about 850 men toward Harrisburg, and the Texian army, of about the same strength, lay between him and the town. Paralleling Santa Anna's column, about twenty miles away, was a 540-man force under his parole-breaking brother-in-law, Martín Perfecto de Cos. A larger division led by General Urrea marched farther to the west, while a third major force under General Vicente Filísola swept through the coastal plain like ill-tempered locusts.[35]

While the Mexicans were confidently pushing forward, Houston and his army simply marked time between Groce's Landing and the ruins of San Felipe. A few volunteers joined Houston there, bringing with them the "twin sisters," two small but still heavy brass six-pounder cannon. These gifts of a pro-Texas committee in Cincinnati brought cheers from the Texians, who had had so little good news for so long.[36]

President Burnet, never fond of his commanding general, was appalled that Texas's only army was peacefully camped by the Brazos, not fighting Mexicans or even taking up positions to protect Harrisburg. He wrote an insulting note to his general, sending Secretary of War Rusk to deliver it personally (or perhaps to take command of the army himself).

> Sir: the Enemy are laughing you to scorn. You must fight them. You must retreat no farther. The country expects you to fight. The Salvation of the country depends on you doing so.[37]

No matter how stinging the words, neither the letter nor Rusk's presence moved Sam Houston to action. However, almost certainly he confided his plans to Rusk.

Somehow, Houston held the stalemated army together until April 13, when he crossed the Brazos and marched toward Harrisburg instead of moving on one of the Mexican columns. Was this a retreat, as some officers bitterly complained? Was it a maneuver to protect Harrisburg and the government? Or was it an attempt to lure Santa Anna closer to the United States border? Jackson had stationed General Edmund Gaines and a sizeable military force along the Sabine, in Louisiana, and Gaines provocatively sent part of a regular regiment to encamp inside Texas, near Nacogdoches.

"We go to conquer."

SAM HOUSTON, 1836

Still the Texians retreated. Rain made a spongy morass out of the roads; even the high-wheeled wagons had to be manhandled through the mud. To set an example, the general and Rusk put their own shoulders to the wheels of wagons and cannon and, drenched with sweat and spattered with mud, did their share of the inglorious work.[38] Private John Jenkins was full of praise for Houston for "proving himself not only a great general, but also a kind friend to his men," alongside whom he labored tirelessly.

Several days after crossing the Brazos, the general encountered Mrs. Pamela Mann on the road, driving a team of stout oxen. Houston persuaded her—with some difficulty—to "loan" him the beasts to pull the twin sisters, since they were all headed for Harrisburg in any case, but when they reached a fork in the road, a crisis developed. The right fork led to the town—since evacuated by the government, which had bolted to Galveston—the left toward the Trinity River. At the fork the army paused, and Mrs. Mann (later a famous hotelier) and many others felt certain that Houston meant to take the Trinity Road. A tough, profane woman, she branded the general "a dam lier," according to witness Robert Hancock Hunter, cut her oxen loose and led them away. No one moved to stop the irate Mrs. Mann for, as Hunter noted, "She had a pare of holster pistols on her saddle pummel & a very large knife on her saddle." Houston shrugged it off and "put his shoulder" to a cannon wheel again. Many a tale would later be told about the woman who had "bested" Sam Houston.[39]

The army marched toward Harrisburg in any event, arriving across Buffalo Bayou from the town on April 18. As the Texians were pitching camp, fortune smiled, for a patrol captured a Mexican courier. From him and his dispatches it was discovered that Santa Anna, with fewer than nine hundred men, had already passed through deserted Harrisburg, partly burning it before marching on toward Lynch's Ferry on the San Jacinto.[40]

The army moved out the next morning, crossing the bayou, leaving its baggage, sick and a substantial camp guard behind. Sensing combat at last, the Texians marched grimly all day and most of the following night. After a brief rest, they resumed the march, and on April 20, scouts reported a Mexican cavalry screen just ahead, with Santa Anna's main body approaching Lynch's Ferry. Hurrying, the Texians reached the ferry first. Houston apparently intended to cut Santa Anna off and force him to stand and fight,[41] to destroy Santa Anna's column before the other two could converge on his position. He might have known that Urrea's division was marooned on the southwest bank of the flooding Brazos but he could not have known that Filísola's division "became bewildered" and was floundering around far to the south.[42] Here was an opportunity to deal with Santa Anna at almost even odds! On April 19, he wrote Henry Raguet:

> This morning we are in preparation to meet Santa Anna. It is the only chance of saving Texas. . . . We go to conquer. It is wisdom growing out of necessity to meet the enemy now; every consideration enforces it . . . the troops are in fine spirits, and now is the time for action . . . I leave the results in the hands of a wise God.[43]

Those are not the words of a man in blind flight.

Halted in a stand of timber close by the ferry, the Texian army was soon alerted by scouts that Santa Anna's main body was "approaching in battle array," and the general disposed his men to repel the enemy. The Mexicans appeared, advancing in column, a single cannon punctuating the cadence of their march. It seemed that the battle to decide the fate of Texas had begun, but as the Texians' little cannon threw a few salvos at the advancing Mexicans they halted, fired ineffectually and withdrew in perfect order. They marched to a camp less than a mile away, on the bank of the San Jacinto, and there they "commenced fortification," as Houston put it, erecting a low barrier of baggage, brush and tree limbs.[44]

The anticlimactic confrontation had been broken off by Santa Anna when he visually estimated the size of the Texian force to be nearly as large as his own (some 760 to his 900). The Mexican sent orders to General Cos, less than twenty miles away, to join him. He would await reinforcement before moving again on the Texians; the undisciplined rebel ruffians would never dare attack.[45]

If there was confidence in the Mexican camp, there was frustration throughout their opponent's ranks. Only one Texian had fallen in the brief clash and the Texians, barely blooded, were fired up to fight. Many clamored for an immediate attack before the Mexicans could erect a proper defensive position. Most simply wanted action at last and many blamed their general for squandering an inviting opportunity. Turner and some other officers later claimed that if Houston had not trundled out the twin sisters and revealed the Texian strength, the Mexicans would have walked into a devastating ambush. It is difficult to take such an accusation seriously, but many Texians were so frustrated that they did.

That tense evening, as Santa Anna's messenger reached General Cos's camp, one of the most rambunctious of Houston's officers, cavalry commander Sidney Sherman, who had led a company of Kentuckians to Texas the year before, wrung from the general permission to act— within certain limits. After sunset, he led his sixty-one troopers, among whom was Lamar, out of camp for an aggressive scouting of the Mexican position, apparently hoping to spark a general engagement.[46]

Soon the stillness along the bayou was broken by the intermittent popping of gunfire, for the Texians had collided with Mexican cavalry outposts.[47] As the firing increased in intensity, the Texian infantry— two regiments of volunteers and a smaller regiment of regulars—stood to arms and moved forward to cover the cavalry, now in hasty retreat.* It had been a short but sharp brush, and many of the Texians had shown great daring, but as they cantered back to the protection of their camp they brought with them two severely wounded comrades and the saddles and bridles of a number of their valuable mounts.

Inconclusive as it was, the action buoyed spirits in the Texian camp and provided Houston with intelligence about the Mexican position. The baggage, packs and other detritus, he learned, would offer the Mexicans scant protection. Less than five feet high, this "wall" could be swept away by a few rounds from the twin sisters. Most critically, the Mexican position was closed, surrounded on three sides by bayou and swamp and on the other by Texians. Santa Anna had nowhere to

---

* In the nineteenth century, Mexican cavalry had a well-deserved reputation for professionalism, fearlessness and élan.

retreat, which led Houston to believe that the Mexicans were planning to attack him the following day, April 21.[48]

In the early darkness of April 20, after pondering the intelligence gathered by his cavalry, Houston shifted Colonel Sherman to leadership of the Second Regiment of Volunteers, and promoted Private Mirabeau Buonaparte Lamar to command the cavalry, "for gallant and daring conduct" during the reconnaissance.[49] That done, he stretched his exhausted frame on the ground and for the first time gave orders that he not be disturbed.[50]

"There was [now] no alternative but victory or death."

SAM HOUSTON, 1859

When Houston arose, stiff, cramped, but refreshed from his slumber, General Cos was leading his 540 men into Santa Anna's camp; the opportunity to fight on relatively equal terms was lost. What, now, would the Mexican do?[51] According to Houston, he had 783 men, while Santa Anna now had "upward of 1,500."[52] The Texian leader still expected to be attacked and organized his units accordingly: Colonel Sherman's Second Volunteers * on the left of his line, Colonel Edward Burleson's First Volunteers in the center and Lieutenant Colonel Henry Millard's small regiment of regulars on the right. Positioned with the regulars, George Hockley commanded the artillery, whose guns were loaded with broken horseshoes. Lamar's cavalry was posted on the extreme right.[53]

The Mexicans, however, remained mysteriously inactive, making no preparations for attack. The truth was that Cos's men, exhausted from their forced night march, were sound asleep. Captain Swisher, like most Texian officers, was praying that Santa Anna would launch an assault, noting in his diary that Houston's camp was impregnable, with a splendid field of fire.[54] But the hours dragged by in frustrating silence

---

* The Second Volunteers included a company of Tejanos led by Juan N. Seguín, who had been sent out of the Alamo by Travis with a message, probably the last man out.

until, shortly after noon, and probably at the insistence of his officers, the general called his first council of war.[55]

Meeting with Houston and Rusk were six officers: his four regimental commanders, Lieutenant Colonel Alexander Somerville and Major Lysander Wells. Artillery commander (and inspector general) George Hockley was probably also present.[56] The options were stark. The Texians could remain where they were and continue to hope for a Mexican attack, or they could move on Santa Anna. Both alternatives were dangerous. If the Texians remained inactive, Santa Anna might be further reinforced; Filísola was rumored to be in the general vicinity with two thousand men. But the idea of attacking an entrenched, professional enemy of superior numbers defied all military logic.[57]

According to Houston, only the two junior officers favored a Texian attack, the others preferring to wait, at least for a while. His "official" version is supported by another source—Jesse Billingsly—who averred that the majority of the council "were in favor of waiting a reasonable time for the enemy to attack."[58]

Emerging from the council, Houston ordered chief scout Deaf Smith to slip unobtrusively out of camp and destroy Vince's bridge over the San Jacinto, "for it cut off all means of escape for either army. There was [now] no alternative but victory or death," according to the general.[59] He then confronted his other officers, explaining to the resentful subalterns that he could not give battle because the council of war had determined against it,[60] adroitly shifting blame for inaction. Sherman later claimed that the rank and file, learning of the council's caution, protested and voted overwhelmingly for an immediate attack.[61]

His officers' dissatisfaction, protests from the ranks and news from the Mexican camp compelled Houston to act. Clearly visible to the Texians, Mexican infantry were working to strengthen the protective breastwork and were digging firing pits. Not so evident was that most of Santa Anna's army had settled down for their customary siesta.[62]

At three-thirty, with no warning, Sam Houston mounted his horse and ordered the still-formed Texian regiments into a thousand-yard-long line, his battle flag marking the middle. He sent the cavalry out to contain their Mexican counterparts, positioned his two guns and Millard's regulars within two hundred yards of the Mexican barricade and, at four o'clock, led his infantry forward at the "double-quick" onto "an obscure meadow of bright grass," himself a highly conspicuous target.

The twin sisters poured forth horseshoes and grapeshot, gouging holes in the breastwork and tossing Mexicans about like ten-pins, and the mute Texians moved resolutely forward to the rhythm of four musicians playing "Will you come to the Bower with me." The short walk through the open field seemed endless.[63]

"Their brains were dashed out with clubbed guns."

JOHN M. SWISHER, 1836

Stunned Mexicans answered the confused calls of a dozen bugles, grabbed their new English muskets and tried to fall into line. By the time the Texians were within range, some had managed to open a ragged, ineffective fire. It was not returned by the grim, silent, advancing rebels. Soon, according to Swisher, "thick and fast flew the bullets," but even when the range closed to one hundred yards, surprisingly few found their mark.[64] Musket balls flew everywhere around the advancing Texians, whose own cannon advanced closer to the Mexican barricade and were blowing it apart. Swisher marveled, "It really seemed as if some invisible hand had turned them aside."[65]

Although detractors Burnet and Turner later charged that Houston panicked and had his infantry fire at the Mexicans from too great a range, Sherman, normally a harsh critic, testified that the general ordered his regiments to hold their fire until the very last minute.[66] Only when the infantry line was about sixty yards from the breastworks did it begin blasting away at the Mexicans and, without stopping to reload, charged wildly forward.[67] The cacophony of battle overwhelmed its participants. Swisher, in the thick of the fight, recalled:

Much has been said on the subject of inspiring music in battle, but let me observe here that during the fight I was once within three feet of the drummer, and he was beating his drum as though his life depended on his hitting it hard and fast, but so great was the din and uproar that I could not catch the sound of a single flam.[68]

The Mexicans, raked with grapeshot, horseshoes and musketry, fell
in heaps; some dropped their weapons in panic and fled to the rear,
disorganizing units still being formed. The Mexican cavalry disinte-
grated before Lamar's wild charge and soon Texian infantry were crash-
ing over the barricade, catching most Mexicans before they could fix
bayonets. Mexicans fought screaming Texians, flailing away in hand-
to-hand combat, "until their brains were dashed out with clubbed
guns."[69]

Within minutes of the first Texian volley, most of the Mexican line
was crushed and the rest in flight. Screeching "Remember the Alamo"
and "Remember Goliad," the Texians on this occasion fought under a
figurative black flag, dispatching Mexicans, armed or unarmed, with
bullet, gunstock, knife and tomahawk. The slaughter was appalling.
Cornered Mexicans fell to their knees in a largely vain attempt to save
their lives, shouting "Me no Alamo."[70]

The Mexicans, enveloped in chaos, had virtually no leadership that
fateful day. Santa Anna was there and mounted but declined to lead by
example. General Manuel Castrillón was killed in the first minutes
while attempting to form up his men and, of thirteen colonels, four
were soon dead and five wounded.[71] Colonel Juan Nepomuceno Almonte, Santa Anna's chief of staff, managed to keep one battalion relatively intact and did his best to cover the anarchic rout. He was
captured near the end of the battle, his surviving men constituting the
last nucleus of organized resistance. In captivity he was treated with
unusual respect (he would later serve as Mexican ambassador to the
United States).[72]

But hundreds of Mexicans fled mindlessly into the river, the swamp
or the lagoon behind their camp. There, most died by drowning or
bullet. As Robert Hancock Hunter clinically observed, "that lagune was
full of men & horses for about 20 or more feet up & down it, & non of
them ever got out, I think there bones are laying there yet."[73] Hunter,
who later guarded Santa Anna, recalled that "Santa Anna said that it
was not a Battle, that he cald it a massacre."[74]

The battle was decided in the first few minutes and it was over in
eighteen. In that brief span all organized resistance was crushed and
only the scattered gunshots and screams of the mopping up could be
heard. By dusk the field was silent, littered with some 630 Mexican
corpses. Another 208 lay mortally wounded, and the prisoner count

eventually reached 730, including the Napoleon of the West and General Cos. The booty was astonishing, a cornucopia of armaments vital to Texian survival. In addition to the cannon, Texas acquired more than 900 new muskets, 200 pistols, 300 sabers, 300 mules, a hundred horses, mountains of assorted gear, and $12,000 in silver pesos.[75] Individual Texians scavenged the field of battle for personal loot and "large packs of wolves growled as they fought over the corpses" and the badly wounded.[76]

Texian losses were astonishingly modest. Houston's official report, written four days after the battle, tallied six killed in action (three from each volunteer regiment), with two more expiring of wounds a few days later. Twenty-four more were wounded, although some would die many days later of supposedly "light" wounds.[77] This, one of the most lopsided victories of American military history, prompted Burnet to later snipe that "he did not make the battle, but the battle made him."[78]

One of the Texian wounded was General Sam Houston, who had so prominently led his men toward the Mexican lines. As the Texians were swarming over the barricade, he was hit just above the right ankle by a musketball. The projectile, ripping through his boot, shattered the fibula and tibia, causing severe blood loss and excruciating pain. He stayed in the saddle in spite of his agony, though there was little "battle" left for him to direct. Only when his staggering white charger received its fifth wound and sank to its knees was the semiconscious general guided from the field by Rusk and his brother, David.[79]

His blood-filled boot was cut away and one of the army's three surgeons removed some bone fragments and cleaned and dressed the wound, while battle reports flowed in. Chewing on a small plug of opium (the only available painkiller), which he later shared with Santa Anna, Houston had Colonel Almonte summoned to ask where his commander might be. Almonte had not the foggiest notion, for he had last seen his chief riding away from the battlefield.[80]

Dismissing the Mexican colonel, Houston analyzed the reports from the field, briefly interrupted by Margaret McCormick, an Irish widow on whose land the battle had been fought. Horrified by the slaughter she had witnessed that sunny afternoon, she bluntly "told Sam Houston to get the dead Mexicans off her league."[81] Robert Hancock Hunter, standing nearby, heard her explain that the cadavers would haunt her land if they were not promptly removed.[82] Distracted with his responsibilities and with great pain seeping through the opium, he responded that Mexican corpses were Mexican business. The bodies were never buried and, two years later, Gustav Dresel wrote that "the bones on the battlefield still bear testimony to their numbers."[83]

"After the battle, individuals thought of nothing but eating and drinking."

SAM HOUSTON, 1851

One of Houston's most pressing tasks, in his fevered pain, was to recall his men, many of whom were prowling the battlefield and far beyond like jackals. As Marquis James has quoted the general, "a hundred steady men could wipe us out."[84] They had won a splendid victory to be sure, but Filísola and Urrea, with some four thousand troops between them, as well as some smaller Mexican detachments, were still at large, their locations unclear.[85] Years later Houston angrily recalled his soldiers' dangerous lapse of discipline. "After the battle, individuals thought of nothing but eating and drinking . . . they were scattered to the four winds of heaven."[86] Such a victory was heady stuff to the Texians but it was victory in a battle, not in the war.

Later that pain-washed evening Houston took a moment to dash off a brief note to Anna Raguet. With it he sent some flowers: "These are the laurels I send you from the battlefield of San Jacinto. Thine. Houston."[87] He also penned a short description of the battle and sent it to Jackson, dispatching a briefer version to General Gaines. The overjoyed American president was soon jubilantly writing an associate of "the poor mongrel Mexicans! That there is more danger of Texas conquering Mexico than the reverse, admits of no doubt."[88]

"The most distressed crazy creature I ever saw."

AMASA TURNER, 1847

Houston had won a battle, probably his new republic's survival and fame, if not fortune, at San Jacinto, yet he had hardly won universal approbation. Controversy over that battle and his role in it was to defy all logic, dog him for years and force him to defend himself again and again. He had made a raft of enemies during the campaign and, like pit bulls, they were not easily shaken off.

Following the battle, only a few of the ranking officers were on good terms with their general, notably Hockley, Wharton and Rusk.[89] Much, perhaps most, of the enmity later so virulently unleashed on Houston was due more to his political preeminence and his embellishments of his heroism and his "saving" Texas than to the facts of the relatively cut-and-dried battle itself.

Houston no doubt outraged Colonel Sherman on the eve of battle, when following the daring cavalry sally he abruptly shifted the colonel to an infantry command.[90] This led Sherman to criticize Houston's personal behavior in the battle and elicited the latter's riposte that Sherman was "a coward," who during the advance on the Mexican barricade turned command of his infantry over to a subordinate and ran for cover.[91] Years later, on the Senate floor, he had the final word: "Colonel Sherman halted where he gave the order to 'halt,' and I never saw him again until after the battle was over."[92] His depiction of Sherman's want of courage was published for posterity in the *Congressional Globe*.[93]

John Forbes, who had helped Houston negotiate the Indian treaties and who was commissary general at San Jacinto, also had immediate reason to dislike the general. Following the battle, Houston subjected him to a "Court of Inquiry" because of "reports circulated prejudicial to the character of Colonel John Forbes." Though exonerated, Forbes was bitter.[94] Sherman and Forbes were influential men, and their attacks upon Houston often drew political blood.

The antagonism of others is more difficult to pin down. Coleman published *Houston Displayed: Or, Who Won the Battle of San Jacinto*, in

1837, accusing the general of whiskey and opium abuse, absence from his post, abandonment of Travis and Fannin, abject cowardice and incompetence. Coleman also insisted that Wharton devised the plan of attack and Rusk actually led it.[95] President Houston, unamused, had Coleman, then a colonel of Rangers, dismissed from the service.[96]

Moseley Baker, a captain in the First Texas Volunteers and the only other officer wounded at San Jacinto, launched his broadside at Houston nearly a decade later, for partisan political reasons. He repeated most of Coleman's charges, adding abandonment of refugees during the Runaway Scrape and halting prematurely on the field of battle, and he contended that "your imbecility lost to Texas all the advantages" of the victory. "You are an incubus upon the land," fumed the rabid Baker in 1844.

Both Burnet and Lamar, presidents of Texas, orchestrated major long-term assaults on Houston, largely for political reasons. Infuriated by the roseate view of the general published in his 1850s campaign biographies, Lamar denounced him as "the Munchausen President." Burnet, who had been carping at Houston ever since he had so harshly urged him to stand and fight, dismissed the biographies as "disgusting bathos."[97]

Yet, weighed against these many and powerful detractors one finds either silence or praise for the general from Rusk, who for years continued to be Houston's colleague and friend, Colonel Burleson, Lieutenant Colonel Bennett, Hockley, Swisher, Ben McCulloch and many of the rank and file, including future Texas Ranger legend John Salmon ("Rip") Ford, whose only criticism was a wistful regret that the job begun at San Jacinto had not been properly finished. According to Ford, after the battle, the other Mexican divisions "could have been captured easily by the Texas troops" if only a pursuit had been ordered.[98]

As with so much about Houston, both the tragic and the glorious, his role at San Jacinto created controversy, but, as Burnet himself grudgingly admitted, it also "made" him.

Months after the battle, the general received an unintentionally humorous missive from one John Campbell of Washington, D.C. Campbell had planned to run off to Texas and help in the struggle against Mexico, but had not gotten his affairs in order before learning of Houston's triumph. Disappointed, he promised the general that "If your country is likely to be invaded again by the Mexicans you must let me know," and he would hurry down.[99]

EIGHT

President Houston and
the Republic of Texas

"Houston showed total incompetency."

EDMUND RUFFIN, 1857

Sam Houston became brutally reacquainted with physical agony on the bloody field of San Jacinto. Bone chips and splinters clogged his swollen wound and the opium plug, which did not drive away the demons of pain, led to slanderous accusations of addiction.[1] Only after midnight did he fall into a tortured sleep.

The day after the battle, Antonio López de Santa Anna was brought into camp, clothed in a common soldier's uniform, which, however, could not disguise the man within, for this was—even in the eyes of the most loutish Texian—clearly no ordinary conscript, however un-Napoleonic his appearance. If he was seeking anonymity, it was another defeat, for his rustic troops unconsciously gave him away. He had been captured by a Texian patrol under Lieutenant James Sylvester, which had flushed him from a sea of long grass and had shown the good sense to keep the new captive alive.[2]

With Colonel Almonte translating, Santa Anna and Houston had a long interview that day, the nervous Mexican—the object of much angry attention by curious Texians—borrowing a "chew" of opium to help maintain his equilibrium. He was placed under the strictest guard by the general, who recognized Santa Anna as the only bargaining chip he and Texas had. Within a few days the Mexican, still fearful for his

life, sent orders to Generals Urrea and Filísola to cease hostilities and
retire across the Rio Grande.

For the moment, Texians could breathe easily. With more volunteers
crossing the Red and the Sabine, and landing at Galveston almost daily,
the infant republic's strength was burgeoning. Although the external
threat had temporarily receded, internal dissension on the part of some
frustrated officers continued. Prominent among the malcontents were
Baker, Coleman and Millard, whose regulars had suffered no casualties. One diarist recorded that "many of the most respectable of the
men who fought there pronounced that Houston showed total incompetency, & even want of personal courage" at San Jacinto.[3]

But those who made such charges and those who favored hanging
Santa Anna from the nearest tree were vastly outnumbered by those
who idolized their wounded general. "Sam Houston was the most famous and popular leader of the Texians" following the battle, wrote
young Ehrenberg, and his heroism "had won the love and confidence of
all his fellow-citizens."[4] And Secretary of War Rusk, a rock of stability,
praised Houston. He had earlier retained Houston as counsel in a successful case against some swindlers and had great faith in the man.
They had become close friends.

The red-haired, beefy six-foot secretary had been in the thick of the
fight at San Jacinto, despite having no specific rank or command, and
his personal aide, Junius W. Mottley, had been mortally wounded at
his side. Whatever vitriol was directed at Houston, everyone praised
Rusk, and Rusk praised the general.[5]

Devoid of ambition, Rusk was unflappable and respected by virtually
everyone, and Houston leaned heavily upon him. He was de facto commander of the army after the battle and supervised the division of spoils.
Three thousand of the twelve thousand dollars in coin were reserved
for the fledgling Texas "navy," while the rest was distributed among
the troops as a bonus. Houston, at his own request, received none of
the cash.[6] Rusk also labored heroically to regroup the scattered Texian
soldiers, distribute captured supplies and attend to scores of petitions
from officers and men. These included sending General Cos's ornate
saddle to William Christy in New Orleans "to assure him of our heartfelt gratitude towards him for the zeal used by him in our favor in our
darkest days." Christy, a wealthy Texian merchant, had moved to New
Orleans in 1835 and become unofficial quartermaster and banker for
the revolutionaries.[7]

Sam Houston "does not possess talents of the highest order," wrote Julia Ann Conner in 1827, yet, she admitted, he was "the most popular man in the state." This miniature, painted on ivory in 1826 while Houston served in Congress, is the earliest known portrait of him. The soon-to-be governor of Tennessee appears as a handsome, pensive young lawmaker.

1

Andrew Jackson, Houston's mentor and fellow Tennesseean as he appeared at about the time he became the seventh U.S. president.

2

Independence Hall
Washington on the Brazos

3

"Independence is the prize for which we battle," wrote Houston in early 1836, and at Washington-on-the-Brazos, on his birthday that year the independence of Texas was officially proclaimed by Anglo-American settlers in this unimpressive building. Often called "Independence Hall," it had been the home and shop of gunsmith N. T. Byars, and served briefly as the first of many capitol buildings of the Republic of Texas.

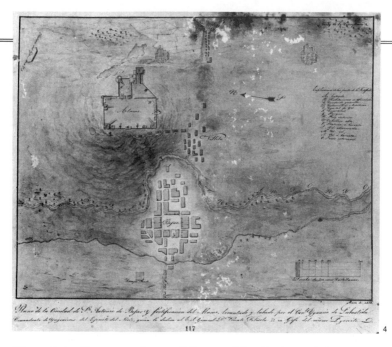

4

"He must give Character to the army," Houston claimed in the regal third person, but his orders to Colonels Bowie and Fannin to abandon, respectively, the Alamo and Goliad were ignored, and both commands were massacred. This map of San Antonio (de Bejar) and its outlying Alamo was prepared by Santa Anna's chief military engineer during the epic February 23–March 6 siege. The five defenders (including Davy Crockett) taken alive were summarily executed by order of Santa Anna.

FALL OF THE ALAMO 5

"All our men are *murdered*. We must not depend on forts," wailed General Houston when news of the Alamo and Goliad massacres reached him. This view depicts one aspect of the final Mexican assault, on March 6. While Santa Anna admitted losing 100 killed and 223 wounded, the true toll was at least twice that. Fewer than 190 Texians had composed the Alamo's garrison.

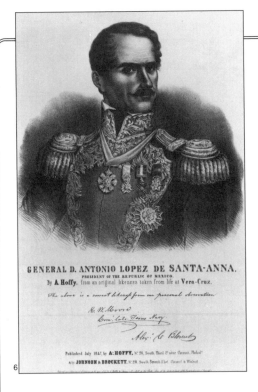

GENERAL D. ANTONIO LOPEZ DE SANTA-ANNA.
PRESIDENT OF THE REPUBLIC OF MEXICO.
By A. Hoffy, from an original likeness taken from life at Vera-Cruz.

The above is a correct likeness from our personal observation

R. W. Moore
Com'dte Texas Navy

Alex. C. Bleroit

Published July 1847, by A. HOFFY, N° 70, South Third Street Corner, Phila²
& by JOHNSON & BROCKETT, N° 28, South Seventh Street, Corner & Walnut

6

Though victor at San Jacinto, Houston often praised the "superior ability of Santa Anna" and never condemned his policy of executing armed rebels. This image of Antonio López de Santa Anna, made about 1840, unlike most, is not a caricature, and its accuracy was verified by Texas commodore Edwin Moore, who knew him well.

"That lagune was full of men and horses," wrote Robert Hancock Hunter of Houston's staff. Hundreds of Mexican troops fled in blind panic into the lagoon when their defensive positions were breached at San Jacinto, and there they were drowned or picked off by Texian troops. With some irony, Santa Anna called it "a massacre."

7

Frank Lubbock wrote of Houston about the time this photograph was taken (1840s) that he had "a piercing gray eye, a mouth and nose indicating character." Hero of San Jacinto and twice president of the Republic of Texas in this period, he was at the zenith of his power and popularity. It was this noble visage that young Margaret Lea of Alabama fell in love with.

8

"Untarnished by the wiles and cold deceptions of the world," Margaret Lea urged her betrothed, Sam Houston, to abandon politics for a bucolic, rural lifestyle. Taken in 1840 in Texas shortly after their marriage, this image of the sheltered, twenty-one-year-old Alabama plantation woman clearly reveals her quiet, mystical nature.

9

©ROGERS Dallas Tex.

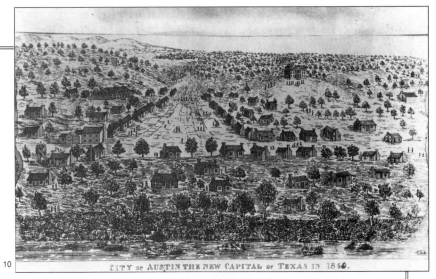

10

CITY OF AUSTIN THE NEW CAPITAL OF TEXAS IN 1840.

Formerly an isolated cluster of huts called Waterloo, Austin was renamed and made capital of Texas by Houston's successor and antagonist Mirabeau B. Lamar. It burgeoned overnight, and within a year, in 1840 when this drawing was made, it boasted some six hundred buildings. Houston, railing that "this is the most unfortunate site upon earth for the seat of Government," did his best to move the capital back to the coast.

The capitol building at Houston, which housed the executive and legislative branches of government from 1837 to 1839, and again, briefly, in 1842, when President Houston evacuated the government from Austin. William Marsh Rice operated the building as a hotel from 1842 to 1900. The impressive edifice was demolished in 1911.

11

Last president of independent Texas (1845–1846), Anson Jones turned against Houston, whom he had served as secretary of state. A Massachusetts-born surgeon, Jones carped that as president, Houston had been so derelict in his duties that it had fallen to him "to administer the Government 'solitary and alone.' " Like many other Texas politicians, he would later take his own life.

12

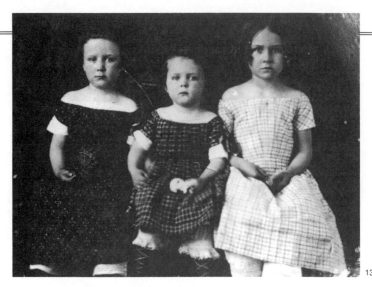

13

"You have around you many of the pleasures which I so much desire," wrote Houston to Margaret from Washington, where he served as senator from Texas. Three of those "pleasures," Nannie, Mary Willie, and Maggie, strike a solemn pose, probably in 1852. Another sister, Antoinette, and four brothers rounded out the Houston "brood."

Antonio López de Santa Anna about 1858, near the end of a political and military career of five decades. Houston corresponded with him for many years. While a highly competent soldier, he proved an inept and corrupt politician, and the "Age of Santa Anna" (1830–1855) so weakened Mexico that President Buchanan bluntly referred to it as "a wreck upon the water," and Houston could urge its annexation on sheer humanitarian grounds.

"Fearless, self-possessed and cunning," according to Rip Ford, Juan Nepomuceno Cortina lacked a "well-defined idea of the rights of property." In the 1850s and early 1860s, he led his army of thugs and rustlers along both sides of the Texas-Mexico border, forcing Governor Houston to mobilize his state.

15

"To do this will be the crowning act of your life," wrote Ben McCulloch to Houston, urging him to invade Mexico in 1860. McCulloch was a feisty, blunt Texas legend—a Ranger, Forty-niner, inventor, Indian fighter, politician and ardent secessionist. He died a Confederate general, leading troops at the Battle of Elk Horn in 1862.

16

17

Austin's Congress Avenue, with the capitol building in the background. Although this photograph was taken in 1866, the view is as it was in 1860, when Sam Houston was governor, for the Civil War and subsequent economic collapse precluded any building. It was in that capitol building that six-year-old Andrew Houston locked the Senate in its chambers.

Houston once introduced his friend Ashbel Smith to Andrew Jackson as "a Gentleman of useful, varied and eloquent intelligence." Smith, a Yale-trained physician who had lived in France, was a wealthy and sophisticated man, who counseled Houston and served the Republic of Texas as diplomat in Europe and the United States. Though Connecticut-born, he supported secession, and leading a company of Texas infantry in which the Houstons' eldest son, Sam, also served, he was wounded in 1862, at Shiloh.

18

"Margaret, I will never do it!" thundered Governor Houston in 1861. He resolutely refused to swear allegiance to the Confederacy following Texas' secession from the Union. That refusal caused his eviction from the governorship and made him an exile in his own beloved Texas. Two years later, his prophecies now sad reality, he died.

19

Rusk also ordered vigilance after discovering that "there are between four and five hundred prisoners and [only] four men as guard!"[8] He did what he could to keep the army from melting away, now that Texas was supposedly "saved," and took a moment to write a short, "official" report of the battle, a model of unassuming brevity: "We have beaten the enemy, killed 630, taken 570 prisoners." He added encouragement to all Texians, actual and prospective: "Tell them to come on and let the people plant corn."[9]

Houston's wound, though treated by army surgeon Alexander Ewing, continued to cause him acute pain and became seriously infected. Because he lacked adequate medical facilities, Ewing urged the general to depart immediately for New Orleans or risk death from infection.[10] Exhausted, Houston resigned command of the army temporarily to Rusk, the only man acceptable to all the officers, and left camp, advising the secretary to send out units to confirm the retreat of the other Mexican columns to the Rio Grande.[11]

As Houston was preparing to leave, Santa Anna signed an armistice. Moreover, he indicated a willingness to negotiate a "permanent" treaty with Texas to recognize its independence as *fait accompli*. This news buoyed the general's spirits almost as much as the raging corruption in his leg depressed him.[12]

Together with Santa Anna and a strong guard, the general churned into Galveston Bay on the steamer *Yellowstone,* which he had commandeered before San Jacinto in the name of the people of Texas, pledging a league of his own land as future payment to the owner.[13] There, where the government's flight had ended, the general was ill-received and shoddily treated by Burnet and his cabinet, who had received letters from some of the disaffected officers. No honors were shown by the ungrateful provisional government, nor even basic civilities. The gaunt, fever-wracked general, his leg in sheerest agony and grotesquely swelled, bade a warm goodbye to Santa Anna, who had been far more civil to him than Burnet, and requested passage to New Orleans on a Texian warship. He was bluntly told that no space was available on any government vessel then at Galveston. In any event, he soon embarked on the fetid little American coastal schooner *Flora*. Since he had no money whatsoever—the government had never paid him a cent—he had to promise to pay *Flora*'s captain for his passage in the future.[14]

"A body of desperadoes from the United States."

W. P. ZUBER, 1905

As Houston sailed for New Orleans, Provisional President Burnet appointed "Colonel" Lamar acting secretary of war while Rusk remained with the army, and he sent Santa Anna under heavy guard to a plantation outside Galveston. No matter the Mexican's glib promises, Burnet agreed with Rusk and Houston that he must be "retained as a hostage," until the government in Mexico City formally recognized both the independence of Texas and the Rio Grande* as its common border.[15] Slippery, canny political survivalist Santa Anna soon (May 14) signed the Treaty of Velasco with Burnet. He pledged to end all hostilities and recognize Texas's independence. Although he had no authority to make such promises, he believed with good reason that they would lead to his release.[16] He was, all the while, completely aware that he neither could nor would honor them. Taken to Washington, he wangled a safe conduct, transportation home and astonishingly, a hefty chunk of the president's petty cash fund.[17]

The creaky *Flora* docked at a crowded New Orleans wharf on Sunday, May 22, and none too soon. News of the arrival of the hero of San Jacinto had preceded the slow schooner and a raucous, cheering crowd of Texas-boosters was on hand. What they saw was not the sturdy, fearless conqueror of the Napoleon of the West they had expected, but a wan, emaciated, taciturn specter, limping feebly with the support of two men, his right leg swollen horribly and wrapped in crude bandages.

The general was quickly spirited to the opulent home of William Christy, where several physicians, including D.C. Ker and a bone specialist named Cenes, were waiting.[18] What they found was what Dr. Ewing had feared, torn muscle and shattered bone and the stench of gangrene as they stripped away the putrid bandages. Ker wielded his scalpel for hours to trim the rotting flesh before Cenes could work on

---

* In fact, Mexico City would not recognize the Rio Grande as its northern border until the end of the Mexican War, in 1848.

the bones.[19] The gangrene was excised and Cenes was as effective as could have been hoped in his specialty. Houston wrote Lamar about his wound that "some twenty or more pieces of bone were taken out of it."[20]

So weak was the hero of San Jacinto that he rested and recuperated in almost total seclusion, seeing only his doctors and Christy. He even disappointed the city fathers by uncharacteristically turning down an appearance at a great celebration in his honor.[21] He did, however, accept a two-thousand-dollar advance fee from a local land company to act as its representative in Texas.[22] He needed the money and the company's fee was well spent to bring a man like Houston on retainer. During his convalescence he also "met a number of Texians there and they requested me to become a candidate for the Presidency." Although he claimed that he rejected such an idea, it remained an option.[23]

In the first week of June Houston, still weak and hobbling clumsily on crutches, departed New Orleans by wagon for Texas. At the same moment, an acquaintance, Ben Currey, was writing him from Washington that Jackson and Vice-President Martin Van Buren considered him "among the great men of the earth."

Houston made a point of tarrying at Nachitoches, Louisiana, where he undoubtedly sought assurances from General Gaines that American troops would remain at the Sabine until all danger from Mexico had passed.[24] Before he could leave, his ankle wound began to fester dangerously and he sought treatment from Robert Anderson Irion, a young physician en route to Texas and a new life. Irion, a Virginian, had married into the planter elite of Vicksburg but had recently lost his wife to cholera and, disconsolate, had taken the road west.[25] They set out together for Nacogdoches, becoming fast friends en route.[26]

Conditions in Texas were deteriorating. The government was ineffective and Burnet was displaying startling incompetence, constantly rotating cabinet members without ever achieving the correct combination. Armed emigrants were swarming into Texas from points as distant as New Hampshire, and the "army" was emerging as arbiter of Texas's destiny. Texas's political style might soon emulate Mexico's. A handful of newly arrived, often self-appointed officers, along with some unsatisfied veterans, were at the heart of the power vacuum caused by Burnet's incompetence.

One of their targets was the paunchy corpus of the Napoleon of the

West, and indeed, Santa Anna was briefly seized before he could sail to freedom by rebellious officers led by "Generals" Thomas Jefferson Green and Felix Huston. Their visions included the execution of the prisoner and a full-scale invasion of Mexico. Men arriving in Texas too late for San Jacinto—including an eighty-man company from Cincinnati—were seeking action, fame and loot,[27] and were natural supporters of such individuals.

Fearing civil war, Rusk wrote Houston on July 2 that Burnet and men like "General" T. J. Green "have been hammering at me and really trying to break up the Army. They have charged me with being a military usurper," and they fiercely resented his "stand in relation to General Santa Anna." Rusk also wrote that Burnet wanted to replace him in command of the army with Lamar, a move "intended by the Cabinet to supercede you." He begged Houston to hurry back, no matter his wound, for only "you have the entire confidence of the Army and the people as well."[28]

Aware of the continued threats against his life, Santa Anna attempted suicide with an overdose of morphine and would have succeeded but for Dr. James A. E. Phelps, at whose plantation he was held.[29] Meanwhile, newly appointed commanding general of the Texian army to "supercede" both Rusk and Houston, Colonel Lamar, received a rude shock. He was overwhelmingly rejected by "his" army, now under the sway of "the mutinous and reckless" Thomas Jefferson Green, recently arrived "with a body of desperadoes from the United States."[30] Houston lamented that in this chaotic epoch the United States "located all the rascals in Texas; did not send any of them to Arkansas."[31]

"Your good wishes unfortunately were not
complied with."

ANTONIO LÓPEZ DE SANTA ANNA, 1836

Green was a true wild card, with murky claims to general's stars based upon a panicky letter of March 20 from the Texas State Department "appointing you a Brigadier General in the Army of Texas" charged with recruiting in the United States.[32] He did little recruiting but showed up in person that summer at Galveston, where he turned his considerable energies to rabble-rousing. His imposing physical stature, biblical rhetoric and promise of booty impressed many newcomers, who had been drawn to Texas by news of war, not peace.

Sam Houston had also been in contact with Green, after the latter had been named brigadier of recruiting. An odd letter written by Houston in the waning days of 1836 helps explain Green's pretensions. Although the two were to become the worst of enemies, Houston wrote Green a placating note in which he swore that "I wished to place you in command of the army. I attempted it and the wish failed." There is no record of this elsewhere. This might have been an attempt to deflect Green's frustrated anger toward another target, probably Burnet, but it alludes to a curious relationship between the two men that has never been elaborated upon.[33]

Green found an ally of convenience in the eloquent and hyperactive Felix Huston, whose general's stars were of even more nebulous origin. He too had been a recruiter for Texas and had expended a great sum of his own funds raising volunteer units in Kentucky and Mississippi.[34] A born filibuster, Huston was hell-bent on invading Mexico.

And so, in mid-July, Lamar, embarrassed, found himself writing Burnet that those "generals" (supported in this case by Rusk) had prevented him from assuming command.[35] At a time when Stephen Austin, for all his fame, was offering to enter the army as a private ("Every man in Texas must shoulder his arms"),[36] the Texian army was degenerating "into a state of mutiny." When Green, Huston and others forced the nonplussed Lamar to abide by a balloting of the entire army, the result was a resounding 1,500 to 179 vote against him.

After all, earlier in the month, with Rusk in titular command, Green, Huston, Memucan Hunt and others were both setting policy and implementing it, seizing Santa Anna briefly with the intention of trying him for war crimes. The Mexican hostage pleaded with Sam Houston, the one Texian he could trust: "By ordering my prompt return to Mexico according to the agreements you will do the greatest service to Texas, although your good wishes unfortunately were not complied with." He begged Houston to use his authority to have him released, contending that the Mexican Congress would never honor the Treaty of Velasco until Santa Anna was safely at home.[37]

So confusing was the situation within the army that Houston had written "the Genl Commanding the Army of Texas" (Rusk, he hoped) to plead with, and order, him to not permit Santa Anna's execution, for "it is obviously contrary to the true policy of Texas—the advantages which his capture presented to us will be destroyed." If Santa Anna were shot, the Mexicans would almost certainly execute any Texians they held, and perhaps the many Americans in Mexico as well. This would lead to a crisis with the United States and end all chance of annexation; far too high a price to pay for mere vengeance. With clear geopolitical logic, Houston, "as Commander in Chief of the Army of the Republic, do solemnly protest against the trial, sentence, or execution of Genl. Antonio López de Santa Anna . . . until* the relations in which we are to stand to the U States shall be ascertained."[38]

Indeed, Jackson was already feeling winds from the edge of the Texian storm. Angry Mexicans, in misguided retaliation against Texas, seized a number of United States citizens at the Gulf port of Tampico, an action Jackson feared might be emulated throughout the republic. In a rage he ordered the United States Navy to Tampico, instructing the commodore in command to inform the city's authorities that "if they touch the hair of the head of one of our citizens, [he would] batter down & destroy their town & exterminate the inhabitants from the face of the earth!" The captives were soon released.[39]

"I would rather vote for you than any other man."

THOMAS JEFFERSON RUSK, 1836

With the Texian army increasing in size and restiveness, Texas was on the brink of anarchy. The soldiers had not been paid and when San Jacinto veterans were given "land certificates" for 320 acres in lieu of salary by their "grateful" government, they found them unconvertible into real money. Hence, according to one veteran, "they would let

---

* A fascinating qualifier.

merchants have 320 acre certificates for a par of pants" or a bottle of whiskey, much as the Cherokees had treated their baffling "certificates of indebtedness" years earlier.[40]

In early August, as rumors flew that Green, Huston and their ilk were planning a coup, Burnet announced a general election for September 5.[41] Houston soon let it be known that he would support Rusk for the presidency, but the latter immediately responded, "I feel flattered that you should think me worthy of filling the presidential chair, but my age [youth] precludes me from running . . . I would rather vote for you than any other man in the country, but we cannot spare you from the army," which had by now swelled to more than two thousand impatient men, two-thirds of whom were newcomers. He again implored Houston to return to headquarters and pledged to support any candidate who would cooperate with the general.[42]

In mid-August, Houston did return to the army—whose "control" Rusk happily relinquished—and his presence did much to restore order. The victor of San Jacinto was immensely popular with the rank and file, both the veterans and the newly arrived. One who adulated him was struck by his "common touch," writing of the unprepossessing general that "notwithstanding his coarse attire, I thought that he was the noblest-looking man that I had ever seen."[43] As if to prove their devotion, the troops took up a collection, purchased Santa Anna's fancy saddle and presented it to their recuperated general.*[44] Agitation to launch an expedition into Mexico receded, as did fear of an Indian uprising instigated by Mexicans, for Houston immediately wrote the various tribes, warning them that while "the Mexicans have told you many things," none of them were true. And, in any case, he reminded Indian leaders, "the Great Chief of Mexico Santa Anna is our prisoner, and he cannot help you to make war" against Texas; a very cogent argument.[45]

---

* He, in poor taste, soon gave it to cousin Robert Houston, of Nashville.

He "paralyzed the arm of the mobocrat."

SAM HOUSTON, 1859?

Stephen Austin and Henry Smith declared their presidential candida-
cies and a divisive campaign began. From the sidelines, Houston calculated that the candidates were evenly matched. He feared that no matter
which politico won, his victory would leave new fissures in the already
torn fabric of Texas politics. Texas needed unity, and who but Sam
Houston could provide it? As he recalled years later, "Not being identified with either of the parties, I believed I would be enabled so to
consolidate the influence of both by harmonizing them." [46]

In mid and late August a number of impromptu mass meetings
throughout Texas proposed Houston for president and, on August 26, a
mere eleven days before the election, he threw his hat in the ring.
While Austin and Smith were hectically "canvassing" (stumping),
Houston, "above" politics, felt little need to campaign at all. He was
serenely confident that his candidacy by itself had, as he noted in the
third person, "paralyzed the arm of the mobocrat by his personal presence." [47] He sounded out Rusk for his running mate, but the younger
man declined, and to Houston's unpleasant surprise, he was to wind up
with Lamar. [48]

The margin of Houston's victory resembled that of San Jacinto, con-
firming both the wisdom of his course of action and his immense popularity. While Austin drew only 587 votes and former governor Smith
743, the hero garnered a mandate of 5,199; 80 percent of the votes
cast. [49] The people of Texas had spoken clearly. A referendum concerning whether Texas should seek annexation by the United States was
even more lopsided, with all voters save 92 in favor.

Houston immediately set about forming his government, attempting
to unite the country by pacifying its real and potential factions. With
Lamar his vice-president, Houston chose Austin for secretary of state,
Smith for the treasury, Rusk for secretary of war, Robert Barr for
postmaster, and wealthy North Carolinian James Pinckney Henderson
for attorney general. He not only placated interest groups, but co-opted

obvious talent.[50] Now, he believed, he could work for swift admission to the Union.

"THE ALL-HORRIBLE DEMON IN HUMAN SHAPE."

S. H. EVERITT, 1836

His cabinet in place, President-Elect Houston convinced Burnet to relinquish his office before the expiration of his term, prompting Lamar to charge him later with "a palpable violation of the Constitution."[51] Burnet, for his part, stung by growing public criticism, was positively relieved to turn the turbulent new republic over to the general. With perhaps "indecent haste," the transfer of power occurred on October 22 at Columbia, and Houston took the oath of office at a rude table covered with an old blanket.[52] He faced truly daunting tasks: annexation to the United States or, failing that, recognition and binding treaties; maintaining discipline, trimming and taming the fractious army; cementing a lasting peace with the Indians, which hinged on Senate ratification of the treaties; and negotiations with Mexico, which still represented a very real danger. In addition, he needed to negotiate treaties with major European nations, if Texas were not annexed, and consequently seek recognition, loans and trade. Finally, he needed to create a national economy in a land already heavily burdened by debt. In short, he had to create, safeguard, maintain and nourish a nation, even if, as he hoped, only briefly.

He plunged into his work with manic energy. He authorized Thomas Toby and his brother at New Orleans to serve as general commercial agents for the new republic.[53] He inaugurated small "ranging units" (forebears of the famed Texas Rangers), including some composed of Cherokees, to patrol the frontier. He fortified Galveston and formally solicited volunteers from the United States, but only if armed and provisioned at their own expense. He accepted private foreign aid such as two cannon "presented by the ladies of Havana," and commissioned privateers to prey on Mexican commerce. Scrip for public land was issued in lieu of currency to be used to purchase supplies. All the while, he dealt tactfully with the captive Santa Anna, who claimed to be representative of the Mexican people.[54]

Somewhat grudgingly, he approved a congressional resolution to "open a secret correspondence with Gen. James Hamilton* of Charleston, South Carolina, to ascertain of him whether or not he will accept the commandancy of the army of Texas, if the emergency requires it."[55] Houston, who knew Hamilton only by reputation, bowed to the will of Congress, but the general was never summoned west.

Santa Anna wrote Houston two weeks after the inauguration, incensed that the Treaty of Velasco, predicated on Texas's becoming an independent nation, was being violated. He considered that the overwhelming popular vote for annexation had annulled the treaty. In any case, Mexico, he predicted, would never accept the United States on its border.[56]

Houston promptly announced that the Mexican president would be sent, in company with Texian commissioners, to Washington, D.C. The commissioners, who included Spanish-speaking Barnard E. Bee and Houston's old friend William Wharton,† were to press Congress for swift annexation. But the release of the national hostage brought howls of rage from many Texians, who preferred Santa Anna in chains or in a pine box. S. H. Everitt, in a public speech at Galveston, vehemently protested such lenient treatment of "THE ALL-HORRIBLE DEMON IN HUMAN SHAPE," but to no avail, for Santa Anna and the commissioners left Texas on November 26, unmolested.[57]

---

* Former governor of South Carolina, friend of John C. Calhoun, diplomat, financial wizard and kinsman of Barnard E. Bee, whom he had sent to Texas early in 1836 to purchase land for him.

† Wharton fatally shot himself in 1839, supposedly while cleaning his pistol. More probably he was just another of the ubiquitous Texas suicides.

"The President's cabin has no glass."

MARY AUSTIN HOLLY, 1836

As Houston scrambled to organize his fragile nation during the critical autumn of 1836, his past returned briefly to haunt him. John Campbell sent him disturbing news of Eliza. Campbell had met her in the spring, in Gallatin, and he informed the Texian that she had been thrilled by the news of San Jacinto: "It is said that she showed great pleasure at your success and [was] fairly excited." More to the point, the writer noted, "I heard that some of her friends wanted [her] to git a divorce, and she positively refused, and said she *was not displeased with her present name;* therefore she would not change it on this earth but wanted to take it to the grave with her . . . *she is certainly a most estimable woman.*"[58]

Campbell's reportage, if accurate, indicates, and indicated to Houston, that Eliza did not consider the marriage ended, and that she was unaware of the rigged 1834 Texas "divorce" arranged by her husband. Corroboration came when trusted cousin Robert McEwen wrote from Nashville that Eliza and her family would welcome a reconciliation. Houston, however, felt it far too late for that, or perhaps believed that it would be for the wrong reason; his new fame.[59]

The president was, after all, infatuated with Anna Raguet, in his words the "richest ruby, and fairest flower" in all Texas.[60] Miss Anna hardly returned his attentions but she had fashioned for him the rather gaudy crimson sash and sword belt that he had worn at San Jacinto and he had sent her "laurels" (actually, magnolias) from the field of glory.[61]

As the year of Texas's independence drew to a close, tension was on the increase. Mexican agents were again among the tribes and Secretary of War Rusk melodramatically warned Texians that those agents sought "to induce them to commence an indiscriminate massacre of your wives and children." Continuing a pattern of long standing, Rusk was again inciting anti-Indian sentiment, never far below the surface in Texas.[62]

Despite the lopsided vote for Houston, Texas was not destined for political consensus, save on the single issue of annexation. There were strong differences of opinion in Washington D.C. on that particular matter, fueled by many Americans' fear that annexation of Texas would precipitate war with Mexico. Should the nation go to war, many asked, to add another slave state to the Union? Jackson, the consummate politician, would have been proud to bring Texas swiftly into the nation but made no move to do so, given the mood of Congress.

In addition, he feared that the specter of the Houston-Jackson conspiracy to pirate Texas might revive. He wrote Texian agent William Wharton that "Texas must claim California," so that they could both come into the Union at the same time. Admitting one free and one slave state might make Texian statehood more palatable to congressional abolitionists.* [63]

In California, as if on cue, a federalist revolt was brewing, ostensibly to restore states' rights under the constitution of 1824. Further, the states of Sonora, Zacatecas and the Yucatan were also restive and on the brink of revolt.[64] Whether this would be an opportunity or a threat to Texas remained to be seen.

On Christmas Day—two days before Stephen Austin's unexpected demise†—Mary Austin Holly jotted in her diary a brief description of Houston's presidential "palace" at Columbia: "The President's cabin has no glass—slats across the windows with blankets interwoven supply the place,"[65] and Houston himself lamented to his friend Henry Raguet that "Our accommodations are miserable here."[66] Only rarely was he paid his salary, and consequently he was forced to survive on credit.

The president wrote cousin John that he was weary of responsibility, a refrain he repeated often but never acted upon. "By all means get Texas annexed to the U. States—I wish to retire, and spend the balance of my days in peace, and to review the past, as a Philosopher shou'd do."[67]

As Mary Austin Holly "Drank Champagne—sung & danced in the new year" at Brazoria,[68] Henry Morfit, a special agent sent across the

---

* The 1820 Missouri Compromise had established a line drawn from the north of Arkansas west, prohibiting slavery north of that line. California lay to the north.

† Houston was shocked by Austin's untimely death, writing of it "as the greatest misfortune & calamity that the country had ever sustained." "The Father of Texas is no more! The first Pioneer of the Wilderness has departed!" he wrote, ordering twenty-three-gun salutes throughout the republic.

Sabine by Jackson, reported that Texas was growing with spectacular rapidity, estimating its population at 45,000 Americans, 5,000 slaves, 3,000–3,500 Tejanos, and 12,000 Indians.[69] Clearly, this new nation would soon have to be dealt with.

"Showing all the Cherokee traits of defiance."

ANDREW JACKSON, 1837

Unfortunately for Texas, the United States suffered financial collapse in the "Panic of 1837," caused largely by Jackson's bizarre banking policies but blamed on incoming president Martin Van Buren, the first president born in the independent United States. He had pledged to continue Jackson's policies and press for the annexation of Texas but found himself facing both abolitionist resistance and doubts about the constitutionality of annexing an independent nation.

Like the financial temblor of 1819, the Panic of 1837 stimulated more emigration from the Old Republic to the New, but it also painfully constricted Texas's credit, its ability to borrow in the cash-poor United States, and the willingness of Americans to speculate in Texas bonds and land scrip.

As the new year dawned, Houston continued to press his mentor to work for annexation or, at the very least, recognition of Texas. William Wharton, now Texas minister plenipotentiary to Washington, often rebuffed by antislavery congressmen, pointedly began to court the diplomatic representatives of Britain and France.[70] Michigan became the twenty-sixth (free) state in January, but Jackson did not press for annexation and, in fact, informed Congress that the time was simply not propitious to make any move concerning the frontier republic. To his protégé's dismay, he did not even urge recognition, though Houston had written that Texas had at least as legitimate a claim as did the new Latin American nations recognized a decade earlier.[71]

Jackson, in his last months as president, continued to avoid the Texas question as adroitly as he could. He occasionally became irritated by

Houston's "demands" concerning annexation and remarked sarcastically that his Texian friend "was showing all the Cherokee traits of defiance."[72] Yet, with virtually no warning, on March 3, his 2,992nd and last full day as president, he officially recognized the Republic of Texas and nominated Louisianan Alcée la Branche as United States chargé d'affaires at Columbia, the Texian capital. That same day he did something else Houston had long desired; he officially remitted the Texian's five-hundred-dollar fine in the Stanbery case, dismissing it as "excessive."[73]

Beyond the manifold tasks of the presidency, Sam was heavily occupied with courting and excessive drinking. He wrote Miss Anna, "I will not marry until I can once more go to Nacogdoches and see how my matters are there!" The Raguets, of course, lived at Nacogdoches, and if he found all in order there with her, "Why then I may look out for a 'spare rib' to appropriate to myself."[74] Miss Anna blithely affected to miss the point.

The president, once more, had to deal with problems in the army. The new commanding general, Felix Huston, was attempting to make the army a personal vehicle for fame and loot by organizing an expedition to capture Matamoros, just south of the Rio Grande. Houston considered this dangerous and counterproductive, certain to stir up a diplomatic hornet's nest and goad Mexico to war. The president dismissed the general and replaced him with Albert Sidney Johnston, a West Pointer and professional soldier, destined to be the highest-ranking officer in the Confederacy in 1861.[75] Enraged at being sacked, Huston challenged the new commander to a duel and wounded him grievously. The president left Johnston in command despite his convalescence and Huston, having retained his honor, if not his position, left Texas to sulk in New Orleans.[76]

Aware of the undercurrents of discontent within the army and embarrassed by the government's total want of funds, Houston chose a gravely risky course.[77] In the spring he instructed Rusk to begin furloughing company after company from the army, until no more than six hundred select men remained. It was a brilliant escape from a potentially explosive situation, for legally, furloughed troops were subject to instant recall in time of emergency and, as Houston grimly admitted, he could not actually disband the various companies, "as there was no money to pay them." In fact, he had recently pledged most of his own lands as collateral to provide supplies.[78] Despite some grumbling, the jury-rigged demobilization worked.

Houston had never been content with little Columbia on the Colorado as the national capital, but most Texian towns were too exposed to the Comanche or Mexican threat, or located on the periphery. Texas was a new republic, and, as Mary Austin Holly put it, "The rage is now for making towns."[79]

Once such town-in-the-making had been "platted" and laid out in August 1836 by the enterprising brothers John K. and Augustus C. Allen, "shrewd speculators from New York State." They had purchased 6,642 acres near the ruins of Harrisburg, close to the juncture of Buffalo and White Oak bayous. As they were surveying, they had the brilliant idea of calling it Houston.[80] They also constructed what might pass for a capitol building, which Columbia lacked, and offered to rent it to the government "for a nominal fee."[81]

The Texian government could hardly refuse, and in November the new "city" became the capital of Texas, although it would be months before the government could relocate there. Before the capitol building was framed, Sam Houston, in a gleeful letter to his friend Robert Irion, admitted that the Allen brothers had given him twelve prime city lots, which he estimated "should be" worth at least a thousand dollars each! He perceived no conflict of interest, and in fact, gave away many of his town lots to friends in the coming years.[82]

The new capital fairly mushroomed. As Houston himself noted in April, "On the 20th of January, a small log cabin and 12 persons were all that distinguished it from the adjacent forests, and now there are upwards of 100 houses finished . . . and 1500 people." And there was a thriving social life worthy of a frontier capital: "There are more than 100 ladies resident in town," wrote the gratified president, "and at a ball given on the 21st, 73 attended!"[83] Mary Austin Holly noted that dances were popular in Houston, especially in the winter, where they served the population well "to keep warm."[84]

The president did not reside in rustic opulence. Far from it. John James Audubon, passing through Houston in 1837, described the presidential "manse" in a few words, for there was little to describe: "a small log house, consisting of two rooms and a passage . . . the ground [dirt] floor, however, was muddy and filthy."[85] Frank Lubbock, a Houston merchant, sold his own retail store to Congress in 1838 to be used as the "Executive Mansion," because he was distressed to see the president living in "a small rough log cabin about twelve by sixteen feet . . . there was no fireplace—nothing but a small clay furnace in the room for him to get over and warm his fingers, Indian style."[86] Houston, though, rarely complained.

"Sam Houston . . . has not drawn a sober breath."

ANON., 1837

Cramped, "muddy and filthy" it was indeed, but also, the "Executive residence was a scene of Rabelaisian entertainments," as Houston and his friends frequently drank themselves insensate.[87] Both Houston the man and Houston the city were hard-drinking and nearly every visitor to the town was struck by its boozy rowdiness. Lubbock marveled at its huge tent saloons, and Gustav Dresel waxed fondly eloquent about his compatriot Kessler, who owned the "Round Tent," on Main Street near Congress Avenue, a watering hole crowded with veterans of the revolution who used their bonus land scrip and a few coins to buy "brandy cocktails, gin toddies, claret punches, cherry brandy" and other exotic potables, which brought a certain sophistication to their revels.[88] John Hunter Herndon wrote distastefully in his diary that less than a year after its founding, Houston had become "the greatest sink of discipation & vice that modern times have known."[89]

Frustrated Baptist minister-missionary Z. N. Morrell sadly concurred, declaiming that "drinking, fighting, and wrangling" were the town's only pastimes. In two years of heroic effort, the Reverend Morrell converted not a single soul in rambunctious Houston![90] The fact was that in 1837 and 1838, spirits were the only bargain to be had in Houston. Ice sold for an incredible fifty cents a pound, coffee for half that, eggs for an astonishing six dollars a dozen and flour for an astronomical thirty dollars a barrel, but a quart of popskull could be had for a dollar![91]

Few in that ambience of barleycorn fumes noticed the behavior of the president or would have strongly disapproved of it. As one source has noted, "The Texians being an entirely military people, not only fought but drank in platoons," and Sam Houston was, after all, their favorite general.[92] One who did disapprove described the president and his "suit" of friends as "as miserable and drunken a set of vagabonds as ever disgraced a community," snorting that during an eight-day visit to Nacogdoches, "Sam Houston . . . has not drawn a sober breath."[93]

The only restraint on Houston's almost constant tippling was his closest confidant, Dr. Ashbel Smith, who lived with him for several years before the president remarried. Smith, a Connecticut Yankee with a Yale medical degree and honors in Latin and Greek classics, was a cultured, sophisticated, well-traveled man. He had studied the latest medical techniques in Paris, spoke fluent French and moved in the highest social circles. He was the author of influential works on cholera, and his treatise on yellow fever, written after he had worked with victims in Galveston, was "still a recognized work" decades later.[94]

While not a teetotaler, Smith, who had a "redoubtable talent for mixing classical quotations with frontier profanity," was an exceptional doctor, and he tried to moderate his friend's assault on his liver. Smith also helped found the Texas Philosophical Society, and later, the University of Texas, and was recommended by Houston to Andrew Jackson in 1838 as "a Gentleman of useful, varied and eloquent intelligence." But he was not notably successful in limiting Houston's consumption of spirits during his first presidential term.[95]

In 1838, according to Jesse D. Lum, the president went on a monumental bender with his future brother-in-law Vernal Lea and some other bent-elbow friends, draining an entire "barrel of whiskey." About ten in the evening, as Lum was walking near Courthouse Square, "I heard moaning and . . . I saw a hole [and] in the inside a man in it on his back. As soon as he saw me he spoke and said 'Jesse, my friend, I am so glad to see you. I, while with my friends, have drank too much of that Dutchman's mixture, it has taken the use of my legs from me, please help me to the hotel.' " As Lum vividly recalled, "Sam Houston was a very heavy man & his legs so limber it was with difficulty that I got him on his feet." He deposited the president at the hostelry and noted that while he often saw Sam Houston in his cups, he was no ordinary inebriate: "Whiskey could limber Gen. Houston's legs, but could not affect his mind. Let his legs give way from too much whiskey

—prop him up and he could make as clear and plausible a speech as if he had not drank any spirits."[96]

<hr>

> "He was a most perfect specimin
> of physical manhood."
>
> FRANK LUBBOCK, 1837

Not all was "limber" legs in 1837, even for Sam Houston. The diplomatic and economic scenes were dark. Simply winning independence had saddled the new republic with $1.25 million in debt.

William Wharton was getting nowhere in Washington. The annexation issue had become a shrill abolitionist forum, with such foes as Congressman John Quincy Adams stalling congressional debate on the issue—once holding the floor for three full weeks![97] Nor was there movement on proposed treaties of trade, friendship and, perhaps, defense. Texas was too hot a potato for Congress—or President Van Buren—to touch. As a result, Texian agents seeking loans of up to $5 million met failure.[98] Wharton was soon replaced in Washington by the ill-tempered, penniless Memucan Hunt, an unfortunate choice. By nature undiplomatic, Hunt, rudely buttonholing congressmen and cabinet members, undoubtedly retarded rather than aided the cause of annexation.[99]

Nor were relations with the European powers cause for rejoicing. Although on San Jacinto Day, 1837, the parade was pointedly led by the president and a Mr. Crawford of the British Consular Service, London had reservations about recognizing Texas. Not the least of these concerned slavery, an institution long abolished in the British Empire. Despite Houston's proclamation on December 19, 1836, ending the slave trade (save with the neighboring United States), the British found as much fault with the institution as with the trade that perpetuated it.[100]

J. Pinckney Henderson, envoy plenipotentiary to both Britain and France (appointed in part because he could subsist off his own funds), had his hands full. Henderson, to whom Houston had recently sold two city lots in the capital for a token five dollars,[101] wrote from London in October that he had wangled an audience with Lord Palmerston. "The question of slavery in Texas, will cause the greatest difficulty with this Government," he had learned, but not the only one. A Texian privateer had mistakenly captured a British merchant vessel in the Gulf, and this "caused some excitement here against Texas."[102]

The embryonic Texas navy, in fact, was proving itself a liability. While one privateer, the *Tom Toby* (outfitted by the Toby brothers), managed to take a Mexican prize in 1837, others took British prizes instead, and the United States brig *Pocket* as well. The latter caused a diplomatic flap at a sensitive moment, requiring formal apologies and a cash indemnity, which Texas could ill afford.[103] When Houston was inaugurated in October 1836, Texas boasted four small naval vessels and a few privateers, but *Liberty* (four cannon) was detained by American authorities at New Orleans for many months, *Independence* (seven) was captured by Mexicans in April, *Invincible* (seven) was wrecked on Galveston bar in September, and *Brutus* (eleven) was driven ashore in a storm the following month.[104] No wonder the Texian government was skeptical about its naval expenditures! The president was especially rankled, for he had personally pledged "a first rate league of land on Red River at Port Bolivar, belonging to me" in February, to raise money to outfit *Independence,* only to have it towed as a prize into Veracruz two months later.[105]

Slavery and clumsy privateering bothered British statesmen, but so too did a less moralistic problem. The British feared that recognition of Texas might put at risk the millions of pounds Britons had invested in Mexico and also jeopardize their thriving trade with that country. Mexico was already unstable and unpredictable and anything beyond informal British trade arrangements with Texas could well have serious repercussions. The only motivation for cordial relations with Texas was to prevent annexation by the United States, thus limiting American expansion, while courting Texas as an alternative source of cotton. That source might even someday become a British economic satellite. In the short run, however, the British would simply observe developments and restrict their relations with Texas to commerce. The same path was chosen by France.[106]

Diplomacy, then, moved at a glacial pace, and later in the year, when

the United States Congress ended its session without formally considering annexation, Houston withdrew both Texian application for it and
envoy Memucan Hunt, who, broke and—like everyone else—unpaid,
had to skip out on his Washington boardinghouse bill.[107] When Anson
Jones was later sent to represent Texas, he was advised to stay at a
different hostel.

But Texas was firmly established, and even had its own (instantly
depreciated) currency, the famous "Star" bills, complete with the new
"Lone Star" emblem of the republic, which graced the official flag as
well. The truncated army was under a semblance of control, although
Houston still railed against "some evil disposed" officers,[108] the navy
was slowly being rebuilt and Mexico, while repudiating the Treaty of
Velasco, was taking no steps to reconquer Texas. Revolts in New Mexico were being ruthlessly dealt with, and a federalist rebellion in California had collapsed.[109]

No clear and present danger hung over Texas, save perhaps from the
Indians, including the president's friend Bowl, who were rapt audiences for Mexican agents promising vast expanses of land. Those agents
foretold endless waves of American immigration, which would swamp
the Cherokees and other tribes unless they now took a stand. Such
immigration, of course, was precisely what the Texian Congress hoped
for, and why it would not ratify the treaties made by Houston and
Forbes.[110] Land, land scrip, and Star bills (whose modest solvency was
based upon public lands) were all the government had, and the Indians
occupied real estate needed to stimulate more immigration.[111]

By late 1837, however, there was less conflict in Houston's personal
life, despite repeated summons to the dueling ground, which he always
refused, and the odd rumor of impending assassination.[112] Tiana had
died of a fever, and Houston himself had obtained a more legal divorce
from Eliza, who had just divorced him. He was at last free to pursue
the elusive Miss Anna.[113] Unfortunately, while she appeared to enjoy
the game, she deftly dodged Cupid's darts.

In addition to the sheaves of letters the president dispatched to Anna,
he often wrote Robert Irion, who lived with the Raguets at the time,
begging to be informed "how the Peerless Miss Anna is & does."[114] He
often postscripted letters to Irion "Salute all my friends, and don't forget
the fairest of the Fair!!!"[115] Anna herself he normally wrote late at
night, when "the toils of the day have passed by, and all the recollec-

tions of friendship and affections recur."[116] A mutual friend wrote Houston from Nacogdoches in November that "Miss Anna is well, she has many admirers . . . Candidates for her fair hand . . . I wish you were here to defeat these fellows."[117] So too did Sam Houston.

No matter booze, frequent illnesses, overwork and unrequited love, Houston was an imposing force in Texas. Most who saw him during his first term were struck by his bearing: "Houston was then a splendid specimin of manhood," remembered admiring Rip Ford. He had "a form and features which would have adorned the walks of royalty, a fund of conversational powers almost unequaled, the matchless gift of oratory, a vast grasp of intellect—all marked him a great man."[118] Frank Lubbock was similarly taken—"no person ever met Sam Houston in the early days of the Republic without being impressed with his greatness," wrote the future governor, "a piercing gray eye, a mouth and nose indicating Character, of fine proportions, and as straight as a majestic Indian, he was a perfect specimin of physical manhood."[119] One who saw the president at an 1837 ball recorded that he was "dressed in a rich silk velvet suit," and "moved among the throng with a gallantry and grace which have always distinguished him when he chose to assume them,"[120] a judgment Julia Ann Conner had made a decade earlier.

N I N E

Texas on the Brink

"Misery is the lot of man, and miserably
do I realize it."

SAM HOUSTON, 1838

Before 1838 was a week old, Sam Houston wagered that he could remain cold sober until the year ended: total abstinence. He would pit his ego and will power against his favorite vice. The bet was made with Augustus C. Allen, and the winner would gain a five-hundred-dollar suit of clothes, a worthy prize for sartorially conscious Houston. He pledged not to "use any ardent spirits, wines or cordials, and is only to use malt liquors" during 1838. If he could cling to the wagon as it jolted down its potholed road until January 1, 1839, "the clothes are to be paid immediately thereafter."[1]

He tried mightily to prevail, but the road was bumpy and rutted and he was early pitched onto the familiar ground. One who saw him before his fall was impressed, writing his brother: "I called on the President, found him in good health, and perfectly sober. He told me he had resolved . . . not to 'touch, taste, or handle the unclean thing' until the first of January next." Not only would the president's health benefit but his abstinence would "be a fine thing for the Republic of Texas" as well, an indication that his drinking was affecting affairs of state.

However, Houston was marooned and overworked in "this great City of Mud, Sickness and Death," in one observer's description;[2] he was surrounded by revelers and was all too far away from the abstemious

Miss Anna. His resolve began to shrink. When he wrote his beloved that he was "fated to pass some eleven months in petty splendor and magnificent misery," he was not referring only to his political tenure.[3] Within three weeks of his leap onto the wagon, his feet were dragging in the dust and he lamented that "misery is the lot of man, and miserably do I realize it."[4]

All around Houston the Texian capital roared and shook, lustily awash in grog. In mid-February, John Hunter Herndon jotted in his diary about a classic bender he had shared with some friends. One of the revelers, a Doctor Watson, had been the life of that party, for "Dr. W. drank whiskey out of a scull that had yet brains in it."[5] The capital was hardly the venue for overworked Sam Houston to wrestle his demons.

Saloonkeeper Ben Fort Smith, whose watering hole the president had frequented in the past, sent the president some bills in late April that indicate that Houston's wagon had overturned. They included board for Houston, for the gallant president had left his official residence so that the bereaved Mrs. Barker, a touring thespian, could make use of it. Her husband had committed suicide by downing a gill of the powerful narcotic laudanum, and Houston permitted the grieving widow to stay in relatively genteel surroundings before she left town with her stock company.[6] Houston was surrounded by temptation and his heavy-drinking friends at Smith's raucous emporium, and the inevitable transpired. Following the San Jacinto Day ball, Houston and a gaggle of veterans went on a toot,[7] and publican Smith was soon dunning Houston for champagne, liquors, three bottles of whiskey (which even at his upscale tavern cost only a dollar each), and a special charge for "Glasses & breaking at Champagne party," as well as fifteen dollars "for 1 bedstead, etc.," suggesting some collateral damage.[8]

Houston contested some of the charges, irately protesting to Smith that he "broke no Glasses—the bill I will never pay—as I am satisfied it is unjust," but he did pay for the three bottles of whiskey.[9]

The mad rowdiness of the capital was underscored while Houston was at Ben Fort Smith's tavern. Diarist Herndon recorded laconically that on April 14, in Congress, a Mr. "Ward made an attack upon [Frank] Lubbock, Comptroller, who after being knocked down and arising shot at Ward without effect." Shortly thereafter, Congressmen Leavy and Armstrong had a fistfight (with much cheering from appreciative lawmakers), following which "Leavy went and provided himself with a pistol, returned and shot A. in the back of the head from which wound he died immediately." Leavy was jailed, and, Herndon surmised incorrectly, "will unquestionably be hung." [10] Even the halls of the Capitol resembled a tavern's back room.

In such chaotic conditions, the president attempted to maintain the façade of sobriety only for the distant Anna, to whom he wrote in May, "I never drinks nothing." [11] No doubt Anna herself heard tales of her suitor's boozing. Only in 1840 would Houston achieve general sobriety, and his slave, Esau, an accomplished bartender, had many more drinks to fix. [12]

"I was *devoted!*"

SAM HOUSTON, 1838

If he lost his bet in the spring of 1838, he nearly lost his "fairest of the fair" as well. In early June the Nacogdoches belle wrote her suitor with what seems affected pique, accusing him of having toyed with her affections while still married. It is difficult to believe that Anna had just learned of Houston's separation from Eliza, although it is possible that she had been told he had been divorced long before. At any rate, learning of the 1837 divorce, she claimed to feel deceived, for Houston had been paying a great deal of attention to her since 1833. It is more probable that she had enjoyed the attentions of so famous a man until, legally divorced, he could seriously contemplate marriage.

Stung by her accusations, he wrote that he had been free of Eliza since the alcalde's divorce decree of 1834: "I believed that I was as free from all legal and moral hindrances to any union, which might be created as the mountain air which I so much delight to breathe. I was *honest,*" he insisted, "I was *devoted!*" to her alone. Pathetically, he appended documents to the letter, as if he were trying a case at the bar. "The enclosed letters contain the opinions of Gentlemen eminent in the profession of the Law—obtained on the abstract Question as to the legality of my divorce!" [13]

Although somewhat placated by Houston's defense, Anna grew ever more distant, writing him less and less often. Eventually, her coolness sank in and Houston's letters contained less of the playful rhetoric of courtship. Houston's "mobile and persuasive" tongue had utterly failed to win the heart of Anna Raguet.[14] In fact, his letters to Anna soon revealed him in the role of matchmaker. If he could not have her, some excellent fellow of his acquaintance should.

"My words shall not sink in the earth."

SAM HOUSTON, 1838

During 1838, President Houston was preoccupied with the very thorny Indian question. The Cherokees claimed and occupied all of today's Cherokee and Smith counties and more, territory they had been promised by Houston in 1836, nestled in a region thickly settled by land-hungry Texians.[15] And, while "Texans kept the pot of rebellion simmering south of the Rio Grande," Mexicans applied their own fire to the caldron of Indian discontent in Texas.[16] The generous promises of Mexican agents, the Texian Congress's cavalier repudiation of the 1836 treaties and a rising incidence of almost casual Indian-white violence all led the Indians to seriously consider open warfare. In light of the continuing influx of American immigrants, they would have to act soon, if at all.[17]

Houston had done his best to argue the Indians' cause before the tribunal of Texian public opinion, but on this issue he found almost no support. He had also parleyed, bestowed gifts, drunk and feasted with councils and had written various chiefs frequently and eloquently ("they will be well treated and I will take them by the hand"),[18] but those who had elected him now openly denounced him as an "Indian-lover," blind to Indian preparations for war. The criticism was so hostile, and so many (including Burnet) came forward to challenge him to duels, that he began to go about armed. Samuel Colt, seeking publicity for his fine new firearms, sent "a pair of handsome dueling pistols," which Houston routinely carried.[19]

When surveyors from the Texas Land Office entered Cherokee lands in 1838, violence erupted and some Indians raided nearby farms and ranches.[20] This coincided with the minor but panic-inducing "Córdoba Rebellion," led by a disenchanted Nacogdoches Tejano egged on by Mexican agents. Vicente Córdoba and his band of plundering malcontents were joined in September by some warriors; Texas appeared ready to explode.[21]

To add fuel to the fire, when one Pedro Juan Miracle was killed in a clash with Rangers* on the Red River, an incriminating diary and communications from Mexican General Filísola † to Bowl and other chiefs were found on his body. It seemed clear that the Indians were more responsive to Mexican cajoling than Houston had wished to believe, or than he had been led to believe by the Indians.[22]

Houston labored feverishly to defuse the situation, writing virtually all the chiefs in August and September. To his Cherokee friend Big Mush he explained:

> There is now some trouble between the Mexicans and the Americans. I wish you to stand by the treaty which I made with you & my Red Brothers. I will never lie to that treaty while I live, and it must stand as long as [a] good man lives and water runs. . . . Listen to no bad talks from the Mexican agents who wander your camps.[23]

Confiding to Rusk his fears that Bowl and other chiefs might "compromise with the enemy,"[24] he wrote the old Cherokee, formally addressing him by his Mexican rank, as "Colonel Bowl." He bluntly warned that he was gathering a force of a thousand Texians, "and I hope to the Great Spirit, that my Red Brothers will not make war nor join our enemies, for if they gain a little now they must soon lose all."[25] With Córdoba and some Indians on the warpath, and chiefs like Bowl and Big Mush contemplating the same course, the president had to talk and act tough. Promising a Shawnee chief that "my words shall not sink in the earth," he worked ceaselessly for peace, while his constituents forced him to prepare for war.[26]

---

* In 1837, the Texas Legislature formalized their standing, authorizing Houston to raise six companies of men to be called "Texas Rangers," to patrol and garrison the dangerous frontier.

† Filísola's interest in Texas was more than merely patriotic, for in 1831 he had been granted a large empresario contract in the Department of Nacogdoches.

He also immediately ordered a cautious and diplomatic survey of the Cherokee boundaries, as set by the moribund treaty of 1836, which he pledged to attempt to resurrect. "If it is done speedily it will tranquilize the Indians, secure their confidence, and give security to at least a portion of our frontier,"[27] he wrote with stunning naiveté while he was gathering Texian forces.

Any chance of resuscitating the treaty disappeared before the boundaries could be plotted, for on October 5, Indians massacred eighteen members of the Killough family near Larissa. The Texian "War faction," led by Lamar, who had been elected president in September, and the bellicose Rusk, could be placated no longer. Dejected, Houston at last authorized the use of force.[28] A series of minor running fights took place and, on October 16, a band of Córdoba's men and Indians were defeated in a major shoot-out.

The war faction was briefly pacified[29] but there would be no treaty. There would, in fact, be no survey. There would only be crackling tension between two armed camps, one a great deal larger than the other.

Coming when it did, the Córdoba-Indian imbroglio helped decide the September 3 elections. Anson Jones, Houston's favorite, crashed in defeat before the ticket of Mirabeau B. Lamar and David G. Burnet. The winners had campaigned on a prodefense (that is, anti-Indian) platform, excoriating Houston for supposedly leaving Texas defenseless. Lamar promised that he would resolve the Indian problem the way Jackson had in the United States, through removal.[30]

Just before Lamar's December inauguration, Houston instructed Washington envoy Anson Jones to press Secretary of State John Forsyth to help neutralize the Indian threat to Texas. Large numbers of Cherokees, Caddos, Kickapoos, Choctaws and others were "preparing to assail the settlements of the whites," goaded by Mexican agents. Jones was to stress that warriors in Indian Territory would cross the border in an all-out war against the Texians. He was to request that the United States "interpose a force" along the frontier to avoid widening the expected war, with its resulting diplomatic complications.[31] Houston himself had earlier reassured Rusk that "If the Indians cut any capers, the U. States will march over and put them at peace."[32] What his source was for such assurances is not known.

"We must await a more auspicious moment than the
present, to exterminate [the Indians]."

HUGH MCLEOD, 1839

Most of the good news in 1838 was in the area of diplomacy. In November, Texas and the United States signed a convention settling outstanding claims upon the former for its erratic navy's seizure of two United States merchant ships, *Durango* and *Pocket*. Texas was constrained to dredge its treasury for $11,750 in damages, but it was well worth the crucial cash, for the settlement led to an important treaty of amity, navigation and commerce on December 8.[33] Further, France was showing official interest, sending Alphonse de Saligny, secretary of the French Legation at Washington, to Texas "with a view to an examination of a country" soon to be recognized by Paris.[34] On September 25, 1839, France recognized Texian independence, signed a commercial treaty with the republic and posted Saligny there as chargé d'affaires.

The Texian economy was expanding almost as swiftly as the nation's debt, and Americans continued to stream into Texas. Customs collections at Galveston soared,[35] and sale of public land produced substantial revenue. Progress was not assured, however. "Much to our *surprise, regret and mortification*," according to a Texian loan agent in Philadelphia, a large loan, which "we expected to close with Mr. Biddle,"* had fallen through. "He has been compelled by the anti-Texas and anti-slavery feelings of his board to decline anything to do with the Texas loan, on *any terms*, much to *his* astonishment and mortification."[36] This was a rude blow, for Texian loan agents in Europe had also come a cropper and for the same reasons.

Lamar was inaugurated December 10, 1838, in a ceremony shamelessly upstaged by Sam Houston. The outgoing president, dressed in the style of George Washington, complete with powdered wig, literally and figuratively towered over the diminutive Lamar. He delivered a

---

* Nicholas Biddle, former director of the Bank of the United States, was, in 1838, that nation's most influential private banker.

booming three-hour farewell oration that sounded suspiciously like a campaign speech. He dwelled on his manifold achievements and the folly of a policy of hostility toward the Indians. Frederic Gaillardet observed that "Samuel Houston was as free of his words and speeches as his successor is guarded in his."[37] So rattled and apoplectic did Lamar become that he could not articulate his own brief inaugural address, delegating that anticlimactic task to his secretary, and leaving Houston, literally, the last laugh.[38] Lamar's victory at the polls had provided him something less than a clear mandate. He had been one of three candidates, but would never know for certain if he actually was the people's choice, for the other two contenders both committed suicide before the balloting. Attorney General Peter W. Grayson shot himself during a painful illness, and former chief justice of the Supreme Court James Collinsworth, in a fit of alcoholic despondency, drowned himself in Galveston Bay.[39]

Lamar's proxied inaugural address dealt with real and perceived threats to Texas, and with annexation, which he denounced. "The step once taken would produce a lasting regret, and ultimately prove as disastrous to our Liberty and hopes as [would] the triumphant sword of our enemy."[40] Lamar was not one to mince words, and he made it clear that Texas must guard its independence, its ties to Europe and its territorial expansion. On the last point he was supported by most Texians, including Houston and Anson Jones, who in this epoch were fond of asserting that the republic should stretch "from the Sabine to the Rio Grande, and from the Gulf of Mexico to the Pacific Ocean."[41] Houston's "Dream" now had wide currency.

When the Texian Congress convened a few days later, the new president presented his budget, a lavish spending plan for an impecunious nation. His civil appropriation for 1839 (which included $2,300 for an opulent carriage) came to a whopping $550,000 (Houston's 1838 equivalent had been only $192,000). The president's salary was a comfortable $10,000, plus very generous allowances (Houston had received less than $1,000 the previous year*), and members of Congress were to receive an adequate five dollars per diem, plus an enormous twenty

---

* His salary had been a mere $200 monthly, and allowances for four servants and travel, but it was only rarely made available to him, and when he left office, the republic owed him almost $6,000.

cents per mile travel allowance. More ominous was Lamar's military budget of $1,523,445 (up from $881,000) to finance his plans for defense, plans predicated on Indian war.[42]

To accent his point, a few days later, Lamar informed Congress that "the Indian warrior in his heartless and sanguinary vengeance recognizes no distinction of age or sex or condition. . . . The wife and the infant afford as rich a trophy to the *scalping knife,* as the warrior." He emphasized the role of Mexican agitators among the Indians, employing patriotism to cloak racist animosity and land fever.[43]

The president also appointed a professional soldier, hard-drinking, Indian-hating Hugh McLeod, to head his military hierarchy. McLeod had earlier written with evident regret that "we must await a more auspicious moment than the present to exterminate [the Indians]."[44] In the wings stood Felix Huston, back in Texas and writing Lamar that he would like to "locate on the Rio Grande or anywhere within the hereafter limits [near the border with Mexico] five thousand or upwards military colonists," if the president would but grant him the land.[45] Even Lamar was skeptical of that scheme. He wished to settle the Indian question before provoking Mexico.

"The Cherokees can no longer remain among us."

MIRABEAU BUONAPARTE LAMAR, 1839

Lamar did not tarry, pushed along by McLeod, who blamed the entire problem on "the mismanagement of Houston,"[46] and Green, who resurfaced in Texas to clamor shrilly for action. Green, now in Congress, wrote Lamar that "Negotiation, negotiation, negotiation" had been the former president's policy, and it had "left him in a state of political bankruptcy and the country had not benefitted." "I say, GET MONEY, GET AN ARMY, and which first to get I am at a loss to advise."[47] With such counsel, and with eager Indian fighter Colonel Edward Burleson commanding the First Infantry, open warfare was only a matter of time.[48] The Indians all too soon gave Lamar whatever additional justification he might have felt he needed.

Early in the spring, Texas Rangers killed Manuel Flores, a Mexican Indian agent working out of Matamoros. He was carrying documents linking Cherokee and other Indian chiefs including Bowl with negotiations with Mexico, and perhaps an actual treaty as well, pledging the Indians to "an unceasing war against Texas."[49] A report also reached Acting Secretary of War George Hockley from Rangers in the field, about "marauding parties of Mexicans in this vicinity . . . murdering, plundering and making captives" near Aransas.[50] Clearly, the Mexicans were upping the ante and the Indians were impressed.

Lamar was almost ready to move, but without the latest in military technology. George Hockley, also colonel of ordnance, had rejected the new Colt repeating pistols and rifles that had been sent him for evaluation. They were too complex for any but "cool," veteran troops, and he feared that even they would waste prodigious amounts of ammunition. Instead, Hockley wanted screeching, British-made Congreve rockets, to "excite terror and probable confusion" among the Indians.[51] Lamar also scorned modernity, rejecting Memucan Hunt's recommendation that Texas adopt Samuel F. B. Morse's new "Electro Magnetic Telegraph," which he had just seen demonstrated.[52] The coming conflict would be a traditional, low-tech affair.

With reports of Indian raids, Cherokee collusion with the Mexicans, Mexican raiding parties and the reappearance of Vicente Córdoba barraging them, Lamar and his new secretary of war, Albert Sidney Johnston, addressed to the chiefs a stern ultimatum. Johnston wrote Bowl on April 10 that it had been "incontestably" proven that the Cherokees had "entered into a compact with Cordova" and the Mexican government "to carry on the war,"[53] a charge Bowl vehemently denied.

When that chief and his warriors prevented Texian troops from constructing a military post on tribal land, Lamar wrote Bowl, "You have committed an error . . . an outrage. . . . The forked tongue of the Mexicans has beguiled you; and you are running into dangerous paths contrived by the enemies of Texas for our own injury and your ruin." The brief note was virtually a declaration of war by the "aggrieved" party.[54] To a Shawnee leader the president wrote of this Cherokee perfidy, warning that they had been seduced by the Mexicans, "who are always women in war, and wily serpents in peace." His message was unmistakable: "The Cherokees can no longer remain among us."[55]

Lamar sent Vice-President Burnet and Johnston to negotiate and

enforce a definitive Cherokee removal, either westward or north to
Indian Territory. Bowl, intimidated, agreed verbally, to the ire of many
of his warriors, to return to Indian Territory, begging only sufficient
time to prepare.[56] Too much time was spent in those preparations for
Lamar, however, and a powerful expedition was sent to speed the Indians up or to provoke a fight. The spark was on the fuse and the brief
"Cherokee War" finally erupted on July 15, with a large but inconclusive fight. Bowl and his warriors fell back but his band was overwhelmed a few days later by a Texian force that counted Rusk, Burnet,
Johnston, McLeod, Burleson and Rip Ford in its ranks. Bowl, eighty-
three, died fighting, dressed, as Ford remembered, in "a red silk vest
said to have been a present from General Houston."[57] The latter angrily
thundered that the chief "was a better man than his murderers," who
partially skinned the old warrior to provide souvenirs for the less sensitive Texian volunteers. Houston's friendship with Bowl would be constantly used against him.[58] Big Mush died that day as well, along with
perhaps a hundred braves,[59] and the spirit of Cherokee resistance was
broken. The bulk of the tribe was herded north on its second "Trail of
Tears." *

The observant Shawnee permitted themselves to be disarmed and
were soon on their own trail out of Texas, and the Delaware and other
sedentary tribes anxiously signed treaties and migrated as well. The
doubly cursed Kiowa were first devastated by a smallpox epidemic and
then forced to move.[60] Before the Northers howled their first cries of
winter, removal was a fact and vast new areas of eastern Texas were
now available for settlement.[61]

Now only the Comanche represented a genuine threat and, as was
their wont, they were scorching the frontier again, killing, rustling
cattle and taking numerous white women and children captive. They
were still smarting from a freelance attempt to wipe them out in 1838,
when some Texian Borgias, feigning friendship, poisoned 350 braves at
a parley.[62]

Lamar sent agents to the Comanche villages and agreements were
made with several chiefs, including the much-feared Muguara. They
would travel to San Antonio, release their white captives and talk peace.

---

* Cherokee claims to east Texas, however, refused to die, and were in the Texas
courts as late as 1964.

Given the poisoning affair it is odd that Muguara would consent to a parley, especially on his enemy's ground, but on March 19, 1840, he cantered into San Antonio with some thirty braves, a few women and children and one lone white, although he was known to hold more. The captive, Matilda Lockhart, was in shocking condition, even given the circumstances. Fifteen years old, she was emaciated and badly bruised, and her nose had been burned off by live coals applied to her nostrils each morning to awaken her. The whites were incensed as the Indians filed through a muttering crowd into the San Antonio Council House. Outside, Colonel William Fisher had three companies of Rangers surround the building and, before long, firing broke out. Some Indians and Texians had carried concealed weapons into the Council House, and within minutes, the fight spread, as Indians bolted for the doors and windows. When the powder smoke cleared, Muguara and thirty-four Indians lay dead, along with seven Texians. Taken prisoner were twenty-seven women and children and two very old men. One woman was released and sent back to the Indian camp to warn that such would be the fate of all who dealt in bad faith with the Texians.[63] The other Indian women were parceled out "among the respectable families" of Austin as servants.[64]

The results were predictable. After torturing some of their captives to death, the Comanches declared war, putting a thousand warriors in the field, all eager to punish the Texians who had violated the sanctity of the Council House. No quarter was given. Victoria was ravaged, ranches put to the torch, farms destroyed, and travelers butchered. On August 8, the coastal town of Linnville was razed, the surviving townspeople watching the destruction in shocked silence from boats offshore.[65]

At the Battle of Plum Creek, four days later, a Ranger force led by Huston, Burleson and Ben McCulloch defeated a Comanche war party, and veteran Indian fighter John Moore soon massacred a Comanche village on the Red Fork of the Colorado, reclaiming much of the loot taken from Linnville.[66] The Comanches reeled westward from the blows of the vengeful Texians, but Lamar had started a war that would sputter on for years and keep the treasury empty.

Perhaps aware of this long-term financial drain, the president and Anson Jones convinced the Senate, in "secret" session, to permit the sale of the expensive new navy steamer *Zavala* and the brig *Potomac*, a decision later incorrectly ascribed to Houston.[67] Ironically, President Houston had earlier named Jones "agent of this Government, for the purpose of procuring a Navy in the United States," and had appointed him minister to the United States,[68] a post he never assumed.

"Nor will Caesar be rivalled by the Commentaries of Lamar."

SAM HOUSTON, 1840

While Lamar was resolving the Indian problem to the applause of most Texians, Houston was in the United States in search of the fortune that had so long eluded him. Instead, he found love.

He had written the aloof Miss Anna in early February that he would soon travel to the United States for six months or so, perhaps stopping in Tennessee, for "I am anxious to see my sisters." He wanted to see Jackson as well and, as he was again agent for a land company, he would seek to peddle Texas real estate.[69] Just before his departure he again wrote Anna, gushing with praise and protesting that "I do not flatter, but speak the words of truth, and *soberness!*"

Rusk and he had finally fallen out over Indian policy, and about Rusk's bragging about his heroism ("when a little *tight* he claims the 'laurels of San Jacinto' "). Also, Rusk, a heavy drinker, was not, according to Houston, happy about "my reformation in habits." Of the president's Indian campaigns he sniped, "nor will Caesar be rivalled by the Commentaries of Lamar."[70] He also pointedly recommended two suitors to Miss Anna. General Dunlap would give half his considerable fortune to "secure your affections. . . . He is a fine looking fellow, and younger than myself." Also a potential beau was "Our friend Irion. . . . He is great and excellent in his qualities. All love him, who know him." Houston had given up on his Nacogdoches love.

If he had a "reformation in habits" in 1839, it was short-lived, for he was barely out of Texas before he got beastly drunk again. According to Memucan Hunt, his coat was burned off him by a ship's stove as he drunkenly lurched about.[71] Hunt, in Mississippi when the former president passed through, wrote Lamar from there in July about Houston's constant boozing: "Only think how contemptible he acted," he lamented.[72]

Sam Houston, however, was in the Gulf States to make money, and since that was normally best accomplished when at least relatively sober, he began to count his drinks. He was there to interest prospective speculators and immigrants in a townsite near Galveston. At one promotional meeting he met the stern, fatalistic widow Nancy Lea, a woman of set ideas, grim certainty of her own mortality, and disposable cash. Although Lea was fascinated with Texas, she was a bit cynical concerning promoter Houston, whose reputation as a careless husband and heavy drinker had preceded him.

At Mobile, Houston befriended Nancy's son Martin, who at a garden party one lovely May day introduced him to his sister, Margaret. A beautiful, introverted woman of twenty, with "arresting, violet eyes," she was also possessed of hero worship for the tall Texian. What transpired was almost literally love at first sight.[73]

Unknown to Houston, handwriting expert Dr. William B. Powell of Columbus, Mississippi, penned a blind report on the Texian's scrawl that same spring, a basic graphoanalysis of the former president's character:

> His issues and plans are always upon a large scale. There is nothing in his character that is small, or contracted, except that he is probably somewhat close in money matters. He is ambitious, energetic, and persevering . . . he is fond of his family . . . and he adheres to his friends as long as they adhere to him, or so long as he can make them mutually serviceable . . . [he] would make a bad soldier, but a good leader—calculated for learning and science . . . when acting under a special motive he is concealed and prudent, but his general manner is communicative and frank.[74]

While one might question the subject's fondness for family, and his supposed aptitude for science, the report is in striking consonance with the man. Certainly his plans were "always upon a large scale," and as Miss Conner had earlier noted, he was a manipulator.

"Say, will he cherish me, and love me, too,

in that dark hour?"

MARGARET LEA, 1839

Margaret, daughter of Nancy and the late Temple Lea, a Baptist minister of Marion, Alabama, had grown up sheltered, introverted, and
asthma-plagued in the Greek Revival mansion of her brother, state
senator Henry Lea. Her three brothers, two sisters, mother and other
relations in the Marion area constituted a tight-knit clan, a self-contained family.[75]

Educated by Dr. L. J. and Mrs. Goree at the nearby Judson Institute,
Margaret was a wistful reader of the saccharine romances of Sir Walter
Scott (*Ivanhoe* was a favorite). Although her eyes were poor from an
early age, she was embarrassed by her spectacles and rarely wore
them.[76] A professed Christian from her early years, at age nineteen she
had been "reborn" and converted to a more melancholy, fatalistic faith
that would be one of her dominating characteristics.[77] This shy, retiring
young woman, described as five feet six inches tall, 110 (later, 140)
pounds, "with beautiful dark brown hair . . . noble, gentle, spiritual
minded," fell deeply, romantically in love with the Texian Ivanhoe
(whom, coincidentally, she had once seen from a distance at New Orleans, when he landed for surgery in 1836).[78]

Houston was in Mobile only briefly before passing on to Nashville,
but he too was thoroughly smitten. While he had been discussing real
estate with Nancy, he was already talking matrimony with Margaret.
On the road to Nashville he paused to write his new beloved, couching
his note in highly atypical religious rhetoric. "I met thee first on the
holy sabbath-day. We walked to the house of God & took sweet counsel
together." He understandably neglected to mention that it had been
many years since he had entered any house of worship.[79]

As Houston conferred with his aged mentor and others in Nashville,
Margaret emerged from her shadows to write a poem, "Lines to a Withered Pink," referring to a flower he had given her, which she had
preserved. The somewhat mordant poem nervously alludes to marriage

while asking, "Say, will he cherish me, and love me, too, in that dark hour [old age] as now I Cherish thee?"[80]

Aware of her daughter's infatuation, Nancy attempted to dissuade her or at the least put the brakes on the relationship. She was worried by what she had heard concerning the general's character and habits, the legality of his "divorce" and his apparent impecunity. Imperiously, she summoned the Texian back to Marion. So did Margaret, albeit hardly imperiously. The young woman wrote Houston at Nashville on July 17, blushingly confessing that the note was "the first I have ever addressed to any gentleman." Describing, as she would so often in the future, her love of the bucolic life, she dwelt upon her happiness in rural Alabama, "untarnished by the wiles and cold deception of the world," and urged her beau to leave the big city and join her. She hinted, embarrassedly, that her entire extended family wished to meet and examine him.[81]

And so, on his way back to Texas, Houston appeared, no doubt with trepidation, to court Nancy's daughter and face inspection. He was successful in both. His proposal of marriage was accepted by Margaret and her family, although they demanded a decent delay and insisted that the nuptials take place in Marion rather than in Texas. Nancy, almost convinced to invest in Texas lands, agreed to visit later in the year to inspect Houston's townsite. Buoyant on both personal and business counts, the general departed for home, pausing only long enough to purchase some "blooded stock," paying an unusually steep two thousand dollars for one select "chestnut filly."[82] He was not so penniless as had been thought; at least not for the moment.

> "Her little son found her dead in a closet."
>
> MARGARET LEA, 1840

Houston lost something also. Upon his return to Texas he learned that his slaves, Tom and Esau, had run away to freedom in Mexico. The latter became a respected hotelier in Matamoros and no doubt continued the bartending sideline he had perfected while living with the general.[83] Houston, who had been born into a slaveholding family, was ambivalent about the Peculiar Institution. While he rarely defended slavery publicly, neither did he attack it, and with the racial assumptions common in his day, he was content that people wrenched from Africa remain in bondage. All his life he would own slaves, twelve at the time of his death.

He threw himself into politicking, criticizing Lamar brutally—especially on his Indian policy—and he drank as he nervously awaited the arrival of the Leas. He was sorely disappointed, for the proper widow Lea, still beset by doubts about her daughter's betrothal, was not about to bring her to Texas. Instead, she appeared with a son in December and, masking his disappointment, the general played promoter and convinced Nancy to purchase a prime tract of land near Galveston. The two also set a February wedding date, which in the event had to be postponed to allow Houston to attend the Texian congressional session to which he had been elected. In addition, he now really had no cash. He had to borrow $250 from Ashbel Smith before heading east that May to tie the knot that would never be untied.[84]

While Houston was busy in Texas, Margaret was crafting her trousseau, teaching herself Spanish to please her fiancé, and writing him a steady stream of letters and poems. Contemplating a small portrait of the general that he had given her, she wrote wistfully:

> Dear gentle shade of him I love,
> I've gazed upon Thee till thine eye,
> in liquid light doth seem to move,
> and look on me in sympathy.

Margaret was to have a great deal of time alone in the future to search for "sympathy" in the many images Houston was to provide her.[85]

Just weeks before the wedding, the future Mrs. Houston worriedly wrote her mother, who was again in Texas, that she had learned "that General Houston's health was bad." She also relayed the local news and gossip, characteristically dwelling upon the morbid. "A very melancholy thing happened a few days ago, Mrs. Vincent Sanders committed suicide by hanging herself. Her little son found her dead in a closet." Barely skipping a beat, she followed that with "I have made me a white satin dress, a purple silk and a blue muslin." Her trousseau, she beamed, was now complete.[86]

Ill or not, Houston rode into Marion in early May to be married. The ceremony took place on May 9 in brother Henry's manse, with the Reverend Peter Crawford, who had baptized the bride, officiating. The groom displayed his usual sartorial exuberance and Margaret wore the white satin gown she had crafted. Her old teacher, Mrs. Goree, stood matron of honor, while the Gorees' slaves prepared the feast that followed.[87]

This marriage of Margaret, twenty-one, and Houston, forty-seven, seeming opposites, was expected by most to fail before the year was out, yet it would produce eight children and endure through his lifetime, even though he was often away from home and she never accompanied him to his political posts outside Texas.

There is no doubt that the evangelical Margaret had one overriding goal in her marriage and her life: the "reformation" and "rebirth" of Sam Houston. Others saw this clearly, and Margaret's letters make it obvious. She would change the general, no matter what the cost. One of their slaves heard her admit it often[88] and, not long after marriage, a "dry" Houston himself wrote a friend, "You have, I doubt not, heard that my wife controls me and has reformed me."[89]

Her effect was immediate, for from the moment they set foot in Texas, which was described that year by a British wanderer as "the Desert of Villainy," Houston drank no whiskey, brandy or other "ardent spirits" and was soon a member of the Houston Sons of Temperance.[90] This is not to say that he forswore all alcohol, however, for he embraced bitters, and for years he convinced Mrs. Houston that the "old Texas recipe" of bitters with orange peel was good for him. He did not explain that the bitters of the day contained about 40 percent alcohol, almost the potency of twentieth-century whiskey.[91] Oddly, both Eliza and Anna Raguet were also married in 1840, the latter eloping with Houston's good friend Dr. Robert Irion.[92]

"bankrupts, swindlers and felons"

ANON., 1842

Texas in 1840 was, albeit mired in debt, booming, while Sam Houston's finances were quite the opposite. American immigration continued on a grand scale, stimulated by the availability of emptied Indian lands, and thousands of Europeans disembarked as well. Cotton production and exports doubled every few years, and new towns mushroomed. One such, which would embroil Houston in controversy and crises, sprang up in 1842 and was called Austin (distinct from San Felipe de Austin).[93]

In early 1839 Lamar sent a congressional commission scouting around for potential sites for a "permanent" capital.* A tiny cluster of huts called Waterloo, situated more than 150 miles inland on the hilly north bank of the Colorado, was selected. Lamar liked the site for two reasons. It had grated on him to have the government in a town named for a man he despised, and on a more calculated level, he believed that a capital in the interior would help develop Texas by pulling settlers away from the relatively crowded coast. Galveston, which claimed three houses in 1837, had more than six hundred in 1840, and a population exceeding four thousand.[94]

In October 1839 government offices were transferred to the isolated hamlet, renamed Austin (the only name everyone could agree upon), and the following January it was officially proclaimed capital. As one who witnessed the phenomenon wrote, "The city of Austin, like Aladin's Palace, seemed to have arisen in a night" amidst the thickly wooded hills.[95] No matter its incredibly swift growth, Austin was terribly exposed to the Indians—and Mexicans—on the frontier still known as "the Land of War." But, undeterred, Texians flocked to the new capital and while "Indian fighting was probably the most important municipal activity, it was largely a voluntary affair."[96] Indeed, for many years

---

* After all, in rapid succession, there had already been seven Texian capitals; San Felipe, Washington-on-the-Brazos, Harrisburg, Galveston, Velasco, Columbia and Houston.

cannon were sighted down Congress Avenue, the most likely approach route of attacking Comanches.[97]

Houston was aghast at Lamar's choice for the capital, and not simply because his ego was rooted in the town bearing his name. Moving capitals was "wasteful," and the site was far too exposed to danger: "This is the most unfortunate site upon earth for the seat of Government," be angrily wrote in December 1839.[98] He would do his best to have it changed once more.

Within six months, Austin was a going concern, if not an impressive "city." It then had a population of 856 (550 men, 61 women, 100 children and 145 slaves), and the town center was crowded with nine stores, nine taverns, six inns, six gambling halls, a few ramshackle government buildings and perhaps eighty homes. While one Briton erred in describing its citizens as exclusively "bankrupts, swindlers and felons," Austin was a rough frontier town and would remain so for decades.[99]

But Lamar did more than change capitals and kill Indians. Largely through his initiative, Congress in 1839 passed an act providing for a system of free public education. Three leagues of land (over thirteen thousand acres) were initially set aside in each county for the support of public schools, and later a fifty-league tract was dedicated to provide financial support for two national universities, although this would not soon come to fruition.[100] Lamar, an aristocratic intellectual who considered Sam Houston a "prepostrous Vulgarian," was vitally concerned with public education.[101] Early in 1840, in a rare—if not unique—display of unity, Lamar, Houston, Burnet, Jones and others signed the charter of Galveston University, a charter that grandly proclaimed that "wisdom is necessary to true prosperity, and nations are destroyed for lack of knowledge."[102]

Lamar was to be remembered as the "Father of Texas Education," and properly so, but he will never be revered for his diplomatic expertise, for his dealings with foreign powers nearly brought disaster.

When he took office, the situation was promising. Mexico, no matter its agents among the tribes, had all but been removed as a threat by internal chaos and foreign aggression. During 1838 and much of 1839 a French fleet blockaded Mexico and occasionally landed troops in what came to be known as the "Pastry War." Santa Anna roused himself from restless retirement, raised an army, courageously led it against

French landing parties, lost a leg to a cannonball, gained new popularity and soon was again in power. While the French were pounding Veracruz and Tampico with their naval guns, brushfire revolts erupted in Sinaloa, Tamaulipas, California, the Yucatan and elsewhere, diverting Mexico City's slender financial and military resources. [103]

With Mexico in disarray, Lamar sent a succession of official envoys to Mexico City, including Secretary of State (he had ten in his presidency!) Barnard Bee. They were to negotiate Mexican recognition of independence and a Rio Grande border (rather than the Nueces River to the north) and were authorized to offer as much as $5 million as indemnity (or bribe) to gain those objectives. This Lamar did without consulting Congress, something which became a habit of his. [104] This unconstitutional diplomacy impelled a number of high-ranking officials to resign in protest, among them Rusk, then chief justice of the Supreme Court. [105]

Unfortunately for Lamar's foreign policy, Mexico soon entered a transitory upswing. The French ended their blockade, internal revolts were temporarily silenced and the one-legged despot was feeling truculent, his xenophobia and personal courage endearing him to his people.

While negotiations were collapsing in the Mexican capital, Lamar fell gravely ill, taking leave of absence in mid-December and delegating authority to Burnet. The latter, at Lamar's urging, moved to forge ties with the chronically rebellious Yucatan, a huge, impoverished state that sporadically sought to secede from Mexico. [106] They also sent Colonel Benjamin H. Johnson across the Rio Grande with a small force of volunteers but the filibusters were captured and put to the sword. [107] Similarly, Santa Anna adroitly crushed an 1840–1841 attempt by Mexican federalists to organize the "Republic of Rio Grande" just south of the turgid Nueces. Although battered and bruised, Mexico was still on its feet. [108]

"That courtesy from a British vessel of war."

W. T. AUSTIN, 1840

With some support from the Lamar administration, the Yucatecan rebels declared independence in June 1841 and the protonation's leader, Miguel Barbachano, sent Martín Peraza to Austin in search of alliance. Peraza came well-heeled and presented Lamar with thousands of dollars in gold to outfit the Texian navy. The Yucatecans agreed to pay a monthly stipend of eight thousand dollars in coin to keep the emerging Texian navy afloat in the Gulf, protecting the peninsular republic from Mexican blockade.[109] In Lamar's mind several problems had suddenly been resolved. Texian support of the Yucatan would further weaken Mexico, thus reducing the risk to Texas, and already some Texians were investing in and even moving to the Yucatan.[110] Also, Texas would have its navy almost fully subsidized. Six new ships built to order in Baltimore had arrived at Galveston in 1839 and 1840 but had not been able to fit out and recruit crews for want of funds and were gathering barnacles in the harbor. At Yucatecan expense the new Texian navy and its new and dynamic flag officer, Commodore Edwin Moore, would soon be unleashed.

The same month that the Yucatan declared its independence, Lamar began another rash gambit. Without congressional approval, he sent a military-commercial expedition across the wastes of western Texas to Sante Fe, to incorporate the vast state of New Mexico (then called Santa Fe) into Texas. This union would push the limits of Texas to the Rocky Mountains, almost within sight of the fabled Pacific.

While Lamar was scheming to dismember Mexico, relations with the United States remained static, neither good nor bad. And the same held true for relations with Britain, although H.M.S. *Pilot* offered an exchange of salutes at Velasco on January 21, 1840, "the first time of our receiving that courtesy from a British vessel of war."[111] The British government was openly discussing the establishment of diplomatic relations but the matter of slavery still rankled and Parliament wrestled with the contradiction between moral aims and commercial gain.[112]

Only France seemed interested in relations with Texas;* it was not learned until early 1841 that treaties of trade and navigation had been signed in London in mid-November. Not until August 1842 would chargés d'affaires take up their posts in London and Austin. The French, whose trade with Texas—while still less than Britain's—was expanding, had been the first to recognize the new republic (September 1839) and were angling for interest and influence there. A French squadron paid a courtesy visit to Velasco in 1839 and the balls and soirees that ensued were the hit of the season.[113]

Of more interest to both Austin and Paris, the Texian Congress was soon hotly debating Lamar's Franco-Texian Land Bill. This legislation, favored by French authorities, would have provided a huge tract of land between the Rio Grande and the Nueces for the settlement of eight thousand French immigrants. The president supported the bill, with Houston in opposition, as a way to curry favor with France and also create a strong buffer to seal the river boundary with Mexico. Debated while Texian agents were attempting to negotiate a large loan in France, the bill was eventually killed—as was the loan.[114]

On New Year's Day 1841 Count Alphonse de Saligny was presented with some pomp to the Texian Senate,[115] and his credentials accepted, constituting the best diplomatic tidings in several years. The French Legation at the capital had already become the center of "much of Austin's intellectual and social life" in the few weeks since Saligny's arrival.[116]

---

* The Netherlands did sign a trade treaty on September 18, 1840, which was to lead to recognition.

"I can not be happy but where you are!"

SAM HOUSTON, 1840

The financial picture remained pathetic. Lamar had a taste for extravagance without the wherewithal. Though a small government loan had been contracted in late 1839,[117] attempts to gain multi-million-dollar loans failed despite pledges of almost unlimited public acreage as guarantee. It was money Texas vitally needed, for as early as the closing months of 1839, Baltimore banker Frederick Dawson was dunning Lamar's administration for interest on two Texian government bonds of $280,000 each.[118] A confidential British report of 1840 informed Lord Palmerston that as early as 1837 Texas carried a staggering debt.[119] Also, Lamar had obligated an awesome $800,000 in 1839 to have the new navy constructed from scratch, but those vessels spent their time rotting at anchor.[120] Further, in its financial agony, Congress had literally ordered the president in 1840 to "temporarily" retire most if not all of the new warships and furlough their crews. He refused to do so and the financial hemorrhage continued. While Commodore Moore later that year took some ships to Tabasco, captured and ransomed the port for $25,000 in cash, it would not be until the Yucatecan subsidy regularly arrived that what was left of the navy could be put "on station."[121]

In desperation the president ordered a new currency printed, the "Red Back," but these non-interest-bearing promissory notes depreciated from the day of issue, plunging to 16 percent of par within a few months.[122]

An 1840 British report on Texas claimed that good land could be had for fifty cents an acre and that this lure was attracting five thousand new settlers each month (an exaggeration). There was almost no taxation in Texas, wrote the Briton, for there was almost no money: "There are vast numbers of men in Texas who have more acres of land than half pennies," he correctly estimated.[123]

Houston was one Texian who held land but few half pennies. He and Margaret took up residence in a rude home at Cedar Point, near Houston, which he had probably built with Anna Raguet in mind. Most of their furniture had been donated by Nancy Lea and shipped from Alabama.[124] Houston was obliged to borrow money to cover day-to-day expenses, and he even hired out his own three slaves and perhaps the four that Margaret had brought with her.[125] He still owned several Houston town lots and at least one site at Nacogdoches, but he had no cash to build a proper house. Luckily, as a member of Congress he was beneficiary of Lamar's generous per diem and travel allowance, but this he spent largely in Austin while Congress was in session, for the stark capital was a very expensive town. When he was in Congress, often arguing the cause of the mistreated Indians, he and Margaret exchanged sad and lonely letters. "I must be miserable," he wrote in September 1840, "today is drizling and damp, and I am depressed and melancholy! I can not be happy but where you are!"[126] If this was true, he was embarking on a grim life indeed!

He had assured his new wife that he would retire from politics but he would continue to make such assurances for the rest of his life. He had, in fact, told everyone that he was tired of politics and was ready for the simple life of gentleman farmer. Commodore Moore, who talked with him at Galveston, excitedly wrote Lamar that "he says he does not intend to be a candidate for the Presidency!!"[127] Margaret, wishing this would be the case, wrote a poem at Cedar Point to remind her husband of his stated resolve:

> Yes, dearest, we are happy here
> in this sweet solitude
> of ours, no heartless ones come near
> or tiresome scenes intrude . . .
> At eve beside our cottage door
> we watch the sky's last hue.[128]

Sam Houston, however, was not suited to long recline by his cottage door. He marched to a different drum (and often heard it when others heard only silence) and needed what Margaret considered "tiresome scenes" much more than he needed "sweet solitude." But he would always maintain quite the opposite. By the time his wife had written that poem, he had already decided that Lamar had done so much damage to Texas that he would have to run for the presidency. Of the current president he wrote "mean and base. . . . Poor Lamar! He wou'd no doubt be impeached, but the poor soul is too contemptible to incur hatred." Complaining about money he owed and could not repay, he told an old Nashville friend that people owed *him* twenty-five thousand dollars but could not honor their obligations.[129]

Yes, he would run, despite an expanding catalogue of bitter political enemies, one of whom—S. W. Jordan—attempted to kill him with an axe for criticizing Lamar's Indian policy.[130]

T E N

Texas in Flames and Inflamed

"Its failure arose from causes purely fortuitous."

GEORGE W. KENDALL, 1845

With his foreign policy in tatters, Lamar had one arrow left in his quiver and was determined to score a bull's-eye at last. Undeterred by Congress's refusal to fund a "commercial" expedition to Santa Fe, he simply ordered the New Orleans printer who produced Texian Red Backs to run off and send directly to him an extra half million dollars.[1] An inveterate expansionist, as early as February 1839 he had corresponded with T. J. Jones, who also believed it "desireable that the people [of Santa Fe] should be brought under our direct political control."[2]

The city of Santa Fe, the only sizeable settlement in an area larger than France, had experienced unrest ever since American adventurer William Becknell in 1821 had pioneered the Santa Fe Trail, a slender umbilical cord linking the Southwest settlement to the commercial center of St. Louis. By 1841, a substantial portion of the province's population was American born. Lamar firmly believed that most New Mexicans would eagerly join Texas, if given the chance. In fact, for years, many Texians claimed that Santa Fe lay well within the elastic borders of their republic.

Lamar announced that he would soon send well-provisioned merchants and Texian "commissioners" to both trade and talk.[3] The commissioners were Santa Feans—J. N. Navarro, William G. Cooke, and a Dr. Brenham—whom Lamar instructed to incorporate Santa Fe into Texas if, as he believed, local sentiment and Mexican weakness favored such a move.[4]

In June, the extralegal expedition headed into the trackless frontier from Austin, led by Hugh McLeod, who soon became ill and relinquished command to William G. Cooke, a pharmacist and surveyor.[5] Twenty merchants, with two hundred thousand dollars in merchandise piled high in huge, ox-drawn wagons, were escorted into the unknown by a potent force of five companies of volunteer infantry and a company of artillery, ostensibly to act as guard against hostile Indians.

A confused guide led the column wildly astray, Indians killed a number of stragglers, guides promised by the Lipan Apaches never materialized, food ran out, several officers committed suicide, but the expedition blundered onward into the wastes. However, Santa Fe governor Manuel Armijo was better prepared for a Texian invasion than expected and, to Lamar's consternation, most Santa Feans were not at all keen about casting off their chains.

According to participant George W. Kendall, who claimed the expedition's "failure arose from causes purely fortuitous,"[6] the Texians "were actuated by that love of adventure, which is inherent in thousands of our race." But, after weeks of floundering almost aimlessly in execrable terrain, they were dispirited, emaciated and exhausted. Then, some sixty miles from Santa Fe, faced by Mexican troops and local militia, the expedition simply surrendered. Embarrassingly, they capitulated to what Kendall scornfully dismissed as "a motley, half-naked, ill appointed set of ragamuffins," which Governor Armijo had managed to scrape together. The Mexican, in a classic bluff, had made the tired, disheartened Texians believe that he had thousands of regulares under his command.[7]

The economic loss collapsed several Texian merchant houses and the Red Back fell to 6 percent of face value. More important, the vaunted Texian military prowess, forged at San Jacinto, was dangerously undermined. At the Hermitage Andrew Jackson could scarcely believe what had occurred and warned Houston that "the wild goose campaign to Santa Fe was an ill-judged affair and their surrender without the fire of a gun" would embolden Mexico to use military force against Texas. So badly bruised was the reputation of Texian arms, wrote Jackson, that "it will take another San Jacinto affair to restore their character" in Mexican eyes.[8] And, to be sure, Mexican troops *were* emboldened, and would spend much of 1842 harassing and even openly invading Texas.

Some three hundred Texians, festooned with chains, were soon being paraded through the dusty streets of Santa Fe, whence they were set on the grueling, thousand-mile road to Mexico City, arriving to the curious stares of vast crowds in December. There, the prisoners—soon joined by other unlucky Texians—were demeaningly assigned to public works and street cleaning in chain gangs. Fanny Calderón de la Barca, who saw them at their humble labors, recorded that kindly Mexican families subscribed to purchase "a supply of linen and other necessary articles" for the prisoners.[9]

Although Lamar's last and most gaudy failure incited Mexico to flex its considerable muscle the following year, it seemed in mid-1841 that the huge loan being negotiated in France would at last be approved. But the French, with financial problems of their own, decided not to hazard their resources, or their sizeable Mexican trade. The loan was tabled, though Lamar, by nature sanguine, was already spending the money.[10]

===

"Drily, because we have no *liquor,* and I do not taste
one drop of it."

SAM HOUSTON, 1841

Eighteen forty-one was an election year whose outcome was never in doubt save in the dreams of Margaret Houston, who would have preferred her husband to remain at home. The September 6 vote swept her husband from his "cottage door" and into the presidency (by a vote of 7,508 to 2,574 for Burnet), with Edward Burleson, who had commanded the center at San Jacinto, elected his vice-president.

Houston and Burleson took their oaths of office on December 13. "The day was beautiful," recalled Frank Lubbock, and thousands jostled to witness the ceremonies at Austin.[11] Houston was in rare form, dressed in a rude hunting shirt and buckskins, his habitual broad-brimmed beaver hat jauntily angled on his great head. Burleson, another oversized individual, was similarly decked out, in "his fancy Indian leathered hunting shirt."[12] They were a colorful and rustic pair. Margaret, already displaying acute hypochondria, remained at Cedar Point, and the new president boarded at the Eberly House Hotel instead of the executive mansion, which Lamar was insultingly slow to vacate.[13]

Margaret may have suffered a miscarriage in 1841,[14] and to her chronic asthma she added a number of other "conditions," which kept her husband frantically summoning Ashbel Smith, the only physician they trusted.[15] He wrote a friend at this time with a certain pride that "things move on with me pretty cooly, and very drily—*drily*, because we have had no rain for the last nine weeks, *drily*, because we have no *liquor*, and I do not taste one drop of it, nor will I do it!"[16]

"We have no money."

SAM HOUSTON, 1842

Houston inherited potential chaos and danger when he reassumed the presidency. Santa Anna was said to be preparing an invasion, and Texian defenses and morale were at low ebb. The nation was a pauper state and, with no foreign loan, there would obviously be no quick fix for the economic crisis. Lamar, only two days before the end of his term, slashed all government salaries by half, pared back the bureaucracy and reduced the congressional per diem from five to three dollars, a belated austerity measure often credited to his successor.[17] When Houston reassumed power, he found a treasury so devoid of funds that he had to buy his own firewood to warm the executive mansion![18]

In his first message to Congress, on December 20, the president emphasized re-establishing good relations with the Indians, admonishing his listeners that trading with the Indians both kept the peace and generated profits, while warring with them incurred suffering and unbearable expenditures. He told the unimpressed lawmakers that instead of a chain of forts on the frontier, Texas should construct a string of trading posts. Aware that many in the audience hated Indians, he couched the issue in realistic terms; "View it as we may, it will at least find justification in necessity. We have no money." The projected trading posts would more than pay for themselves and pacify the frontier.[19] He asked Congress to appropriate twenty thousand dollars for an "Indian fund," promising that if it did so, and gave him the "power to restrain whites from misconduct" toward the Indians, he could promise peace. "I will answer for the safety of our frontiers," he thundered, soon to regret his words. Congress, however, was in no mood to accommodate the president or the Indians.[20]

Houston also warned against Texian entanglements or alliances with the rebellious Yucatan, which could easily provoke Mexican retaliation. Like Jackson, Houston viewed "all foreign alliances as wholly unnecessary to the prosperity" and security of the nation. Again, Congress disagreed.[21]

If he could not push Congress to act, there were still a few measures he could implement by executive fiat. He drastically pared back the budget and again eliminated funds for the navy, which he recalled from the Yucatecan coast, where it had been posted (with Yucatecan money) by Lamar.[22]

But Congress, always more hostile to Mexico than it could afford to be, reacted to the news of the Santa Fe prisoners force-marched to Mexico City with a bizarre resolution annexing all of Santa Fe, Upper and Lower California, and all or portions of six other Mexican states. A stunned president saw this dangerously quixotic resolution pass over his immediate and forceful veto. In his veto speech he warned that such grandiose claims would be seen abroad as a "legislative jest" and would jeopardize British mediation with Mexico on Texas's behalf.[23] A prime mover behind the resolution was Congressman T. J. Green.[24]

Just four days later, Houston clashed again with Congress, which legislated that all "free persons of color" be expelled from the republic within two years. Instead of attempting a veto, Houston simply issued a proclamation. The legislation was unjust, and he proclaimed that free blacks could remain, if they were of "good character," and could post a bond of five hundred dollars "for their behavior." Curiously, that bond, if forfeited, was to be "payable to the President."[25]

"Pursue conquest to the walls of Mexico."

SAM HOUSTON, 1842

Ever since Santa Anna's return in 1837, Mexican troops and assorted brigands had sporadically raided Texas, carrying on a cut-rate warfare that stirred up Texas Indians and some of the Tejano minority. Following the Santa Fe *fracaso* and depredations by Texian warships in the Gulf, Mexico upped the ante, prompted by Texian bankruptcy and the surprising aloofness toward Texas of both the United States and Britain.

In 1842 the raids became expeditions, and pressures on Houston rose dangerously. Washington D. Miller, the president's private secretary and confidant, exerted personal pressure for striking into Mexico. He wrote Houston in February, happy to sense war fever in Texas: "A great drama is in progress. Two acts have already passed. The first was the settlement and establishment of the independence of the United States—the second, the settlement and liberation of Texas—the third will be the Conquest of Mexico." [26] Houston recognized a kindred spirit but he knew this was not the time for anything but passive defense. Texas lacked unity as well as funds; its army was small and ill-disciplined, its officers erratic at best. Houston urged, and even plotted, caution rather than revenge or expansion. People began to doubt him, and those who had accused him of cowardice in 1836 levied the same charges now.

Yet Houston's earlier dreams had caught on in Texas, and in the United States as well. On March 5 a Mexican army crossed the Rio Grande and, moving with unusual speed, captured the unalerted towns of Refugio, Victoria and San Antonio. Houston had to act, or at least seem to. Although the Mexicans evacuated within forty-eight hours and slipped quietly back into Mexico, Texians considered the "invasion" a declaration of war.

The president's reaction was swift and aimed at defusing the war fever of his people rather than punishing Mexico. He first sent a force under his vice-president to San Antonio and on into the trans-Nueces no-man's-land. Then he issued a "General Call to Arms" on March 10, ordering each county to prepare its militia for service in the field. He also wrote to General Edwin Morehouse at Galveston, advising him to have his command "in readiness to march at a moment's warning" toward the Nueces. He cautioned that "system and order" must be rigidly enforced "or we will again have the scenes of the Alamo, Goliad, and Santa Fe renewed," and Texas would fall.[27] And he issued an official call for volunteers from the United States, writing that such volunteers—if armed and provisioned—would be warmly welcomed and "will be allowed the privilege of the Texan banner to cross the Rio Grande; and pursue conquest to the walls of Mexico" City.[28] Texas could not pay these volunteers, but he held out the prospect of loot: "The recompense tendered to our friends will be the property captured by them . . . and the soil that they conquer."

On March 26, he reluctantly decreed a blockade of Mexico's Gulf ports, which, as he had foreseen, London immediately protested.[29] Houston also wrote angrily to Santa Anna presenting a bitter history of Texas and of consistent Mexican perfidy. At one point he used Lamar's fiction concerning the "recent trading excursion to Santa Fe," which, he had to admit, had been a "violation of his [Lamar's] duty." Pleading for peace and recognition, he contended that Texas was ready for war, its "patriotism, superior intelligence, and unsubduable courage" more than offsetting the Mexican army's numbers. "Our title to Texas has a high sanction . . . that of conquest," he wrote, warning that if there must be war, "the Texian standard of the single star, borne by the Anglo-Saxon race, shall display its bright folds in Liberty's triumph on the Isthmus of Darien," in southern Panama. Following that saber rattling, Houston formally signed off; "I have the honor to present you my salutations."[30]

Despite rhetoric, bluster and mobilization, Houston was content to maintain a defensive posture. He feared taking the offensive because of the rashness, bravado and lust for loot of his army's officers. Even if a rich booty was gained, war with Mexico would cost a mountain of hard cash that was simply not available. But his measured response angered many Texians, especially the newly arrived. As William Bollaert remembered of this spring, "Every steam boat that has come in from N. Orleans brings volunteers." But, since at the moment there were no armed Mexicans in Texas, the newcomers "have commenced fighting among themselves," just as Houston had feared.[31]

Vice-President Burleson was incensed by Houston's caution, and he threatened to cross the Rio Grande on his own authority. The president removed him from command for insubordination and replaced him with Alex Somerville, but with or without a command, the stubborn vice-president remained in the field, even publishing a handbill criticizing Houston and his "peace policy."[32] He ignored a direct order from Houston to return to the capital, writing: "If any ask why it is that the Vice President is in the field? My answer is that I love my country more than I fear the President's displeasure."[33] The split with Burleson became permanent, and he only rarely appeared in the capital, addressing but one communication to the chief executive during his entire term![34]

"From the impetuosity of our people,
I do fear some disaster."

SAM HOUSTON, 1842

What Burleson did not know was that the president had written Somerville on March 22 to finally slip the army's leash. If Somerville felt himself strong enough, "You are at liberty to cross the Rio Grande . . . taking such towns above Matamoros on the Rio Grande as you think proper." Ordering the general to "be governed by the rules of humane and civilized warfare," he permitted him discretion to invade Mexico, precisely what Burleson and others had been clamoring for.[35] He then informed Secretary of War William Henry Daingerfield that he had authorized "reprisals for the plundering of San Antonio by carrying the war across the Rio Grande." Though he did not broadcast it, he was not attempting to keep this move secret, and while he did not see the impending campaign as a true invasion, he had, at last, decided to move. He also apparently expected more than volunteers from the United States, for, he wrote intriguingly, "Uncle Sam . . . [will aid us] in the work."[36]

To General Pickens of Alabama, who had proposed to lead a unit to aid Texas, Houston wrote on May 1: "You can bring to Texas one thousand emigrants by the last of June . . . you shall have the rank of

Brigadier General," and the opportunity to lead them. But, advised the president, "the emigrants must be completely armed, munitioned, clothed, and provisioned for six months" service.[37] In platoons and companies, they flocked to Texas, but Houston found many "destitute of every needful supply," and Texas had little to offer them.[38] Once again, armed, directionless men threatened the stability of Texas.

Unaware of his orders to Somerville, many accused Houston of timidity or worse. James Hamilton, Jr., who had spent time in Texas, railed from his Alabama plantation against Houston, and "put out a call for soldiers and threatened to march to Texas, displace Houston, and take action against Mexico" himself.[39] Albert Sidney Johnston was barely restrained from similar mischief. So general was vilification of the chief executive that Washington D. Miller felt obliged to reassure many prominent Texians that "the President is firm in his determination to prosecute the war. He has his plans well devised. They will not, of course, be published to the world," for that would be "execrable generalship."[40] He also denounced Burleson, who, he claimed, "has been made a *tool*" of the ever-intriguing Thomas Jefferson Green.

Meanwhile, although he had authorized action against Mexico, blockaded its ports and issued letters of marque to privateers to ravage Mexican commerce, Houston feared uncontrolled military chiefs leading Texas to ruin. To a Brazoria committee that had urged him to immediate action he snapped, *"Parties* have *destroyed* nations, but they have *never* created a country . . . Texas can maintain but one party and that must be the *Texas Party."*[41]

No matter the pressures upon him, Houston refused to move precipitiously, aware that it would take Somerville, who was no hothead, many weeks to get his expedition ready. Reflecting on the lack of discipline that had resulted in the disasters of 1836, he wrote presciently that "from the impetuosity of our people, I do fear some disaster."[42]

Congress, meeting in special session, horrified the president on June 27 by passing a special War Bill effectively declaring war on Mexico and giving the president extraordinary powers to conscript up to one-third of the male population, dispose of ten million acres of public lands, and launch a major invasion.[43] He immediately vetoed the measure, even though he knew that would be seen as further proof of his hesitancy.

In his veto speech Houston declaimed, "If Mexico is invaded, it must be by a force whose term of service will not be less than one year, and whose numbers shall not be less than five thousand men," intuiting that Texians were not ready to face the cost of full mobilization. Six months training and stockpiling vast supplies would be necessary, yet "the Executive has not one dollar" at hand. The operation would cost at least two million in coin, and simultaneously "impair the value and credit of our currency." Perhaps worse, the power to conscript and use militia outside Texas was patently unconstitutional. He would not be a party to subversion of the sacred constitution, he piously proclaimed, although he was "resolved to annoy and injure the enemy" in any practicable manner.[44]

The treasury was bare, but Houston, with no fanfare, on June 15 "advanced about $450 on my own individual account," to purchase supplies for the troops.[45]

"If Chihuahua is taken, I will be grateful."

SAM HOUSTON, 1842

Houston's reasoned veto was not overridden, and Andrew Jackson, who always watched Texas closely, congratulated his friend on his unpopular stand, writing, "If you had not vetoed this bill, it would have led to the destruction of your Country . . . you have saved your Country, and yourself from disgrace. *Stand on the Defensive!*"[46] Few Texians would have agreed, and Memucan Hunt, never a friend, wrote Houston after the veto, warning of an incipient "civil revolution," because "you have been accused of being a traitor."[47]

William Kennedy, a British agent in Texas, and a newly arrived chargé d'affaires, naval captain Charles Elliot, reported to London that Houston was readying five thousand men, and Indian levies, "for the invasion of Mexico," which he would personally lead.[48] Houston himself wrote William Christy that he would soon unleash his invasion, which he hoped would be "successful and honourable to those engaged in it." He tellingly let slip that "If Chihuahua is taken, I will be grateful."[49]

When, on September 11, a large Mexican force under French adventurer General Adrian Woll fell upon unlucky San Antonio and captured it easily, another shock wave roiled Texas. Woll held the town for nine days and took hostage some fifty prominent Texians, including former governor James Robinson, when he withdrew. On the eighteenth, some two hundred Texians from units near San Antonio intercepted Woll and a sharp fight erupted at the Salado, an action chiefly notable for the massacre of about forty Texians following their surrender.[50] The Mexican force continued its withdrawal without further incident."

"The authority of the Government is not respected."

WILLIAM KENNEDY, 1842

As General Woll recrossed the Rio Grande, Burleson raced to San Antonio, impudently writing Houston that he wanted Texian troops to elect him commander so he could get on with invading Mexico. If the Mexicans were not severely punished on their own soil, he prophesied, the nasty little war would drag on and Texas would never be secure.[51] Houston ignored his vice-president and ordered Somerville to select twelve hundred of his best men to lead across the river into Mexico. Capturing Mexican pueblos on the way, he was to push westward along the river as far as Mier, which he was to take, if he could do so with little risk. He was specifically enjoined to "let no outrage be committed upon the peaceful inhabitants."[52]

Rip Ford, with Somerville, later wrote that the plan of operations was too cautious, that in fact Houston had lost a splendid opportunity to seize northern Mexico with a humanitarian justification. Houston, at a later date, would morosely concur.[53]

Somerville reached the Rio Grande with one thousand men, but he soon found that he had scant control over the rambunctious Texians. His army was really a congeries of gangs, led by boisterous, arrogant *caudillos*: T. J. Green, Fisher, Hunt, future Texas governor Peter Bell, and a pantheon of legendary Rangers, including Ben McCulloch, Jack

Hays, Sam Walker and Big Foot Wallace. The latter, himself a hard-boiled adventurer, claimed that Somerville's army included many "renegades and refugees from justice."[54] Ignoring Houston's injunction to conduct "civilized warfare," Texians ruthlessly sacked and plundered Laredo, a town inside the borders claimed by Texas,[55] according to a British diplomat in Mexico. They had volunteered, he contended, only "for the sake of plunder."[56]

British agent Kennedy waxed pessimistic about Texas in his fall 1842 reports. "The authority of the Government is not respected" and, rhetoric notwithstanding, the Texians were unprepared for real war. In fact, "The bad state of the roads seems to be the Chief existing obstacle" to a Mexican invasion of Texas.[57] Houston's worst fears were being realized.

At the Rio Grande, Somerville grasped at last that his men were not in his control, and led most of his putative command back to the Nueces. Some 310 men, including most of the stronger personalities, refused to abandon the potentially lucrative project, and they elected Colonel Fisher their commander. In mid-December these free spirits splashed across the Rio Grande, bound for Mier, taking it easily on the twenty-third. Like Laredo, it was promptly stripped bare.[58]

"Seduced by the reckless or misled by
the improvident."

SAM HOUSTON, 1845

Tall, erudite Colonel William S. Fisher—who had done a stint in the Mexican army[59]—was not to savor his "victory." On Christmas Day, Mier came under assault by a strong Mexican force led by General Pedro Ampudía. The fighting was close and brutal and Fisher, in agony after his right thumb was torn off by a musket ball, soon ran up the white flag. Twelve Texians had been killed and twenty-three wounded but hundreds of Mexicans were said to have died, and Ampudía himself might well have been on the verge of breaking off the action.[60]

The dispirited Texian prisoners, under heavy guard, were put on the road to Mexico City, relieved that they had not been shot out of hand. After a week or so of forced marching, many began to plot escape. They elected Ewen Cameron, a Scot, their "escape commander," and at the village of Salado 193 men bolted for freedom. Only four would make the Texas border, for the prisoners were deep in the almost trackless northern Mexican desert. Several escapees died, some were killed by Mexican soldiers, a few were killed by Indians, and a few simply disappeared. A total of 176 were soon again in Mexican chains. As the march resumed, orders arrived from Santa Anna that all Texians should be executed for the sack of Mier, but the governor of Coahuila, General Francisco Mexía, interceded and ordered the Texians "decimated" instead. So 176 common beans—seventeen of them black—were mixed in a clay pot and each prisoner was forced to draw one. The unlucky seventeen were promptly shot, and the others set again on the road to the capital, where Cameron, by presidential order, was executed.[61]

The Mier prisoners, among them Washington D. Miller, gave the Mexican government the leverage of hostages and Houston a major political headache.* He had to denounce Fisher to the British, French and United States governments, but within Texas,[62] while he railed against "want of discipline and subordination," he praised the common soldiers ("patriots") captured at Mier and pledged their release.[63] "They were a gallant band of men," he said, guilty only of having been "seduced by the reckless or misled by the improvident."[64] He was also careful to stress that those "gallant" men had been decimated because the Mexicans were properly enraged by the looting of Mier and, he thundered, "Thomas Jefferson Green was the first man who broke open a house, and incited the men to outrage."[65]

Later, in the U.S. Senate, Houston retorted to Green's account of Mier, denouncing his "dastardly cowardice, his utter want of chivalry," and claiming that compared with Green, "Santa Anna is one of the most magnanimous men in the world!"[66]

---

* Ten eventually escaped Mexico, including one plucky man who wandered undetected to Veracruz, enlisted in the Mexican navy and later jumped ship in Charleston.

"When your hand is in the lion's mouth it is safest to
withdraw it quietly."

SAM HOUSTON, 1842

If the army caused the president political grief, the ill-starred navy complicated his life far more seriously, though it was, in 1842, hardly an impressive force. The only war steamer, *Zavala*, had run ashore and was a useless hulk. Schooner *San Bernard* was wrecked in September, and a month later, schooner *San Antonio* disappeared at sea.* [67] Two small brigs, never fitted out for want of cash, became feasts for marine worms, and only brig *Wharton* (sixteen guns) and ship *Austin* (twenty) were operational. [68]

Worse yet, Britain had just built two state-of-the-art war steamers for Mexico, the *Guadalupe* and the *Montezuma*, the latter the second armor-plated warship ever constructed. [69] Ashbel Smith, now chargé d'affaires in London, protested and claimed that British abolitionists had underwritten construction, but the two imposing vessels were delivered on schedule, with British captains and partial British crews. The Texian coast was at risk. [70] Houston had to dissuade his friend in London from overdoing his protests, for he was then attempting to persuade the British government to mediate with Mexico for recognition and the return of Texian prisoners. He admonished Smith that "when your hand is in the lion's mouth it is safest to withdraw it quietly without slapping the lion on his nose." [71]

By late 1842 the two powerful Mexican warships were fitting out and training in the Gulf, and Commodore Moore, to secure a renewal of the temporarily lapsed Yucatecan subvention, on his own authority offered to defend the peninsula's coast with his two-ship "fleet." [72] Houston was aghast, for in addition to its unconstitutionality, Moore's gambit threatened the president's attempt to "normalize" relations with Mexico and endangered the Texians held in that nation. Congress, mindful of this and the empty treasury, passed an act in secret session to sell what was

---

* "Lost at Sea in the Gal of Septr. or Octr. 1842 and nothing ever heard of her."

left of its navy. Hastily, the president named three commissioners to race to New Orleans, where the *Wharton* and *Austin* were berthed, to arrange the sale.[73]

But by the time the commissioners reached New Orleans, so too had Colonel Martín Peraza from the Yucatan, "with his welcome sacks full of money for the Texas Navy."[74] The Yucatecans, terrified by the new Mexican war steamers, considered eight thousand dollars a month a bargain price for protection. As a result, Moore was feverishly fitting out when the commissioners arrived, and in short order he gained the support of one, James Morgan, and the acquiescence of the others. In early April 1843 the *Wharton* and *Austin* weighed anchor, Yucatan-bound, despite the commodore's receipt of a proclamation from the president. That document relieved him from command and summoned him back to Texas, and asked "all nations in amity with Texas to seize Moore and his ships," should he sail.[75] Houston wanted the navy out of the Gulf and himself and Texas absolved, should the commodore do anything to upset the British.

Ignoring the proclamation, Moore sailed, en route hanging four men for an earlier "mutiny."[76] Early in May, off the hazy Yucatan coast, the commodore's two ships fought two inconclusive but still successful actions with the new Mexican warships (the *Guadalupe* illegally flying the Union Jack), boosting morale and thwarting a Mexican blockade.[77] Unbeknownst to Moore, however, a furious Sam Houston issued a proclamation on May 6 of unusual harshness, stripping the commodore of his command and accusing him of piracy:

> The Naval Powers of Christendom will not permit such a flagrant and unexampled outrage, by a commander of public Vessels of war, upon the right of his nation and upon his official oath and duty, to pass unrebuked; for such would be to destroy all civil rule and establish a precedent which would jeopardize the commerce on the ocean and render encouragement and sanction to piracy.[78]

Moore was now an outlaw, fair game to any navy that cared to bag him. The accused pirate, considered by many "the Nelson of Texas," became an almost incoherently bitter enemy of Houston's, and would soon pen the tiresome 201-page *To the People of Texas* in his own defense.[79] He would also, to Houston's annoyance, emerge unscathed from a formal court-martial for neglect of duty, embezzlement, fraud, disobedience, contempt and defiance of the nation, treason, murder and sixteen other charges brought by the president. After seventy-two days of trial, the court found the commodore guilty only of four infractions so minor that no punishment was mandated.[80] Ironically, a year later, Congress again voted overwhelmingly to sell off all navy assets, using the slender proceeds to pay off naval personnel, including Moore.[81]

Houston was flabbergasted by the court-martial verdict, and boiling with anger, he wrote a friend: "You speak of that miserable Col'el Moore. The poor soul will fall by his own poison, or rather he will be strangled with his own venom! . . . He like the bloated maggot, can only live in his own corruption!"[82] He had just read part of the commodore's book!

Edwin Moore's actions had jeopardized relations with Britain and retarded negotiations with Mexico, putting the lives of hundreds of Texian prisoners at risk. Also, as noted by Houston in his piracy proclamation, he had openly challenged the authority of his own government.

"You Dam old drunk Cherokee."

JOHN WELCH, 1842

Even before the various crises of 1842 had stirred, Houston coupled his antipathy to the Texian capital, Austin, with its vulnerable geographical position, and using the latter as pretext, ordered the government to shift its personnel, offices and paperwork to far safer Houston (later, to Washington-on-the-Brazos). He would rather cope with a peripatetic capital than have it remain on the frontier. There was a great deal of grumbling about this "emergency" measure, but the government did indeed move coastward, leaving Austin with virtually no raison d'être.

As early as March 1842, Secretary of War and Marine Hockley expressed his own fears concerning Austin. He expected to see Mexican banners on the horizon at any moment, and he assured the president that "I will defend the archives to the *Knife,*" reiterating his promise the following day: "*I am burying the archives* under the different offices, so that if they, or we burn [the town] the valuable papers will be safe."[83]

A month later, with no clear Mexican threat to validate the fears of Houston and Hockley, one jealous citizen of Austin wrote Lamar that "we are holding on to the Archivs like death to dead Negro & are determined they shall not be taken from here 'till ordered by a higher power than Sam Houston."[84] It was one thing for the government to "flee" to safety, but where the papers were, the seat of government was, even with no personnel present to govern. The famous "Archive War" had begun.

Further revealing the strong sentiments of the people of Austin, James Webb, former secretary of state, wrote in May that "we have now but a small population—no business—& are living under great privations—we have however, held on to the '*Archives,*' & will battle for them to the death."[85] Those dry official records (and Sam Houston) stirred up surprisingly strong passions.

So inflamed was public opinion in the Austin area that the Texian Senate ordered an investigation in the summer and demanded the president explain his actions.[86] Houston was destined to lose the Archive War, but until the capital regained the government's personnel, it languished, one visitor remarking that "the largest body of visitors [to Austin] in 1844, was a herd of buffalo which wandered down Congress Avenue on the way to water at the river."[87]

In late 1842, with the government operating from makeshift quarters at Washington-on-the-Brazos, Houston issued a proclamation ordering the transfer of the official archives from Austin to the temporary capital. Because he foresaw resistance, he entrusted the transfer to a company of hard-bitten Rangers, commanded by veteran Captains Eli Chandler and Thomas I. Smith.[88]

As he suspected, the denizens of Austin, a feisty and irreverent lot, knew that so long as they retained the records, Austin would remain legal capital of Texas. Thus, on the crisp night of December 30, a patrol of local citizens discovered the Rangers loading large crates of state papers onto wagons. Mark Lewis and Angelina Eberly (local hotelier and rabid Houston-baiter), and the town's Vigilance Committee, sprang to the defense. When the good folk of Austin actually opened fire on the Rangers with a cannon, and an armed, muttering mob began to advance, the Rangers beat a hasty retreat.[89]

One in that triumphant mob—John Welch—wrote an insulting, semiliterate note to the president a few days after the cannon's discharge:

> . . . the truth is that you are afraid you Dam old drunk Cherokee . . . you Dam blackguard Indian drunk . . . now old Fellow if you want to try Ned Burleson's spunk just try to move these papers, and old Ned [Vice President!] will serve you just as he did your Cherokee brother when he took the Hat what you give to your Daddy Bowles,

from his dead, skinned body. Promising that Burleson could raise a force of a thousand men to defend the archives, Welch openly dared the president to risk what amounted to civil war.[90]

Although he backed down, the president was not a man to concede defeat gracefully. When early in 1844 Congress proclaimed Austin the permanent capital, he lashed out: "Austin is unsafe, inconvenient and expensive," and in any case, "the Act of Congress fixing the seat of Government there is unconstitutional." He never explained how, but unconstitutionality was often his fallback position, and one senses that he identified himself and his policies so strongly with the constitution that opposition to one was opposition to both. Houston went down for the count on the archive and capital controversy, but he went down fighting.[91]

"Grief has sounded in your camp."

SAM HOUSTON, 1842

Other problems were festering before Houston's eyes, hinting at Texian ungovernability. One of these was the "Regulator-Moderator War." This outburst of violence originated in a series of disputes over forged land titles and spilled over into the county-level political arena, as charges of election fraud soon had much of east Texas in arms. The epicenter of unrest was Shelby County, "a mean and dangerous place," but it spread to Harrison and Panola counties as well. It became a low-intensity civil war, which littered the landscape with corpses and the dispensaries with angry wounded. Suppressed in late 1842 by militia dispatched by the president, the conflict burst out anew in 1844. With the death toll exceeding fifty, Houston sent militia general Travis Broocks and Alexander Horton, now a colonel, to the turbulent area "to arrest ten of the leaders of each faction" and essentially hold them hostage, and to declare a temporary state of martial law.[92] The Regulator-Moderator slugfest came to a grudging end, but its coincidence with a congeries of other threats complicated an already very tense situation.

One of the few upbeat notes in this period was an absence of serious Indian hostilities. This was in large part due to herculean efforts by the president, who had written to virtually every remaining chief in Texas, assuring even the implacable Apaches on the western frontier that "your enemies are our enemies," and convincing them, if only temporarily, that trading could be more rewarding than raiding.[93]

There is no better example of this frontier diplomacy than the case of the Lipan Apaches. In late 1842, their chief, Flacco (with whom Houston had earlier negotiated), died mysteriously. The Lipans had been quiescent for longer than was their norm, and Houston moved to keep them that way. He wrote a long poem for the Lipans about the death of their great leader, which began:

> My heart is sad!
> A cloud rests upon your nation.
> Grief has sounded in your camp;
> The voice of Flacco is silent.
> His words are not heard in council;
> The chief is no more.
> His life has fled to the great Spirit,
> His eyes are closed;
> His heart no longer leaps
> At the sight of the buffalo.
> The voices of your camp
> Are no longer heard to cry
> "Flacco has returned from the chase."
> ....
> Grass will not grow
> On the path between us.
> Let your wise men give counsel of peace,

Let your young men walk in the white path.
The gray headed men of your nation
Will teach wisdom.
Thy brother, Sam Houston.[94]

"Brother" Houston supplemented this eulogy with gifts, including plugs of tobacco for Flacco's son, and "to his wife I send eleven shawls." With manipulative frontier brilliance, he also attempted to pin Flacco's probably natural death on the enemies of Texas: "It is said that Mexicans from the Rio Grande killed him." After all, should the Lipans decide to again stain their lances with blood, better it be Mexican.[95]

"Adds affliction to my perplexities."

SAM HOUSTON, 1842

Despite these "stern alarums and dreadful marches," Texas was a growing, flourishing nation. Several consecutive bumper crops of grain and a vast expansion of the cotton belt and ranching areas all added up to prosperity for most Texians, even though their national treasury would echo if a silver dollar were tossed into it.

The population continued to spiral dizzily upward no matter the Mexican threat, and large numbers of Germans established thriving communities such as New Braunfels. President Houston signed a great many colonization contracts in this period with immigration societies in England, Ireland, Belgium, France, the German states and even Sweden.[96] And the immigrants moved to diversify the Texas economy, some English colonists, for example, bringing a new economic motor—"large flocks of some of the finest wooled sheep of Great Britain."[97]

The prosperity was general, and even the growing number of slaves shared in it to some degree. Mary Austin Holly noted that many slaves were permitted their own garden patches and any profits they could wring from them. A few even raised cotton commercially, and "some of them make $70 per year." According to the diarist, "This is the case within all this neighborhood & generally" through Texas.[98] Indeed, as one new arrival to Texas appraised his new country, it was destined "to become the Store house of the western world."[99]

Houston, however, was one Texian who did not noticeably prosper, and when the government moved to Washington-on-the-Brazos he had to board with a friend, John W. Lockhart, because he simply had no funds, personal or public, to pay for rooms. He even had to rent out one of his own houses for a mere fifteen dollars a month. It was at the Lockharts' that the president went on his last recorded toot, probably in January 1843.[100]

Margaret, then pregnant, went into old-fashioned seclusion at Grand Cane. She had been ill much of 1842, which, bemoaned her husband, only "adds affliction to my perplexities" in that dreadful year.[101] One night the lonely president pulled out a gallon jug of Madeira wine and drained it at a sitting. Totally intoxicated, he became fixated on one of the ornate bedposts of Mrs. Lockhart's prized mahogany four-poster. He resolved this peculiar fixation by ordering his slave Frank to hack off the offending object with an axe. As Frank enthusiastically flailed away, the Lockharts, fearing that their guest was being assaulted, charged upstairs. They were—at least initially—relieved to simply find the president drunk on the bed and Frank looking confused.[102]

In fact, there was a basis for the Lockharts' concern. Houston's reluctance to order a major invasion of Mexico had angered many, as had his attacks on the navy. Not for the first time, threats and rumors of assassination reverberated through Texas. Later, he admitted to Ashbel Smith without elaboration that he had discovered and thwarted a Mexican-style "pronunciamiento" against his government.[103] Houston-basher Moseley Baker spoke for many when he wrote the president that "this is the first year of your second term and already they [the Mexicans] have three times invaded the country and they will continue to invade it until the people of Texas should be convinced that you are an incubus upon the land."[104]

Houston did become worried for his safety. In a letter to Washington D. Miller marked "Private!!!" he enjoined: "I think you have two fine pistols. If you can spare them, I want them, and the [bullet] moulds."[105] Not long afterward, he confided in British chargé Elliot that he was the only man in the government who could or would make decisions, "Hence the necessity of my bearing the sins of the people to the wilderness in imitation of the Israelitish custom." [106] He bore those sins and Miller's brace of pistols well, though in very deep loneliness.

Margaret remained in what she considered proper seclusion with her mother for fully six months, from December 1842 until May 25, 1843, when she gave birth to a healthy, sturdy boy, who was given his father's simple name. [107] Anna and Robert Irion also had a boy, and they named him Sam Houston Irion.

During Margaret's long isolation her brother Martin had died by his own hand, and her mordancy deepened. [108] In February, indulging perhaps in an unusual moment of guilt, Houston wrote a friend that he but rarely saw his wife. "Now only reflect that one half of this time Mrs. Houston is unwell, can see no company," and hence must be very lonely. [109] Indeed, his absence hardly improved Margaret's general outlook. While protesting that he was only happy when with her, Houston contrived to be almost perpetually absent.

"The fittest man in this Country for his
present station."

CAPTAIN CHARLES ELLIOT, 1842

Relations with Britain improved noticeably with the posting of Captain Charles Elliot to Texas. This celebrated "hero" of the sordid Opium Wars was a canny man, a loner who often incurred the wrath of his government, but he got on well with Houston, despite early reservations. Originally worried by Houston's fabled "drunkenness," Elliot soon came to consider him "the fittest man in this Country for his present station." [110] Three treaties had been signed in 1840 (commerce and navigation, a loan agreement and an agreement for suppression of the slave trade), and all were ratified in 1842, although Texians ignored the slave trade convention. [111]

There was some friction caused by the Texian blockade of Mexico's Gulf ports, [112] which British merchants continually protested, and there was rancor in Texas over Britain's construction and crewing of the

Guadalupe and *Montezuma*,[113] but those were fleeting contretemps. Britain's major goals were to see that Texas was not annexed to the United States and that it not hamper British interests in and trade with Mexico. Independent Texas was a firm roadblock to United States expansion, which the anonymous writer of "A Memorandum Relative to Texas" saw as essential to Britain, for "so dangerous a people have never before existed," and they must never gain the entire continent.[114] In regard to British investments, as early as 1837 Britons held over $50 million in Mexican government bonds alone, a staggering sum they did not care to jeopardize. As a result, the foreign secretary, Lord Aberdeen, attempted to halt what he termed the "fruitless and desultory war" between Texas and Mexico.[115]

For their part, Texians sought British trade, loans and diplomatic help in Mexico City. Trade mushroomed, loans were finally contracted and a temporary truce was arranged with Mexico in mid-1843.[116] In this the Mexicans caved in to British pressure, but they also believed wild promises made by James Robinson, captured at San Antonio in 1842. Claiming authority he did not have, Robinson pledged to arrange a peace based on Texian recognition of Mexican suzerainty.[117] This absurd idea was rejected peremptorily by Houston (falsely accused by some of complicity in the scheme), and the disabused Mexicans scrapped the truce.[118]

Relations with France were in stasis, or worse. The failure of the Franco-Texian Land Bill and loan negotiations were complicated when Chargé Saligny stormed out of the country. He had been thoroughly offended by treatment he received in a dispute over his servant's killing some pigs belonging to a neighbor. He was succeeded in 1843 by Viscount Jules Edouard de Cramayel, a far less irritable envoy.[119]

Also, George McIntosh, Texian chargé in Paris, was unable to entertain, or maintain even a modest lifestyle. Unpaid for many months, he anxiously wrote Houston that "I am at this moment in Paris entirely *destitute* of funds and nearly $4000 in debt." McIntosh had even had to "pawn my watches and other little valuables" and feared that when his replacement arrived he would be jailed for debt, for until then his diplomatic immunity was "the only bar between me and imprisonment."[120] Houston found little money for his embarrassed diplomat, and the Paris legation was added to Ashbel Smith's London post (as was Madrid, later). Smith had both the wherewithal and the knowledge of Paris to function as a diplomat.

Smith probably advanced McIntosh enough money to leave France. The president's friend was a godsend to the Texian government, not only because he spoke fluent French, but because he had been appointed "on the condition that [he] pay his own expenses."[121] In addition, he was effective, establishing close relations with Foreign Minister Guizot, who began working seriously for Mexico's acceptance of Texian independence.[122]

Relations with the United States were at an impasse. Talk of annexation was merely rhetorical, and Washington's mediating leverage with Mexico was slight. Houston wrote Elliot at this time that Texas was being treated shoddily: "Heretofore Texas has been looked upon as an appendage of the United States. They cannot realize that we now form two nations." Most Texians, he assured, no longer desired annexation. "It is not selfishness in me to say," he wrote Elliot, "that I desire to see Texas occupy an independent position among the Nations of the earth."[123] That, at any rate, was what he wanted the British diplomat to relate to Aberdeen.

Waddy Thompson, United States envoy to Mexico, used his little leverage but considerable charisma to ameliorate the harsh treatment of the Texian prisoners, and in September 1844 was instrumental in obtaining their freedom, but this did not warm relations between his nation and Texas.[124] The great game continued, with Houston manipulating the specter of perpetual independence, the Mexicans freeing Texian prisoners to assuage public opinion in the United States, and the British and French willing to do nearly anything to protect their investments. Of all the combinations, however, the relationship between the United States and Texas was the most difficult to fathom.

A minor brouhaha in that relationship developed in 1843 when Houston "permitted" Colonel Jacob Snively, an old friend, to lead "volunteers" on an expedition to prey on Mexican pack trains plying the Santa Fe Trail. Following a brief, successful clash with a small Mexican patrol, Snively's column collided with a United States Army unit, which claimed that the Texians were on United States soil, from which they were rudely expelled. Houston, in high patriotic dander, claimed that Snively and his men had never left the legitimate bounds of Texas, filed an official protest to Washington and demanded reparations. The gap between the two English-speaking republics seemed to be widening.[125]

E L E V E N

The End of the Republic

"Pioneers . . . whose political power will not halt
short of the Isthmus of Darien."

SAM HOUSTON, 1843

Of all issues facing Texas as the election year of 1844 approached,
annexation loomed paramount in the concerns of five countries: Texas,
the United States, Mexico, Britain and France. At stake was the future
of a vast continent. In such a high-risk game Sam Houston was the
most competent player and perceived a wider range of options than any
of the other players. Texas could be annexed by the United States. It
could continue independent with eventual Mexican recognition and
British protection, or it could—as Houston often proclaimed—unite
with the Oregon Territory, the Californias and Santa Fe into a transcontinental power. Finally, it could turn south and absorb much of
underpopulated northern Mexico. "If we remain independent," he
promised Texians, "our territory will be extensive—unlimited," bound
only by the Pacific.[1]

Ever since extending recognition in 1842, Britain had striven to win
the Texas market and keep the Lone Star Republic friendly and independent. An 1836 memorial to Parliament by concerned British merchants
stressed their huge investments in Mexico and adjacent Spanish-speaking
lands. They posed a vital and hardly fanciful question: "If the United
States were suffered to wrest Texas from Mexico, would not Cuba and
other Mexican possessions* fall a prey to the United States?"[2]

---

* Cuba was never a "Mexican possession."

The United States, however, declined to seize the opportunity, for a number of reasons: the generally isolationist policies and mind-sets of Jackson and his successor Van Buren; the increasingly well-organized abolitionist movement; the "Panic of 1837" with its aftershocks; and the belief that annexation would lead to war with Mexico.

In Texas, many prominent figures openly opposed annexation, among them Lamar, Burnet, Washington D. Miller, Ashbel Smith and Barnard Bee, although most would later change their stand. In his 1838 inaugural address, Lamar had stated bluntly that he could see no advantages to Texas in becoming a state, rather problems and dangers, and he urged continued independence to preserve "our liberty and hopes."[3] Also, waves of European immigrants arriving in Texas "tended to render the people indifferent to annexation."[4] Time appeared to be on the side of continued independence.

Houston himself, vocal advocate of annexation at first, set the issue aside as well, appearing blasé about annexation by 1840, even when invasion by Mexico seemed imminent. Under his and Lamar's guidance Texas became a member of the world community, recognized by and trading with a score or so nations. By 1843 Galveston counted consular representatives from twenty-four countries and sixty-nine foreign steamship companies maintained offices there. Texian consuls were stationed in Dublin, Bremen and Stockholm as well as in Baltimore, Charleston and New York.[5]

Following ratification of treaties with Britain, Houston worked more assiduously than ever through Captain Elliot to mobilize British influence to lessen the threat from Mexico. He was also reviving his old imperial vision. In the spring of 1843 he wrote Elliot that if Texas remained a republic, it would write its own proud chapter in the saga of the inexorable advance of the Anglo-Saxon race. Texas would become "a cantonment for the pioneers in the van of that mighty advance whose political power will not halt short of the Isthmus of Darien."[6]

Relations between the president and the British chargé seemed so cordial that Washington D. Miller had to reassure President John Tyler, who favored annexation, that "a large majority, amounting to almost unanimity, of the people of the Republic, at the head of whom stands their illustrious President, desire most warmly the consummation of a treaty of annexation." He added, "General Houston, *I am sure,* entertains for the measure the liveliest wishes," a coy hint that Houston's position was not what it publicly seemed. Miller purposefully described Britain as puppeteer with many strings on Texas, asserting that only Tyler could prevent Britain from dominating Texas as it did Mexico. Annexation must be hurried along: "Let it be done. Let it be done before peace with Mexico is obtained," he warned, pointing out the obvious.[7] Houston probably put Miller up to writing this letter to goad his American counterpart to action.

Tyler was worried about the British and there was growing anti-British sentiment in the United States over joint occupation of the Oregon Territory,* whose population was overwhelmingly American. The last thing he wanted was another British presence in North America. In September 1843, after annexationist Abel P. Upshur became secretary of state, Tyler ordered secret negotiations between the two nations, certain that Texas and Britain were similarly engaged but with the opposite goal.[8]

At this juncture, annexation received support from an unexpected quarter. In London Ashbel Smith was becoming suspicious. He wrote Houston that it "is my deliberate and solemn opinion [that] Britain is extremely anxious to abolish slavery in Texas." According to the envoy, "The ultimate purpose is to destroy the agricultural interests of the South and thereby the maritime and manufacturing interests" of the United States. Now a skeptical Anglophobe, the doctor prescribed annexation as the lesser of two evils.[9]

"Oceans of blood and millions of money."

ANDREW JACKSON, 1844

As 1844 manhandled 1843 aside, Sam Houston, no longer an open supplicant for annexation but instead the object of much courting, laid out to Isaac Van Zandt and James Pinckney Henderson, Texas's representatives at Washington, the basic terms for negotiations. The most

---

* Still galling, though less important, was the expanding enclave in Central America that would become known as British Honduras, as well as British machinations in Panama and among the Misquito Indians of the Caribbean shore.

important were the assumption of the Texian public debt by the United States, the acceptance of slavery in Texas and guarantees of military protection during the period between the signing of an annexation treaty and its ratification. Further, his envoys were to seek to have Texas annexed as a territory rather than as a state. This would permit Texas, as its population grew, to subdivide and later enter the Union as a number of states, which would bolster Southern strength in the Senate. Finally, in the event of rejection of the treaty by the United States Senate, they were to obtain at any cost an offensive-defensive alliance.[10]

He also contacted Andrew Jackson to prod him to use his venerable influence in Washington. "Texas, with peace, could exist without the United States," he warned for effect, "but the United States can not without great hazard to the security of their institutions, exist without Texas," a message rich in geopolitical wisdom and veiled threat.[11]

Deeply concerned, Jackson responded with alacrity, sketching a geopolitical nightmare of his own and lecturing his younger friend: "Great Britain [clings] to the Oregon Territory, and if she got an ascendancy over Texas, by an alliance, she would form an iron Hoop around the United States, with her West India islands, that would cost oceans of blood and millions of money to Burst asunder." That very real threat, if properly explained, would convince even "that arch fiend J. Q. Adams" to accept annexation.[12] Texas, independent, would find itself an unwilling participant in war between the two great English-speaking nations, should it rashly accept close ties with London. Now, that was a warning!

By the time Jackson wrote this apocalyptic letter, intrepid Washington D. Miller had arrived in Washington, D.C., sent by Houston to help Van Zandt and Henderson, to keep him fully informed and to broadcast, by his very presence, just how seriously the president of Texas took the upcoming negotiations. In a letter of introduction to the old man of the Hermitage, Houston advised that "he knows all my actions and undertakings, all my motives. I have concealed nothing from him—nor will he conceal anything from you."[13] He never claimed the same for any other man.

"Texas is presented to the United States as a bride
adorned for her espousal."

SAM HOUSTON, 1844

The Master Game-Player wrote Miller in April that fewer Texians favored annexation with each passing day, "and at any time, if some five or six individuals would ride throughout the Republic and advocate independence upon a guarantee of France and England, annexation would be rejected" overwhelmingly. He was feeding Miller lines to be repeated in Washington, but what he left unsaid is far more revealing. He, the hero of San Jacinto and president, could have unequivocally declared for or against entering the Union and have had far more influence than any "five or six individuals" riding the frontier. He was clearly ratcheting up the tension in Washington by his silence.[14]

These rumblings in Texas reached Secretary of State Upshur, as they were meant to, both officially and informally, in the early months of 1844. He assured the Texian diplomats that the Senate would vote for annexation, although perhaps not accept all of Houston's specific terms. On January 20, following an especially cordial meeting with Upshur, Van Zandt wrote Houston that "I am authorized by the Secretary of State, who speaks by the authority of the President . . . to say that the moment a treaty of annexation shall be signed, a large naval force" would be sent to the Gulf, and army regiments "will be ordered to rendezvous upon the borders of Texas."[15] In other words, one of Texas's greatest fears—invasion by Mexico—would be banished. This understanding, however, was in verbal form only, for there were grave constitutional doubts within the executive branch concerning what might be construed as placing United States military forces at the disposal of another nation.[16]

Houston again wrote his aged friend at the Hermitage, his rhetoric graphic, blunt and colorful. "Texas is presented to the United States as a bride adorned for her espousal. But if now so confident of the union she should be rejected, her mortification would be indescribable." He wrote in this quasi-ultimatum: "were she now to be spurned . . . she would seek some other Friend."[17] This "flirtation" gambit was well understood by the men he posted to Washington, and they played their parts well. J. Pinckney Henderson wrote that he thoroughly enjoyed the president's game: "You would be amused to see their jealousy of England. Houston has played it off well and that is the secret of success."[18]

Fate, however, undid the plan, for on February 28 an experimental cannon exploded aboard the USS *Princeton* as it was being demonstrated to President Tyler and a gaggle of political notables.[19] Killed outright were the secretary of state and several other prominent supporters of annexation.* The president and his betrothed escaped death only because they had gone below decks to freshen their champagne, but her father, America's richest man, David Gardiner, died on the spot.[20] Just the night before he was blown to pieces, Upshur had penned the draft of a treaty of annexation.[21]

As soon as he had shaken off his shock, Tyler cast about for another staunch annexationist to replace Upshur and, in misguided political maneuvering, chose John C. Calhoun, paladin of states' rights and slavery. The South Carolinian favored annexation with almost rabid zeal, largely because he saw Texas as another slave state needed in Congress.

Calhoun's fanaticism kept the abolitionists in a state of alarm. By the mid-1840s John Quincy Adams was the elder statesman of the antislavery movement. He openly denounced "John Tyler and his cabinet of slave-drivers" who "swill like swine, and grunt about the rights of man," while they sought to expand the "peculiar institution." Tyler was a mere "slave-monger," and moderate Daniel Webster "a heartless traitor to the cause of human freedom" because he refused to stand against slavery.[22]

A temporary boon from Calhoun's appointment was his April 11 transmission to Henderson and Van Zandt of written guarantees of United States protection during "the pendancy of the treaty of annexation." This communication was unequivocal and sanctioned by President Tyler.[23]

A new treaty, drawn up by Calhoun and modified by a Senate com-

---

* This explosion was by far the greatest disaster to ever befall high-ranking personnel of the government, with more key officials killed and wounded than in any other misadventure. President Tyler in any case had to rebuild his cabinet. In addition to Upshur, Secretary of the Navy Thomas W. Gilmer, and John C. Calhoun's best friend, editor Virgil Maxcy, prominent voices in favor of annexation, were among the dead.

mittee, was less advantageous to Texas than Houston had expected, prompting him to complain that "the terms are dictated, and the conditions are absolute."[24] Washington was proving a poor suitor, and "selfish in the extreme." He advised his envoys in high dudgeon that "you may rely upon it if the Govt. of the U. States does not act immediately and consummate the work of annexation Texas is lost to them."[25] They duly communicated his message to all senators who would listen.

On May 6, Houston again turned up the heat. He wrote United States chargé William S. Murphy in bluff anger, warning that Texas could go it alone. Texas needed the United States far less than the United States needed it. If annexation failed, "a rival power will soon be built up, and the Pacific, as well as the Atlantic, will be component parts of Texas . . . the Union of Oregon, & Texas will be much more natural and convenient, than for either separately to belong to the U. States."

"I am free to admit," he continued, "that most of the Provinces of Chihuahua, Sonora and the upper and lower Californias, as well as Santa Fe which we now claim, will have to be brought into the connection of Texas and Oregon." The dream had logic and geographical symmetry. "It is impossible to look upon the Map of North America and not perceive the Rationales of the project . . . they are the results of destiny over which I have no control." For this immense new nation, "Population would be all that would be needful," and that would come from overcrowded Europe. Nations are by nature selfish, he cautioned, and "recognize no *mentor* but interest," and he even ruminated whether "the Union should last" without Texas.[26] He ended with the stark admonition that "the present moment is the only one that the U. States will ever enjoy to annex Texas."

Houston was toying with his grand scheme, and the observer is hard put to determine how serious he might have been. There is no record of him sending agents to Oregon or the Californias to prepare the way for his vision. Perhaps he simply believed that conditions favored his plans and that his famous name would be catalyst enough. More likely, he realized that his plan was a pipedream and was merely using it to goad the Senate by capitalizing on his reputation as a filibuster.

"The Pacific alone will bound the mighty march of our
race and our empire."

SAM HOUSTON, 1844

Though Murphy was rattled, Houston's escalating threats had surprisingly little effect in Washington, where on June 8 the Senate rejected the treaty and what it saw as Calhoun's expanding "Slaveocracy" by a dismaying vote of thirty-five to sixteen.[27] Shortly after this debacle, a satisfied William Kennedy reported to London on the results, quoting Texas Secretary of State Anson Jones: " 'Annexation for the present has failed. We have been shabbily used.' " The diplomat urged Aberdeen to swiftly take advantage of Texian disillusionment and assured him that Houston had now abandoned all hope—and desire—that Texas join the Union; that he planned to "seek some other friend," as he had earlier warned.[28]

The failure of the treaty nullified any hope of United States protection as well and, responding to an anxious query in this regard by President Houston, General Zachary Taylor wrote in August from the border that "under my present instructions I am not at liberty to cross the Sabine," no matter what might transpire in Texas.[29]

Some prominent Americans, including the infirm Jackson, were unsettled by the failure to annex Texas and foresaw grave complications. In December, he wrote his nephew Andrew Jackson Donelson, newly appointed United States envoy to Texas, urging him to warn his former protégé not to abandon his quest to join the Union. Jackson painted a macabre canvas of two independent nations competing in North America: "Texas and the United States will be plunged into a war against each other" someday, because Texas would inevitably become a satellite of Britain. "How much more honorable to be a Senator representing a free and an enlightened people," he cajoled, "than the president of . . . a mere colony of England." Annexation was a cause not yet lost.[30] The rhetoric was escalating, and talk of war between varying combinations of nations was becoming almost casual.

Sam Houston was busily probing other options. One of these was to have Ashbel Smith gain Spanish intercession with Mexico. If this could be accomplished, along with a trade treaty permitting Texian access to Spanish Cuba's slave market, "Texas would prefer to remain independent." Smith immediately related this ploy to a British diplomat.[31] In his farewell address on December 9, Houston talked confidently of independence: "If we remain an independent nation, our territory will be extensive—unlimited! . . . the Pacific alone will bound the mighty march of our race and our empire."[32]

He was still counting on British pressure, if Texas remained independent, to bring about peace with Mexico, and the British were thinking along the same lines. As the year ended, Lord Aberdeen wrote Elliot that "we consider that independence [of Texas] the highest importance to Mexico—for Texas itself—and eventually to the United States" as well. This was because in his view, annexation "Wd. scarcely fail, in no long time, to become a serious source of contention between the northern and southern states." He ordered Elliot to avoid the appearance of meddling, as he worked to steer Texas away from the idea of statehood. Discretion was crucial, wrote the wily Aberdeen, lest the captain "inflame the wild and dangerous spirit, which . . . has been roused and sustained by demagogues in the United States" who favored annexation. Let no hint of rivalry for the affections of Texas be slipped.[33] And in late 1844 a special British envoy to Mexico City reported that he had been able to dissuade Santa Anna from launching a huge expedition against Texas, agreeing to shelve the invasion out of "deference" to London.[34]

New president Anson Jones, who wrote at this time of Texas that "she was in a condition, physically & moraly, to maintain & continue her independent position," was ambivalent about joining the United States. As secretary of state he had developed a close working arrangement with the crafty Captain Elliot, and perhaps even fallen under his sway.[35]

According to equally ambivalent Ashbel Smith, as Houston prepared to leave office he charged his successor to instruct Smith to propose a treaty with both London and Paris. This treaty would pledge Texas to remain independent if the two European nations forced Mexico to recognize Texas and cease hostilities. Smith wrote that the Europeans would have jumped at the offer and most Texians "would have . . . accepted with shouts of joy. Such was the opinion of Sam Houston.

Such was the opinion of Anson Jones. I had it from themselves." He further recalled that Houston had written him that he would "take the stump against annexation for all time to come," unless the United States Congress reversed its position on annexation by inauguration day in the United States (March 4) when his old friend, James K. Polk, would be sworn in.[36] Houston was being less than candid with his old friend (he was, in fact, lying), and Smith was later to note of Houston that "this seeming passion was all pure judgment and calm calculation."[37]

Smith recalled that Andrew Jackson Donelson was so anxious to keep annexationist sentiment alive in Texas that he promised a wide range of benefits for the new state, aware that Congress was unlikely to sanction them, even if it did bring Texas into the Union. Further, a nervous Washington sent a stream of notables to "visit" Texas, including famed navy commodore John Stockton, to manufacture public opinion.[38] Perhaps in part because of this propaganda blitz, Lamar, Burnet and some other famous Texians reconsidered and publicly endorsed annexation. Others, however, remained steadfastly opposed, such as Houston's secretary of war and marine Barnard E. Bee, who had also served as Lamar's secretary of state. So distraught was Bee (a "Nullifier") that when annexation did occur, he returned to South Carolina in anger.[39]

Lord Aberdeen instructed Elliot to inform the Jones administration that "H.M.s Govt. are firmly convinced that the *dignity* and *prosperity* of *that country* are *more secure* in its own *keeping*" than in that of the United States. The Briton was convinced that his nation would benefit from a permanently independent Texas, for this would create "a more permanent balance of interests in the North American Continent," and he ordered the chargé to push Texas into negotiations with Mexico. At the same time, he advised that Secretary of State Calhoun had recently warned France to cease meddling in Texian affairs.[40]

For his part, the chargé reported to London that "General Houston has since I have known him, always been more emphatic in his determined opposition against annexation than the present president and more sanguine in his avowed belief that the people of his country would never sacrifice their independence if its acknowledgement could be secured from Mexico." Elliot wondered that Houston's "true" sentiments never seemed to work their way into his public speeches: "What the result might have been if General Houston . . . had decisively opposed it at an early stage of independence, I cannot say," but his great influence among his compatriots would no doubt have borne fruit.[41] Though a skilled diplomat, Elliot never fathomed that the seemingly rustic Sam Houston was capable of sophisticated maneuvering.

The American Congress was well aware of foreign efforts to perpetuate Texian independence, and it was feeling pressure from its Anglophobic constituents, who were daily becoming more bellicose on the Oregon Territory issue, where "manifest destiny" collided with British geopolitics. Polk had been elected in the autumn on a platform that included annexation of Texas and the slogan "Fifty-four Forty or Fight" on the Oregon boundary question, and outgoing President Tyler frequently berated the Senate for its unwillingness to annex Texas. In this situation the issue was reopened and the Senate voted with unusual speed on February 28, 1845, to annex Texas, by the most slender margin: twenty-seven to twenty-five. The House assented the following day, and on March 1, three days before leaving office, Tyler signed the annexation bill.[42] But, would Texas, twice "spurned," ratify?

The British thought not, partly due to their misreading of Houston. Elliot reported in late March that "we shall act with perfect conceit, and with utmost caution. Very much depends upon General Houston, and we have satisfactory intelligence of his temper."[43] By "conceit" and "caution" the chargé meant that he was about to undertake a clandestine mission. About Houston's "temper" he was simply mistaken.

So, while Aberdeen—unapprised of Elliot's covert trip—was writing to urge him to persuade Texas to moderate its wild boundary claims, the intended recipient of those instructions, in mufti, was in the Mexican capital. There, he worked directly upon the Mexican government, with minor aid from the British and French diplomats stationed there.[44]

Elliot's energy, coupled with direct orders from London and Paris to their chargés in Mexico City "to obtain an unconditional recognition" of Texian independence, swiftly paid off.[45] Elliot dashed back to Texas with the good news: Mexico would recognize Texas by treaty, halt all hostilities and negotiate a mutually acceptable boundary. Aberdeen applauded Elliot's victory, and his initiative, but "admonished [him] to beware how he again acts in this secret and clandestine manner, wh. still may lead to injurious effects," should the United States learn of his mission and see it as part of a sinister plot.[46]

The people and government of Texas now had two treaties to consider; two paths to the future.

"A great public measure has been perverted into
private intrigue."

THOMAS P. ANDERSON, 1845

Just what did Houston think of all this? As in past crises, he guarded his silence, confounding all around him, including Ashbel Smith and Captain Elliot. In fact, there is a curious gap in his extant correspondence for the first four months of 1845. Donelson feared that he might publicly endorse the treaty with Mexico. So did Ashbel Smith and President Anson Jones,[47] but citizen Houston refused to speak out. In a July letter he referred to the views of others without elaborating his own: "I find every body in favor of annexation—poor Jones is effectively dead."[48] Aberdeen, however, clung to the fragile hope that most Texians, including Houston, would prefer independence, provided that it was guaranteed by British money and bayonets.[49]

The sly Briton was in error, for shortly before Texians voted on annexation Houston wrote his old Tennessee friend President Polk that "there will be no war declared by Mexico against the U. States" when Texas was annexed and this was why he had not sought a military commission, as so many others had. He would, however, offer his services, "if they can be useful to Texas, or the U. States." While playing down the possibility of war, he admitted that he had taken the precaution of sending his family to Alabama on a visit.[50]

In a speech at Huntsville, after the Texian Congress had approved the annexation treaty on June 28 (unanimously rejecting the Mexican alternative) but before a referendum on that vote, Houston let slip what he had been up to. "If ladies are justified in making use of coquetry in securing their annexation to good and honorable husbands, you must excuse me for making use of the same means to annex Texas to Uncle Sam."[51] He had, in effect, played both sides of the street. His ultimate goal had been annexation, but had annexation failed, he would have tested other waters. Under the protection of Britain, he would opt for independence and attempt to realize a dream he had expounded so often: Imperial Texas!

On October 13, the voters overwhelmingly approved annexation, and a new state constitution. Now, although Congress still had to formally accept Texas as a state* (December 29), the main work was done.[52] On February 16, 1846, when Anson Jones transferred power to newly elected state governor James Pinckney Henderson, the Lone Star flag was lowered and the Stars and Stripes proudly raised.

Well before the new flag rippled in the breeze, Thomas P. Anderson complained to Lamar that it was criminal that Houston was taking credit for statehood: "A great public measure has been perverted into private intrigue" and converted into political mileage.[53] Lamar even published broadsides accusing him of treason by working for "annexation to the Mexican Government."[54]

While the sharks swarmed in on tough-hided Houston, Aberdeen, the dejected geopolitician, was writing a confused Elliot. The now postless diplomat was to inform the outgoing Jones administration "that the voluntary surrender of their independence does not annul the treaties, and therefore as long as the treaties remain *in force* G. Britain will have a right to require their fulfillment."[55] His Lordship did not lose with good grace.

"Every body who can will rob me."

SAM HOUSTON, 1844

The 1844 Texas presidential campaign had not been fought over the issue of annexation. In fact, it had not been much of a campaign. Rusk tested the water but dropped out early, convinced that expected support

---

* Texas came in as one state—although an odd provision in the treaty could have led to creation of three others—rather than as a divisible territory, ceding to Congress the right to determine its boundaries. Its public debt was not assumed by the United States.

from his friend the outgoing president would never materialize. Houston, in fact, wrote a friend that he had planned to back Rusk, but had realized to his dismay that "I could not confide in his firmness or stability."[56] This left the contest to sulking Edward Burleson and Anson Jones. While affecting the fatherly fiction that he was "above" politics, Houston let it be known that he favored Jones and considered Burleson unstable.

Jones, a Massachusetts-born surgeon of wide political experience, had gradually developed a heartfelt antipathy to Houston while serving in his cabinet. Many of Houston's written communications to Jones were annotated by the latter with snide, acerbic comments. Ironically, while Houston passively supported his presidential bid, Jones accused him of "crawfishing about, trying to defeat my election."[57]

No proponent of annexation, Jones, with his running mate, Kenneth Anderson, swept to an easy victory in the 1844 elections. Once in office, the new president did his best to ignore his predecessor.

Surprisingly little is known of Sam Houston during the annexation period. That he was absent from the capital a great deal while president was one of Jones's principal complaints, for he felt that he, the secretary of state, had had to run the government. Because the president—and the almost invisible Burleson—were so often unavailable, wrote Jones, "I have been consequently for months left to administer the Government 'Solitary and alone.' "[58] In 1844, he claimed, "It will be seen from Gen. Houston's letters and other documents that he was absent from the seat of Government nearly all the year 1844 and much of 1843."[59]

Some of the time, the president was with his wife and son, for Margaret was increasingly morbid. Apologizing for being at home rather than at his presidential desk, Houston wrote Jones in the autumn of 1843 that his family was ill and, as a family man, "I must yield to circumstances when sickness obtains, for it is an act of God."[60]

Houston contended with financial demons as well as with family illnesses. His salary as president was paid only sporadically and in "Exchequers," the heavily depreciated new currency he had created in 1842. The records for 1843 and 1844 show that he withdrew salary only when there were sufficient Exchequers in the treasury. Even then, he usually withdrew his pay in irregular amounts of $24, $36, $100, or $350, and never received constant monthly pay.[61]

So strapped for funds was Houston that he had to hire out most of his slaves at bargain rates, one to Anson Jones for $12.50 a month. John Shackleford (of the Red Rovers from Alabama) bought at least one of Houston's slaves, "Your girl Martha," in 1844, adding a much-needed $450 to the family coffers.[62] The former president also was forced to sell off his remaining Houston town lots and, still desperate for cash, asked a friend to rent out his Cedar Point house for fifteen to twenty dollars a month. He also enjoined the friend to ascertain how much he owed, imploring, "Do pray prevent me from being cheated if you can. Every body who can will rob me," because he was too enmeshed in national affairs to monitor his finances. A pathetic postscript testifies to the seriousness of his plight: "Please see if you can sell my papers for anything."[63] They were not sold.

In contrast, Margaret "lived in anonymity" with her girlhood slave, Eliza,* visited only by her mother Nancy and sister Antoinette Power. She cared for and doted upon young Sam, practiced playing the pianoforte (a gift from Nancy) and Spanish guitar and watched, waited and pined for her husband.[64] She also wrote poetry; long, syrupy rhymes to the absent Houston, such as "My Husband's Picture,"[65] and scores more simply entitled "To My Husband." One of those, written after Houston relinquished office, was Margaret's naive celebration of his "retirement" from politics, and eventual return to the tranquil bosom of his wife:

> Dearest, the cloud hath left thy brow
> The Sunshine of content is there
> Never might thy Country's woes
> again that hallowed light dispel,
> and mar thy bosom's calm repose
> Thy task is done; another eye
> than thine, must guard thy Country's weal
> ....
> Thy task is done: the Holy shade
> of calm retirement awaits thee now.[66]

The lonely Mrs. Houston was deceiving herself to think that her Sam, for two decades a frenetic politician, could be content as gentle-

---

* Often referred to as "Miss Eliza," or "Sister Eliza." They had a close, lifelong relationship.

man farmer and devoted family man. The "cloud" had not left his brow, it had merely shifted position. Not that Houston was an uncaring man. He was simply preoccupied, even obsessed, by the great events of his times and the certainty that he had a large role to play in them.

In 1843, he had bought his wife one of the rare gifts he presented her, a bright yellow wagonlike coach. She was thrilled and proudly used it for the rest of her life.[67] He also purchased a parcel of unimproved land for a family home fourteen miles east of Huntsville, sending his slave Joshua on ahead to get construction under way. A skilled black-smith, Joshua was a second-rate carpenter and, when in early 1845 the "retired" Houstons moved to the farm—named "Raven Hill"—they found but a small, crude log house. No matter, to Margaret it was home.

Not, however, for long. Word reached Houston that the guiding light of his political life was flickering out, and with young Sam in tow, he set out posthaste for Nashville. Riding from that town toward the Hermitage on June 8, the two Sam Houstons encountered Jackson's physician, who informed them that Old Hickory had expired just hours earlier. It is said that, arriving at the plantation, Houston personally closed his mentor's eyes, tears running down his cheeks, while his son looked on.* He then sat down at Jackson's desk and wrote President Polk of the sad event: "12 o'clock at night. . . . In deep sorrow I address you this hasty note. At six o'clock this evening General Jackson departed this life."[68] Both politicians had lost their mentor.

"The most splendid looking man I ever saw."

HARRIET VIRGINIA SCOTT, 1845

While in Tennessee, Houston was feted as a hero and, without his knowledge, was elected in Texas as a delegate to the July 4 convention to decide on annexation.[69] A pleasant message came that autumn from Senator Benton, who was still monitoring his former subaltern's career.

---

* This is almost certainly apocryphal. The physician would have done this.

Congratulating the Texian for manipulating annexation, Benton expressed his conviction that they would soon again be "serving together in the same field, the Senate being substituted for the camp."[70] This was something Margaret had for some reason not foreseen, although her husband had, for in December he announced that he would consent to serve if asked. He was, of course, and on February 21, 1846, the Texas legislature overwhelmingly elected him and Rusk United States senators. By chance, it was Houston who received the short (two-year) term, while Rusk drew the full six-year mandate. This, at least, must have tempered Margaret's disappointment.[71]

Harriet Virginia Scott, visiting from Kentucky, met the Houstons in this period. While she totally ignored Margaret, she waxed enthusiastic about the senator-to-be:

> He is decidedly the most splendid looking man I ever saw, one of Nature's noble men the most intellectual countenance and the most fascinating address . . . walking up town with his Mexican blanket thrown over his shoulder, with an air of lordly superiority—intellect and nobility stamped on every feature you would declare that he was a man born to govern.

By now Margaret was accustomed to being invisible, and her husband, "born to govern," was soon off to do so. In March he was in Washington, where he boarded at Brown's Hotel, and he took his Senate seat less than a month before Mexico declared war on the United States.[72]

"Killings were merely a form of spectator sport."

J. ROSS BROWNE, 1847

The Texas Houston represented in the Senate in 1846 was a far cry from the Texas he had helped found. What James Hamilton had described to Aberdeen as "an intelligent and warlike population" was growing phenomenally.[73] There were almost 200,000 Texans in 1846

(45,000 of them slaves), with more swarming in daily.[74] As early as 1841, despite bad weather, Texas exported a respectable 39,000 bales of cotton, a figure that would increase more than 1,000 percent by 1860.[75] Texas also exported a cornucopia of cane sugar, hides, tallow and a variety of other goods bound for the United States and Europe. There were now thirty-six organized counties, yet these covered less than one-fifth of the area claimed by the state.[76] As someone in Texas at the time wrote, "Agriculture blesses with abundance plains that were desolate and unproductive; the axe rings in the forest, the towns resound with the hum of industry."[77]

Colonization bills passed by Texas in 1841 and 1842, at Houston's urging, prompted a flood of foreign immigrants, some arriving in large, organized groups, others as individuals or families. Henri Castro, who contracted for a colony with President Houston, soon had boatloads of French settlers tying up at Galveston and, in recognition of his Texas-boosting, was named consul-general of the republic in Paris.[78] Between 1843 and 1847 Castro brought in 485 French and Alsatian families and 457 single men.[79] Germans from the various states and principalities came in even greater numbers, often settling as communities. An estimated 7,000 arrived in the years 1841–1846 from the port of Bremen alone, while perhaps 8,000 Germans from Prussia, Saxony and other states debarked in 1846.[80] By then Germans were predominant, or very nearly so, in De Witt,* Victoria and Goliad counties, with other large communities at Galveston, Houston and various other towns.[81] Founded in 1838, New Braunfels had a population of over 1,500 in 1846, almost all German. A sophisticated town, it was liberally supplied with lawyers, physicians, clergy and apothecaries and boasted many "manufacturies."[82] By 1861 many German-language newspapers were being published in Texas, including the respected *San Antonio Zeitung* and *New Braunfels Zeitung,* and the state government had to issue its secession decree in English, Spanish and German.[83]

While before 1845 there had been a plethora of crude frontier types in Texas, the European immigrants, largely hard-working farm and artisan families, spread civilization across the rowdy scene.[84] To French and Germans were added sizeable contingents of Czechs, Serbs, Sile-

---

* Where, for instance, one finds Hochheim, Nordheim, and Lindenau snuggled in among Cotton Patch, Cuero and Yorktown.

sian Poles, English and Norwegians, and where they settled, malcontents did not. In truth, there was little now in Texas to attract or hold the footloose, often larcenous wanderers so common in the previous decade. Many of their ilk now sought adventure farther west, where a gigantic new frontier beckoned.[85]

This is not to imply that Texas was urbane and tranquil. Far from it. There was still the "Comanche Barrier," where the Indians "hated Texans with a bitter hate . . . [making] a distinction between Americans and Texans," to the latter's disadvantage.[86] Then there were the Apaches, the comancheros, the "Mustangers," Mexican *bandido* gangs and the ever dangerous trans-Nueces, claimed by both Mexico and the United States, in addition to the still rowdy, brawling and violent towns, of which New Braunfels was hardly typical.

Houston itself was a hard place. To the west of Main Street was a perfect wallow of sin and lawlessness. "The town was a paradise for saloon-keepers, dance-hall men, and Knights of the green cloth [gamblers]," recalled one who saw it. There were so many murders in Houston and nearby Richmond that some enterprising gamblers rigged up a toteboard and "would then bet on which town would have the most daily or weekly killings." This wagering, the "shooting scores," was normally won by the former capital.[87] Gangs of churlish youths also made life less than civil in Houston; "small boys who roamed the streets undisciplined, chewing tobacco, swearing, fighting, and tormenting passersby."[88] As late as 1840 there had been but one solitary clergyman in town.[89] Nor were other towns paragons of civilization. Bastrop boasted a newspaper, a Methodist Academy and "the usual accompaniment of barrooms and billiard saloons," and "killings were merely a form of spectator sport" for the townsfolk.[90] Texans in general were "a hard-smoking and hard-drinking lot," and at San Antonio, "Religious activity was haphazard at best."[91] This was the Texas that Sam Houston was to represent in the Senate, a thousand miles from his lonely wife.

TWELVE

Senator Sam Houston of Texas

"Though the decision may bring misery upon me,
beyond description, I will try to bear it."

MARGARET HOUSTON, 1846

Washington, D.C., was crackling with excited anticipation in the spring of 1846. It was generally understood that on January 13 the president had ordered General Zachary Taylor to move troops into the disputed trans-Nueces, a region regularly patrolled by Mexican cavalry. Polk had boldly declared the Rio Grande a border worth fighting for,[1] and Taylor was to provide that fight.

In fact, most Americans, and certainly the government, were positively spoiling for war, for while Mexico was hardly the easy prey often depicted,* the potential gain was stupendous.[2] The high tide of "Manifest Destiny" was in full flow, eating away at the Hispanic nation to the south, and while Mexico had impeccable legal arguments, the United States had the implacable will and the necessary weaponry. Few in Washington doubted that war with Mexico—which General Taylor was to precipitate—would mean California and Santa Fe falling like ripe avocados into Yanqui hands. There was dissent, especially on the part of abolitionists, but there was also a lust to realize the beckoning

---

* The Mexican regular army was at the moment four times as large as that of the United States, with superb cavalry and plentiful, modern artillery. Later, in 1862, a Mexican army all but destroyed an invading army of French professionals some thirty thousand strong.

fate of a transcontinental power. It was the United States' birthright to dominate the continent, as Houston had so often contended. It was Mexico's tragedy to be "so far from God, so close to the United States."

In this unfolding scenario, the imperial visionary, Senator Houston, was influential, and he was immediately drafted onto the Senate Committee on Military Affairs. The Texan, described by a Senate staffer as "a magnificent barbarian, [only] somewhat tempered by civilization,"[3] cut a heroic figure: "The most extraordinary of all the Senators was Sam Houston, newly arrived from Texas. By his height of six feet four and his remarkable dress, he would have been conspicuous in any assembly. His waistcoats were sensational: one of flaming scarlet cloth, another of cougar skin. He carried himself with formal grandeur"; not at all the border ruffian many had expected.[4]

Houston moved among giants of American history. John Quincy Adams harangued the House, and in the Senate sat some of the finest thinkers and orators since the founding of the republic. Henry Clay had retired, but then rejoined the Senate when Houston was serving. As a lawyer Clay had dreamed up the plea of "temporary insanity," and as a representative had engineered the Missouri Compromise.[5] Debt-ridden New Englander Daniel Webster was in his seat (when not at the podium or in a tavern), a spellbinding orator and logician, "radiating eloquence." Although often in his cups, Webster was an awesome presence—"No man could be as great as Webster looked," according to one who saw him.[6] Hulking Thomas Hart Benton, lion of the frontier even in old age, still cut a powerful figure, while his frenetic son-in-law John C. Frémont—a captain of the Topographical Engineers and noted explorer—was already on a secret mission to "subvert" California.[7] Houston's perpetual saddle burr, Calhoun, was back in the Senate, with his sharp and passionate intellect. He and Houston had one common friend in the Senate, Rusk, who had lived on Calhoun's South Carolina plantation and read law under him.[8] Edmund Ruffin represented New York with brio in this session, and Jefferson Davis, soon to resign and serve with exceptional gallantry in the war, keenly looked after Mississippi's interests. Described by Houston as "cold as a lizard and ambitious as Lucifer," Davis worked to create a powerful Southern political force, while the Texan was dedicated to national concerns.[9] Soon most of these political behemoths would be gone, and Houston and Rusk would be among the most influential men in Congress.

On March 29 Senator Houston paid a call on President Polk, whom he had not seen in years. "I was much pleased to see him," the president scrawled in his diary; "I found him thoroughly Democratic and fully determined to support my administration."[10] Almost certainly they discussed a possible military command for the Texan in the impending war, and Houston himself wrote that both he and Rusk had been offered, but declined, the rank of major general.*[11] Some have conjectured that Houston, by demurring, threw away an almost guaranteed presidential bid. In truth, both of the war's leading generals, Winfield Scott and Taylor, did become presidential candidates, the latter gaining the White House despite a rather pedestrian war record. Jefferson Davis, a true war hero though only a colonel of volunteers, parlayed his battlefield distinction into the presidency of the Confederate States of America.[12]

Houston seriously considered a field command, and in a letter, Margaret, six months pregnant, indicated that she had been consulted on the matter:

> Dearest you tell me, that I shall decide whether or not, you are to go out with the army. . . . Have I not invariably ascertained your views, and then coincided with them, let my own sacrifices be what they might . . . I wish you to be governed entirely by your own judgement, and though the decision may bring misery upon me, beyond description, I will try to bear it without a murmur . . . I will indulge no longer, in this melancholy language.[13]

Polk, who in March had been confident of Houston's support, was soon disabused, writing that "Genl. Houston was dissatisfied with the Administration," or was pretending to be, for "the truth is that Senator Houston desires to be a candidate for the Presidency" in 1848. Polk also alluded to Houston's disappointment about army rank. The president had been urged by Congress to appoint an overall commander, with the rank of lieutenant general, and it was soon known that he was considering Benton, and not the Texan.[14] Polk—dismissed by a disappointed Houston as "a victim of the use of water as a beverage"—had passed him over.[15] If Houston had been eyeing the 1848 presidential race, he should have taken to the field at any rank he could wangle.

* Although this is possible, there exists no proof of such an offer.

"with my arms around your neck, the happiest,
the most blest of wives."

MARGARET HOUSTON, 1846

In mid-April General Taylor presented the United States with the war it sought, when one of his cavalry units was cut to pieces by Mexican lancers "on American soil," in the trans-Nueces. On April 23 Mexico declared war, and on May 11, so did the United States House of Representatives, by a vote of 173 to 14,* with the Senate eagerly following suit the next day, voting 40 to 2.[16] The following month the Oregon issue was amicably settled, freeing American energies to be directed southward. In place of the blustery "Fifty-four Forty or Fight," the United States realistically accepted the forty-ninth parallel, and the lion's share of the disputed region.

Oddly, Houston had been more hawkish on the Oregon question than he had been with Mexico, sternly warning against compromise. He even went so far as to accept the possibility of war with Britain over the northern territory, thundering that "war . . . is preferable to national degradation, or the loss of empire."[17]

With Oregon defused, the United States turned its resources against Mexico, where, as Geoffrey Perret has noted, "the rubber man of the century, Santa Anna, bounced back" into command of the army. He worked wonders to prepare that corrupt and neglected service for offensive action against the Yanquis.[18]

Almost the moment war was declared, Senator Houston urged the invasion of Mexico, and in fact, its dismemberment, bruiting about a number of schemes, one of which even called for immediate annexation of the Yucatan.[19] This rang responsive bells in Texas, where politicians were giving speeches "which scarcely concealed a desire to acquire all Mexico." Democratic newspapers in the East took up the cause, mass meetings demanded it and the Michigan legislature endorsed it as well.[20] Houston's private dream was at last in the public domain.

---

* The naysayers, led by John Quincy Adams, were mostly New Englanders.

Ironically, many Texans—including Houston—soon felt that it was Texas that was being dismembered. Colonel Stephen Kearny, with sixteen hundred troops, crossed through the state and occupied Santa Fe in August. Kearny ran up the Stars and Stripes, and "since his fiat now made the people of New Mexico U.S. citizens," he wrote a constitution, declaring the region's people citizens of the United States Territory of New Mexico.[21] Texans felt cheated, for their official state maps—not yet disputed by Congress—embraced the whole of Santa Fe and far beyond. Hurriedly, Texan "commissioners" were dispatched westward with counterclaims. The issue led to years of contention between Austin and Washington before being resolved in the latter's favor.[22]

Sam Houston was eager to return home that summer. Margaret was pregnant and depressed, and her letters pricked his conscience. One, on May 16, informed him that she had belatedly received a batch of letters he had sent long before while on his way to Washington. "You can imagine my state of mind, for a few weeks past. It amounted almost to desperation," and those weeks were "wasted in useless melancholy." In her distress she had briefly considered following her husband to the capital, but was at the last moment dissuaded by "our dear Sister Eliza," who wanted no part of the big city. Nor, it seems, did Mrs. Houston, who would avoid it for thirteen long years. In her anxious seclusion, Margaret passed the time perusing her well-worn Bible, often reading aloud to her young son. She noted with feigned surprise that three-year-old Sam "is horrorstruck at Abraham's willingness to slay his son." That she missed her husband is painfully apparent; she implored him to pay attention to her needs: "Oh, my Love, if you could only look into my heart this moment, I know you would never leave me again."[23]

Her deep religiosity would not permit her the release of anger, even as the first wartime session of Congress dragged on far longer than normal. In late June she wrote, "My heart seems to sink almost to despair when I found in your last [letter] no encouragement to hope, that you would soon be home," but, she reproached herself as she so frequently did, "I will indulge no longer, in this melancholy language." Instead, she expressed the hope that "I shall be sitting, as in bygone days, on your lap, with my arms around your neck, the happiest, the most blest of wives." A postscript, supposedly written by toddler Sam, was also aimed at the senator's conscience: "My kittens too, are great

things. They are my only youthful associates . . . as Ma does not allow
me to play with the little negroes."[24] Two Houstons, lonely and somewhat depressed, and another on the way.

"I am often enveloped in clouds of gloom which I
cannot understand."

MARGARET HOUSTON, 1846

On August 10, the first session of the Twenty-ninth Congress at last
came to an end, and Houston was on the road the following day, arriving
home by September 6, when his first daughter, Nancy Elizabeth
("Nanny"), was born. Margaret, rejoicing at his return, was further
cheered to learn that he had attended church several times while in the
capital.[25] She had labored since their marriage to introduce Houston to
religious faith, but he had remained a skeptic. He was hardly the only
skeptic in his state; one missionary wrote at the time that Texas was a
place "calculated to dishearten and dispirit the most resolute" of Christians.[26]

The senator was not always "home" when he was home in Texas.
His short Senate term meant that from the beginning it was necessary
to campaign and press the flesh, and there was a war on, which added
to his duties. Texas mobilized more thoroughly than any other state,
sending three regiments into the field under Governor Henderson, as
well as Ranger companies, which rendered distinguished service as
scouts and light cavalry.[27]

Houston wandered Texas, giving speeches, inspecting troops, politicking and basking in tremendous popularity. This despite the fact that
he had been one of the few Southern senators to favor a ban on slavery
in the new Oregon Territory, a stance taken to preserve the Missouri
Compromise of 1820. While it endeared him to many in the North, it
angered many Texans and other Southerners.[28] He did, however,
strongly oppose the Wilmot Proviso when it was introduced in Congress
to prohibit slavery in any territory taken from Mexico. He felt that

Congress had no right to legislate on the slavery question in any state or territory. This did not contradict his position on Oregon, for that had been based on a congressional decision long since in force. He objected only to new decisions concerning slavery in the states and territories.[29] However, many Southern politicians began to feel that the Texan was "soft" on the vital slavery question, and hence not a true Southerner.

Even before Polk had scented the senator's presidential aspirations, many other noses caught it on the wind. Ashbel Smith convinced his friend to "permit" an official biography, and Charles Edward Lester was commissioned to write it. This, a "campaign biography," *Sam Houston and His Republic,* published in 1850, was designed to acquaint the public with Houston's heroism, sagacity, wit and selflessness, which caused his enemies much gnashing of teeth.[30]

All too soon for Margaret, her husband was packing his bags for the second congressional session, which began in early December. His plans were somewhat clouded, however, by Margaret's fragile health. In addition to chronic asthma and a catalogue of other ailments, she had a sore breast, which soon became dangerously inflamed. Encumbered by baby Nanny, who sapped her strength and tortured her breast, she slipped into depression when she discovered a lump in her breast and realized that it was probably cancerous.[31]

Tumor or no, Houston only briefly delayed his departure, setting forth from Raven Hill with no assurance of Margaret's health. He took his seat in the Senate on December 21, several weeks after the session convened, and within days was opening a letter from his wife: "I am often enveloped by clouds of gloom which I cannot understand." Her tumor had grown considerably.[32]

Pushing his worries aside, the senator was soon caught up in his work in frantic wartime Washington. Since few doubted that the war would be won, the major issue was what geographical spoils the United States would reap. How many future states could be molded from the clay and sand of northern Mexico? This in turn roused the specter of the expansion of slavery, and essentially lit the long fuse that Eli Whitney had fashioned in 1793. It would sputter and hiss all the way to the cannon touchholes around Fort Sumter in 1861.

America was bursting its geographical seams. A virtual traffic jam clogged the Oregon Trail as thousands headed West every month, risking everything in the process.* Brigham Young made the first settlement in Utah in 1847 with 140 or so of his Saints, creating a magnet at Great Salt Lake that would draw thousands of the faithful from as far away as Europe, and present the United States with a preview of secession a decade later.[33] Literary themes focused upon people caught up in movement and new lands, and Henry Wadsworth Longfellow's *Evangeline* was an instant best-seller.

The slavery issue, simmering quietly on the back burner, began to boil, and many were scorched, for land seized from Mexico would lie almost entirely south of the Missouri Compromise line, and hence be open to slavery. While Houston was only vaguely committed to slavery, he joined other Southerners in Congress to defeat the Wilmot Proviso,† clashing noisily with congressional abolitionists. The Proviso actually passed in the House, but Calhoun, whose oratory often included bluster and threat, led Houston and other colleagues to defeat it in the Senate.[34]

Still, the experience had alerted the South to its declining voting power in Congress. The alarm bells rang even more jarringly as two new political parties, both dedicated to the abolition—or limitation—of slavery, were organized. The Liberty and the Free Soil parties, while small and sectional, merged in 1847, adopted the latter's name, and under the leadership of Martin Van Buren, began to spread across the Northern states. Growth was further stimulated by a large wave of "liberal" immigrants to the United States fleeing the failure of Europe's optimistic revolutions of 1848.

---

* The infamous Donner Party, lost and trapped in the icy Sierra Nevadas, gave cannibalism a bad name this winter.

† The Wilmot Proviso would have prohibited slavery in all lands seized from Mexico.

"I fear it has deranged my system in
every possible way."

MARGARET HOUSTON, 1847

Senator Houston found time to do some canvassing for the presidency, most likely thinking of 1852; he sowed some seeds but they were not yet ready to sprout.

He was often on the floor of the Senate in 1847. One pet project was to keep the United States Army small, even in wartime (it had numbered only about eight thousand in 1846). He favored volunteer regiments instead, raised by the states for short-term federal service. He had developed a virtual disdain for the Regular Army, and especially for West Point graduates, whom he depicted as a snobbish, even dangerous, elite. Repeatedly he spoke against each army expansion bill, "and the expenditure inseparable from it."[35] He also spoke, both in and out of Congress, on the wisdom of absorbing huge portions of Mexico, ironically clashing with Calhoun, who opposed a major land grab on the grounds that it "would degrade American whites and destroy American institutions" if a large mass of Mexicans were added to the United States.[36]

The radical rhetoric of pro- and antislavery senators also prompted him to speak out. Especially galled by the intemperate remarks of men like Davis and Calhoun, whose defensiveness drove them to consider extreme states' rights options, he lashed out: "Disunion! It was a monster; and if he could, he would seize upon its mane, drag it forth, and if it had a penetrable spot, he would strike it to the vitals!"[37] With prescience, Sam Houston, almost uniquely, already feared a civil war.

His antidisunionist tirades boosted his popularity in the North, but on his mind by late February was his distant wife. Margaret's tumor had grown threatening, and she was in great pain. The tumor finally burst, and Margaret, in agony, summoned a physician to deal with the wound. Modest to the extreme, she would not permit that frustrated medic full access to her breast, but luckily, Ashbel Smith answered her next summons and the family friend examined her fully and decided to operate at once. Refusing brandy as an anesthetic, Margaret simply clenched her teeth on a silver dollar as Smith excised the tumor.[38]

Houston, apprised of her crisis, left Washington before the session's end and sprinted for Texas, unbeknown to Margaret, who continued to write him. In one letter, penned just before he arrived at Raven Hill, she adroitly avoided any mention of the operation: "After an illness of 10 or 12 days, I am again able to sit up and write you a few lines. My symptoms at one time were very bad . . . and I fear it has deranged my system in every possible way." She appended a simple, disapproving postscript: "In your last, you say nothing about coming home in the Spring. Are we to see you or what?"[39] A great wave of relief swept over her when he walked through the door in the third week of March. He helped her recuperate, admired his children, oversaw planting and bought some sheep.[40]

Unfortunately, Margaret's condition failed to improve. The stitches in her breast irritated her day and night, and she believed she had located a new cancerous growth. So, in late April the senator again summoned his physician friend to Margaret's bedside, relating that "Mrs Houston has more anxiety than is agreeable about the condition of her breast. The *ligature* remains in the wound, there is diagonally across the stomach, bearing to the left side, something like a cord, or tendon, which is quite sore, and she is fearful that it may be a root, of the Cancer."[41] Smith traveled posthaste to Raven Hill and the Houstons' fears receded.

Houston was worried by Margaret's condition, to be sure, but since he remained "a man who sang the praises of home and its serenity mainly when he was away," he was soon restless. His short Senate term was more than half over, and he lusted for a full, six-year tenure. That meant politicking, for it would be the legislature's decision, and many of its members had been dismayed by his argument against slavery in the Oregon Territory. So he spent much of the summer and autumn on the road, mending political fences while Margaret mended her body. When he returned to Washington at year's end he had the second term he sought.[42] And Margaret was again with child.

"We are to decide in favor of civilization
or barbarism."

SAM HOUSTON, 1848

Eighteen forty-eight was a critical year for the United States. The war had gone swimmingly for the northern republic, despite Santa Anna's best efforts. His main army had bravely shattered itself against Taylor's regiments at Buena Vista in northern Mexico early in the war;* Winfield Scott's army pulled off the first large amphibious assault in United States history and occupied Mexico City in late 1847 after having fought a dozen stiff battles. Smaller American forces took California, Santa Fe and even Chihuahua.[43] American arms presented the government with a geopolitical dream at surprisingly modest human cost—1,721 Americans had been killed in action, and 4,102 wounded. The financial cost was somewhat more sobering—almost $100 million—but such immense territorial gain would certainly justify the expenditure.

On February 2, 1848, a week after gold was discovered in California, the two countries signed the Treaty of Guadalupe Hidalgo, which formalized one of history's most grandiose real estate transfers. In return for $15 million and United States assumption of its citizens' claims against Mexico (some $3.25 million), the latter recognized Texas as part of the United States (with the Rio Grande border) and ceded to its northern neighbor over half a million square miles of its territory.† A transcontinental nation had been born, and British fears validated.

Not everyone in the United States was pleased by the booty. Abolitionists were horrified by the vast new possibilities for the Southern slavocracy. Many Southerners, coveting fertile California—soon awash in gold—argued that the Missouri Compromise line should be erased, while many, including Houston, felt that far more of Mexico should

---

* The Battle of Buena Vista was a very close-run thing, and Jefferson Davis and his Mississippi Mounted Rifles gained great distinction there, as did the Texas Rangers.

† Included in the cession were the future states of California, Nevada, New Mexico, Arizona and Utah, and substantial portions of Colorado and Wyoming.

have been taken. Also, as a Texan, he was deeply suspicious that the treaty gave the trans-Nueces and New Mexico to the United States rather than to Texas.[44] There was something in the Treaty of Guadalupe Hidalgo to offend everyone.

His eye fixed on a future White House bid, Houston gave a spate of speeches in the Senate and across the Northeast, where he was in much demand. It was his poor luck that peace came early in 1848, for the treaty unleashed a gaggle of victorious generals, which the major political parties fairly battled over.

In the Senate he spoke glibly of an almost genetic imperialism: "I would recommend to you, if the country should be acquired, to take a trip of exploration there, and look out for the beautiful *senoritas,* or pretty girls, and if you choose to annex them, no doubt the result of this annexation will be a most powerful and delightful evidence of civilization."[45] In New York he rhapsodized about seizing all of Mexico, claiming it was destined that "the Anglo-Saxon race pervade the whole southern extremity of this vast Continent." This was a duty thrust upon the United States, for Mexicans were patently "incapable of self-government."[46]

During debate on the treaty he had introduced a resolution calling for the absorption of all of northern Mexico, as far south as the port of Tampico. Jefferson Davis, who wanted even more, seconded him.[47] He also supported Polk when he recommended military occupation of the Yucatan, which had been requested by one local faction. On May 8, Houston, using the fiction that the Yucatan was as independent as Texas had been, "entirely separated from the Mexican Republic," advocated sending troops there, skillfully blending humanitarian concern and fear of European intervention with patriotic expansionism. He stressed "the propriety of taking possession of Yucatan, if there is even the slightest possibility of its falling into the hands of any other nation . . . Yucatan has appealed to this Country for relief. She has offered us in return her 'dominion and sovereignty.' . . . We are to decide in favor of civilization or barbarism," he thundered,[48] conjuring up an early version of the imperialist justification later known as the "White Man's Burden." Britain's presence just south of Yucatan in what became British Honduras gave substance to his argument. The Yucatan soon lapsed once more into relative calm, no European nation was seen seriously poking about, and the peninsula's distance from the United States did not offer the rationale of propinquity. With a touch of regret, Congress failed to act on the president's request.[49]

The treaty itself was ratified by the Senate on March 10, 1848, by a vote of thirty-eight to fourteen, with four senators abstaining: a single Democrat (Houston) and three antislavery Whigs. The Texan thought the treaty demanded too little of Mexico and too much of Texas, while the three Whigs believed just the opposite.[50] His abstention looked peculiar to most Texans despite his rationale, for all other Southern senators, including Rusk, had approved it while most antislavery men had not. His vote was greeted by gales of applause in the North, where he was already a legendary figure, and this, in turn, worried many Texans.[51]

If the senator was warming up for the 1852 presidential race, he would need Northern support, and as sectionalism divided the republic, his articulation of Unionism and constitutionalism made him appear a *national* man rather than a Southerner. He carefully fostered that image, speaking to large gatherings in New York City, Philadelphia, Hartford and other Northern cities.

Busy in the Senate and on the speakers' circuit, he was not at home for the birth of his second daughter, Margaret Lea, on April 13. He did, however, send a steady stream of endearing letters. He often mollified his wife by telling her about his frequent attendance at church and his reading of the Scriptures, assuring her as well that he continued to abstain from strong drink and other unseemly vices. He even avoided theaters, parties and taverns in the capital, once admitting that "it is only a sense of propriety and regard for the feelings of my Dear, that keeps me away . . . yet were I otherwise situated, I have no doubt but what I might attend them."[52] He thus permitted Margaret to feel that she exercised some control over his life. Still, he was not with his family, and Margaret was "sinking into fits of depression and then succumbing to ardent Southern Baptist evangelism" as solace.[53]

"His very bursts of tempestuous passion
were premeditated."

ASHBEL SMITH, n.d.

Washington was far more exciting than Huntsville, especially in 1848.
The Democratic party convention named Lewis Cass of Michigan in
May, a week before Wisconsin became the nation's thirtieth state. The
Whigs gleefully pounced upon the popular Zachary Taylor, hoping to
revive the party's sagging fortunes, and the small Free Soil party went
into righteous battle with Van Buren in its van. Despite his flag-
wrapped battle fame, Taylor found himself in a tough race, and the
election was so close that had all Free Soilers voted Democratic, Cass
would have been elected.

Houston's attention was drawn in 1848 less to the presidential campaign than to what he interpreted as a sinister and stupid move by
Southern radicals, whose weapon of choice had become the rhetoric of
threat.

Archetypical Southern zealot Calhoun was deeply perturbed in 1848
as Wisconsin was admitted as a state. He saw the "peculiar institution"
under serious attack, as evidenced by the Wilmot Proviso and the ban
on slavery in Oregon, which had not been part of the United States
when the Missouri Compromise was accepted and ought not to be
bound by it. The ban on slavery there was unconstitutional and a direct
attack upon the South.[54] Houston took the opposite tack. He had voted
for the Oregon Bill precisely because of the Compromise line. As if to
prove Calhoun's paranoia founded, the House introduced a bill to abolish the slave trade (not slavery) in the capital.

To Calhoun, this confirmed Northern conspiracy and Southern
weakness, and he grew more strident in debating the cankerous issue
of slavery. If he meant to frighten Americans both North and South,
he succeeded, but that fright only produced a hardening of positions
and strengthened the antislavery movement.

In a speech at Charleston that summer, Calhoun, frail but still com-
bative, advocated that South Carolina abstain entirely from the upcom-

ing elections. While not raising the skeleton of Nullification from its crypt, he urged the South to unite, perhaps even form its own political party to safeguard its interests. The first such step should be a convention of Southern politicians. Implied was that someday the South might have to secede for self-protection. Some perhaps recalled that when Calhoun had resigned as Jackson's vice-president in 1832, medals had been struck in his home state bearing his likeness and the legend "John C. Calhoun, First President of the Southern Confederacy."[55]

Houston bridled at such talk. In a Senate speech he sneered that he "would never go into any Southern Convention," nor "aid in any scheme to bring about dissolution of the Union. What would a Southern Convention do," he asked sarcastically, "raise troops to cut off emigrants to Oregon, because they were going there without Negroes?"[56] Metronomically, Houston, the former lieutenant, and Calhoun, the former secretary of war, confronted each other. While Houston boomed against disunion in all its guises and posed as the chief shield of the Constitution, Ashbel Smith tartly testified that "his very bursts of tempestuous passion were premeditated."[57]

Late in the year, Calhoun helped summon a caucus of Southern congressmen in Washington. Eighty-two attended, but pointedly, neither Texas senator was invited. Houston came to watch in any event and became an unwanted spokesman for moderation.[58] This was but a first flexing of Southern muscle and helped defeat the House resolution to end the capital's slave trade. Before the caucus broke up, it appointed a committee to draw up a "Southern Address" to the nation, cataloguing the region's grievances. Calhoun drafted the entire document.[59]

The Southern Address, according to one authority, "was written for maximum shock value"; a ringing indictment of abolitionism that came close to being an outright attack upon the North, which Calhoun accused of manipulating territorial policy in order to encircle the South with antislavery crusaders. These, if permitted, would destroy the economy, polity and society of the South. The document was so intemperate that some committee members refused to sign it, and when it was passed to all Southern congressmen, only forty-eight appended their signatures.[60] As for Houston, "Rusk and myself . . . would not indorse him [Calhoun]," he wrote Henderson Yoakum. "It is 'the Union' or 'disunion.' You know that I am as unionfied as General Jackson was," and Texas was "among the last to come into it and being in, we will be the last to get out of it."[61] His words were directed in part at his Texas constituents, and from this point on he would do his best to remind them of their unique heritage, so different from that of the rest of the South.

Calhoun's address utterly failed to unify the South but it did galvanize the region's radicals. So his next step was to call for a Southern Convention to meet later in 1849 to produce a "Southern Position." He intended the meeting as an unmistakable warning to the North. Southern politicians were urged to attend if they loved their South, and this prompted irate Sam Houston to bellow in the Senate: "But upon what authority does Mr. Calhoun assume the character of guardian of the whole South?" Where did he get the gall to order other senators around? "What apostolic mission warrants the extension of his infallibility beyond South Carolina, and the visitation of the excommunicating power upon the representatives of other States?" He announced that he, for one, would boycott any such convention. He declared himself in "opposition to all the schemes of mad fanaticism at the North and mad ambition at the South, which would embroil the country in civil war," concluding that "the Federal Union, it must be preserved!"[62] The National Man had spoken.

Preservation was about to be made far more complicated, for the 1848 gold strikes in California led to the nation's first true gold rush. Gold was not the problem, of course; people were. No one had expected California to have the minimum required population (sixty thousand) to apply for statehood for many years, but the magic figure was surpassed in 1849. California would soon request statehood, and the divisive issue of slavery would emerge red-eyed and snorting fire.

"There would have been no appropriation for the
current year but for me."

SAM HOUSTON, 1849

With the Union exploding in rhetoric about him, Senator Houston turned his attention to other important issues, including building a nation-unifying transcontinental railroad. His first step, an early 1849 resolution, urged that a Senate committee investigate the railroad's military applications, and also urged that it be constructed as a strategic necessity. Unlike his later proposals, this one did not call for a Southern railroad, but one "between San Francisco on the Pacific" and some suitable point on the Mississippi.[63] While others sought to divide, Houston struggled to unify and defend.

He also wrote frequently to his family, at times with uncharacteristic sentimentality. To Margaret he admitted that he had been recollecting their first meeting, "in an old ladies garden near Mobile! . . . My Love, do you recollect anything about the incident? I do!" then passing on to an accustomed refrain: "Every hour which passes increases my anxiety to reach my house, that I may embrace my all on earth." He explained his absence by portraying himself as indispensable to the work of government. He confided to Margaret that "I am fearful my Dear that there would have been no appropriation for the current year but for me. The wheels of Govt. would have been stopped and anarchy would to some intent [extent], at least, have succeeded and the Government been endangered! As it now is; we can look forward to years of prosperity for our country." Certainly forestalling anarchy and guaranteeing national prosperity justified his absence from his family! A few days later, he further mollified his lonely wife, writing that he had heard two sermons the previous Sunday, "from our friend Mr. Samson . . . an excellent & intelligent Gentleman," with whom he had discussed the Scriptures.[64]

He was back in Texas in May, again making an effort to fit into the domestic mold, overseeing farmwork, attending church with his family and giving a rousing speech at a "Temperance blowout" on the Fourth of July.[65] But even familial bliss and bucolic splendor, Margaret's twin ideals, could not insulate Houston from national issues, and he found himself engaged in a long epistolary debate with James Gadsden, a fellow Jackson protégé, a railroad promoter and Southern nationalist. In 1853 he would negotiate the Gadsden Purchase of the Mesilla Valley from Mexico for use as a site for a future *Southern* railroad to the Pacific.

Gadsden had written the Texan to criticize his aloofness from the Southern "Cause," and Houston shot back that while the Founding Fathers had labored to construct an "imperishable" Union, "The Nullifiers [his term for Southern radicals] seek to destroy that Union." Hence, "The course pursued by Mr. Calhoun, and the *Abolitionists*, tend to the same end. So far they are co-workers," undermining the Union. He cogently argued that the "fanatics inhabiting the North" were but few: "Are Southern rights and Southern institutions in any real danger of subversion or invasion, from such a source?" Southern radicals were exaggerating the danger and, in the process, aggravating sectional rancor.[66]

Houston's argument was sincere and logical, but events were taking on their own convoluted logic. In March Congress established the Minnesota Territory, with slavery prohibited, and with California's population magically doubling and trebling, a convention there created an antislavery government in September and petitioned Congress for statehood. The balance in Congress was cascading against the South. In 1850 Sam Houston and his colleagues would shift the course of United States history.

THIRTEEN

Sam Houston and the Union

"Sir, the Union is not dissolved!"

SAM HOUSTON, 1850

The 1850 census showed the United States to be no longer an "infant" republic but a full-blown nation with a population of 23,191,876. In that same year, many of these flocked to theaters to worship the "Swedish Nightingale," Jenny Lind, on her American tour. A sizeable portion of the population was swept away by a cholera epidemic in the mid–United States, but their places were soon filled by the 369,980 Europeans who disembarked in 1850. Despite congressional rhetoric, the United States was tranquil, even cocky, enjoying peace along all its borders. So secure were Americans that they entrusted their protection to a mere 10,540 army and 7,500 navy personnel, probably the smallest military-to-civilian ratio in the nineteenth-century world.

In the absence of external threat, Americans seemed bent on becoming their own enemies. Northerners demanded cessation of the slave trade in the capital. Southerners saw this as another step in an abolitionist conspiracy. California demanded statehood, as did New Mexico, and John C. Calhoun, terminally ill, lashed out in his last Senate speech. In a March 4 tirade he delivered his final warning, that if the stronger North would not protect the rights of the weaker South, "Let the States we both represent agree to separate and part in peace."[1] An appalled Senator Houston heard Calhoun's call for a constitutional amendment designed to guarantee a political equilibrium between the free and slave states. But even the brilliant Sage of the South could not specify the provisions of such an amendment, and the idea expired with him on March 31.* Despite his contentiousness, "Calhoun's death brought a sense of loss that was nationwide," according to his biographer.[2]

In the fall of 1849 a bipartisan Southern Convention in Jackson, Mississippi, had called for a representative convention of all slaveholding states in Nashville the following June. Houston and a shrinking coterie of Southern moderates did their best to discredit the coming conclave, but their criticism isolated them in their own states.[3] In January, Houston presented a resolution in the Senate that Congress had no power over slavery in any territory or state, and that when a territory applied for statehood, the issue of slavery should be left to the wisdom of the voters. This, he said, was democracy![4] Many agreed, and later that month Henry Clay introduced what was to become the Compromise of 1850, which the Texan heartily applauded. Houston, however, was the only major Southern politician to support Clay's imaginative way out of the slavery impasse.[5]

The Compromise sought to be all things to all men, its basic provisions being that California would enter the Union with slavery prohibited; that the slave trade (not slavery) would cease in the District of Columbia; that a strong federal fugitive slave law would be passed to guarantee Southern property; and that the debt of the Republic of Texas would be assumed by the United States. At the same time, the almost autonomous Mormon empire, "Deseret," became the smaller federal Territory of Utah.[6] Newly inaugurated president Millard Fillmore, bowing to the inevitable, named Mormon leader Brigham Young Utah's first governor.

The Texas debt question, resolved in the distinct Texas and New Mexico Act, caused howls of outrage in the nation's largest state, for the price to be paid included its geographical pretensions and imperial dream. The act stripped Texas of its claim to at least half of the enormous New Mexico Territory.[7] Texas's presumptuous claims to all lands north and east of the Rio Grande from its mouth on the Gulf to its source in southern Colorado were peremptorily dismissed.

---

* It was reborn in 1860 and early 1861, but failed to gain enough support to avert the Civil War.

Texas took its inflated claims seriously. As late as 1849, the legislature prepared to send militia and Rangers as far as Santa Fe. However, Santa Feans proved uncooperative, and the Texans were ejected from the territory by presidential decree.[8] New Mexico soon formed its own —illegal—state government with a constitution banning slavery. Arrogantly, New Mexico sent representatives to the United States Congress, where they were, of course, rebuffed.[9] Many Texans blamed the loss of Santa Fe on Houston, staunch supporter of the Compromise of 1850. He was harshly criticized for selling out his state's future to cancel the republic's past.

On February 8, Houston gave an impassioned speech, one of his finest, in support of the Compromise. He pilloried the divisiveness of the slavery debate and fiercely attacked Calhoun. Punctuated by bursts of enthusiastic (Northern) applause, the speech revealed a national statesman as well as a nationalist. He defended first the rights "which all free people have to regulate their own domestic institutions," flagellating Congress for interfering with the people's choice for or against slavery. Next, he tackled Calhoun and all the other "Nullifiers," sounding his ringing battle cry: "Sir, the Union is not dissolved!" He finished amidst tumultuous cheers:

> But I beseech those whose piety will permit them reverently to petition, that they will pray for this Union, and ask that He who buildeth up and pulleth down nations will, in mercy, preserve and unite us. For a nation divided against itself cannot stand. I wish, if this Union must be dissolved, that its ruins may be the monument of my grave, and the graves of my family. I wish no epitaph to be written to tell that I survive the ruin of this glorious Union.[10]

"I was nursing a viper."

MARGARET HOUSTON, 1850

Because of its complexity, the Compromise of 1850 generated seven months of well-publicized debate before it was enacted. Houston's focus

on the "Union" rather than on Southern grievances caused him to
be vilified throughout the South but increased his popularity in the
North and West. Many Texans viewed his speeches as stepping-stones
to the White House, but it is hard to determine just how much
of his public exposure was truly premeditated. The convergence of
his views with those of the great Henry Clay gave him a new credibility outside the South, and he was soon swamped with speaking
requests.[11]

Instead, in late February, during the most heated debate over Clay's
proposals, Senator Houston packed his bags and departed Washington
without explanation.

Margaret was in trouble. Near term with their fourth child, Mary
Willie (born April 9), she was ill and, in addition, had just been accused
of criminal assault. The case involved Virginia Thorne, an orphan
adopted by Margaret's sister-in-law Mary Lea, who had become a legal
ward of the Houstons when Mary died. To all intents and purposes,
she was a servant. As she grew into her teens, she resented her status
and relations between her and Margaret grew tense, while relations
between her and the much older overseer of the Houston farm, Thomas
Gott, grew embarrassingly warm.[12]

One day, accusing Virginia of mistreating little Nannie, Margaret
thrashed the girl with a strip of cowhide, drawing blood. Not long after,
in her habitual Tuesday letter to her husband, she informed him with
relief that "last night Virginia eloped with Gott." As soon as Thorne
decamped, wrote Margaret, several people had stepped forward, and "I
can now find from various sources that I was nursing a viper," a vindictive and "loose" young woman. With the vixen out of her hair, Margaret
had also sold a "troublesome" slave, for a much-needed five hundred
dollars.[13]

At the now-discharged Gott's urging, Virginia filed assault and bat-
tery charges against her former mistress. Houston arrived in Texas in
early March, hired a lawyer and helped get the preliminary hearing
postponed. But he had to depart again for Washington just days before
the overwrought Margaret, still in poor health and suffused with gloom,
gave birth.

The preliminary hearing resulted in a deadlocked grand jury, which
permitted the case to be settled by elders of the local Baptist church, of
which Margaret was a very prominent pillar. Following several weeks

of investigation and testimony, to no one's surprise Mrs. Sam Houston was acquitted.[14]

While Margaret was wrestling with her peculiar demons, her husband, back in the Senate, was again jousting in defense of the Union. There, he lashed out at detractors such as Edward Hall—"I challenge you or any other panderer or pimp"[15]—while he dispensed medical homilies to his wife: "Do not bathe her [Nannie] at any time in less than two hours after eating. . . . See that her clothing is uniform and changed once or twice a day, as clothes ought always to be!" How odd that Sam Houston would presume from afar to offer pediatric advice to his wife! He also took the time to buy India rubber balls and live canaries for the children, worrying over how best to send his gifts to Texas.[16] After inspecting them, he recommended that Colt revolvers be issued to the Rangers, for "the great number of discharges render them terrible to an enemy."[17]

For the most part, however, he was writing and delivering speeches, fulminating against disunion and radicals North and South. The Nashville Convention, which he noisily boycotted, was a perfect target, for it epitomized the destructive forces threatening his nation.

"the South alone would be a trifle."

SAM HOUSTON, 1850

Nine Southern state delegations converged on Nashville for the convention on June 3. John C. Calhoun would have been disappointed by their general tepidity. There was little unity, less agreement, and only a smattering of radicalism. It turned into a symposium, almost a retreat, on Southern grievances and produced no lasting document, Union-threatening or otherwise.[18]

But to Houston, the very act of meeting was a threat and insult to the Union. His speeches throughout the summer excoriated the concept. In late June he accused the convention delegates of violating the Constitution, which "declares that no one or more states shall enter into any compact or agreement without the consent of Congress," and Congress had not given approval.[19] In a major speech in August just after President Taylor died of typhoid fever,* Houston defended his vote to admit California as a free state and attacked the Southern conventioneers. "By whom were they constituted a great assembly to dictate to the *Congress* of the United States?" he roared. He cautioned that "the evils connected with such a measure as disunion would be fraught with utter destruction not only to the South, but also to the North. We would be a distracted, wretched people; a people without a nation." He urged Southerners not to defy the Constitution and create a weak country, ripe fruit for any European nation to pluck.[20]

Two days later he again lectured the Senate: "Why talk of resorting to a dissolution of the Union for the cure of even real evils?" The radicals should turn instead to the Supreme Court. He noted that "the President's veto is another safeguard," as was the possibility of amending the Constitution. He all but accused the Southern senators of stupidity for considering secession without exploring legal constitutional options. "I will stick to the South" no matter what, he conceded, but made the bitter point that "the South alone would be a trifle" on the world stage. Likening the Union to a rim holding together the spokes of a wheel, he concluded grimly, "The unity is one; that cannot be severed without destroying the whole. I need not dilate upon that which is too painful to contemplate": secession and ensuing civil war.[21]

Once again the Texan gained kudos and respect north of the Mason-Dixon Line, where he was lauded as a man of reason. And once again he was vilified in the South, despite his protestations of loyalty. Future president Andrew Johnson, another Tennessean who knew Houston well, and who himself was a "Union" Southerner, wrote at the time that "Houston is much Spoken of here for the next President," and would win the Democratic nomination, if he would but try to gain it.[22] With Houston, the question was always "if." Ironically, his friend and fellow Unionist Thomas Hart Benton was then writing John A. Dix about the Texan's presidential chances, noting that "he has flaws in him that would make him fall to pieces in our hands."[23]

That Houston was laconically seeking the presidency was underscored by the publication of the almost embarrassingly self-serving *Sam*

---

* Succeeded by Millard Fillmore, who had run on another ticket.

Houston and His Republic in 1850. Author Lester had spent a great deal of time with the senator but very little time with anyone else, for while the campaign biography thrilled the average person, it enraged many who knew Houston and "His" Texas. One, J. A. Jones, wrote Andrew Johnson: "I did not care to know when or where or how Sam Houston was born & read no further" than the first page. He claimed that "my yard dog Salam [is] . . . every way more worthy of a Biography than the Texas rowdy. If at any time you should hear of the death of Sam Houston I shall be pleased to receive the intelligence."[24] T. J. Green, always apoplectic on the subject, condemned "the corruptions of Sam Houston . . . the most infamous Falsehoods," and may have coined the sarcastic sobriquets "Sam Jacinto" and "Sham Houston."[25] Lamar, whose anti-Houston broadsides were largely ignored because they were so expected, began referring to him as the "Munchausen President" of Texas.[26]

Houston had no time to worry about his critics that summer and autumn as he worked indefatigably to drive Clay's Compromise through the Senate. He argued fruitlessly against the Texas–New Mexico Bill, declaring at one point, "It is her boundary she asks—not your millions,"[27] knowing full well that the money was the best he could hope for. Such an argument was less than politely brushed aside, and the bill passed in Congress.

On September 9, Houston returned to the attack in the Senate chamber, implicitly accusing the Southern senators of treason—"Disunionists, *per se,* therefore, sink below [Benedict] Arnold in the scale of infamy." As for those who contemplated secession, Houston reminded them that the Union represented shelter, not oppression. He spoke from personal experience, reminding his colleagues that unlike most of them, "I have experienced the inconvenience of being out of the Union."[28]

He frequently wrote home in this period, increasingly to his son. His letters were peppered with parental advice, such as, "Boys should always be kind and generous to their Sisters. No man is either good or great, who is unkind to Women!" He implored the seven-year-old to do what he himself could not: pay attention to Margaret. "The greatest of all earthly friends is the Mother to her son, while she lives. The Father may be a great friend to the Son, but he can never know and feel the cares of a Mother for her sleeping infant, or her helpless child. Should you live to be a man . . . you will then understand, how much a son owes to his Parents, and particularly to his Mother! I may love you as much as your Ma does, but I cannot feel for you as she has done!"[29] Houston often placed his children's mother on a pedestal, without once mentioning his own "Ma."

Another, similar letter, written a month later, urged Sam to show kindness, "even to dumb animals," for kindness and love are the twin characteristics of a good person. "The wicked are bad, because they are the children of the Devil, and not children of Light," he penned, lacing the missive with generalized versions of the scriptural lessons he himself was learning: light and dark, sin and redemption, God and the Devil. "You are a blessed Boy, because while you are young, you have a kind Mother to teach you to be good, and pray with you, and for you!"[30]

<hr>

"I do not think you will leave me again."

MARGARET HOUSTON, 1851

By 1851, Sam Houston was a genuine teetotaler. Abstinence, and his new interest in religion, showed the effect Margaret had upon him. He often felt constrained to apologize to friends for not having strong drink around,[31] but he never moralized about others' drinking habits. A member of several temperance societies by 1851, he steadfastly refused to support their demands for Sunday prohibition laws. He found that such laws would violate religious and civil liberties and run counter to the concept of separation of church and state; hardly a popular stand among the "drys."[32]

Houston was still courtly in dealing with people. One who met him remarked that "his manners were . . . quite aristocratic, smooth and cordial. His mind was keen, quick, and rather wily, but defenseless against flattery."[33] Another who observed him in the Senate wrote that the Texan "carried himself with formal grandeur," but, "while other Senators orated, Houston whittled. For hours each day he would fashion little wooden hearts, about the size of a quarter. He carried them in a snakeskin pouch to offer ladies who pleased his fancy, saying 'Lady, let me give you my heart.' " [34] The man who basked in flattery gave as good as he got.

This odd mix of "grandeur" and simplicity extended to his wardrobe as well, although as he grew older he became more dandified, often wearing several large gaudy rings and a hefty, prominently displayed gold watch, and carrying a gold-headed cane and a gold-encased pencil." [35] He certainly cut a figure, especially in conservative Washington, as witnessed in scores of portraits and formal photographs that he commissioned. [36]

Eighteen fifty-one was not a banner year for the Houston family. The senator, always careless with money, was consistently broke, despite his above-average salary and allowances. Nor was he much of a farmer, rancher or small businessman. He purchased, for example, a large herd of swine in 1850, but all but one soon died. [37] He might have lived and dressed with some elegance while in Washington, but in Texas he, Margaret and their children just barely "got by." [38]

Margaret's health was a constant problem. In 1851 and 1852 her asthma became dangerous. Many nights she could not even lie down, "for fear she might strangle." To combat major asthma attacks her slaves filled every dishpan and bucket with dry leaves, placed them around their mistress, and set them on fire. "The smoke from the burning leaves always did her more good than all the medicine she ever tried," recalled one of the family's slaves. [39]

In part because of the asthma (and her fifth pregnancy, known by May 1851), Margaret began to brood about death. [40] It hardly helped her mood that Nancy, who lived now in nearby Independence, was truly steeped in morbid thought, constantly broadcasting her own imminent demise. Nancy not only spoke of death incessantly, but also had a plastered limestone tomb built conveniently behind her house, complete with an ornate iron gate. The pièce de résistance, however, was a weighty metal coffin she ordered from New Orleans. This rather exotic item she stored in her bedroom. [41]

Nancy's fixation on her demise showed up in many of Margaret's letters to her husband. "Mother is not well, and I fear her health is seriously failing," she wrote in one, and "Mother's health seems declining very fast . . . she is talking every day about arranging her temporal matters for death . . . it is a mournful thing." These are typical updates on her mother, a staple of her correspondence with Houston. Yet her mother remained active and spry (if grossly overweight), relaxing her tenacious grip on life only in 1864.[42]

The morbidness of mother and daughter received a big boost in 1851 and 1852. First, Margaret's brother Henry died unexpectedly and, a few months later, so too did her other brother, Vernal. To complete the ill luck, Margaret's sister Antoinette and brother-in-law Charles Power were left penniless when their coastal sugar plantation was literally swept away by a hurricane.[43] The ambience in the Houston household was sepulchral, and the senator's almost continual absence deepened the gloom.

So deep did those shadows become that Margaret seriously—albeit briefly—considered moving to the capital to be near her husband. In February 1851 she wrote him a letter revealing the depth of her despair. "I am completely unnerved," she informed him, and then delivered what amounted to an ultimatum: "Well I do hope, that I shall never again be required to exercise my fortitude in the same way. Not that I expect you to resign . . . but I do not think you will leave me again. . . . As I mentioned to you before, I would like for you to select a pleasant boarding house for us about 8 or 10 miles from the city." Nothing ever came of this idea, and she never so much as visited Washington. For one reason, she became pregnant within days of the senator's return in April. In addition, Houston wanted to separate his public and private lives, and preferred that she remain in Texas with their growing brood.[44]

Home in early spring, just as Herman Melville's *Moby-Dick* appeared in bookstores and a young German socialist named Karl Marx began writing for the *New York Tribune,* the senator tried his mightiest to jump into the family circle, and in the process dispel some of the palpable gloom enveloping it. Briefly he was again the gentleman farmer, husband and parent. "I am farming in a small way . . . planting peas, corn, rice, and millet," he wrote a friend, and raising some "fine milk cows" as well.[45] His son he damned with faint praise in a letter: "Sam is a tall, long and homely lad, fairly smart in some things. I hope he will make a good man if not a great one."[46]

Religion was a balm for the Houstons. By 1851 the senator was a regular, but still unbaptized, Baptist churchgoer. Most Sundays in Washington he attended the E Street Baptist Church, where, according to one witness, he "always occupied a pew near the pulpit. And there he would stand, his commanding figure wrapped in a Mexican blanket in cold weather," often whittling.[47] Much to his wife's pride, when he was back in Texas Houston began to offer prayer and read from the Bible at the end of each meal, even summoning the slaves to participate. Formal conversion, sighed Margaret, was but a matter of time.[48]

The Houstons now owned ten or eleven slaves. Some, like Margaret's wedding present, Eliza, functioned as nannies, chasing after the diminutive Houstons. Others worked in the fields, but the one with the most respect was Joshua. The senator permitted his slaves to earn what they could in their "free time," and Joshua, a skilled blacksmith, generated a handsome income. He had his own small smithy, and through careful saving amassed a great deal more cash than his master. When the senator died, Joshua was by far the wealthiest member of the household.[49]

Houston for a while gave himself over to what most people considered "normal" life, far from adoring crowds, political brokers and ambitious power-seekers, life with his "homely" son and three daughters, who were "as wild as antelopes."[50] But in the autumn he would again be absent, and one can almost sense his eagerness to return to the fray.

"Houston never has exhibited any evidence of
uncommon talent."

EDMUND RUFFIN, 1857

Houston's dream of empire had never died. He continued to monitor
events in Cuba and Mexico. From 1830 or so Cuba was the main source
of illegal slaves for Texas and the Gulf States, all the while sporadically
racked by revolutions. These uprisings attracted American sympathy—
and volunteers—and encouraged expansionists who coveted the island.
In the summer of 1851, while Houston was watching his millet grow,
Cuban freedom fighter Narciso López invaded the island with a band
openly recruited in the United States. The Spanish army crushed the
López insurrection, and a wave of indignation swept American public
opinion—but not the government, which officially apologized—when
the Spanish executed a band of yanqui volunteers.[51] Just before that,
Houston wrote Henderson Yoakum: "No news from Cuba; this promises
well for the revolutionists." He was sorely disappointed by news to the
contrary.[52]

For generations Americans had been fascinated by Cuba. By 1850,
several "organizations" dedicated to renewed national expansion were
evolving. In the South they aimed at the expansion of slavery, which
was denied increase within the bounds of the United States. One such
group, which Houston might have joined, was the Lone Star of the
West. It was a low-profile group that passed itself off as a manifest-
destiny organization created to "complete" the process begun with the
Mexican War, but expansion of slavery was its primary concern. "Star"
members talked openly of acquiring Cuba and northern Mexico by any
means necessary.[53]

Better known than the Lone Star of the West, and perhaps springing
from it, was the Knights of the Golden Circle, formed about 1850.
Theoretically a "secret" society, the Knights' goal was the "setting up
of a slave empire encompassing a great circle with Havana as a center
and with a radius of 1,200 miles." This ambitious radius would embrace
the Caribbean, Mexico, Central America, the northernmost portions of

South America and, of course, the slave states of the American South.[54]
Whether or not the Knights were involved, as suspected, in William
Walker's conquest of Nicaragua in the mid-1850s is not proven, but the
organization was real, and in the heat of the slavery debate, was growing. It would exist for at least a decade, and Houston later contemplated
using its resources to conquer Mexico.[55]

Houston had another dream. The White House was much on his
mind in 1851 and 1852. *Sam Houston and His Republic* sold well; his
endorsement of the Compromise of 1850, his firm Union stance, and
his excoriation of all radicals made him a popular figure. His many
speeches in the North boosted his visibility, and his pronouncements
on temperance endeared him to an increasingly large and vocal interest
group. He was inducted into New York's influential Tammany Society
in 1851 and gave dozens of speeches on Texas history, San Jacinto,
temperance, and the Indian, rarely failing to captivate his audiences.
Rip Ford relates that in 1852 Houston traveled to Austin—hardly hos-
pitable territory—to give a political speech despite threats against his
life by veteran antagonists James G. Swisher and Thomas Ward. Ford
and some other friendly Rangers acted as unofficial bodyguards, but the
senator spoke with such "impassioned eloquence" that Swisher and
Ward, converted, personally escorted their old nemesis from the podium, arm in arm![56]

In a Philadelphia speech later circulated as a pamphlet, the Texan
wrapped himself in Jackson's mantle ("He was a man whose memory I
venerate"), dissociated himself from parties-qua-parties ("Neither party
can play the rascal long with impunity") and assured all that he had
personally snatched Texas from the maw of Mexican despotism.[57] He
also spoke widely about the mistreatment of the Indian, as he did in
Hartford, in January 1852, although, as one source notes, "This speech
could not have gained him a single vote. Even the Abolitionists of
Hartford hated Indians."[58]

Some Southerners, men like Virginia "Nullifier" Edmund Ruffin,
hated Houston for his lack of sectional patriotism and considered him a
"despicable wretch." Ruffin was perplexed as well as angry, for "though
other as base men have stood as high, most of these (as Benton) had
great ability as well as Villainy. But Houston never has exhibited any
evidence of uncommon talent."[59] The uncompromising Ruffin would
fire the first cannon of the Civil War.

Houston was never reluctant to strike back, especially at the leadership of South Carolina, a state he had seen no good in since his flirtation with "Miss M." from Cheraw. In a letter to John Letcher, he argued that the only purpose served by the Nashville get-together was "to furnish a sort of safety-valve for the overcharged patriots of South Carolina and Mississippi to let off their *extra gas*," but even this, he wrote, "can just as well be done in town meetings," without the trappings of disunionism.[60] One constant refrain was his criticism of the South Carolina "Oligarchy." He claimed that a small, privileged elite ran the state undemocratically, with property requirements for holding office, no popular vote for the governor, and a carefully limited suffrage.[61]

By late 1851 Andrew Johnson, among other political insiders, considered Houston a distinct front-runner for the Democratic nomination. He wrote in December that "the democratic party can go into the next contest with Houston or Cass . . . the party can elect either of them."[62] Yet, beyond his speeches, Sam Houston did nothing to gain the nomination. He was curiously silent on the issue of his candidacy—or even availability—and this drove most of his actual and potential supporters away. Even after the Whig party nominated Mexican War hero Winfield Scott, Andrew Johnson was writing of Houston that "he is the only man in our ranks that can defeat General Scott."[63] But the senator made no declaration and unveiled no proto-platform. His inaction drove his own state's politicians to distraction.

One Texas presidential elector, Guy M. Bryan, began a correspondence with the senator that lasted years. Bryan wanted to know two things: whether Houston was serious about the White House (Bryan decided that he was), and whether Houston had been a detractor of his relative, Stephen F. Austin, as rumored. Bryan did not want to help "to elevate to the presidency of the U.S. a deadly enemy of my Uncle."[64] He was assured that such was not the case. In July, after the Democratic convention nominated Franklin Pierce and William R. King, Andrew Johnson lamented the absence of the Texan from the ticket, which he incorrectly saw as doomed. "If we could have Succeeded in procuring the nomination of Houston at the National convention we could have elected him without any kind of doubt." But Johnson also noted that the Tennessee delegation had refused to consider him.[65] That state would never forget the Houston of 1829.

"I love all my children, but I love them to be
industrious, and try to make Me happy."

SAM HOUSTON, 1853

As 1852 began with Houston's vacillation wasting his chance at the presidency, the balance of power in Congress hardly reassured the Southerners. There were sixteen free and fifteen slave states, resulting in a slender plurality for the former in the Senate, but a crushing imbalance of 144 to 90 in the House, due to the heavier Northern population. The signs were ominous, and many Northern states passed stringent "Personal Liberty" laws designed to emasculate the new Fugitive Slave Law that had emerged from the Compromise of 1850. The appearance of the simplistic antislavery novel *Uncle Tom's Cabin, or Life Among the Lowly,* by Harriet Beecher Stowe (seen as anti-South in that region), made abolitionist converts in the North and increased the defensiveness of the South. That the book sold an astonishing three hundred thousand copies the first year indicated the breadth and depth of feeling in the North.

The Houstons' fourth and last daughter, Antoinette Power, was born January 20, while the senator was in Washington, eulogizing Hungarian patriot and revolutionary Louis Kossuth. Little else is known of him in 1852. There was an odd silence from and about him, though he did go on a speaking tour on behalf of the Democratic party in the fall, touting Pierce with faint praise in Pennsylvania, New York, Ohio and Tennessee.[66]

The election surprised most political pundits, including Andrew Johnson. Despite being far better known and respected, Scott was handily defeated by the relatively obscure Pierce, in large part because of Scott's frequently aired abolitionist sentiments. The Free Soil party also suffered, attracting barely half its 1848 tally. Here was a hiatus in the heated politics of slavery and antislavery. The nation was taking a last, deep breath of moderation.

The year 1853 was as quiet for the United States as it was for Sam Houston: It was the eye of a national and personal storm. Yellow fever ravaged New Orleans once more, but Commodore Matthew Perry sailed past bristling fortresses into Tokyo Bay to "open" Japan to the West. From Galveston, inventor (and local tax collector) Gail Borden applied for a patent to protect his process for making canned, evaporated milk.[67]

Also, a new political party was born: the Native American (or American) party, also known as the "Know Nothings" because in its early days that was the response given by members to any questions about what it stood for. It was a nativist response to recent massive immigration, and was anti-Catholic and anti-Semitic. Know Nothings sought to slow or halt immigration, impose strict naturalization laws and make it more difficult for those not born in the United States to hold public office. One Know Nothing, inventor Samuel F. B. Morse, was convinced that the Catholic church was plotting armed insurrection in the United States![68] Although a party of negatives, it attracted a large number of well-known politicians, whose sensitive antennae detected a large potential constituency. Among those drawn to the Know Nothings were former president Millard Fillmore, Andrew Jackson Donelson and, for a while, Sam Houston. The new party would briefly have a great deal of influence, especially on the state level.

Senator Houston spent more time in 1853 at his writing desk, in both his public and private capacities, than he had the year before. He made a sincere effort to write more often to his two eldest children, and his letters characteristically displayed a combination of guilt and piety. He advised Sam in January to draw less and study more and "while I am absent, do pray seek to make your dear Mother, and all of the family happy. It would make me unhappy if I thought you would not be Noble in your feelings and good in your Conduct." Following that came his ritual yearning to be at home: "Far distant from my family whom I love so much, all that I can do for them is to love them and pray for them, both of which I never cease to do."[69]

A few days later he wrote Nannie, then six. "I send you a comic Newspaper," he began, promising to send along others so that Nannie would have something light to read. He also had a gift for his oldest daughter; "I have a pretty locket for you, my Dear, that has two likenesses of me in it." He complained to Nannie that Sam had not written him recently, and that "I am fearful; that he is too *selfish*" to care about other people. Finally, he told the girl that he would soon send "some evergreens from the *tomb of Washington*," which he wanted her to plant at Huntsville.[70] A few weeks later he again wrote Nannie, urging her and her siblings to be "good," adding that "I love my Children, but I love them to be industrious, and try to make Me happy."[71]

He adopted much the same paternalistic tone with President Pierce, a man he neither liked nor respected. Even before his inauguration he wrote to instruct the president-elect to be exceedingly careful in his choice of cabinet members. He wrote, "I declare to you, Sir, that I have found . . . a disease at the heart of the government, which, unless arrested, must eventually . . . surrender the government to speculators," machine politicians who served special interests rather than the public good. He exhorted Pierce to choose his cabinet members for their proven qualities, and not in order to satisfy one or another wing of the party.[72] This marks the point at which Houston became thoroughly disenchanted with the two major parties, for Pierce selected men abhorrent to him. He was soon to cast about for a "cleaner" vehicle for his own ambitions.

"Will you not marry, Miller? You must do so!"

SAM HOUSTON, 1853

Houston was early disheartened about the president. Just weeks after Pierce took the helm, the senator wrote Washington D. Miller, giving friendly advice ("Will you not marry, Miller? You must do so!")[73] and carrying on about the stupidity of the new cabinet, lamenting as well that "we have no President." He was upset that neither he nor Rusk had been permitted their "fair share" of patronage, and he felt that Pierce considered him a rival. Pierce "is jealous of me," he penned, and he promised that "*if God wills, I will make him more so!*"[74] By September he considered the president "a poor, a very poor dog skin."[75]

Houston's interest in a transcontinental railroad resurfaced in 1853 and focused on a southern route, which would benefit Texas. Ever since 1849, California-bound emigrants ("argonauts") had been trekking through Texas with their wagons and carts. With a direct rail link, would not the millions in bullion spurting from the California mines flow through the state in the opposite direction?[76] Such traffic would generate revenue for Texas, and the southern route would be the simplest, for there were virtually no mountains, no snow zone, few rivers, and an almost imperceptible grade.

For once, Houston and Jefferson Davis (now secretary of war) were in agreement, and the senator was more than happy to cast his vote to appropriate funds the Mississippian requested for a railroad survey of all "practicable" routes west.[77] Ironically, the final survey reports favored a central route, even though the southern route was least costly.*[78]

This thrust for a southern transcontinental route led to the Gadsden Purchase, signed December 30. Santa Anna, incredibly president once more, needed money to maintain his lavish "court," so he was willing to negotiate with James Gadsden. The resulting treaty obligated the United States to pay $10 million for Mexico's Mesilla Valley, over twenty-nine thousand square miles of flat land ideal for railroad construction.[79]

In September Houston bought another farm, at Independence, some two hundred enclosed and almost as many timbered acres. He paid $2,000 down, and agreed to pay another like amount in three installments, with an additional $804 for a flock of 268 sheep.[80] Soon thereafter he and the family—Margaret again with child—moved there, happily close to Nancy, and Sam was promptly enrolled in the nearby new Male Department of Baylor University.[81]

Much to the chagrin of many, Houston managed to get re-elected senator by the Texas legislature that fall, probably because the slavery issue was momentarily quiescent and the senator was so loudly beating the drum for a Texas-based transcontinental railroad. Also, Houston was still stronger than the state Democratic machine, which had all but disowned him.[82]

As 1853 faded like a daguerreotype left in the sun, two major fissures in the American political system could be discerned: One would annoy the nation, while the other—and Houston saw this with startling clarity—would all but destroy it. The annoyance was the surprisingly swift

---

* The first transcontinental railroad, whose construction *was* on the central route, was built between 1864 and 1869, linking Omaha and Sacramento.

growth of the Know Nothing party. In the off-year 1853 elections the new party (more accurately, *movement*) proved itself extremely strong in such diverse states as New York, California, Maryland and Massachusetts.[83] It might prove a proper vehicle for a man who distrusted, and was distrusted by, the two major parties.

The true danger was to come out of an agreement pulled off by a presidential commission with scattered tribes on the frontier. The government's sleight-of-hand tricked the Indians out of more than thirteen million acres of land in what would soon become known as the Territories of Kansas and Nebraska.[84] One of the first matters Congress had to deal with in 1854 would be how to organize these new territories. Houston would warn, prophesy and even threaten but his dire forecasts would be ignored.

FOURTEEN

Sam Houston, President?

"You are putting the Knife to the throat of the South."

SAM HOUSTON, 1854

In 1854, as the nation began to noisily unravel despite Senator Sam Houston's best efforts, he underwent a twofold conversion: He abandoned the political faith of Andrew Jackson, the Democratic party, and he embraced the religion of his wife.

The new Senate session had barely begun when Stephen Douglas of Illinois unveiled his plan for the newly acquired Indian lands. As expected, he proposed creation of the Territories of Kansas and Nebraska, but the bedrock of immediate contention was his fervent demand for the vox populi, "popular sovereignty," which would permit the settlers themselves to decide on slavery when the territories applied for statehood. Before then each territory might permit slavery, unless prohibited by its territorial legislature.

Houston was horrified, although he personally favored the concept of popular sovereignty . . . in the abstract. He recognized that it would exacerbate the slavery debate and could lead to bloodshed, since both Kansas and Nebraska were north of the Missouri Compromise line. If Douglas's bill (supported by Pierce) was passed, the Missouri Compromise would be voided and a mad scramble to control the territorial legislatures would ensue, inevitably widening the gaping wound of sectionalism. Even the remote possibility that slavery might expand would spark a strong Northern reaction and would slip the leash from the radicals on both sides of Mason's and Dixon's invisible line.

Douglas (called "the Prince of Demagogues" by Houston [1]) introduced his bill on January 23, and a vehement debate exploded, with Northern Whigs leading the attack. Houston had no opportunity to address his colleagues until mid-February, but then, in a passionate, prescient, two-day speech, he limned the manifold dangers posed by the bill. First, the territories had virtually no white population as yet, but the Indians would soon be brutally swept away. "They are human beings," he cried out to an unimpressed audience accustomed to his humanitarian tirades. More important, however, was the voiding of the Missouri Compromise, which had somewhat muted the slavery question since 1820. "Has not the Missouri Compromise been of great benefit to the Country?" he asked, noting that it had kept the slavery crisis confined to verbal rather than physical exchanges. "I deem it essential to the preservation of the Union, and to the very existence of the South. It has heretofore operated as a wall of fire to us. . . . Repeal it, and you are putting the Knife to the throat of the South, and it *will* be drawn" by Northern radicals. The slavery issue would be resurrected far more vehemently. He pleaded with the Democratic party to "resist all attempts at renewing, in Congress or out of it, the agitation of the slavery issue." [2] He feared the party of Jackson would permanently split, permitting a radical party to rise to power. His clairvoyance, ignored at the time, was remarkable.

It was a magnificent speech, and despite its length, no senator was bored by it. Unfortunately, Houston's words fell on ears tuned to a different frequency, and upon minds long since made up. Only one other Southern senator, John Bell of Tennessee, opposed the bill, for he too intuited its implications. [3] He and Houston were almost cast out of the Democratic party, and the latter was savagely denounced by the evolving Texas state machine.

Notwithstanding his critics, Houston again spoke against the bill on March 3, noting that "the extremes of the Abolitionists and secession parties had become Siamese Twins." He thundered, "Depend upon it, Mr. President . . . it will convulse the Country from Maine to the Rio Grande. The South has not asked for it. I as the most Southern Senator upon this floor [hisses] . . . repudiate it." He then put the matter dramatically: "In my opinion, upon the decision which we make upon this question must depend *union or disunion.*" Most senators dismissed his harsh verdict as gross exaggeration.[4]

Houston's speeches were recognized even at the time as brilliant, although many saw them as political posturing for the next presidential race. One who heard both major speeches and considered them superb claimed that Houston had thereafter told him that he was determined to seek the presidency in 1856, because he had a duty to heal the ailing Union.[5] Ironically, John Bell was beginning to feel also that only he could save the Union.

If the speeches continued to boost his popularity in the North and West, they also continued to sorely wound him in the South, and in Texas politicians and editors flayed him mercilessly, in part because Rusk was known to favor the Douglas bill, as did all Texas members of the House. The Texas legislature was so enraged that it adopted a resolution disapproving and repudiating his position, and Houston was nearly recalled.[6]

On March 4 the bill passed in the Senate by a vote of thirty-seven to fourteen. Eased through the House, it was signed by President Pierce on May 30.[7] Houston, frightened by what Congress had unthinkingly wrought, wrote despairingly: "I see my beloved South go down in the unequal contest, in a sea of blood and smoking ruin." He openly predicted civil war.[8]

The senator was not alone in grasping the implications of the Kansas-Nebraska Act. As early as April 26, Eli Thayer and some other abolitionists founded the Emigrant Aid Society, to channel antislavery settlers into Kansas, whose climate and terrain were held to be more amenable to slavery than those of Nebraska, and the society's first settlement, Lawrence, was established later in the year. It became a race, North and South, and "squatters immediately began pouring across the border" into Kansas, the majority of them antislavery zealots. Money was raised throughout the North (and, to a lesser degree, the South) to propel settlers into Kansas. Propagandists feasted upon the "threat" of one group or another, adding substance to what Houston viewed as self-fulfilling prophecy.[9]

Angrily watching as Kansas filled with truculent Northerners, some seventeen hundred proslavery Missourians charged across the border bent on mischief. They claimed residence in Kansas only long enough to vote for a proslavery delegate to Congress and then skipped back into Missouri. The following year, when it came time to elect territorial legislators, enough heavily armed Missourians, boasted one man, "to kill every God-damned abolitionist in the territory" churned into Kansas. "Bleeding Kansas" entered its time of anarchy and agony. Two separate governments were formed; Transcendentalist preacher Henry Ward Beecher sent money and Sharps rifles ("Beecher's Bibles") from his New York pulpit; a colonel stereotypically named Jefferson Buford led four hundred armed men up from Alabama; and intermittent violence broke out as the nation looked on in horror. Abolitionist and Nullifier, each saw validation of his fears and convictions, and the blood that ran in Kansas ate away at the weak glue of union. As Houston said in a Texas speech, "I saw in that bill what the results have proved it to be—disruption and disunion." [10] He was immensely sad.

When South Carolina congressman Preston Brooks caned Massachusetts senator Charles Sumner nearly to death in the Senate over remarks on the Kansas bloodbath, the rabidity spread. Typified by messianic John Brown, who murdered settlers along Pottawatomie Creek in 1856 in the name of freedom, border ruffians, thugs, would-be guerrillas, hired guns and the simply lunatic killed hundreds, burned farms, razed villages, destroyed crops, pillaged and raped, and they proved Sam Houston a prophet. The Kansas-Nebraska Act had fatally poisoned the nation. [11]

"The Democratic Party has more wings than the beast
of Revelations."

SAM HOUSTON, 1856

As immigrants sprinted toward Kansas, Houston's presidential hopes soared, for with the chaos there, his efforts to establish himself as the National Man might well bear fruit. "San Jacinto" and Houston clubs began to spring up, chiefly in the North, with New York, Massachusetts, New Hampshire and Ohio in the vanguard. [12] People were frightened, and many turned to the man who had warned them. Mass meetings, fawning editorials and nomination by a New Hampshire citizens' committee soon followed. [13] Nor was the senator caught off guard.

Early in 1854 he had contracted with C. Edward Lester for a new, improved campaign biography, which was in bookstores early the following year. Lester unblushingly admitted to Houston that "I have used what discretion I could muster, in preparing the work." The new title, *Life of Sam Houston*, was less abrasive and egotistical, the volume was heftier and it was now laced with Know Nothing vignettes critical of immigrants, Catholics, Jews and others. Houston was not quite ready to openly leave the Democratic party, which by now considered him persona non grata, but he let Lester tantalize the Know Nothings.[14]

Disgusted by his own party, he was also disappointed by the waning Whigs and repulsed by the Free Soil and evolving Republican parties. Cautiously, he moved into the orbit of the dramatically expanding American party. Declaring that "we find that the Democratic Party has more wings than the beast of Revelations,"[15] the senator adopted, bit by bit, the major tenets of the Know Nothings, publicly advocating such ideas as a twenty-year waiting period for citizenship.[16]

This political jockeying absorbed Houston and, consequently, he spent very little time at home in 1854, again missing the birth of a child, this time their sixth, Andrew Jackson, on June 21. A few days before, Margaret, suffering the late-stage pregnancy blues as well as loneliness despite her squalling covey of children, wrote her husband a remarkably depressing letter:

> Every day I feel the want of your society more and more, and often feel as if my fortitude would fail entirely. Our children are great comforts to me, but they can not sympathize with me in my trials and sufferings. At present my health is so fine, that I feel that it is wrong to complain of anything . . . but without you, everything seems so dreary and desolate that my spirit, after looking around in vain for sympathy and congeniality, shrinks into its wonted solitude . . . I am striving hard to attain a perfect resignation to the will of God, and if it should be His blessed will to call me away at this time, I trust I shall be enabled to confide our little ones and their dear Father to His care . . . [the children] are all in fine health, and talk more about you than I ever knew them to do. Little Antoinette grows sweeter every day, and talks more and more about you. . . . Sam only remained at school two weeks, and I am now teaching him myself at home. . . . Mother's health seems declining very fast . . . she is talking every day about arranging her temporal matters for death . . . it is a mournful thing.[17]

Margaret's distant husband must have reeled. Nancy appeared to at last be dying and, although admittedly in superb health, Margaret herself expected to be snatched away by the Lord. The children were "great comforts," but their mother was disconsolate, "dreary and desolate," while Sam for some mysterious reason had abandoned or been expelled from school. Margaret felt it necessary to assume the added burden of teaching him herself, while all their progeny gabbled incessantly about their absent father!

Margaret was not the only person to feel the effects of Houston's absence and neglect, for if he was not at home in Texas, he was often absent from his Senate seat as well. The lure of the White House thrust him onto the speaker's circuit, and he gave dozens of speeches throughout the North. His colleague Rusk bitterly complained of his prolonged absences, noting that "Houston does little else but electioneer for the Presidency and as usual the work falls on me."[18]

Adding to Houston's burdens was a spate of nasty attacks on him from his dedicated detractors, who were like lampreys to his shark. Prompted by his presidential ambitions, such men as Green and former commodore Moore fired double-shotted salvos at the Texan. Both in and out of the Senate, he defended himself, launching into an odd series of rambling speeches lauding his actions while lambasting his assailants. There must have been dazed stares in the Senate as he droned on about his history and that of Texas, and Moore's "Contumacy," which, according to him, was "unparalleled in history."[19] Carping at Moore, Green and company, while the Union shuddered and shook from gunfire in Bleeding Kansas, he did not appear the National Man.

By late October, the senator was again at Independence, acquainting himself with his rotund son, Andrew Jackson, and reacquainting himself with the rest of his clan. One evening, to Margaret's pleasant surprise and relief, he made a quiet profession of faith to her, the best news she could have hoped for.[20] The very next morning, a chance encounter with Baptist brother George W. Baines led him to ask for formal baptism into the faith. Margaret's pastor, Reverend Rufus Burleson, was happy to oblige, and proudly readied his unique, coffin-shaped baptismal font for the distinguished convert.[21]

On the appointed day, a very chilly, blustery November 19, Burleson was shocked to find his baptismal device vandalized. Because of this Devil's work, the venue was changed to a nearby stream, and in the presence of hundreds of the faithful as well as his beaming wife, Sam

Houston and the reverend immersed themselves in the icy water. According to one witness, when they emerged they "looked to me like they were about to freeze to death, as their teeth were chattering" audibly.[22]

One of Margaret's consuming worries was no more, and Houston's letters to his children in succeeding years make it clear that his conversion was not cosmetic. He had at last come into the fold. Perhaps to underscore his conversion, he donated three hundred of his scarce dollars to Baylor University for the education of future ministers.[23]

"Have not Catholics cursed and threatened us?"

SAM HOUSTON, 1855

As Sam Houston rattled once more toward Washington in the waning weeks of 1854, two new, dynamic political parties were striking sparks in the public awareness. The newest, the Republican party, had been founded only in July. Its early members were Whigs abandoning their sinking political ship, distempered Free Soilers who had lost faith in the effectiveness of their small party, and Northern Democrats willing to cede the party mantle to the strident Southern radicals. Considering the Kansas-Nebraska Act a sellout, Republicans shared an antipathy to slavery. So rapidly did the party grow that within two years it was set to challenge the Democrats on the national plane, its chosen standard-bearer Benton's charismatic and erratic son-in-law, explorer John C. Frémont.

The Know Nothings, who adopted the patriotic name American party in 1855, also surged in numbers and influence, capturing state after state. However, the party's curious determination to ignore the issue of slavery became a stone around its collective neck. In the North, silence was interpreted as support for the peculiar institution. Things had gone too far for a party to feign indifference to the national tripwire, especially as mayhem in Kansas daily generated headlined martyrs. As a result of Know Nothing silence concerning slavery, it never became a national party.

But Houston was still casting about for the presidency, adding strong "Americanist" speeches to his campaign biography.[24] In March he attacked the "polluting" effects of large-scale immigration. He declared that half a million were arriving from Europe each year, "sent here by European governments . . . vessels are chartered to convey paupers and criminals from European prisons and poorhouses to this Country," many of them Catholic. Further, almost all the immigrants, "violently opposed to slavery," went to the Northern states, daily augmenting the North's domination of Congress. It was "to the interest of the South to extend the period of naturalization" and restrict future immigration.[25]

Lester, who released his new biography to the public in March, worked hard to have his subject nominated by the American party. The Texan sent Lester "lists of individuals and newspapers" throughout the country known to be friendly to him, and the publicist worked through those to promote Houston's candidacy.[26]

Speaking at an American party barbecue at Austin in late 1855, Houston asserted that "the Democratic Party . . . have got into a prodigious pickle" over the issue of slavery, and was ignoring other crucial problems, such as immigration. There, he finally left the political closet: "I adopt and admire the principles of the American Party . . . it is the only party in my opinion whose principles will maintain the perpetuity of our free institutions." He was now committed.

Criticizing Pierce and his cabinet—composed of disharmonious Nullifiers, abolitionists, and women's rights crusaders—he moved on to tackle the pope. Sensitive to burgeoning anti-Catholicism, he disclaimed bigotry, but then—the former Mexican Catholic—he declared, "I will resist the political influence of Pope or Priest. Have not Catholics cursed and threatened us?" Mexico lay supine in chaos "because priestcraft rules, and civil liberty is subordinate. There is no freedom where the Catholic Church predominates. Do even Catholics in our own Country enjoy the fullest Liberty?" Of course not, for they were oppressed by their priesthood, which in turn was manipulated by a shadowy, ermine-draped figure in Rome.[27]

The senator was now aligned, at least verbally, with the Know Nothings. In 1855 and 1856 he coursed the speaker's circuit, flailing away at the other parties, writing that "the Whig party lives only in the memory of its great name . . . [while the Democratic party] although it retains the *name of democracy* has no memories to which the present organization can refer without a blush of shame," and the Republican party was sectional and small-minded. He accordingly repudiated them and promised to campaign for the Know Nothings.[28] Strangely, beyond his powerful stump speeches he did little to gain the party's nomination, announcing well in advance that he would not attend its national convention. Many correctly saw this as political suicide. Nonetheless, in early 1856, shortly before the party convention in Philadelphia, he wrote Margaret that he had visited the White House: "Yesterday I was there, and told the doorkeeper that he must keep the House in good order, as I might have to take it for the next four years."[29] Margaret was not amused.

When the American party convention met in late February it did not consider Houston a serious candidate. On the first ballot he received a few votes, but the party decided instead on former president Fillmore, and Houston's old friend Andrew Jackson Donelson as running mate.

Houston was less than enthusiastic. "The masses were for no one else but me," he imaginatively lamented, and he blamed the party machine for opting for a more pliable standard-bearer. "I assure you, I was glad that I was not nominated by such an incongruous Body," he insisted. He swore that he would eschew all political conventions and appear before the American voters as a solitary man, a "National Candidate" with no platform save "the Union & the Constitution."* As for Fillmore and Donelson, he could not support the former, and he had personally told the latter, "kindly & calmly, that I would not speak in behalf of the Ticket." In any case, he could not favor the party platform, for it avoided the major issues.

Despite his protestations, Houston did reluctantly campaign for the American party ticket, because the Republican candidate was the inflammatory abolitionist Frémont, while the Democrats went with James Buchanan, a man Houston knew and liked, but believed would lose, permitting a Republican victory by default. That the small Whig convention endorsed Fillmore, and that their endorsement made the candidate articulate a slightly stronger commitment to save the Union, also made campaigning more palatable.[30]

During the campaign Houston often invoked Jackson's memory, insisting that he had never deviated from his mentor's policies, and claimed that Jackson had wanted all Americans "a little *more* American-

---

* Coincidentally, John Bell would sound the same slogan in the election of 1860.

ized." To one political skeptic he wrote that he and the American party were not antiforeign, but simply nationalistic: "All faithful naturalized citizens, though of foreign birth, who can not be controlled by any foreign allegiance, can come forward to their support as national men."[31]

No matter this professed liberality, the election result was a foregone conclusion, and the American party, "whose tenets were so abhorrent to the ideas of free government,"[32] went spiraling down to defeat, never to rise again in the national arena. While many Americans did indeed fear they would be submerged in a riptide of immigration, and many detested Catholics, the reaction of the vast majority to Fillmore was described as "almost cosmic boredom."[33] Buchanan and John C. Breckinridge led the Democratic party to victory on November 4. The only unsettling surprise was the extremely strong showing of Frémont and the fledgling Republican party. They did awesomely well, garnering 1,335,264 popular votes (114 electoral) to the Democrats' 1,838,169 (174), and the Whig/American party's 874,534. A wave of fear passed through the South, for two new, ideological parties had taken over 54 percent of the votes cast.

"I am the only one who keeps cool.

Others evince passion."

SAM HOUSTON, 1856

In 1855 and 1856, Sam Houston was home even more rarely than before and Margaret, aghast at his putative presidential bid, languished. Complicating her moods was a move from Independence back to Huntsville. She had been happiest at Independence, and when she left that town she pined for that "Sweet Village! Thou loveliest spot on earth to me."[34] No matter, Houston sold one home and bought another at Huntsville, and the family moved.

All Margaret heard from her spouse was politics, and while for some months the senator was optimistic about his presidential chances, she was not. He wrote her in this period that "they are sanguine that I will be nominated" by the American party, and "the general if not universal sentiment is if I am nominated, I will easily beat" any other candidate. But, he continued, "I have no clique, nor have I made any promises of place or favor," a proper moral stand that might be his undoing. In the same letter he confided that "dear Love, I think more, and much more intensely about you, than I do about the Presidency, or any thing else in this world. Our young Barbarians come in for a share in my thoughts, and affections" as well. But Margaret, he sought to reassure her, was paramount in his dreams. He promised that "I will leave (if nothing else) to my family an unsullied escutcheon. I know my Love, you would prize this far above place or power."[35] In fact, that escutcheon was nearly all he did leave his family. Another letter, written in the Senate a few months later, assured her that "I am the only one who keeps cool. Others evince passion."[36] Exactly what Margaret was to make of this is unclear. She was steeped in mordancy during his prolonged absence, as obsessed with death as her mother, during one of the most brutally severe winters on record. She wrote the senator, "Some dark cloud hung over me . . . threatening to fall upon me and extinguish the feeble light of my soul."[37]

Sensing his wife's excruciating loneliness, Houston began writing her almost daily, short notes written at his Senate seat. One of these may have caused Margaret to bridle. "I have to write to you or listen to persons in whom I feel little interest." Margaret, apparently, was the lesser of two evils! At about the same time, he informed his wife that he had finally met Harriet Beecher Stowe, who was still basking in the glow of *Uncle Tom's Cabin* fame. "She is certainly a hard object to look on" was his single observation.[38]

Despite his seemingly endless absences and usually dispassionate correspondence with Margaret, the senator was wont to think of himself as the quintessential family man. He wrote a friend at this time:

> Just think of the little Addendas, no less than six little Houstons to dandle on my knees, & kiss them and call them dear Children. Is not this worth more than all the honors, now a days. . . . About the 23rd of April I have to visit my Dear Wife Maggie, & the brats, so you see, by Heaven's blessing, I have abundant resources of happiness.[39]

When she learned of his impending visit, she wrote him a prescriptive letter of her own. She had had quite enough of Houston's absences and excuses. "I believe it is wrong for us to be separated as much as we are, and if we should be spared to meet, I intend to preach you a perfect sermon on the subject." She had just recovered from another ill-defined malady and recounted her agonies and fears in full. She had, in fact, also experienced another conversion, and explained that though she had embraced God while young, "I wandered far, far away from the Cross," and since, "have never passed a day of my life without sin." During her recent illness, she wrote, the specter of death brought on "new birth."[40]

In Huntsville, Margaret busied herself planting a fairly elaborate garden, filled with cape jasmine, iris, phlox, pinks, ivy from Washington's tomb, and clover seeds her husband had sent from the capital.[41] She probably read and reread one short letter from the senator that included what she considered the year's best news. He would take his first communion at Washington's E Street Baptist Church in early March. She may have wondered why this all-important symbolic event would take place so far from the woman who led him into the fold.

"The true field for the extension of slavery is in Central America."

WILLIAM WALKER, 1856

In Washington, Houston continued to politick, boosting his popularity in the North while diminishing it in the South, consistently voting against what he felt to be wasteful military expenditures and railing loudly against any expansion of the army, an institution he disdained, considered antidemocratic and, seemingly, feared. He scored his colleagues for lavishing millions on the army, when "$300,000 judiciously expended would secure peace with every Indian tribe on the Continent."[42] He fought "the naval and military academies, as . . . nurseries of favoritism."[43] Fearing a large army officered by elitists, he preferred reliance on armed citizens for defense.

His support in Texas had by now eroded to bare bedrock, and in the late summer of 1856 some stage drivers in the state even refused to let him on board![44] His stand on the Kansas-Nebraska Act, his rejection of the Democratic party, his espousal of Know Nothingism, and his open courting of the Northern electorate, all extinguished his appeal to most Texans. His colleague Rusk, on the other hand, was held in great esteem, and as a "moderate" elder statesman, was even being touted as presidential material, much to Houston's annoyance.[45] "Great without ambition and pride," in the words of Rip Ford,[46] Rusk was elected president pro tempore of the Senate in 1857, but "in a fit of despondency," committed suicide that year, apparently in grief over the death of his beloved wife.[47]

No matter the Texas antipathy, Houston found himself on the road politicking more often than at home. Rumors had reached him that the state legislature was determined to elect somebody else for the next Senate term (which would begin in 1859). Rumor very soon became fact, as that body insultingly elected his successor fully two years ahead of time! Undaunted, he decided to run for governor. That he had no party or machine backing nor any prospects of such did not deter him. He was not at all ready for Margaret's version of reflective retirement and would rely on a grass-roots, "people's" mandate.[48]

In 1856, his most enduring dream seemed to revive. Mexico, again awash in anarchy, looked vulnerable, and the Knights of the Golden Circle, especially robust in Texas, as well as certain influential individuals, such as Rip Ford, Ben McCulloch and Edward Burleson, Jr., were salivating.

The moment seemed propitious, for not only was Mexico disintegrating (Santa Anna was ousted, and with him went his relatively stabilizing influence), but William Walker appeared to be firmly in control of much of Central America. Walker, with several hundred American adventurers—many of them Knights—had seized Nicaragua, made himself president, and re-established slavery. He was certain he could "regenerate" the poor and chaotic region and was convinced that "the true field for the extension of slavery is Central America."[49] He saw himself working for the good of the South. While many in the North saw his filibuster as proof positive of the slave power conspiracy, others throughout the nation saw it as the inevitable trend of Manifest Destiny. In the event, Walker was overthrown and executed by Central American forces, but his briefly successful coup de main rekindled dreams of American expansion.

At the same time, the Indian frontier in Texas again burst into flames as the growing white population surged westward. In the autumn of 1855 Texas Rangers under Edward Burleson, Jr., had a close-range, four-hour fight with seven hundred hostiles, described by a witness as a mix of "Mexicans, Seminoles, Lipans and Muscaleros [Mescalero Apaches]." The Rangers triumphed despite poor odds thanks to their Colt revolvers, but most of the hostiles faded away to fight again. Many Texans called for finishing the job by pursuing the enemy into their Mexican sanctuaries.[50]

In February 1856, Rip Ford wrote Burleson, a major figure in the expansionist scheme, in blunt and specific terms: "If you, or McCulloch or Callahan,* would go up on the Brazos you could get money" for the invasion of Mexico. That invasion, wrote Ford, was "a political necessity—a duty we owe to Texas and the South; it has occupied my thoughts for years." He ached to emulate Houston and Burleson's own father: "Why may not others of less note secure another slice from the grasp of anarchy and place it under American control?" The time to strike was upon them, for in Mexico "everything is in confusion." Invading Mexico would gain "indemnity for the past and security for the future," and this could only be achieved by "placing the Country between the Rio Grande and the Sierra Madre under the control of Americans and by giving protection to slave property in Texas and the South."[51] Ford was a friend of Houston's, and the latter was well aware of the scheme.

* James H. Callahan, a survivor of Goliad, a Ranger and a noted Indian fighter, was killed in a clash with Indians later in the year.

FIFTEEN

Houston, Texas and the Coming of the Civil War

"I am indeed an exile, interdicted from
all that is dear."

SAM HOUSTON, 1857

Sam Houston expended barely more energy seeking the governorship than he had campaigning for the presidency. Certain that he could defuse his state's growing radical faction more effectively in Austin than in Washington, he announced that he would not seek re-election to the Senate, as if the legislature had not already decided that issue. He immediately began a laconic campaign for the governorship, expecting that his name and his place as a "Founding Father" of Texas would boost him to certain victory over the state Democratic machine.

That machine was thoroughly oiled by a clique of radicals who on May 4 nominated secessionist lieutenant governor Hardin Richard Runnels for the statehouse. To no one's surprise—certainly not Margaret's —the senator announced his own candidacy eight days later. He stumped the state that summer in a borrowed red buggy, doing what he considered a full canvass, but his campaigning was less than energetic. Since there were few concrete issues to debate (the abstraction of Union or disunion for some reason fell flat), the race quickly became personal and nasty. In a crescendo of character assassination, Houston was branded anti-Southern and a closet "Black Republican," and he salvoed back against "Nullifier" Runnels. In a single, ill-attended speech at Austin, Houston accused his Senate successor, radical L. T. Wigfall, of swindling, accused James Pinckney Henderson of forgery, accused Judge Oldham of "discreditable conduct," vilified Frank Lubbock ("that man has all the attributes of a dog save one—fidelity!"),[1] labeled Hugh McLeod and T. J. Green "arrant cowards" and pilloried Anson Jones,* former president Pierce, Stephen Douglas and a galaxy of other politicos, noting in passing that "he could find forty niggers who could make a better speech than Dick Runnels." He professed that Runnels sought "plunder," while "he [Houston] was the only Democrat having any principles." Urging the women present "to pour hot water down their husbands' backs if they should resolve to vote for" Runnels, Houston, according to one witness, presented "a melancholy picture of imbecility, vindictiveness and hate in old age." From the crowd "applause was very seldom and very feeble."[2]

The race was negative, unenlightening, and expensive. Houston, with no organization to sponsor, sustain and finance him, very nearly went bankrupt, and the election results reflected Houston's lack of a constructive platform and his habitual reluctance to share his views. For the first time in his life he lost an election, attracting only 27,500 votes to Runnels's 36,257.[3] He muttered darkly again about retirement from the dirty game of politics, a game, he said, that was rigged against the interests of the people. As he muttered, however, he was slyly beginning his 1859 campaign, his watchword and motto "Union."

The senator's wounds acted up severely in 1857,[4] and his gait had deteriorated into a shambling limp. Relations with Margaret—again pregnant—changed not a jot, and for the first time she lamented that he had not won an election, for success would have kept him in Texas. Houston, lame duck senator, wrote her from Washington with unusual feeling at this time: "When I reflect on the distance from this to where you are and our flock, I feel that I am indeed an exile, interdicted from all that is dear to me on earth." In short, he marveled, "You have around you many of the pleasures which I so much desire." In one letter at this time he spoke not only of returning home, but also of his interest in helping shape the piety of his progeny to "advance our children in all that is useful and excellent in life."[5]

The outgoing senator did yeoman service for a nation that was visibly coming apart. Early in the year, militant abolitionist William Lloyd

---

* Jones joined a long list of noteworthy Texan suicides in 1858.

Garrison pronounced that there could be no compromise on the "moral" issue of slavery. It would be better if the South made good on its threats to secede.* "No Union with slaveholders" was his angry battle cry, and it was soon adopted by thousands, including many leading intellectuals of the North.[6] Garrison was to experience more anguish later in the year, for in *Dred Scott* v. *Sandford,* the Supreme Court decreed that slaves could not testify in court, and that territories could do as they pleased concerning slavery.

In the South there was also a hardening of an already ossified position, because of bellicose Northern public opinion and the continued violence in Kansas. And King Cotton was firmly on his throne. The South was producing prodigious quantities of a raw material for which there appeared to be an ungluttable market. That product constituted about one-third of the value of all American exports over the years 1820–1850 and produced a torrent of wealth. The figures were startling; average annual exports showed an increase from 729,524,000 pounds (1846–1850) to 1,383,711,200 (1856–1860).[7]

Cotton fueled the Southern economy, and Southern radicals perceived a certain leverage in both the North and the wider world. British and French textile mills depended almost entirely upon American cotton, and those countries might recognize an independent Southern nation. Clout with Europe was matched, the radicals thought, by clout with the North. After all, a key component in the nascent American industrial revolution was the network of textile mills in New England. Without cotton the mills would close and the economy would collapse. Southern radicals had an exaggerated view of their section's power, but they did agree with Garrison on one matter: the formation of a distinct Southern nation. Only independence, said men such as Jefferson Davis and Hardin Runnels, would protect the South's institutions and way of life. As Houston had foreseen, the "Ultras," North and South, were now working to the same end.

---

* It is worth noting that among independent Latin American nations, only Brazil (until 1888) permitted slavery.

"I have always denounced Filibusterism."

SAM HOUSTON, 1858

The senator, watching developments sadly during his gubernatorial campaign, simultaneously attempted to meet his Senate duties. He again voted against increased military appropriations, even though the United States, with a population of over thirty million, maintained a minuscule army of some fifteen thousand officers and men. His resistance to military expansion was consistent, but 1857 demonstrated a need for a larger army, for while the Indians were for the most part quiescent, Utah's Mormons were not. The Latter-day Saints were behaving as a separate people, flaunting their "social peculiarities," such as polygamy, ignoring laws that offended them, and forging a state within a state, Deseret.[8]

By 1857 it appeared that the Mormons had informally seceded from the Union, and when President Buchanan felt that he had to replace Brigham Young as territorial governor, he was openly defied. The "Mormon War" of 1857 was not much of a conflict, but it graphically demonstrated how ill-prepared the United States Army was.

Under an executive order, Colonel Albert Sidney Johnston managed to collect a few regiments and, after months of delay awaiting supplies, finally moved them to Utah. Luckily, the Mormons did not fight, for they might have won, and thoughtful observers, including Houston, knew it. By year's end Utah was tranquil, if sullen, and the Mormon War's chief impact was to prove that a transcontinental railroad would be crucial to national security.[9]

In 1858 Sam Houston continued his lifelong dreams. His quest for the statehouse was partly motivated by his certainty that the South would secede. Perhaps he could keep Texas in the Union, or at least return it to independence, which might constitute neutrality in a future civil war. With Texas independent he could attempt to realize his oldest dream; indeed, the lure of Mexico might be manipulated to help create an independent Texas. Certainly the Texas of 1858 was viable, with six hundred thousand people, a diversified and vibrant economy and few potential enemies. It was far stronger than the republic had been in 1844, when Houston suggested expanding it by force, should annexation fail.

As the new year opened, the senator was again in his seat, whittling absent-mindedly but listening closely to the debates. He wrote Margaret in January that he had but one purpose in Washington: "I am for UNION and OUR union as it is!!!" [10]

He also elaborated upon his dream. While adamantly opposed to a sizeable army, on February 15 he introduced the ultimate and most grandiose version of his vision: "A Resolution Proposing a Protectorate over Mexico and Central America." Reborn was the idea he had shared with Santa Anna, Captain Elliot, Lieutenant Maury and many others. The flag—Lone Star or Stars and Stripes—should fly over the fabled Isthmus of Darien. [11] Responding to inevitable charges of "adventurism," he calmly replied that "I have always denounced Filibusterism. . . . This resolution is not offered with a view to extending our dominion [but] with a view of improving our Neighborhood." He meant the word "Protectorate" to be interpreted literally; it was the duty of the United States to "protect" revolution-gutted Mexico, for it clearly could not protect itself. Just how Central America became part of the scheme is not so clear. [12] Although the senators knew that Buchanan favored a similar plan, they found the resolution too much to handle, especially in view of its implications concerning slavery, and it was packed off to die in committee. [13]

Despite his disclaimers, an acquaintance of the senator remarked that "Houston, according to an account given by his warmest friends, was, *in principle,* a filibuster." [14] In any case, he pressed the protectorate idea, his old dream in modern garb, perhaps to divert attention from slavery-related questions and dangers. Apparently lost on him was the contradiction that a Mexican "adventure" would exacerbate the slavery issue, and at the same time make army expansion inevitable.

On March 1 he introduced a bill to provide for organization of, and federal pay for, a regiment of mounted Texas Volunteers (Rangers) to protect the state's frontier. He also sought authorization for the president to call up when necessary four more such regiments into federal service. [15] Some senators saw this as a ploy to obviate the need to expand the Regular Army, but others saw a more sinister plan. Houston had been hinting broadly that if the United States did nothing to settle the

Mexico question, Texas might. Many felt that federal funding, including modern arms and supplies, for this proposed regiment was part of Houston's larger design, and the bill was shunted aside.[16]

While the senator was angered by such cavalier treatment of his bills and resolutions, news from Texas rankled yet more. The state legislature passed a joint resolution on March 9, permitting the governor to call for election of special delegates to meet with other Southern designates should a sectional convention be called to discuss events in Kansas.[17] This was precisely the type of "disunionism" Houston detested and feared. Texas was still regarded as a "Moderate" state, but if its legislature could pass such a resolution, moderation was flagging.

So Houston returned to the attack, fighting army growth while arguing for expansion into Mexico. On the first of April he ruffled Jefferson Davis's feathers in a speech against the "New Regiments" Bill to expand the army, declaiming that he saw no need for more regiments, and that in any case, he did not want any further army units sent to Texas. Largely infantry, they were useless against Comanches, Apaches and Mexican banditti. Further, the few cavalry units were mounted on grain-fed horses that could not subsist off the local grass. Thus, said the senator, regular troops on the frontier "are as useless as so many post oak trees." He also backhanded the officer corps, which in his view "are now becoming sufficiently numerous to form a privileged class in society, and that is never favorable to the perpetuity of free institutions."[18] Some must have wondered how he could argue for absorption of Mexico with an army he averred was not even capable of guarding the existing frontier of Texas![19]

"I cannot control the destiny of this Country."

SAM HOUSTON, 1858

Shortly after fulminating against the New Regiments Bill, the Texan raised the Mexico question anew, assuring his colleagues that a force of five thousand men (his projected five regiments of Texas Volunteers?)

could pacify that benighted land and provide internal order and efficient administration. "The protectorate must be self-protecting—the expense incident to it defrayed by the protected. The general Government of Mexico could probably be administered, taking a term of ten years, for $6,000,000," a sum that could easily be repaid by Mexican customs revenues. Reminding his audience that of all 261 members of Congress only Sam Houston had served when Monroe articulated his famous "Doctrine," he asserted that European nations would soon control Mexico should the United States fail to act.[20] Again, his prescience was not to be appreciated until the French moved in 1862 to take advantage of yet another Mexican upheaval. Although his speech was front-page newspaper copy and well-received in Texas, it drew little applause in the Senate.[21]

Just two days after that speech, Houston despondently wrote some troubled lines to his nearly full-term wife: "I cannot control the destiny of this Country," he scrawled bitterly, but, "were I its *ruler,* I could rule it well."[22]

"Ma would have written but she felt too unwell."

NANNIE HOUSTON, 1858

Throughout the spring of 1858, Houston also advocated a southern transcontinental railroad and a Homestead Bill to stimulate settlement of the West, and at night he wrote frequently to his faraway family. He admonished Sam to adopt "practical" studies rather than waste his time on art, Latin or Greek. And the study of human nature, he told his son, was far more valuable than the study of mathematics.[23] To daughters Maggie and Nannie he counseled patience and even temper. "By watching ourselves we can guard against bursts of passion," he wrote from experience. Not only did displays of anger offend others and solve no problems, but "anger gives to the countenance a harsh and unamiable cast, and causes the features to become coarser." That would be tragic for such fine-looking young ladies as the senator's daughters.[24]

Margaret, again ill during her seventh pregnancy, wrote her husband only infrequently. Nancy, still awaiting her imminent demise, had taken her special coffin and "stood it up in the closet of her bedroom," bizarre solace for the old woman, but surely no comfort for her lonely daughter.[25] No wonder that Nannie, now twelve, wrote her father a letter in April, pleading that he return as soon as possible: "Do make haste, won't you?" The senator was needed at home, and his wife's unwonted silence must have concerned him. Nannie's postscript simply informed him that "Ma would have written but she felt too unwell to do so."[26]

On May 17, Houston wrote Margaret about the tension he felt, which in turn had affected his health. "I had a fearful attack of nightmares last night, never suffered so much in all my life from the same." He wrote again the following day, admitting illness and that "I have for some time purposed getting bled," a practice he often resorted to.[27] A week later, on May 25, William (Willie) Rogers Houston was born, without complications, erroneously described as a "pale little cripple" by his father upon his return to Texas.[28]

The senator drenched his wife in more bad news. Not only would he campaign for governor when he came back, but attendant expenses, added to debts run up in his 1857 campaign, meant a major change in their scarcely opulent family lifestyle. Hence the Houstons' expanded house at Huntsville was sold to pay the senator's obligations, and the house at Independence rented out, leaving only the modest residence at Cedar Point, far from Nancy and her metal coffin.[29] Margaret bore all this with equanimity and wished him well in his bid.

In the Senate, Houston would not permit his Mexico vision to die a dignified death, but continually exhumed it. On April 30 he made a long "protectorate" speech, in late May "a motion to take a vote on the Mexican Protectorate Resolution," which failed, and on June 2 a strong speech "Concerning a Mexican Protectorate," which encountered only bored tolerance from his colleagues.[30]

"I had not the gratification of sitting by her."

SAM HOUSTON, 1858

Back in Texas only in July, Houston was constantly canvassing the state, advocating Union, defense of the Texas frontier, a Texas-spanning Pacific railroad and, of course, a protectorate over Mexico, all things most Texans wanted to hear. With such a program to offer the voters, it was less necessary to malign his opponent's character.[31]

While he was stumping Texas, his feisty foe, Mirabeau Buonaparte Lamar, was in the steamy jungles of Nicaragua, which had been recently pried from the dead hand of William Walker. Lamar, who had applied to President Buchanan for a diplomatic posting, had been sent to the unstable, Yanqui-hating nation, and he was soon fuming with frustration. Speaking openly about the wisdom of an American protectorate, Lamar shattered diplomatic etiquette. He even filed an official protest against the host nation's government, harshly criticizing "the deep malignity and lying propensities of this miserable race of people."[32] Using rhetoric he normally reserved for Houston, Lamar for once saw eye to eye with him.

Not long after Lamar's "protest" from the Central America he loathed yet lusted to acquire, Houston, at a campaign rally, pushed the protectorate idea upon a receptive audience. On this occasion he admitted frankly that he himself "might be willing to lead a filibuster," but doubted that his age would permit it.[33] He had found an issue that ignored party and ideology and avoided the fighting words of Union and disunion. Perhaps he could tighten the fraying bonds holding the United States together with his dream of expansion?

While the aspirant was canvassing Texas, the famous Lincoln-Douglas debates began in Illinois, and in the autumn off-year elections, the still infant Republican party made impressive gains. Within a year it would outnumber the Democratic party in the House and have twenty-six men in the Senate to the thirty-eight Democrats and two lonely Know Nothings.[34] To Southerners, there was grim handwriting on the walls of Congress before the year ended.

By the time the fall election results were tallied, Houston was for the last time on the road to Washington, leaving behind a family he understood but superficially and a spouse again bedridden by illness. Guilt surfaced in his letters, as he wrote to Maggie. "I was much distressed to hear that your Dear Ma was not well . . . I feel pained . . . that I had not the gratification of sitting by her every moment of her illness, and waiting upon her." But, "It has been otherwise ordained by Providence. . . . Dear Daughter, you ask me to come home. . . . Every hour that I pass from home, I regard as a blank in my existence," but national crises required him to sacrifice this pleasure.[35]

"Life's sand is running fast and is almost out."

SAM HOUSTON, 1859

In 1859 Houston's plans and speeches grew more concrete. In January he alluded to a curious scheme, backed by British capital, in which he would play a central role. The British, wishing to protect large investments in a Mexico torn by the destructive War of the Reform (a nationwide civil bloodbath), would finance a huge filibuster to pacify Mexico.[36] In a speech that month in which British "interests" were again mentioned, Houston told his fellow senators that "I think it very probable that our extreme Southern border will [soon] extend to the city of Mexico."[37] The speech's context indicates that he was referring to the Texas border, not that of the United States.

The times again appeared opportune, for Mexico was tearing itself apart. The president, in his annual message to Congress, actively pushed for American occupation of the southern republic, like Houston, citing the Monroe Doctrine. Mexico, according to Buchanan, was "a wreck upon the ocean, drifting about as she is, impelled by different factions." Rhetorically, he asked, "Shall we not extend to her a helping hand to save her? If we do not, it would not be surprising should some other nation undertake the task, and thus force us to interfere at last."[38] Nationally, there was rising interest in expansion to the south, in part because of the president's lead. It was known that he coveted Cuba also, and prominent figures such as Florida senator Stephen Mallory were openly urging acquisition of the Pearl of the Antilles.[39] Frederick Law Olmsted, traveling in Texas, noted talk there of making Baja California into a new slave state as well.[40]

The lame duck clung to the vision—and politically acceptable project —of expansion with great tenacity, and also to the southern transcontinental railroad, on which he spoke in the Senate three times in January alone. Both issues were popular and bipartisan, and while he had long boosted both, it appears that he now stressed them for political reasons, for he needed issues that would find wide approval in the South, and in Texas.[41]

"My Dear Daughter [Maggie] how anxious I am to be at home, and see your Dear Mother, and all of you young ones," he wrote early in the year, but seven months later he was writing the same words.[42] To his wife, who knew that he was campaigning for the governorship while planning an invasion of Mexico, he unblushingly promised to at last retire—"I can, and if spared, I will throw off the cares of politics, for I cannot control them!"[43]

The capital years were at an end, and the Capitol's janitors would no longer face mounds of Sam Houston's whittling debris. Thirteen years in the Senate had made the Texan friends as well as enemies, and the *Washington Evening Star* eulogized a man it had rarely agreed with: "No other public man ever made more, or more sincere, friends here, nor was severance of a gentleman's connection with American public affairs ever more seriously regretted." Truly a scarce commodity in the 1850s, a National Man was, sadly for the country, returning to his state.[44] The effusive goodbyes cheered him a great deal, no matter their source, whether an editorial, a Senate page—"Sam Houston was one of the gentlest and most kindly natures I have ever known . . . a gallant gentleman"[45]—or a political adversary. He proudly wrote Maggie in July that "I got letters expressive of regrets at my going into private [life] from thousands I met, and indeed many to whom I have been politically opposed. . . . It is gratifying for me to know that this far my life has not been spent in vain."[46] He was already an American legend. Now it was time for the outgoing senator to return to Texas, make another bid for governor and try his hand at stock raising: "I hope to find it more profitable" than politics, wrote the famous man whom fortune had so long eluded.[47]

It was in the summer of 1859, embracing "the cares of politics" he had promised to cast off, that Houston gave his only gubernatorial campaign speech. It was a memorable one, rasped out in muggy Nacogdoches on July 9, and it touched every base. Responding to Southern radicals who called for the relegalization of the slave trade, Houston warned that "the South will be deluged by barbarians," the value of slaves would decrease, the cost of wage labor would fall to the point that whites could not compete and it would enrage the North and increase the odds of civil war. He then praised President Buchanan as "an honest man . . . a patriot," because he had urged intervention in Mexico, and "has he not advocated the acquisition of Cuba?" But he sternly warned the crowd that the United States was becoming like poor, benighted Mexico, with rival "chieftains in every state in the Union." Look at Mexico, he demanded, "her people mad with anarchy and misrule," a nation that "will disgrace the character of this century, by bloodshed, debauchery, and riot." The United States should immediately establish its protectorate, because "the infusion of American energy would develop her incalculable stores of wealth." Mexico, he declared, was destined for "incorporation into our Union. . . . Avoid the result as we may, it is bound to come."

Although Mexico was a sorry spectacle, the United States, said the candidate, might face even worse. "Mark me, the day that produces a dissolution of this Confederacy will be written in history in the blood of humanity." The Union, he repeatedly hammered, must be preserved, for "it is our only ark of safety." After reiterating his standard positions, he oddly confessed the frailties of his advanced age. Perhaps unique in a campaign speech was his admission that "life's sand is running fast and is almost out," hardly a qualification for political office! [48]

That steamy day in Nacogdoches he warned, reassured, threatened and cajoled. His stand for the Union mollified many German-Texans who were concerned by his flirtation with the American party, while the average Texan favored frontier protection and intervention in Mexico. This was a candidate on the correct side of the major issues. [49] It was a well-thought-out speech, although he denied it, writing disingenuously that he had spoken at Nacogdoches only "as I was there purchasing sheep & cattle." [50]

The August election was a mirror image of that of 1857, this time with Houston defeating Runnels by a vote of 36,257 to 27,500. Margaret must have felt relieved, for her husband would at last remain in

Texas.[51] Unionists throughout the nation shared her relief. The nation just might remain whole if more such moderate, national men would step forward.[52]

"Cortina did not seem to have a very well-defined idea
of the rights of property."

RIP FORD, 1859

Trouble was brewing in Texas; trouble that Sam Houston would endeavor to manipulate to his own—and his state's—ends.

By September, Juan "Cheno" Nepomuceno Cortina (or Cortinas) was on the warpath. Cortina had been a minor-league border scourge and bandit in both nations for years, but in mid-1859 his charisma and anti-Anglo disposition made him a magnet for disaffected Tejanos, Mexican ne'er-do-wells and assorted border thugs. Described by Rip Ford as "of medium size, with regular features, and a rather pleasing countenance," Cortina was also "fearless, self-possessed, and cunning."[53] By October he was leading five hundred or more mounted ruffians, and a large stretch of the border area was in his hands. Not a real threat to Texas, he had simply gotten out of hand, and as Ford, who fought him, recorded, "Cortina did not seem to have a very well-defined idea of the rights of property." Something, alas, would have to be done about him.[54]

On September 28, Cheno and a large mob of his "troops" descended on Brownsville like a plague of locusts, seizing the town to the cry of "Death to all Americans!"[55] The so-called "Cortina War" had commenced. Word flashed through Texas telegraph lines of what sounded like, but was not, a massacre. John S. Campbell, in a panicky letter to his brother, claimed that Brownsville and Corpus Christi had fallen to the bandit horde, their citizens butchered.[56] In reality, Corpus Christi was not even threatened, and only a handful of civilians were killed at Brownsville, which was soon abandoned by the banditti. But Texans were alarmed, all the more so when Ranger units came off second best in a number of minor shoot-outs with Cheno's gang.[57]

On November 23 Cortina issued a rather odd "Proclamation" insisting that he was a man of peace—most certainly not a bandit—and that he wished only to safeguard the rights and dignity of the Tejano community. The proclamation, issued as if he were governor, was rational, not at all threatening, but contained an odd sentence: "The Mexicans of Texas repose their lot under the good sentiments of the governor elect of the State, General Houston."[58]

Houston, for his part, was not amused by Cortina's endorsement. He sounded the alarm, blew the bandit raid out of proportion, and sowed fears that Cheno might be planning to create a Mexican state within Texas. In response, the frustrated Rangers were at last joined by army units under Major Samuel P. Heintzelman, and together they swept after Cortina along the Rio Grande. After a series of minor brushes, the Rangers and some army troops crossed into Mexico, and on December 6, in a brisk fight, with minimal losses, killed sixty raiders of an estimated six hundred.[59]

Cortina had not been with his "army," and while he again protested his desire for peace and harmony, he was soon raiding once more, blissfully unaware that he was now a building block in the edifice of Houston's plans to intervene in Mexico.[60] The governor, who as senator had done his best to keep the United States Army small, now complained loudly that it was far too small to protect his state. If, as Ford wrote with hyperbole, "One of Cortina's projects . . . was the reconquest of Texas," one of Houston's projects was surely the conquest of all or much of Mexico![61]

The Indians were also restive, and although their raiding was minor, it too was exaggerated by Houston. John Campbell noted that hostile bands were spotted near Austin that autumn, and he reported Texans' fears that if the Indians on reservations joined the Comanches, all hell would break loose.[62]

"Poor little fellow, he cries for you so piteously."

MARGARET HOUSTON, 1859

On December 21, 1859, while Cortina was causing trouble along the Rio Grande, Sam Houston became governor of Texas. Margaret was not with him in Austin, but at home at Cedar Point, ill and pregnant again.

Houston's brief inaugural speech was devoted to the twin themes of Union and defense, and he bluntly advised that if the United States could not protect Texas, he would marshal the state's resources and do so himself—using them against Mexico.[63] The human resources available, he noted, included the Rangers, Minutemen militia companies then being raised, friendly Indians and dissident Mexicans.[64]

The stage was craftily set. The governor was fixing the gaze of Texans on Mexico rather than on the deteriorating scene to the north. Tension gripped the nation in late 1859. John Brown, would-be extirpator of slavery, had taken the federal arsenal at Harpers Ferry, Virginia, with his armed insurgents in October. His admitted intent was to arm the slaves of the South and drown slaveholders in a sea of their own blood. Army troops captured the conspirators, and despite Northern protests and petitions, John Brown was hanged on December 2. His bizarre act had electrified the nation, and to the dismay of Southerners, abolitionists, including many ministers, and much of the Northern press portrayed Brown as a hero and martyr. To Southerners he was a murderer and a madman. The chasm between the sections yawned unbridgeable. When Oregon entered the Union that year, the balance in Congress tilted yet further against the South.

Houston had to turn the attention of his people toward Mexico. All he needed was money, men and the aid—or at least the indifference—of Washington, D.C.[65]

SIXTEEN

Houston and the Grand Plan
(or Two)

"I will either be rich or flat broke in one or
two years."

BEN McCULLOCH, 1859

Sam Houston's fixation on Mexico was shared by many. The Order of the Lone Star of the West, dedicated to dismembering the southern republic, was strong in Texas, and the governor was probably a member. Rip Ford, who was, recalled its supposedly secret nature and its initiation ceremony: "It was impressive and intensely unique. Its cabalistic passwords were indelibly impressed on the mind."[1] The more widespread Knights of the Golden Circle (K.G.C.s) were especially strong in the South, and many prominent Texans were members of both secret societies and ready for action.

One such man was Ben McCulloch, a blustery soul very close to the new governor, with whom he had been friends for more than two decades. Disdainful of Mexicans in general,* McCulloch was in and out of their country often. In mid-1859 he was in Sonora for some unexplained "business" and later that year, the businessman-adventurer wrote that "I have just obtained an interest in a gun which will require my personal attention this fall and winter." He announced to his mother, "I will either be rich or flat broke in one or two years."[2]

---

* McCulloch had written his mother from Mexico that "a more indolent stupid & worthless race does not exist."

Ranger, Forty-niner, and man in perpetual motion, McCulloch was a central figure in Houston's reinvigorated grand design.

When the legislature convened in January of fateful 1860, the governor pressed to settle the Mexican "issue," and demanded funding. Texas had accumulated a special university fund of one hundred thousand dollars, plus interest, and Houston wanted access to it, but not to further education. He argued that the money was desperately needed for defense, and that in any case, "the establishment of a university is in my opinion, a matter alone for the future."[3] Promptly, the legislators authorized him to draw upon the "University Fund which is to be used alone for frontier defense,"[4] and as early as January 20 he was raising and issuing orders to a large number of "Ranging Companies." He micromanaged this mobilization, detailing exactly what areas they were to patrol, and forbidding gambling, horseracing, and other frivolous pastimes. He even mandated that no "intoxicating liquors of any kind" were to be permitted within five miles of any Ranger camp![5]

He also turned to Washington, where he still had considerable influence. He wrote Secretary of State Lewis Cass, recommending Henry L. Kinney as minister to Mexico. Kinney, a fellow Texan, a veteran filibuster and wealthy rancher who had purchased land in Nicaragua in 1854, had collaborated with William Walker. He had previously been involved in abortive revolts in the north of Mexico. Cass was wise enough to pass on this highly undiplomatic choice.[6]

The governor instructed his friend Ranger Captain Edward Burleson, Jr., to take his company south of the Nueces, and "select six good Mexican guides to be regularly enrolled in your company." Other Ranger officers received similar orders. The need for six "Mexican" guides hinted strongly at his purpose.

Escalating his preparations, the governor had the legislature pass a new militia bill, which provided for thirty-two brigades, with a total strength of ten thousand.[7] At the same time, he begged Secretary of War John B. Floyd for more modern arms.* "Texas can and will, if appealed to, in thirty days be able to muster into the field ten thousand men . . . to make reclamation upon Mexico for all her wrongs. Can we hope for aid from the Federal Government?"[8] It was out in the open. Texas was asking Washington to support its quest for "reclamation."

---

* For more than three decades the federal government had allocated a certain number of new weapons to each state, to help it keep its militia respectably armed.

Floyd—like President Buchanan—was leery of the Texan's request. He felt the arrogant governor had presented him with a fait accompli. The border was unusually pacific as far as Floyd knew and Texans were already sufficiently heavily armed. What on earth was Houston really after? What did he mean that his people would act "if appealed to"? By whom? Did he really believe that Washington would unleash ten thousand angry Texans upon Mexico? Floyd was noncommittal, which prompted Houston to send a frantic telegram asserting "that the territory of Texas has been invaded," although by whom was not clear. Unless Floyd acted decisively, "Circumstances may impel a course on the part of Texas which she desires to avoid." It was hardly necessary to read between the lines; he was threatening to take his state to war on the flimsy excuse that Texas, under attack, would do so "reluctantly."[9]

At the same time, Houston received an offer from the shadowy "General" Elkanah Greer,* putative commander of the Knights of the Golden Circle, proposing a joint Texas-Knights invasion of Mexico.[10] The offer was tempting, for the Knights had substantial economic and human resources. He accepted Greer's offer on February 28, for the legislature had "adjourned without leaving me a dollar," omitting mention of the university fund.[11]

Soon, probably at Greer's orders, suspicious numbers of heavily armed men were finding their way into Texas. Major General David E. Twiggs, commanding the army's Department of Texas, became suspicious, "directing post commanders to scrutinize armed parties . . . and to arrest those discovered to be organized for any unlawful projects."[12] About the same time, Ranger James Pike met a Captain Davis, purportedly a recruiter for the Knights, who told him that his organization's purpose was "to raise a force of twelve thousand men to invade Mexico, under command of General Sam. Houston . . . to be paid by English capitalists." Chihuahua, Coahuila, Nueva Leon and Tamaulipas were to be seized and annexed. Houston himself "was not taking any public part in the matter, for State reasons, but . . . [soon] would declare his purpose." The British "were to pay the General a fabulous sum."[13]

* Other sources mention that General George Bickley was commander of the Knights.

"To do this will be the Crowning act of your life."

BEN McCULLOCH, 1860

While on the surface Davis's tale might appear fanciful, events indicate it was not. In 1859 and 1860 Houston was receiving offers of volunteers from all over the Union, as well as tenders of loans and bargain-rate arms.[14] At the same time, McCulloch was departing Washington for Texas, "as there is trouble brewing on her frontiers & I wish to participate in any war . . . Genl. Houston talks of the stirring time that there will be on the Rio Grande ere long . . . this looks like war." Happily, McCulloch demanded a piece of the action, and of the spoils.[15]

Edward Burleson, Jr., was also primed and ready for action with his Ranger company on the Rio Grande. He wrote the governor: "If there is a war with Mexico . . . I want to be ordered there. I have lived there, speak the language, know the Country and the people."[16] Houston had to restrain him from turning his Rangers loose on Mexico without orders.[17]

The project, it seemed, was finally afoot. As governor, Houston was asking Washington for arms, but not troops; armed "emigrants" were swarming into Texas; and he was courting the services of the army's new commander of the Texas frontier, Colonel Robert E. Lee, who was taken by surprise and a bit offended. In response to Houston's thinly disguised request for United States Army cooperation across the Rio Grande, he wrote the governor's emissary, Albert M. Lea, that while he was "aware of [Houston's] ability" and applauded his strong Unionism, "should military force be required to quiet our Mexican frontier," it must be ordered by Washington, "& I hope in conformity to the Constitution."

At the same time, Major Heintzelman assured Secretary Floyd that all was quiet along the Rio Grande,[18] and Lee himself wrote Houston directly to chide him for exaggerating the threat. To Lee, the case was closed, and he had, on his own authority, dismissed the Ranger companies along the Rio Grande, for, he explained, they were not needed there, and in any case he would not use them "upon the Conditions proposed," whatever those were.

Gruff Ben McCulloch, who probably never in his life marked a letter "confidential," was unequivocal in an April 6 letter to his friend the governor, providing a clear view of what was transpiring. He attempted to goad Houston, who he correctly feared was vacillating. Although he claimed that "the K.G.C.s' have for the present abandoned their intended campaign into Mexico," McCulloch urged Houston not to follow their timid lead:

> In truth no one could succeed so easily as yourself, a declaration from you to the people of Mexico, saying you came for the purpose of giving them a good Government & not to annex them or their Country to the U.S., would be believed and more than half of them would joyfully welcome you . . . if the opportunity offers and you decline to act, *others will,* and there is no telling the effusion of blood that will be saved by the use of your name, any other person than yourself will be looked upon by those ignorant people as a filabuster & will be resisted by all parties. Reflect, gravely reflect, Genl., on this subject. You need not fear wanting *men* or *money,* thousands of men and millions of money will be placed at your disposal, to do this will be the Crowning act of your life & will make your name greater than if you were President of the U.S.[19]

Through the first four months of 1860, however, instead of taking action, Houston bombarded the War Department with virtual demands for weapons to defend a frontier declared pacific by the army's ranking officers on the scene. Further, almost one-fifth of the army (2,651 officers and men) was already in Texas, with more units en route from New Mexico![20] Exactly what was the threat? Washington wanted to know.[21]

The governor responded that Cortina was still a menace (he was not), and that in the first months of 1860 Indians had killed fifty-one Texans, wounded more, taken others captive and stolen eighteen hundred horses.[22] This strained the credulity of John B. Floyd, a reasonable man worried about preserving an unraveling Union as militia drilled incessantly in many Southern states. And, at the moment, while he was depicting Indian depredations, Houston was sending his own agents among the frontier tribes. Indeed, he requested that he be appointed by Washington to administer the affairs of all Texas Indians! Secretary Floyd was not about to cooperate.[23] Perhaps he remembered Houston's scheme to use Cherokee "auxiliaries" to help free Texas from Mexico.

In March, Houston learned that some of his Ranging Companies, long on active but boring duty, were getting out of hand. But despite the want of discipline on the part of a few Rangers, Houston informed Floyd that he could "offer" 5,000 Texas volunteers (rather than accept more army troops) to pacify the frontier. All he needed in return were 2,000 percussion rifles, 1,000 new Sharps repeaters, 3,000 Colt revolvers, and a mountain of other gear: "an immediate supply of arms."[24]

Acting Secretary of War W. R. Dunkard responded that "under the law," Texas was to receive but 169 somewhat antiquated muskets in 1860. "In an emergency" this could be doubled. Even that would cost the United States Treasury $5,000 but, wrote the bemused bureaucrat, Houston's request for 3,000 state-of-the-art rifles and 3,000 pistols was outlandish, and would cost "within a fraction of $100,000." According to Dunkard, the president himself had denied Houston's request.[25] A piddling 338 muskets would hardly be adequate for Sam Houston's purpose, so the wily old governor took a new tack.

"A suspicion in the minds of some that Texas has a
covert design."

SAM HOUSTON, 1860

Aware that the president—like everyone else—believed he was planning to invade Mexico, Houston coolly reassured the War Department that such was not the case. "Tis true that since 1857 I have been written to from various parts of the United States urging me to invade Mexico . . . and assuring me that men, money, and arms would be placed at my command." But he had consistently refused to take part in such illegal undertakings, and that was why he needed arms from Washington.[26] Ironically, the same day he disclaimed responsibility, the Texas secretary of state, E. W. Cave, at his request proposed to an arms manufacturer that Texas would like to exchange five hundred old muskets "for Rifles or revolvers (Army Size)" of more recent vintage.[27] Why a businessman would contemplate accepting bad weapons for good is not clear, unless he was informed about, and sympathetic to, the plan.

Less than two weeks later, to calm the Buchanan administration, which had a surfeit of major worries, Houston formally put on the brakes, issuing a "Proclamation Declaring an Expedition to Mexico Unauthorized," asserting placidly that he had just learned that such a project might be afoot. In the proclamation—which did not specifically declare the project "illegal"—he noted that armed bands of Texans were gathering at Gonzales, apparently the jumping-off point for the expedition.[28]

Few, of course, were taken in by such protestations of ignorance and innocence. Four days later he wrote a group of concerned citizens about the inevitable protectorate over Mexico: "Politicians may shirk the issue, but destiny will force it on our people," and probably soon.[29] Yet Houston himself was displaying timidity, confusing the issue and everyone connected with it. In March, Houston's mind was almost made up for him. A mixed force of Rangers and army regulars again briefly invaded Mexico under Heintzelman. They crossed the Rio Grande on March 14 and struck deep into Mexico, in search, it was said, of Cortina and his cutthroats. They never found the border bandit, but instead blundered into and captured a Mexican army garrison. "Apologies were offered" to the Mexican government, and the disconcerted strike force withdrew, leaving Cheno highly amused.[30]

In a letter to the nervous secretary of war describing the inept south-of-the-border foray, Houston again evinced a nonchalant contradiction. He again urged Floyd to call up a regiment of Texas Rangers, because "they are excellent horsemen, accustomed to hardships, and the horses of Texas" can feed on the local grasses. Also, he charged that the army had proven "entirely useless" in containing Indian incursions, which he again willfully exaggerated. He failed to understand, he claimed transparently, why "there still seems to be a suspicion in the minds of some that Texas has a covert design upon Mexico."[31]

Belying that statement, a few weeks later he instructed Colonel Middleton T. Johnson, then commanding all Rangers, to hunt down hostile Indians "wherever they may be found and upon whatever soil."[32] Probably because of Texan military mobilization, some Indians really did go on the rampage in west Texas. Although Houston continued to exaggerate the threat, several farm families near Austin were butchered by Comanches, their deaths touching off a minor panic.[33]

Colonel Johnson, in a "Private" letter to the governor, wrote on May 16 that, sanctioned by Washington or not, he himself had organized a

Ranger regiment and would lead it wherever Houston ordered. "I have made it a little larger than I intended," he admitted, because so many were so eager to enlist. Would Houston please move ahead with his plans?[34]

"The Union is gone & civil war will follow."

BEN McCULLOCH, 1859

While Houston redreamed his dream in the first half of 1860, he also juggled family matters and his puzzling political future. With the nation so obviously dissolving, perhaps his hour had at last arrived. Such a thought may well have kept him from seizing the proferred moment to strike into Mexico, as that move would have cost him treasured Northern support, because it would have resulted in the extension of slavery. Sam Houston, the National Man, with no party and no platform standing in his way, stood unique in the paranoid American political arena of 1860, and in truth, the nation needed him.

So too did his family. Margaret, who would give birth to their eighth and last child, Temple Lea, on August 12, was almost constantly unhealthy in 1860. Nor was she ecstatic in the governor's mansion, for she considered it far too opulent (no wonder, given her rude quarters of the past two decades); its rooms disconcertingly large and airy, its furniture ostentatious.[35] In January, Houston worriedly wrote her spiritual mentor, "Brother Baines," that "Mrs. Houston has not enjoyed an hours health since she came" to Austin. Also, she had been injured when her carriage overturned, but at least her contusions were healing nicely.[36]

Teenage Sam was studying at Colonel R. T. P. Allen's Military Academy at Bastrop, and, attempting to heed his father's advice to eschew the less "useful" arts, he would try to avoid becoming what his father considered "a graduated fool."[37] The two Sam Houstons were in regular communication, swapping news and gossip, the elder salting his letters with Unionism and practical advice. At sixteen, Sam, in a

Southern military school, was certain to be inundated by the secessionist sentiment so much in vogue, and this worried his father. Stay away
from poetry, dead languages and Nullifiers, counseled the father; "I
hope you will be more profitably employed in the studies of the Military
Art,"[38] an art he hoped his son need never practice.

To boost Margaret's spirits, Houston bought her gifts, including "a
pretty match of carriage horses,"[39] and, as the receipt indicates, "one
first class Wheeler and Wilson sewing machine," fully warranted, and
costing a hefty $125.[40] In this period he purchased many gifts for his
children as well; various pets for the younger of the brood, "some ivory
Bracelets, and Thimbles" for the girls, a painting of "Caius Marius
sitting on the ruins of Carthage" and a magnificent Mexican sombrero
for his eldest son. ("It cost $4.50. It is worth it.") In several letters
Houston noted that the word "Mexico" was somewhere printed on it,
mentioning on one occasion that "if the word 'Mexico' is not in it, you
may yet have a chance to write it there" yourself.[41] The dream survived.

This flurry of letters, a large proportion of them to Sam, continued,
almost daily. On the twenty-fifth he wrote that "your Dear Ma has just
heard that the Scarlet fever is raging in Bastrop, so you can judge of her
anxiety about your safety." He implored his son to write home once a
day, "until your Ma's alarm is over."[42] He also transmitted Margaret's
folk medicine instructions to the boy. Whether the youngster wore the
noisome herbal concoction around his neck as recommended or not, he
was not felled by fever and soon received an exciting letter from his
father, who had just been sent "three fine guns and a pistol" as gifts.
When Sam returned home at the end of the term, he could have his
pick of the new weapons.

That spring, with the first settlers rolling into Idaho Territory—
certainly not a fertile field for slavery—Winchester's repeating rifle and
Darwin's *On the Origin of Species* both hit the American market. The
political skein unraveled at a faster rate, and Sam Houston began to
believe that he might have a chance at the presidency. But he demanded
it on his own terms.

The first public support for his candidacy surfaced in December
1859, when hundreds of "Houston men" rallied at Austin.[43] Two days
later a similar rally took place and appointed a committee of correspondence to write potential Houston backers throughout the nation. At
about the same time, McCulloch, in Washington, repeated a warning

he had issued the previous year, that if the Republicans won the presidency, *"The Union is gone & civil war will follow."*[44] It was this fear, this stark perception of a Republican victory, that drove many into Houston's camp. Also, other "moderates," such as the founders of the Constitutional Union party (formed in early 1860), were convinced that Houston should—and would—be their paladin.[45]

In March the governor wrote a Texas committee formed to draft him into the race. Railing that "sectionalism has been the canker-worm, which has feasted on the [Democratic] party," and decrying "the serpent of sectionalism," he offered his own strong arm to smite it. He would not, however, serve the interests of any party, nor be constricted by any platform. "A man who would consent to be a mere tool because it secured him the Presidency, does not deserve to be the head of a Nation!"[46] This cost him nothing to declaim, since no major political party was interested in his candidacy.

"We take old Sam Houston to be a low, spiteful,
cunning, hipocritical man."

SAM D. CAROTHERS, 1860

The Democratic National Convention, meeting at the epicenter of Nullification, Charleston, was a political brawl from its April 23 opening until the last gavel. Many Southern delegations, including that of Texas (chaired by Hardin Runnels), walked out in protest over the details of the slavery planks in the shaky platform. The party was shattering, as many had predicted, along sectional lines.[47]

On San Jacinto Day, two days before the Charleston maelstrom began, a large meeting at the battlefield resolved that the governor should declare as "the people's candidate," a bridge between the two feuding sections. They went so far as to choose four presidential electors and speed them off to Charleston.[48] The idea of a "people's candidacy" appealed to Houston, as it did to many, but the Democratic party would have none of him.

Soon newspapers in other areas of the country picked up the concept and touted it as the answer to sectional strife. The *New York Sun* proposed Houston for president, as did the same city's *Express,* the Augusta *Daily Chronicle and Sentinel,* the *Arkansas Gazette* and dozens of others across the land, as well as most of the Texas German media, including the Galveston *Die Union.*[49] In May, as the Constitutional Union party* was sending electors to its Baltimore convention, there was also harsh criticism heard. One newspaper observed of Houston that "his appreciation and respect for the Constituted authorities was exemplified in his recent proposition to invade Mexico!"[50] Another, the *Constitutional Union,* noted of the quasicandidate that "General Sam Houston [is] a rather good old soul, as we all know, but the most shallow of the shallow politicians"; a man who merited no attention. Similarly, the Austin *State Gazette* portrayed him as "testy in temper, crafty in policy and shallow in information."[51] Houston's friend Rip Ford had doubts about his presidential qualities also, remembering that he had not only been a Know Nothing, but "its great high priest in the Lone Star state."[52] And Frederick Law Olmsted, in Texas at the time, recounted a conversation about the governor he had heard: "There was much laughter at his expense . . . he seemed to be held in very little respect . . . the greater part of the old fighting Texans hated and despised him."[53] Sam D. Carothers wrote disdainfully, "We take old Sam Houston to be a low, spiteful, cunning, hipocritical man."[54]

Characteristically, Houston displayed his availability in every way possible but did little campaigning. Despite strong support in the Constitutional Union party, he declined to attend its convention. He seemed to be making the point that only the "People" could elect him and that he wanted to be drafted by the common American or not at all. He wrote Sam at the time that "discord is rife" and threatening the nation: "My son I wish you to love and revere the Union. . . . Mingle it in your heart with filial love."[55]

The Constitutional Union party convention opened on May 9, with twenty-two state delegations. No party had a more critical mandate: to stave off secession and civil war. Many a glowing speech and endorsement was made, a number championing the absent Houston. The chair-

---

* The Constitutional Union party sought to maintain the Union in part by guaranteeing continuance of slavery only where it then existed by constitutional amendment.

man of the Texas delegation speculated that if Houston were
nominated, he would carry all the slave states, New York and enough
of the North and West to win the election.[56]

When it came time for nominations, Texas declared for its governor,
instantly seconded by New York. The first ballot drove out some minor
figures and resulted in fifty-seven votes for Houston and sixty-eight and
a half for Tennessee's former senator John Bell, a man of Houston's
stamp, but without his vacillation. The Texan had gotten the votes of
his own state, New York and Arkansas, and partial support from Ohio,
Pennsylvania and Connecticut, but he was drubbed on the second ballot, 125 to 68. John Bell and Edward Everett became the party's nomi-
nees.[57] Had Houston campaigned, had he been in Baltimore to speak,
had he exerted any real effort, combined with his unsurpassed name
recognition, he could have had the nomination. And, given the frac-
tured state of American politics, he might have been elected. But, as
before, he showed hesitation, aloofness and unwillingness to share his
plans. He was never candid about his alleged candidacy. In a letter to
Sam he wrote that the boy should not be disappointed, for "if I really
desired the Presidency, I would not consider the action at Baltimore as
any hindrance to my chances. I will recognize no action of a caucus or
convention. The people only are sovreign." If Sam should be taunted by
other cadets, the governor urged him to respond that "my Father never
authorized his name to be used by any convention or caucus." The
truth is, he would have accepted the nomination of any party, save the
Republican, that had a chance to win.[58]

The Republican party nominated Abraham Lincoln and Hannibal
Hamlin on May 18,* and a month later a reconvened Democratic convention (now at Baltimore) nominated Stephen A. Douglas and Her-
schel Johnson. That ticket, seen by Southern radicals as far too
moderate, prompted dissenters to meet in late June to nominate John
C. Breckinridge of Kentucky (Buchanan's vice-president and a strong
proslavery man) and Joseph Lane of Oregon. The election of 1860 was
to be a four-way race—or was it?[59]

---

* Ironically, Houston received a few votes at this convention, for vice-president, a
fact used against him politically in Texas.

"I am with politics as Falstaff was with
strong Potations."

SAM HOUSTON, 1860

What the governor had in mind following the Constitutional Union party convention can be gathered from his letter to his eldest son quoted above. Claiming to "recognize no action of a caucus or convention," Houston would, in extremis, turn to the "People." [60]

Almost as soon as John Bell expressed his thanks for the nomination, Houston announced that he would accept the invitation of the San Jacinto mass meeting and run as the people's candidate, for "no period could be more propitious than the present, for the assertion of the rights of the masses." [61]

With astonishing swiftness, large pro-Houston meetings took place in Texas and elsewhere, several in New York City in May and June. The *New York Herald* on May 30 endorsed him, devoting most of its front page to the Hero of San Jacinto and his "people's candidacy," which, it opined, "might actually be the solution of the ugly problem before the nation." [62] The same newspaper later ran biographies of the four party candidates, and Sam Houston, whose "platform is [simply] the record of his public life." [63] The candidate himself proudly declared his freedom: "The Constitution and the Union embrace the only principle by which I will be governed if elected!" [64] He briefly believed that the "People" both could and would elect him.

At this juncture he was applying for a free league of Texas land under provisions of an 1837 act to reward wounded veterans of the Texas Revolution (there were remarkably few). With less than perfect candor for a man who had worked like ten beavers for twenty-four years after the battle, he enclosed medical affidavits "declaring that Houston's wound, received at San Jacinto, was a permanent disability." [65] He shortly afterward wrote Ashbel Smith, who had signed one of the affidavits, admitting with rare frankness, "I am with politics as Falstaff was with strong Potations." He always had been, as Margaret had learned. [66]

"It must not sink into the character of spoil
and robbery."

SAM HOUSTON, 1860

Governor Houston, although he gave a number of campaign speeches in Texas, knew by the first of August that he had no chance—even within his home state. That sad fact was dramatically driven home to him by the results of the August 6 Texas election for three state executive positions. The candidates Houston had supported were all swamped by the Democratic machine.[67] He was soon resignedly writing a friend that "as to my having any wish to be President, I can say before high Heaven, I have not a single wish or desire to be placed in that office."[68] That no one believed him did not faze the governor one bit. A few days later he publicly bowed out. In a letter "To Friends in the United States,"* he withdrew a candidacy, he wrote, that he had not sought, but which had been thrust upon him by the "People" and his own love of Union. He failed to mention which of the four candidates—if any— he might support.[69] Now, he would return to his vision of Greater Texas.

There was little doubt in Houston's mind by mid-1860 that the South would soon secede, and that Texas was also poised to do so. The 1860 census revealed that Texas had a population of 431,000 whites and 182,000 blacks (almost all slaves). With such a population base, and prospects for considerable immigration, Texas could survive and flourish as an independent nation. A return to independence—rather than statehood in a Southern confederacy—and control of northern Mexico would make Texas a power, and might keep it out of the civil war Houston had long predicted.

So, despite his vacillation in the first half of the year, he turned again to men like McCulloch, Burleson, and Colonel Charles L. Mann, who was acting as his personal agent in New York City. Mann had—at the governor's request—been in communication with British financiers

---

* As if it were a *foreign* country.

whose large investments were trapped in war-ravaged Mexico. Desperate, those investors were still willing to support any measure to stabilize Mexico.

In one letter to Colonel Mann that has survived Houston hints at his attitude toward the renewed scheme. Noting that "I have had a Protectorate at home to claim my attention," he mentioned that money for the Mexican adventure simply could not be had in the United States. Of the British he wrote, "If the bondholders cannot be approached, it would take years to raise a reliable force to achieve any glorious result." He instructed Mann to press those bondholders for the cash, for "if this matter succeeds—no matter under whose direction," great riches were to be gained. The only question he had was, "Will men in London trust any man so far from home?" He was betting that they would, and Mann was to assure them that "as to the plan of operations, that is a small matter," for he had long contemplated the move. He would write McCulloch, he promised, to sound him out: "Ben will do for a very 'big Captain' as my Red brothers say."[70]

Had the United States not been sliding down the flume to civil war (South Carolina seceded in December), Houston's vision might have been realized. The day after writing Mann, the governor addressed himself to McCulloch in Washington, explaining that "I am for some work if it is undertaken. We look on it as a mission of mercy and humanity, and it must not sink into the character of spoil and robbery. It must be to elevate and exalt Mexico to a position among the nations of the world," and not be merely a crude conquest. He asked his old friend to ascertain how quickly ten thousand of "his rifles" could be manufactured, warning that "it is best to keep it *sub rosa*." As to politics, "I am arms folded," and no longer an aspirant. In an odd postscript he scrawled, "Don't get married."[71] The plan was progressing, but Houston had thrown away his chance in the spring and must have realized it. The idea that a renewed project could await the design and manufacture of ten thousand rifles—perhaps two years—was preposterous.

While McCulloch was making his inquiries in the Northeast, Governor Houston was ordering Colonel Johnson to raise another unit of Rangers, this time a battalion, sending similar orders to a number of trusted Ranger captains, including Burleson and William Dalyrymple.[72] At precisely the same time, however, he was mustering out other

Ranger companies and relieving some officers. He was, in short, purging the state military of unreliables as the nation approached election day and probable crisis.[73] The governor—for the first time—also appointed numerous "Volunteer Aides de Camp" to advise him, and soon had a military staff larger than that of Santa Anna at his peak! These included Burleson, whose position was commander of Texas militia, Dalyrymple, with the rank of cavalry colonel, Francis Duffan with the same rank, and Colonel Johnson himself.[74] Houston was surrounding himself with many trusted men of military experience, influence and now, elevated rank. In a crisis, they could take over a vastly expanded state defense establishment.

A wave of malaise and unrest swept Texas—and much of the South —prompted by fear that radical abolitionists were stirring up the slaves. Things commonplace—fires, unsolved murders, runaway slaves—were increasingly seen as abolitionist-inspired crimes. Near panic reigned that fateful autumn.[75] Typical of the building social tension was a letter written by Sam D. Carothers to his brother. "Horse thieves, murderers & Abolitionists from Kansas" were "slipping into Texas to foment unrest," he claimed. At Austin, the sheriff had arrested "a Negro for burning a house . . . he confessed." Grimly, "hundreds met & with one voice said hang him and did so in two hours." Carothers saw the social fabric badly shredded.[76]

A few weeks later, George T. Strong jotted in his diary a rumor that someone had found "about one hundred bottles of strychnine to be used by some nigger toxicologist to poison the wells of a whole county." The totally unfounded rumor led to panic, and the local vigilance committee spilled a rivulet of blood—of whites and blacks—before a semblance of calm could be restored.[77] It was not a safe time for strangers to wander Texas.

"The Union is worth more than Mr. Lincoln!"

SAM HOUSTON, 1860

In this initial stage of mass hysteria, the governor made a Unionist speech in the somewhat hostile state capital. On September 22, in one of his most memorable orations, he attempted to explain the consequences of disunion. Of the possible collapse of the Union he passionately proclaimed: "I might ask that I might not survive the destruction of the shrine that I had been taught to regard as holy and inviolate, since my boyhood. . . . Do you believe it will be dissevered and no shock felt to society?" Before secession was considered Americans should turn to the judiciary and the Constitution for redress: "Are we to sell reality for a phantom?" States leaving the Union would be but "petty states," squabbling and fighting, abused by European powers and prey to "British Abolition, which in fanaticism and sacrificial spirit far exceeds that of the North." Only a minority in the North are hostile to Southern interests: "Shall we cut loose from the majority" for their sake? If Lincoln were elected, the Constitution would bind him and protect Southern rights: "The Union is worth more than Mr. Lincoln!" he thundered. Labeling Texas radicals "transplants from the South Carolina nursery of disunion" and "men of convenient politics," he cogently asked, "But where are their Washingtons, their Jeffersons, and Madisons?" Once out of the Union and unprotected by the Constitution, "Aristocracy will rear its head," and the common people would suffer, he foretold, crying out that his own children would "share the fate of your children. Think you that I feel no interest in the future for their sakes?"[78] It was a brilliant speech and it made a strong impression on the thousands who heard it, but the verbal edifice of the Union that he hammered together was soon to be swept away by the wind-shear of radicalism.

That fall Houston campaigned lackadaisically for the Constitutional Union party ticket, but in a letter to a friend admitted that "I like Breckinridge more than either of the other candidates . . . [however] my wish and object is to beat Lincoln with any man in the field."[79]

On November 6, 1860, a nervous American electorate went to the polls, and the results soon sang nationwide over the copper wires. Abraham Lincoln had won a hollow victory, elected president of the dis-United States with only 38 percent of the votes cast. The Republican gathered in 1,886,252 popular votes (180 electoral), as against 1,375,157 (12) for Stephen A. Douglas, 849,781 (72) for John C. Breckinridge, and 589,581 (39) for John Bell. The vote had been very largely sectional.[80] Hence on the electoral, rather than the popular vote tally, Lincoln won.

The vote in Texas devastated the governor. Breckinridge took the state by storm. Unionism had been nowhere near as strong as Houston had hoped. Stephen Douglas ran second nationwide, but in Texas received a paltry 410 votes because of his stance on slavery, and Lincoln could boast no recorded votes whatsoever![81] To many Southerners the real issue on November 6 had been that of secession, and in their minds, secession, not Lincoln, had won.

***

"Dear Colonel, hurry by all means."

SAM HOUSTON, 1861

A month before the election, South Carolina governor William H. Gist had written his counterparts in all fifteen slaveholding states save Texas. He informed them that South Carolina would in all probability soon secede, and he asked them to consider the same course of action.[82] Within days of Lincoln's election, Gist's state legislature called for a special convention to decide whether to leave the Union. South Carolina would secede in the same manner it had joined the Union—by vote of that special convention. Other seceding states would do the same. The South Carolina convention voted unanimously to secede on December 20 and felt its action wholly constitutional.

Less than a week after Lincoln's victory, Edmund Ruffin, who expected that all Southern states would soon secede, wrote in his acerbic diary that only Texas was in doubt: "The difficulty there will [be] in that old scoundrel & traitor to the South, Houston."[83]

Following the election, Houston ignored a flood of requests and demands to call a special convention to discuss relations with the federal government,[84] but called publicly and privately for a convention of slave-holding states to discuss defense of Southern rights within the Union,[85] to encourage the flying of the Lone Star flag and to mobilize.[86]

Several times he wired Secretary of War Floyd that the state's frontiers were again seriously threatened (they were not), pleading for "the arms to which the State is entitled, for the present year, and in advance for the quota of next year," even though this amounted to only a few hundred muskets.[87] He also called up dozens of Ranging Companies and wrote an alarming letter to Colonel Edward Burleson, Jr., marked "Private."

> You will be here in sometime during tomorrow, *as early as possible,* with all of the men you can bring, *who are true to the Country* and in whom you can rely in any emergency. When you arrive I will explain every thing to you.
> Dear Colonel,
> Hurry by all means.[88]

Burleson and a company of armed Unionists were soon by Houston's side and ten days later the Ranger colonel received a letter concerning mobilization of Unionists to defend the governor and the Constitution: "I have notified Gov. Houston that I stand ready and willing . . . to keep down any sectional party or disunion movement in the State or U. States . . . Ed your Father fought to place you and I in the enjoyment of what we are now enjoying." If blood must flow, so be it.[89] Briefly, it appeared that there might be a civil war in Texas, but the governor calmed the situation and even ironically asked a secessionist committee attempting to form a new militia the same question on Secretary of War Floyd's mind for months: "Why this military display and call to arms in Texas? Have we enemies at home or is an enemy marching upon us?"[90]

To the people of the state Houston admitted that "we must maintain our rights," and that "when the Constitution fails to give them to us, I am for Revolution," but, he stressed, only then.[91] On December 17, under mounting pressure, he ordered a special session of the legislature to convene on January 21.[92]

As Governor Iverson of Georgia was publicly suggesting his Texas counterpart's assassination,[93] Secretary of War Floyd was once again turning down Houston's fervent request to have a Ranger regiment entered into federal service.[94] Floyd patiently reminded the governor that the frontier was quiet, and that the army then had five companies of artillery, ten of cavalry, and twenty-five of infantry stationed in Texas—surely enough to meet any contingency.[95]

With the press of public business compounded by the great national crisis, Sam Houston again saw little of his family as he traveled across the state speaking for Unionism. Margaret delivered their last child, Temple Lea, without complications at the governor's mansion on August 12. To Sam, who desperately wanted a new coat, Houston wrote, "My expenses are so heavy" that the coat must wait, complaining that "I am busy beyond all former times."[96]

His old wounds pained him a great deal in 1860, suppurating freely, and assorted aches and pains—probably arthritis—had by now all but crippled him.[97] Returning exhausted from speaking at Georgetown in October, he found Margaret seriously ill, and family responsibilities fell heavily upon his aching shoulders. Margaret was bedridden much of that autumn, but parenting devolved more upon the Houstons' twelve slaves than it did upon the governor.[98]

He had agreed to call the special legislative session in large part to block a rash move by Texas secessionists, including Rip Ford. These, in a formal address, had urged the people of Texas to hold elections for a state convention to decide whether to leave the Union. Popular response was overwhelmingly favorable, and this impelled the governor to call the legislators into session in the hope that he could convince them to disavow the proposed convention.[99]

S E V E N T E E N

Sam Houston Faces Civil War

"I hear him agonizing in prayer for our
distracted country."

MARGARET HOUSTON, 1861

In the first four months of 1861 ten states followed South Carolina out of the Union. A new nation was formed, America's greatest bloodbath erupted and Sam Houston became an exile in his own land. The flag of the Confederacy, not the Lone Star, was to fly over Texas, and instead of Houston's dream of conquest to the south, the South itself would be the object of conquest.

Events moved swiftly. On January 9 an army resupply vessel, the *Star of the West,* was fired upon as it attempted to reach the small United States Army garrison at Fort Sumter, in Charleston harbor. Outgoing president James Buchanan did his best to ignore the incident, content to let Mr. Lincoln decide what to do with federal property and troops in the departing states.

A week earlier, Governor Houston, speaking before an unfriendly gathering at Waco, assured his restive audience that he would abide by the will of the people, even if they opted for secession. He considered such a move utterly wrong, however, and forcefully advocated an independent "Republic of the Lone Star" should Texas leave the Union. Such a republic would realize a "Manifest Destiny" of its own, unencumbered by alliances of any kind.[1]

At this time he wrote an especially eloquent letter to R. M. Calhoun, of Alabama, who had inquired about the governor's possible cooperation with the nascent "Southern Confederacy." He forcefully warned that such a move "would be worse than suicidal" for Texas. Secession was being railroaded through the South, he claimed, by "the furors of crazy politicians," and not by the logic of rational men. Work within the Union, he implored: "The Federal judiciary have never been appealed to in vain." Secession is "but the distempered dream of Southern enthusiasts who are called upon to fire the Southern heart instead of the Southern mind." Texas had not and would not cooperate in any scheme of disunion. If Texas someday did leave the Union, he promised that it would "provide for her own safety," rather than rely upon the "guarantees" of a weak new Southern nation. Texans' "interests," he continued, "will lead them to avoid entangling alliances . . . she violates no duty to the South in unfurling once again her Lone Star Banner and maintaining her position among the independent nations of the earth. If the Union be dissolved . . . and civil war is to follow, Texas can 'tread the winepress' alone."

Furthermore, Texas—alone of Southern states—had a hostile frontier with a foreign nation. Could the South come to its aid, when the far stronger United States had been able to do so little to protect Texas? As Calhoun no doubt realized:

> Texas has views of expansion not common to many of her sister states. Although an empire within herself, she feels that there is an empire beyond, essential to her security. She will not be content to have the path of her destiny clogged. The same spirit of enterprise that founded a Republic here will carry her institutions Southward and Westward . . . the triumph will be ours; and we will escape the miseries of civil war.

His dream had not faded along with his hopes of preserving the Union. Texas independence actually improved the chances of a successful move against Mexico. The governor concluded by wishing Alabama well, whether or not it seceded. After all, in 1814, "it was upon her soil that I gave the first proofs of my manhood in devotion to the Union." Since then, he reminded his correspondent, "Alabama has risen from an almost wilderness region, under the fostering care of the Federal Government . . . to a great, wealthy, and prosperous people."[2] As his letter was posted, Alabama seceded.

Houston's determination to disengage Texas from the other Southern states and thus avoid their inevitable grim fate ignored certain realities. If Southern secession led the North to use armed force, as he fully expected, could Texas secede in peace? At the very least, Texas would be forced into a defensive alliance with the South. Also, his assumption that Texans would overwhelmingly opt for independence and empire ignored the tenor of Texas politics.

In mid-January, the Texas legislature authorized the governor to call up a regiment of cavalry for state service, under full army discipline and regulations. The regiment would be under his personal control unless Washington accepted it in federal service, which by this juncture was highly unlikely.[3] Houston decided to turn this development to the Union's advantage. In addition to recruiting, he vastly expanded the number of Ranging Companies, creating seventeen new units on January 25 alone, with detailed instructions on conduct and arms, but no explanation for their mobilization. He appointed as captains trusted friends and Unionists, men such as William Tobin, Charles Travis, John Walker and Levi English.[4] He also appointed more "volunteer" aides-de-camp, and most, like S. M. Swenson, were fervent Unionists.*

He also agonized over the collapse of his nation. Mississippi seceded on January 9, Florida followed on the tenth, Alabama the next day, Georgia on the nineteenth and Louisiana on the twenty-sixth, and a convention of seceding states was called to meet at Montgomery, Alabama, in early February, to create a new nation. The clamor for secession in Texas was at high pitch. He was depressed as he considered his few, mostly unpalatable, options. Could he turn his back upon the people of Texas? Upon his deepest beliefs? Could he bring himself to use force against either the uniform he had worn so many years ago, or perhaps worse, against Texas itself?

In late January he wrote to General D. E. Twiggs† at San Antonio, entrusting the note to a "confidential agent." He warned that "an effort will be made by an unauthorized mob to take forcibly and appropriate" federal government property in Texas, claiming "to act on behalf of the State." He told Twiggs to do whatever he felt necessary to protect that

---

* Swenson (a Swede), like many important Unionists, would have to flee to Mexico during the Civil War.

† Under Winfield Scott, Twiggs was senior general of the United States Army.

property and urged him to call upon the authorities of San Antonio "for such assistance as you may deem necessary."[5] Secessionists would have no easy time of it as long as Sam Houston was governor!

Margaret wrote indestructible Nancy the next day (the day the legislature met in special session), noting that "General Houston seems cheerful and hopeful through the day, but in the still watches of the night I hear him agonizing in prayer for our distracted country."[6] Though exhausted from sleeplessness, the governor stood erect before the legislators on January 21, urging caution and optimistically proposing a Southern peace convention. Such a gathering, he promised, could flex Southern muscle within the Union and assure that legitimate Southern needs would be met. The assemblage listened impassively, their minds fixed on the adventure of secession.[7]

On January 28 the Secession Convention met at Austin, with 92 of the state's 152 organized counties represented. Ninety percent of the delegates had been born in slaveholding states, and three-quarters were themselves slaveowners. Observers from South Carolina and Georgia were present to justify their states' actions.[8] On January 31, the day after blood-stained Kansas entered the Union as another free state, a committee presented a secession ordinance, charging the federal government with acting unconstitutionally against "the interests and prosperity" of the South. As a sop to the governor, it also called for Texas to resume its sovereign status on March 2, pending a February 23 referendum.[9]

The governor reluctantly recognized the legitimacy of the Convention the following day and addressed it. "Their fate is my fate," he said of the people of Texas, and "I am with my country,"[10] stressing the latter word. One day later he was present when the Convention passed the ordinance and was visibly shaken by the lopsided vote: 166 to 8 in favor of secession.[11] He had not believed Texans were so disenchanted with the Union, nor had he realized the popularity of the idea of joining a Southern nation. Seven delegates were chosen as representatives to the Southern Congress at Montgomery, a move the governor condemned as illegal.[12] Ominously, the Convention also created a Committee on Public Safety, to serve in some unspecified manner when the Convention as a whole was not in session. The secessionists did not trust Sam Houston, and in contravention of the state constitution, the Convention was bidding to be the real government, with its Committee on Public

Safety a watchdog on the Unionist governor. The implied threat was not lost on Houston.

> "Your sons and brothers, will be herded at the point
> of the bayonet."
>
> SAM HOUSTON, 1861

Throughout this process, Houston was calling up Ranging Companies and asking the legislature's authorization to put Texas on a war footing. He reminded them that secession would mean the departure of more than three thousand United States Army regulars. The frontier would be instantly denuded: "If we are to separate, let us have the means for taking care of ourselves," he pleaded. In any event, he won his point, and was authorized to call up an additional forty-man company in each of the state's thirty-seven "frontier" counties. He finally had his regiment.[13]

As fateful February 23 approached, the governor spoke frequently in defense of Union, foretelling apocalyptic civil war, defeat and utter ruin:

> Let me tell you what is coming. . . . Your fathers and husbands, your sons and brothers, will be herded at the point of the bayonet. . . . You may, after the sacrifice of countless millions of treasure and hundreds of thousands of lives, as a bare possibility, win Southern independence . . . but I doubt it.[14]

As expected, the referendum called for secession by a wide margin; 46,129 to 14,697. However, the turnout was light, and large numbers of Unionists stayed away from the polls out of fear and hopelessness. Eighteen counties had opposed secession, 103 had favored it, and no returns were posted for 31 others.[15]

Houston wearily accepted the verdict, writing with resignation that "I still believe that secession will bring ruin and civil war. Yet, if the people will it, I can bear it with them." The burdens of constitutionality weighed heavily upon him.[16] It would now be his task to make Texas fully independent, and keep it that way, no easy matter. On February 10, Jefferson Davis was elected president of the Confederate States of America, and he and his new Congress were eagerly courting Texas.[17]

Even before February 23, the Convention had "authorized" its Committee on Public Safety to open negotiations with federal authorities for the transfer of all United States property in Texas to the state. General Twiggs found himself in a quandary. Himself a Southerner, he was nonetheless averse to abandoning his forts, posts and supplies to the "mob" Houston had warned him of.[18]

As early as February 10 a delegation from the committee met with Twiggs, and armed Texans began to menace various army posts. The general soon learned to his chagrin that Ben McCulloch, leading a thousand armed men, had camped outside San Antonio on the night of February 15. When the committee delegates demanded that he surrender all United States property under his control on the sixteenth, he complied with as much dignity as he could muster. The War Department promptly relieved him of all duties, citing "treachery to the flag of his country."[19] Commanders of most of the other forts and posts likewise caved in swiftly to the threat of force. At Fort Cooper, violence nearly did erupt, however. There, wrote a Texas Ranger, the situation deteriorated and weapons were cocked: "I hope that Cooper may not be the Lexington of a second Revolution." It was not.[20] Governor Houston was no longer in control.

"Margaret, I will never do it!"

SAM HOUSTON, 1861

There was little the governor could do, especially after results of the referendum were made known. In symbolic protest he delayed the official proclamation of secession from his birthday (and the twenty-fifth anniversary of Texas independence) two days, to March 4. The proclamation was a curious document. He admitted that after a proper electoral count he had found "that a large majority of the votes received and counted of the said Election are in favor of 'Secession' of the State of Texas from the United States of America." He did not spell out that Texas had seceded, or even that it would. But, of course, it had.[21]

Colonel Carlos Waite had been ordered to Texas by the War Department to replace the disgraced General Twiggs, but he arrived only on February 19, by which time he found no positions to hold. He did the only thing he could; he began drawing his scattered units toward the coast. There they could await reinforcement or evacuation.[22]

The day after Houston's tepid secession proclamation, the reassembled Texas Convention passed an ordinance by a 109–2 vote, declaring Texas a state in the new Confederacy,[23] a move the governor denounced as the unconstitutional act of a body with no legal existence. But, rhetoric from the governor's mansion aside, it was by now clear who governed Texas. De facto, if not de jure, Texas was a part of the Confederacy.

Abraham Lincoln, inaugurated the day Houston proclaimed secession, clearly perceived the importance of Texas with a Unionist governor and a sizeable, but overestimated, Unionist minority. Lincoln and his advisors determined to defend Houston as "the outstanding exemplar of Unionism in the South."[24] In fact, serious thought was given to sending massive reinforcements to Texas. Certainly Texas was far more important than lonely Fort Sumter or the only other Union holdout in the South, Florida's Fort Pickens. If Texas could be held in the Union with Houston at its helm, the tide of rebellion might yet be turned. Virginia had not yet seceded,* and a Confederacy without the twin anchors of Texas and Virginia would be adrift upon the diplomatic seas.[25]

In the first week of March Lincoln sent noted Western explorer Major Frederick West Lander to Texas. His secret mission was to encourage Houston to retain power and attempt to keep the state from joining the Confederacy. He was in Austin by midmonth and met with Houston, but elicited no commitment.[26]

As Lander was insinuating himself into Texas, E. W. Cave, writing for the governor, addressed to Confederate secretary of war Leroy Pope

---

* It would do so in mid-April, following the sound of gunfire at Fort Sumter.

Walker a strong refutation of the Confederacy's assumption of power over Texas. Texas was not one of the Confederate states, he asserted, for such had not "received any warrant from the people of Texas," but only from the Convention, which "represented but a minority." Despite innate sympathies for other Southern states, Texans had "just resumed their nationality," not at all "subject to a Government which her people had had no share in making." Texans felt no obligation, explained Cave, and would never "sanction the course pursued in annexing them to a new Government without their knowledge or consent."[27] If Lincoln learned of this communication, as he may well have, it must have given him hope that Texas could still be saved. The matter, however, was soon academic.

On March 14, the Texas Convention ordained that all state officials swear an oath of allegiance to the Confederate States of America, a nation Houston refused to admit that Texas had joined. "Margaret, I will never do it!" he roared in anger and frustration.[28] Yet he knew that to refuse would be to court personal disaster.

The Convention, realizing that Houston could still be a formidable antagonist, sent a delegation to convince him to endorse the new Southern nation, but the old man would have none of it.[29] So, on March 16 the state's highest officials, including Houston, gathered in the Capitol for the oath taking. The governor cordially greeted everyone, then simply descended to the basement. As name after name was called and men stepped forward to signal their allegiance, Houston sat and whittled. Then, recalled an observer, "The call thrice repeated—'Sam Houston! Sam Houston! Sam Houston!,' but the man sat silent, immovable, in his chair below, whittling steadily on."[30]

Only the governor and one friend, Secretary of State Cave, refused the oath. The Convention then declared the governorship vacant, ordered Houston to leave the executive mansion and on March 18 swore in his lieutenant governor, Edward Clark.

Sam Houston, however, was not quite out of the picture. That same day he made a bitter proclamation "To the People of Texas." Calling the Convention unconstitutional, arbitrary and a mere "quasi government," he warned his compatriots that "you have been transferred like sheep from the shambles. A Government has been fastened upon you [and] . . . you are to pay tribute to King Cotton." He assured both the government and the people that he was not planning a coup (as rumor had it), for:

I love Texas too well to bring civil strife and bloodshed upon her. To avert this calamity, I shall make no endeavor to maintain my authority as Chief Executive of this State, except by the peaceful exercise of my functions. When I can no longer do this, I shall calmly withdraw from the scene . . . but still claiming that I am its Chief Executive.

With true passion he declared that "I stand the last almost of a race . . . stricken down because I will not yield those principles which I have fought for." He lamented, "The severest pang is that the blow comes in the name of the State of Texas." Then, in full capital letters he made his last bid to stand fast: "I PROTEST IN THE NAME OF THE PEOPLE OF TEXAS AGAINST ALL THE ACTS AND DOINGS OF THIS CONVENTION, AND I DECLARE THEM NULL AND VOID." He concluded that "I will lay the same before the people, and appeal to them."[31]

No wonder that Texas Unionists took heart and read into this protest that Houston would attempt to remain the legal governor of Texas.

"My God, is it possible that all the people
are gone mad?"

SAM HOUSTON, 1861

Returning home dejected, Houston and his slave Jeff were overtaken by a rider on a winded horse. The rider was probably the mysterious George H. Giddings, a Pennsylvanian who had migrated to Texas in 1846. A fervent Unionist, he had been chosen by Lincoln to deliver a desperate message.[32] Lincoln had written that Washington would make a serious effort to hold Texas in the Union if Houston and his Unionist friends would collaborate. Army troops in Texas were to concentrate, dig in, and await reinforcements. If he would openly declare for the Union Houston would immediately become major general and commander of all United States forces in his state. He was promised fifty thousand troops, to "put down secession in Texas and help Mr. Lincoln save our Union."[33] Troops were indeed being marshaled at New York, and one diarist noted that they were "destined neither for Sumter nor Pickens, but for Texas, to strengthen the hands of Governor Samuel Houston."[34]

Houston raced to the governor's mansion and sent for four trusted friends to seek their advice. It is not known who the four were, but they probably included Cave and Burleson. When they had gathered, he read Lincoln's letter aloud and asked their counsel. Only one urged him to accept the offer and make his stand; the others viewed such a move as dangerous folly. Remarking with immense sadness that if he were but ten years younger he might well accept Lincoln's risky proposal, he dismissed his friends and threw the letter into the fireplace.[35]

Anticipating Houston's resistance to the secessionists, on March 19, wily General Winfield Scott ordered Colonel Waite "to fortify and hold Indianola, Texas and support Houston or other state authorities in defense of the Federal Government."[36] That same day, a band of armed Unionists appeared at the executive mansion and offered to keep Houston in power by force. He was appalled: "My God, is it possible that all the people are gone mad?" He sent them home, telling them flatly that he would not be responsible for a Texan civil war, for "the civil war now being inaugurated [across the South] will be as horrible as his Satanic Majesty could desire."[37]

But, although he did not avail himself of the proffered aid, rumors abounded that he was plotting to move against the Convention. The *Texas Republican* reported on March 23 that "General Houston is raising troops on his own account," claiming that fifteen hundred armed Unionists "are at hand near Brownsville."[38] There probably were gatherings of Unionists in Texas (as in other Southern states), but even if they were ready to act, Houston was not. After all, the overwhelming vote of the people had been cast for secession, and the vast majority seemed to favor statehood in the Confederacy. He could not go against "his" people. That decision disheartened Unionists throughout the South—men who might well have taken a stand had Houston done so.

"The hiss of the mob and the howls of their jackal
leaders can not deter me."

SAM HOUSTON, 1861

Most doubts concerning Houston's allegiance were resolved when the former governor wrote Colonel "Charles" Waite on March 29. He had just learned that Waite had orders to rally his troops "at Indianola, in this State, to sustain me in the exercise of my official functions." Houston strongly declined such aid and asked the colonel to evacuate the state "at the very earliest day practicable."[39] Prudently, he made certain that the contents of this letter were made public. No traitor to Texas, Sam Houston; rumors to the contrary be damned![40]

Federal troops were soon embarking, as the state mobilized for the civil war to come. Rip Ford, now a colonel, was dispatched to the Rio Grande with fifteen hundred men by Governor Clark, for Mexico was still considered a threat.[41] But Texas would need more than Ford's small army and turned to Confederate Secretary of War Walker, requesting Confederate military aid for the frontier. A blunt warning was given: "We can assure you that nothing contributed more to destroy the bonds of affection which bound the people of Texas to the United States . . . than the reckless denial of adequate protection." Walker did authorize Texas to raise a regiment for frontier duty, to be paid for by the Confederacy.[42] Very early in the war, however, that regiment was ordered elsewhere by the Confederate government. One of its soldiers angrily wrote Burleson that "our Regiment is ordered to Missouri," leaving the long frontier again protected only by Ford's force and volunteer Ranging Companies.[43]

On the last day of March the Houston family moved out of Austin in several dangerously overloaded wagons, bound for Nancy's place at Independence. Stopping at Brenham, the former governor could not resist calls for an impromptu speech. He told the quizzical audience that "the vox Populi is not always the voice of God," and that "the hiss of the mob and the howls of their jackal leaders can not deter me nor compel me to take the oath of allegiance to the so-called Confederate Government." Just two weeks before shots were fired at Fort Sumter, he prophesied darkly, "The soil of our beloved South will drink deep the precious blood of our sons."[44]

The penniless Houstons somehow crowded into Nancy's house, and Houston brooded alone in one bedroom for days, utterly disconsolate. Nancy, in her dotage, had become so fat that she feared she had outgrown her special coffin. Margaret coped.[45] After several weeks of familial strain, the Houston clan moved on to the old farm at Cedar Point.

"We are not wanted or needed out of Texas."

SAM HOUSTON, 1861

Although he counseled his eldest son to be patient and remain in school, Houston could sense the young man's restlessness. In fact he was now unofficially drilling with the Bayland Guards, a company formed and outfitted by Ashbel Smith. Though originally a "Connecticut Yankee," Smith, now fifty-six, was an ardent secessionist, determined to defend his new nation.[46]

Margaret, burdened with the care of eight children, was not well. All but Sam had in recent years been educated at home for fear that rabidly anti-Houston zealots might harass or even harm them.[47] Andrew's leg had been seriously infected by a dog bite. And Nannie, having experienced a religious upheaval, was now in the disquieting throes of her third religious rebirth.[48]

On April 12, 1861, General Pierre Gustave Toutant Beauregard permitted Edmund Ruffin to fire the first cannon of an epoch-destroying war, a war that would cause nearly twice as many American deaths as would World War II. Just two days later, little Fort Sumter surrendered after a token defense, Lincoln declared a blockade of the South and the war was at last on. Brother-in-law Charles Power, who apparently had ignored Houston's funereal predictions, wrote him petulantly on April 16 that "I wish all this fuss was at an end, and that we had quiet once more."[49]

On May 10, with North and South mobilizing on a scale undreamed of in North America, Houston at last declared formally for the Confederacy. In a speech at Independence he admitted that now, with the smell of gunpowder in the air, "the time has come when a man's section is his country. I stand by mine. All my hopes, my fortunes, are centered in the South." It was better to go to war "than cringe before an enemy whose wrath we have invoked." He was ready, even at age seventy (actually, sixty-eight), to bear arms, "though others may lead, I shall not scorn to follow, and though I may end life in the ranks, where I commenced it, I shall feel that the post of duty is the post of honor."[50]

To his son at Bastrop, Houston wrote in a different vein: "Attend to business, and when it is proper, you shall go to war, if you really wish to do so," but only in defense of the state, for "we are not wanted or needed out of Texas."[51] The younger Sam, however, was eager to take part, no matter where the venue of action. Like many young Southerners, he was thrilled by the "great victory" at the First Battle of Manassas (Bull Run) in northern Virginia, on July 21. Surely the war would come to a speedy conclusion. Even more inspiring to Texas was the Confederate victory at Wilson's Creek in Missouri on August 10, where Ben McCulloch shared command with Sterling Price and led his Texans to glory. McCulloch rode into battle dressed in a simple suit of black velvet, without "any uniform or badge of rank, neither did he carry a sword," despite his general's rank. So dressed, he would be killed in battle the following March.[52]

Young Sam, offered an officer's commission because of his academy training, and easy duty at Galveston due to his name, disobeyed his father and enlisted in Ashbel Smith's spiffily uniformed company, which was soon merged into the Second Texas Volunteers. His father was both disappointed and proud, and when the Second Texas had been officially mustered in, drilled and readied for service, he traveled to Galveston to see his son off. The famous father turned the occasion into a media event when the regiment's colonel, John C. Moore, asked him to formally review the "splendid regiment of eleven hundred young men."

An astute eyewitness recorded the event. The tall, somewhat stooped Houston, arrayed in the suit he had worn at San Jacinto, his old sword and an ancient, weather-beaten hat with one side of the brim buttoned, addressed the troops sardonically. " 'Do you see anything of Judge

Campbell or Williamson S. Oldham here?'* 'No' was the emphatic reply. 'Do you see anything of Judge Campbell's son here?' 'No, he has gone to Paris to school,' responded the regiment. 'Do you see anything of young Sam Houston here?' 'Yes,' was the thrilling response. 'Do you see anything of Old Sam Houston here?' Regiment and citizens together responded in thunderous tones, 'Yes!' " He then put the regiment smartly through its maneuvers.[53] He had donated Sam's uniform, and Margaret had given their son a new Bible.[54]

The elder Houston later gave a speech at Galveston, despite threats against his life. The same careful observer was in the rapt audience, and his is the most detailed description of Sam Houston in the 1860s:

> There he stood, an old man of seventy years, on the balcony ten feet above the heads of the thousands assembled to hear him, where every eye could scan his magnificent form, six feet and three inches high, straight as an arrow, with deep set and penetrating eyes, looking out from under heavy and thundering eyebrows, a high open forehead, with something of the infinite intellectual shadowed there, crowned with thin white locks . . . and a voice of the deep basso tone, which shook and commanded the soul of the hearer. Adding to all this a powerful manner, made up of deliberation, self-possession and restrained modesty of action, leaving the hearer impressed with the feeling that more of his power was hidden than revealed. Thus appeared Sam Houston on this grand occasion, equal and superior to it, as he always was to every other.

Houston was frank; he "told them he made Texas and they knew it, and it was not immodest for him to say so." In fact, he claimed credit that day for everything from the victory at San Jacinto to the gift of prophecy, "and they knew it." He was perhaps writing his own epitaph: "You have always prospered most when you have listened to my counsels." He then criticized the current war hysteria, predicting that "I and you [will sink] in fire and rivers of blood."[55]

---

* Influential secessionists. Oldham was a Confederate senator.

> "My heart seems almost broken, and yet I am
> astonished that I bear it at all."
>
> MARGARET HOUSTON, 1862

Back at Cedar Point, Houston and his family raised some livestock, planted corn and other staples and generated scanty income by selling firewood to the people of treeless Galveston. In a letter to Maggie, who was nursemaiding Nancy, the increasingly infirm Houston wrote that Margaret "has goslings, young turkeys & about 150 young chickens," but was perturbed because dry weather would reduce the corn harvest.[56] Since because of his deposition his back salary—so long in arrears—was not paid, the Houstons led a hand-to-mouth existence.[57] Although he still owned parcels of land in a number of counties, it was all but impossible to sell in wartime Texas. Cedar Point, though, was no small farm, for Houston had added to the original tract over the years. Renaissance Man Ashbel Smith surveyed the farm on the eve of the war and found 3,642 acres, which Houston had subdivided into eight portions, each assigned to a family member.*

Even after his May 10 declaration of allegiance to Texas and the South (not the Confederacy per se), Houston was suspect in the eyes of many secessionists. In part this was because of his demands that Texas troops remain within the state, and in part because editorials in the North still eulogized the old warrior.[58] And, of course, he was often found in company with other known and vocal Unionists, including Swedish-born business tycoon S. M. Swenson (who fled to Mexico in 1863), William Marsh Rice (who did the same), Cave, Ferdinand Flake (editor of Galveston's provocatively named *Die Union*), future governor Elisha M. Pease, George W. Paschal, Swante Palm and Andrew Jackson Hamilton.[59] The last ("Colossal Jack") fled the state early in the war and was appointed military governor of Texas (in absentia) by Lincoln.[60] This fiction became fact in 1865 when President Andrew Johnson named him Reconstruction governor of Texas.

---

* Oddly, these varied a great deal in size; from 477 acres (Andrew) to 1,035 (Sam), and for some reason, Mary Willie was left out.

Also, it was common knowledge by mid-1861 that Houston had been secretly approached by Lincoln.[61] Suspicion concerning his loyalty persisted, and he complained that while he was loyal, "Yet, I learn that Provost Marshals are especial in their inquisitions about matters which may transpire at my house, or what my Children may say in their prattlings."[62]

In early 1862 the Second Texas was assigned to the Army of Mississippi, commanded by Albert Sidney Johnston, so long ago Texas secretary of war. Although Houston resented that his son (or any Texan) had to serve out of state, at least Sam would be stationed in the "West." Many thousands of Texans served in John Bell Hood's famous Texas Brigade in Virginia. That unit fought in the East throughout the war, was decimated, rebuilt and decimated again.[63] Texas was soon drained of most of its military manpower, its troops serving in all theaters of war, from isolated New Mexico through Virginia. It was a blessing that the Mexican border did not seriously flare up.

Rip Ford, commander of the Rio Grande frontier, encountered a few contretemps with the indefatigable Cheno Cortina, but he was able to write by mid-1861 that "I have endeavored to cultivate a friendly feeling between the military authorities of Texas, and those of Mexico," and had met with success.[64] This had more than military significance, for with the Union blockade tightening each month, trade with Mexico became crucial to the Confederacy.

The Rio Grande had at last been bridged, with a structure of dollars, pesos and mutual interests. Fetid little Matamoros became a thriving entrepôt for Confederate trade with Europe during the war, and as Ford admiringly noted, "was soon crammed with strangers and filled with goods of every class," all desperately needed by the South.[65] It was the only true loophole in the blockade, and for three years and more Matamoros was a genuine boomtown in an otherwise impoverished nation.[66]

At Cedar Point, Margaret fussed and worried. Now that she at last had her husband at her side, her eldest son had been snatched from her by war. News of the Battle of Elk Horn (Pea Ridge), in March 1862, deepened her despondency. Many Texans died in that clash, among them the mighty Ben McCulloch.* Elk Horn provided the first long list

---

* Among his command were Cherokee regiments, and it is noteworthy that Cherokee brigadier general Stand Watie was, in 1865, the last Confederate commander to surrender.

of names in what would become a grim Texan litany.[67] Houston's forecasts were fast becoming reality, and rivers of blood were indeed flowing through the South.

Ten days after the Battle of Elk Horn, Margaret, in deep depression, wrote a gloomy letter to her mother: "My heart seems almost broken, and yet I am astonished that I bear it at all . . . I cannot forget that my boy, my darling, he that was to be the prop of my old age, is from me, probably never to return." She begged her mother to implore Antoinette to write her "cheerful" letters to take her mind off "my bereavement" over Sam.

Soon after that note, Margaret received heartening news from a cousin stationed at Corinth, Mississippi, with Johnston's army. He knew Sam well, and sought to reassure her. "I know full well . . . your anxiety and solicitude about your boy but . . . Sam is in robust health [and] . . . indeed seems to like the business" of soldiering. The cousin advised her to "tell the General to secure a lieutenancy for Sam & save him from the rougher duties of the camp . . . Sam is a boy to be proud of."[68]

"I by no means despair of Sam's safety."

ASHBEL SMITH, 1862

No doubt relieved by this news, Margaret leaped at her cousin's suggestion that Houston use his influence to obtain a commission for Sam. On April 5 he petitioned a long-term political enemy and arch-secessionist, Senator Williamson S. Oldham, who was on a military affairs committee. "Sam is 18 years of age, 6 feet high, and rather a well-made and good looking boy." With those qualifications (and the name Sam Houston), "If you can procure for him a lieutenancy, or any promotion that you may think proper, you will confer upon me an enduring obligation."[69] To place himself under obligation to Oldham was a horrendous burden, but the matter soon became immaterial.

On April 6, General Johnston led the Army of Mississippi in an all-out assault against Ulysses Grant's temporarily divided Army of Tennessee, near Pittsburgh Landing, in southern Tennessee. The Battle of Shiloh, as it is known, was one of the most savage of the war. As James M. McPherson has written, "Shiloh was America's baptism in total war," and the landscape was littered with mangled dead.[70] Johnston, whom Houston had dismissed as "a good man and a gentleman—but not [possessing] one particle of military capacity,"[71] fell mortally wounded among his windrowed men, the command passing to General Beauregard, one of the South's more talented generals. On April 7, the battle resumed, but where the Southerners had held the advantage before, the reunited Union army now went over to the offensive. Technically, the battle was a draw, but failure to halt Grant's inexorable advance through the South constituted a strategic Confederate defeat. Among the staggering 16,500 Southern wounded lay the young Sam Houston.[72]

News of the Shiloh bloodbath cast a pall of gloom over the Lone Star state, for a number of Texas regiments had been chewed up there. And, at Cedar Point, Margaret heard her personal crack of doom. Tidings of the battle had reached her on April 9, and the next day the former governor wrote Maggie, "Your Dear Ma . . . is in a state of painful anxiety until she can hear from your Bro. Sam."[73] Her state of mind was hardly improved by a letter from Ashbel Smith, written April 16. Sam's company commander wrote from a Memphis hospital, where he was recovering from a painful wound.

"I shook hands with Sam on the morning of the 7th," wrote Ashbel Smith, but as he was soon wounded, he lost track of the young man. The Second Texas, according to historian Wiley Sword, "was a hard-luck regiment," rushed from a long forced march into the swirling battle, where it immediately collided with the Seventy-first Ohio and took heavy losses.[74] The following day the Texans were mauled by the Third Iowa while acting as rearguard. Smith later learned that when the remnants of the company camped that evening, "Sam and some 7 or 8 of the others were in no way accounted for," yet "I by no means despair of Sam's safety." Smith eulogized the son of his close friends: "Sam with some others was conspicuous—he fought like a hero, and with the coolness of a veteran." His "conduct and bearing [throughout] was all that his mother and father could desire."[75]

Sam had almost been killed. In a sharp brush with the Iowans he had been shot in the right groin by a minié ball, which spun him to the ground. The legend has it that he would have been mortally wounded had the ball not hit the new Bible in his pocket.* The fallen, Sam included, were left on the field by their back-pedaling regiment "and checked off as dead on the records of Company C," despite Ashbel Smith's disclaimers.[76]

The Iowa regiment's chaplain, checking the scores of rebel bodies for signs of life, found young Houston still breathing, discovered his name from his Bible and did everything possible to save him. Ironically, that unnamed chaplain had known Senator Houston, who had done him a political favor in the 1850s. Sam was nursed back to a semblance of health and then sent to Camp Douglas, near Chicago. While there, he was permitted to spend considerable time recuperating "at the residence of a former friend" of his father.[77]

Only in August did the Houstons learn for certain that their son was alive and a prisoner of war, and by then he was signing his parole papers. So, one sweltering September day Margaret glanced up while weeding her vegetable garden and saw a cadaverous bearded man leaning against a nearby fence rail, a man who "seemed to be all skin and bones. He was on crutches," and obviously weak. It took some minutes for her to recognize her son, so changed was his appearance.[78] The rejoicing was ecstatic, the more so because Sam's wound, although no longer life threatening, appeared severe enough to exempt him from further military service. Mrs. Houston would at last have both her Sams at home.

"His eyes is no better and he has despaired."

MARGARET HOUSTON, 1862

Margaret, however, was to again change residence. The course of the war was clearly against the South. In May, the United States Navy had

---

* The Bible, inscribed "Sam Houston Jr. from his Mother, March 6, 1862," supposedly flattened and slowed the bullet. It can be seen today in the Sam Houston Memorial Museum, Huntsville, and photographs of it appear in several books.

seized the key city of New Orleans, and soon it controlled most of the Mississippi River, effectively cutting off Arkansas, Louisiana and Texas from the eight Eastern Confederate states. Lee's first invasion of the North ended in catastrophe at Antietam in September, and Union forces captured Galveston the following month. Although Confederates would retake the island, Cedar Point was in the path of an anticipated invasion of the Texas mainland, and the Houstons packed up once more and moved back to Huntsville. The state's authorities were relieved, for they preferred the former governor well away from any possible collaboration with Yankee invaders.

At Huntsville, where Margaret felt comfortable, the Houstons rented the eccentrically designed "Steamboat House," named for its appearance from the street. Located next to the town's major cemetery, the house had two fourteen-by-fourteen rooms on each of two stories, with a four-foot-wide gallery on each side. There were two capacious closets on the ground floor, an adjoining dining room at the back and a kitchen and detached servants' quarters in the backyard. It was a spacious and pleasant place, and domestic tranquility was permitted to reign in its rooms as Margaret doted on her wounded son and the rest of her covey. Sam regaled his parents and siblings with tales of army life and his one battle, later writing the sensitive, evocative *Shiloh Shadows*, which recalls in detail the slaughter of the first day's melee.[79]

The only contretemps that autumn came when Maggie, fourteen, was laid low by scarlet fever while studying at Baylor. She had to withdraw from school and recuperate for several months at home, where she contentedly served her father as secretary.[80] As Margaret wrote Nannie at this time, "Your pa says tell Dr. McClintock his eyes is no better and he has despaired" of ever seeing well again.[81] Houston's health was failing as fast as his eyesight, and to compound his troubles, his old wounds were again acting up and draining. But he was probably involved in one last scheme.[82]

By late 1862, discontent with the war began to surface in Texas. This discontent, played upon by Unionists, mounted as horrifying casualty lists came in from Shiloh, the Seven Days battles and, worst of all, the hecatomb of Antietam. "It was reported," recalled Rip Ford, "that the wives of the soldiers wrote to their husbands urging them to come home," causing morale problems throughout the Southern armies.[83]

Houston was long opposed to sending Texas regiments to fight in other parts of the Confederacy, and he may well have considered some plan for getting them back. He was, it appears, again thinking of Texan independence, and perhaps even his beloved Mexican dream. Houston at least sounded out E. W. Cave and A. W. Terrill about this, even suggesting active interference to prevent dispatch of more Texas troops beyond the state, but they dissuaded him. He did, however, intercede at the request of Chief Billy Blount of the Alabamas to obtain the release of his braves from Confederate service.[84] The Cherokees in the army, however, neither sought nor wanted discharge, and served throughout the war.[85]

Governor Clark, worried by a rumored Unionist fifth column and especially by his predecessor, wrote Jefferson Davis that he suspected "an effort will be made soon by the submission party of the State, with General Houston at its head, to convert Texas into an independent Republic."[86] If anyone else's name had been mentioned in this regard, the idea would have been laughed at, but with Houston said to be involved . . . ? That he might have wide support was the governor's greatest fear. And in 1862 and 1863 there were, indeed, Unionist uprisings in Texas, which had to be put down with force.[87]

EIGHTEEN

Quoth the Raven Nevermore

Eighteen sixty-three was the crucible year of the Confederacy, a sad year that doomed the emergent nation as surely as Sam Houston's deteriorating body doomed him. Abraham Lincoln freed no slaves with his Emancipation Proclamation, but he introduced a moral imperative for what gradually grew into a Northern crusade, almost as if Houston had been heard in 1861: "Our people are going to war to perpetuate slavery, and the first gun fired in the war will be the knell of slavery."[1] The Confederacy was vitalized by no moral energy analogous to the antislavery crusade, and internal unrest and uncertainty spread. Grant took Vicksburg, and the Mississippi, the region's great internal highway, became a barrier dividing the South. Lee made a mistake at Gettysburg that gutted his veteran Army of Northern Virginia, shattered Southern morale and left the Confederacy on the defensive. King Cotton withered upon its shaky throne because of the blockade, while Europeans found alternative sources and realized that they did not need the South after all. The revolution begun by Eli Whitney in the year of Houston's birth had run its course.

> "Once I dreamed of an empire for an united People
> . . . the dream is over."
>
> SAM HOUSTON, 1863

At Huntsville, the Houstons "got by." The former governor, still popular with a segment of the population, hauled his tired frame to Houston, Independence and other towns to give speeches, and there were—to Governor Clark's consternation—several calls for him to run again for the state's highest office.[2] The Democratic machine imputed more power to Houston's "canvass" than reality could provide, however, and Charles Power did also, writing the old politician with great confidence that "I make no doubt but that the People will call you out yet for Governor."[3] Houston, who knew better, must have smiled sadly, for Power was as wrong as he had been about the "fuss" called the Civil War.

Expectations of political rebirth, however, were not held by Charles Power alone, and became so general that Houston had to publicly deny such ambitions. That spring he wrote influential Texans, forswearing politics, claiming that old age and a desire for "peace" precluded his candidacy. "Under no circumstances will I permit my name to be used as a Candidate" for any public office, he vowed, this time honestly.[4] Appropriately, Edward Everett Hale's story "Man Without a Country" was published at this time.

Nannie and Maggie remained with Nancy in Independence, caring for the woman-who-would-not-die. They did so in part to take some of the familial burden from Margaret's shoulders, for to the weight of her youngest children had been added the task of caring for an increasingly infirm husband. Young Sam remained at home convalescing, but he was by the spring frustrated by inactivity and by reading about battles fought elsewhere, some by his old regiment. His proud father wrote to E. W. Cave that while "his wound still troubles him," and "the physicians that discharged him said he would not be fit again for active Service," the young man craved action; he is "crazy to be back in the Army." Houston did not share the young man's dementia.[5]

As Sam mended and fidgeted, his father cast about for something to distract him from re-enlisting, and by early April he had cut a deal with Charles Power. "Cousin" Charles was a merchant who traveled often to Matamoros and beyond in search of profitable merchandise. With a sense of relief, Houston wrote Nannie in midmonth that "Sam has to leave to go with his uncle Charles to Mexico," as his assistant, and perhaps guard.[6] Sam did go south with his uncle for several months, and was out of harm's way while rivers of blood were spilled at Gettysburg and the Stars and Stripes were raised over Vicksburg.[7]

Sam Houston meanwhile closely followed the course of the war with growing sadness and anger. Lee, who had taken command of the Army of Northern Virginia in May 1862, he often lauded, but most Southern leaders, military and political, the old man excoriated, and not just in private. His most frequent target was Jefferson Davis, whom he had long before condemned for having the "ambition of Lucifer" and very little talent. Davis, felt Houston, was incompetent and was clearly mismanaging the war. In letters to his friend Cave, he referred to the Confederate president derisively as "Jeffy" and asserted that he was losing the war because of his "disposition to foster pets and West Point gentry."[8] West Point, of course, had long been an object of Houston's scorn, although most pre–Civil War graduates (including Davis) opted to leave the army. It was, in fact, the nearest thing to a national university that the United States would ever boast. But Houston saw it as fundamentally antidemocratic, writing Nannie that Davis's "unhappy penchant for *West Point* scrubs, and other *pets,* I fear will bring disaster upon our cause."[9] A week later, he waxed dangerously blunt in a note to Cave, blustering that "Davis deserves to be shot" for losing the war.[10] Apparently he was not worried about the authorities reading his mail in 1863.

By early that year he had seen his darkest prophecies come true, for true rivers of blood were flowing, and the South was obviously losing the war. He also sensed death's light but insistent tapping at his door. In a speech at Houston in March he again disavowed political aspirations, admitting that he had but little time left: "I have been buffeted by the waves, as I have been borne along time's ocean, until shattered and worn, I approach the narrow isthmus, which divides it from the sea of eternity beyond. . . . Once I dreamed of an empire for an united People . . . the dream is over."[11] In truth, an age was passing, and his audience, knowing that he was an exemplar of that age, was uncharacteristically still.

—————

"Though evidently a remarkable and clever man, he is
extremely egotistical and vain."

COLONEL A. J. L. FREMANTLE, 1863

On April 2, in Steamboat House, Houston drew up his last will and testament. He left virtually all his worldly possessions—and responsibilities—to Margaret, passing on to Sam the sword he had worn at San Jacinto, with the injunction that "it be drawn only in defense of the Constitution."* While the document made only passing reference to his daughters, he ordained that his sons should be rigidly educated: "I wish my Sons to be early taught an utter contempt for novels and light reading," and further, "my sons should receive solid and useful education, and that no part of their time should be devoted to the study of abstract science."

Sam Houston's appointed hour had not quite struck, however, nor was he at all eager that it should. Though immensely tired, he struggled to postpone his final repose. In April, Chief Billy Blount and some of his Alabama braves visited to pay their respects and give thanks for his intercession with the government. They sat council-style in a circle near the house, and according to an observer, "talked a long time in the Indian language." The Alabamas sang their ritual songs for Houston; it was a respectful symbolic farewell to the lifelong friend of the Indians.[12]

Patrician Arthur James L. Fremantle, a visiting British colonel on detached duty to observe the Civil War, encountered the infirm Houston at Galveston in May and left an unflattering portrait of the old warhorse:

Though evidently a remarkable and clever man, he is extremely egotistical and vain and much disappointed at having to subside from his

—————

* One wonders which "Constitution" Houston meant.

former grandeur . . . much given to chewing tobacco, and blowing his
nose with his fingers.[13]

By early June Houston's health was obviously failing. His eyesight
was nearly gone and his old wounds continued to plague him. He left
his family one more time and traveled a rather circuitous route to
popular Sour Lake springs to take the cure. Margaret wrote him worriedly, complaining that he had forgotten to pay the annual tax assess-
ment. "Had you not better attend to it immediately?" she queried, afraid
they might lose what little they had to the tax collectors.[14]

The "cure" failed to ameliorate his condition, and in July, as Lee's
army dragged itself back from the Gettysburg debacle, Houston contracted pneumonia at Huntsville. Bedridden in the downstairs front
room, where he could still have visitors, he grew weaker daily, sliding
in and out of coma. He was obviously dying.[15]

Young Sam was still in Mexico with Charles Power, but the rest of
the family gathered. On July 26, when the old man's breathing became
so labored that it barely wheezed oxygen over his tiny spark of life,
Margaret sent for some of their friends and a neighboring Presbyterian
minister, and the death watch commenced. As Jeff Hunt much later
recalled, "It was almost sundown. Everybody was crying, and I was
moaning with the rest." Perhaps thirty people were in the house when
Sam Houston passed over his isthmus and into the "sea of eternity,"
and Hunt was certain that his last, croaking words were "Margaret!
Margaret! Texas! Texas!"* He was gone.[16]

That evening, Margaret calmly wrote in her family Bible a spare but
fitting tribute:

Died on the 26th of July, 1863, Genl. Sam Houston, the beloved and
affectionate Husband, father, devoted patriot, the fearless soldier—
the meek and lowly Christian.[17]

Sam Houston's funeral was unpretentious and sparsely attended, perhaps at Margaret's wish. In fact, she had so little money that it was
some time before she could obtain a tombstone for the grave.[18] It was a
humble burial, even for a man who had sought the "People's" nomination for president.

---

* These words, which are found in many accounts, are almost certainly apocryphal.

An editorial-cum-obituary in a Houston newspaper not known for supporting Sam Houston reflected that:

Such power over men is unquestionably the most remarkable trait of his character . . . it was not in his virtue, for in the course of his life he passed through what would have been degradation to other men; and from the couch of the debauchee he has risen to the throne of power, his faculties clear, keen, unimpaired, and his authority unquestioned. So, let us shed tears to his memory, tears that are due to one who has filled so much of our affections. Let the whole people bury with him whatever of unkindness they had for him.[19]

"Alas, I am but dust and ashes!"

MARGARET HOUSTON, 1863

The Houston family was in dire straits as the earth fell upon the plain wooden coffin near Steamboat House. The general had never understood money management (nor had Margaret) and had left his family nearly penniless. The inventory of his estate appears impressive, listing a total of $89,288 in assets, but those were far from liquid and could not be translated into money for day-to-day expenses. The inventory also contradicts those who claim that Houston had magnanimously freed his slaves, for they were listed as property.[20] The twelve, ranging in age from four-year-old Lotte to fifty-five-year-old Lewis, were collectively appraised at a substantial $10,530.

Also, he had collected a bewildering scattering of land over the years; some 34,221 acres in all, located in twelve different counties. The land had a total evaluation of $60,910, but the inventory notes that many of the parcels were of "doubtful" ownership. And in war-torn Texas, even land of clear title was almost impossible to sell, a problem that would persist a decade and more following the war, for the state entered a deep depression and cash was almost unknown, the economy largely dependent upon barter. Also, many people owed Houston money, and had for years. All told, $16,748.10 was owed him, but no one had the money to settle. These monies were even more "doubtful" than the land titles. Included in the rather pathetic inventory were a wagon, Margaret's old yellow carriage, an old buggy, five horses, four cows and calves, a Burnside rifle and a brace of "pocket pistols," together valued at a paltry $1,100.[21]

In short, there was almost nothing left behind by Houston that could help Margaret and her flock in everyday life; not even enough livestock to provide sustenance. It is possible that Joshua, the blacksmith slave who had amassed considerable money by working on his own account, offered his mistress cash, but if he did, she declined.[22]

As Margaret pondered her impecunity, she defrauded posterity by informally editing her husband's life to "protect" his reputation. Soon after his death she sorted through his papers and burned trunkfuls of letters, notes and other documents. This no doubt explains the absence of letters from Anna Raguet and many others who figured prominently in Sam Houston's life.[23]

For some months the Houstons lived on credit and the generosity of their friends, especially E. W. Cave, who helped Margaret dispose of some of her real estate, albeit at abysmally low prices.[24] Much to her disappointment, Sam returned to the army late in the year, but she was vastly relieved that he was now a lieutenant and posted for some months near Houston.

Characteristically glum, she wrote him in November about her new and "severe illness." Also, "Poor Maggie has been very ill. Thank God I humbly trust she is prepared for life or death or whatever may be ordained for her," because she was a true Christian. She used Maggie's trauma to urge Sam to convert as well: "Oh, my son, will you not tear yourself away from your gay associates" and attend a revival? "Is it not better to sacrifice a few sinful pleasures, than to be cast with them into Hell?" Then, sounding like her own mother, she indulged in guilt-inspiring self-pity: "Alas, I am but dust and ashes!"[25] If Sam had not been long inured to such gloom, news of Maggie and his mother at the portals of death would have been a heavy burden to bear.

Sometime toward the end of the year Margaret managed to purchase a modest house at Independence, near Nancy, whose health was finally truly failing.[26] The family moved in the first week of January, and Margaret was soon bombarding Sam with news of various acquaintances recently deceased, reminding him once more that true Christians need not fear death: "Oh, what a blessed thing to be 'always ready.' " It was the harshest winter she had ever experienced, she noted, and "a cold bleak Norther is whistling around us today." For a change, everyone but Nancy was well, but she "has been confined to her bed a long time, and I do not think she will ever get up again." [27]

"Sickness and death have been busy among us."

MARGARET HOUSTON, 1867

Nancy never did arise alive from her bed, and on February 7 quietly expired; "a peaceful and happy departure," according to her daughter. Margaret herself was again bedridden when Nancy died, lamenting that she "had not the strength to be present" at the funeral. But she wrote Sam almost proudly that "her remains were put in her metallic coffin and deposited in her Vault," as she had so long desired. "I am told the scene was very impressive." [28] Nancy bequeathed to her daughter her house and a slave (but no money).

Sam, despite his father's injunctions, was writing a great deal of poetry, as well as the much longer *Shiloh Shadows*. He often sent his poems to his sisters, who were utterly thrilled. Maggie boasted of one, "The Soldier's Prayer," that "everybody that saw it said it was *beautiful*." [29] She wrote him later about another of his efforts, "The Southern Flag," which she had found "perfectly beautiful," asking sincerely if "you are going to have it published?" [30] Margaret ignored her husband's disdain for literature and urged her son on with his writing: "I hope you will continue to cultivate your genius." [31] He did.

In scores of letters to the children one can see the emergence of unaccustomed optimism, marred by very little self-pity or complaint of her own illnesses. Margaret was changing dramatically, although her evangelical fervor was still at fever pitch. This change came about despite a poverty so marked that in 1866 an embarrassed state government (pushed by Houston's friend, Union-imposed governor Andrew Jackson Hamilton) finally paid the former governor's back wages. Although Texas was economically imploding, Margaret was relieved to receive from the state treasurer "a draft on Galveston for $1,925.00 *in gold coin,* which you can endorse [and cash] or sell for a premium" anywhere in the specie-starved state.[32]

Most of that money went to settle accounts run up with trusting merchants in the previous three years. In search of additional funds, Margaret contacted William Carey Crane, whom she had known in Alabama. She proposed that he edit Houston's remaining papers and write his life story, some of the royalties to accrue to her. He agreed, but the resulting *Life and Select Literary Remains of Sam Houston of Texas* appeared long after Mrs. Houston's demise.[33] Adding to the strains of penury, a yellow fever epidemic was reaping a rich harvest in Texas, which Margaret sadly reported, but did not dwell upon. "Sickness and death have been busy among us."[34] She was soon writing that "nearly all our friends have died of the yellow fever" in recent weeks.[35]

In November and December the fever ravaged Independence and its environs, and Margaret, sustained by her faith, served as volunteer nurse, comforting the sick and dying. The inevitable occurred. She contracted yellow fever herself, and within forty-eight hours, on December 3, she died. She had wanted to be buried next to her husband at Huntsville, but public health ordinances mandated immediate burial. The evening of her passing, she was carted by E. W. Cave and several of her children to the local cemetery and interred with minimal ceremony.[36] Later, Nancy was removed from her crypt and buried beside her daughter.[37]

In 1875 a sad footnote was appended to the Sam Houston chronicle. Lawyer John Henry Brown petitioned the commissioner of the Texas General Land Office on behalf of Willie Rogers Houston, then seventeen, who was seeking a clerkship: "That the children of General Houston in their poverty should be ignored and overlooked by the state authorities, is a source of pain to thousands."[38]

Fame, but never fortune.

Epilogue

When Sam Houston was born in 1793 the fifteen United States constituted a fragile nation, or experiment, most of whose small population lived within a day's ride of the Atlantic Ocean. When he died seventy years later his nation (despite the bloodbath of the Civil War) was transcontinental, its thirty-five states crowding the Atlantic, the Pacific and the Gulf of Mexico.

Sam Houston had had a great deal to do with this unparalleled growth. His intrigues and leadership had wrenched Texas from Mexico and his voice and pen had popularized Manifest Destiny and the right of the United States to expand not only into Texas, but also into Oregon Territory, today's Southwest and northern Mexico and Cuba (although these last were not realized). His dreams even at times envisioned a single nation spanning the region from the Canadian border to southern Panama.

As a major advocate of, and actor in, this unprecedented national and human drama, Houston was continually wrapped in controversy. Virtually nothing he did, said or even thought escaped his detractors' vitriol. Twice shedding hero's blood on the battlefield, he incurred the enmity of powerful men (most of them veterans of the same campaigns) who questioned his bravery and wisdom. He was governor of Tennessee while a young man, but his failed first marriage generated disillusionment, resentment and anger, which grew apace after he literally fled that state for the frontier. Dogged with allegations of fraud and filibusterism for decades, he nonetheless served two terms as president of Texas, from which position he attracted even more criticism and dedicated foes. His thirteen years in the Senate hardly slackened his enemies' assaults, and well before they were over, he was roundly denounced as anti-Southern in his own region while he explored avenues to the presidency of the whole nation. In old age, as governor of Texas, he sought to preserve the Union, and failing that, to have Texas again an independent nation, but was widely considered a traitor for doing so.

Sam Houston often swam against the popular tide, to be sure, but one can strongly sense that the key to the controversies of his life is found in his penchant for secrecy—or hinting, rather than revealing—and his chronic vacillation at crucial moments. The two characteristics are spliced together into a stout, unravelable cord.

Why did he not reveal the reasons for his separation from Eliza in 1829, calm the passions swirling through Tennessee and perhaps save his reputation? Was he really and seriously considering a filibuster into Texas in the years thereafter as so many believed? If he had openly and soberly committed himself to such an adventure he probably could have gained the support—both financial and human—necessary to achieve his ends. Even in his dotage he left no more than scattered and tantalizing hints. Was the famous victory at San Jacinto of his making, or did "the battle make him," as was charged by one of his subordinates? Why did he, by his own admission, take no one into his counsel in the critical months of the Texas Revolution? Was he forced to stand and fight, as so many veterans averred? He never stooped to sweep away those charges.

Was he serious about invading Mexico while Texian president? He often said so, albeit in vague and general terms, but no concrete actions point to it with certainty. Did the gap between his verbiage and his deeds stem from vacillation? When a United States senator, and again in 1860, he let it be known that he would consider candidacy for the White House, but was he serious? He toyed with nomination from three different parties (Democratic, American and Constitutional Union) in three different election years and appeared to begin a campaign as the

"People's" candidate, yet he failed to commit himself enough to actually campaign, and even his letters to people close to him evinced only allusion. Was he really about to get financing from British sources, volunteers from the Knights of the Golden Circle and friends like Ben McCulloch, and weapons from the secretary of war to invade Mexico in 1859 and 1860? His letters indicate that he was, and men like McCulloch and Edward Burleson, Jr., believed it, but he stopped short of implementing the plan. Was he genuinely expecting to have Texas leave the Union as an independent nation in 1861 as he so often said and wrote? He did not attempt to realize the plan.

For that matter, just how sincere was he as a family man? His voluminous correspondence with his wife Margaret, mother of their eight children, is often saccharine and almost cloying. He missed her so much it physically hurt him and made him feel empty, he constantly wrote, yet he managed to be away from them almost all the time and never really attempted to have them with him in Washington. Even when he was "home," he was rarely with his family, but instead politicking, canvassing, stumping and visiting, crisscrossing Texas as if to establish a record for mileage. But his letters always hark back to the familial hearth around which his wife and children were gathered.

What is one to make of such a man, whose protestations were so much at variance with his performance? His words apparently referred but to things he wanted to do or achieve, not to things he would consistently strive and put himself at risk for. It almost seems as if Sam Houston wanted others to do for him what he was content to only imagine, visualize or propose. He took risks most unwillingly. Julia Ann Conner alluded to his manipulative skills in 1827, and his best friend, Ashbel Smith, almost summed Houston up after his death when he wrote of the man (not for publication), "His self control, his self mastery was perfect . . . this seeming passion was all pure judgment and calm calculation." Sam Houston was not what he seemed to most people to be, and therein lies the controversy.

NOTES

1. SAM HOUSTON AND HIS AMERICA

1. Kenneth F. Kiple, *Blacks in Colonial Cuba, 1774–1899* (Gainesville, Fla., 1976), pp. 4–5.
2. Donald Day and Harry H. Ullom (eds.), *The Autobiography of Sam Houston* (Norman, Okla., 1954), p. 3; Charles Edwards Lester, *The Life of Sam Houston (the Only Authentic Memoir of Him Ever Published)* (New York, 1855), p. 18.
3. G. W. Featherstonhaugh, *Excursion Through the Slave States, from Washington on the Potomac to the Frontier of Mexico; with Sketches of Popular Manners and Geological Notices* (New York, 1844), p. 29.
4. See Marquis James, *The Raven* (Indianapolis, 1929), p. 6.
5. Donald Braider, *Solitary Star: A Biography of Sam Houston* (New York, 1974), p. 18.
6. Houston to Margaret Lea, March 1, 1837 [1839], E.C.B. 2R49, Vol. II.
7. Lester, pp. 18–20.
8. Thomas H. Kreneck, "Sam Houston's Quest for Personal Harmony: An Interpretation." Ph.D. diss., Bowling Green State University, 1981, p. 70.
9. Houston to Colonel M. Arbuckle from Wigwam Neosho, July 31, 1830, E.C.B. 2E250, Vol. II.
10. Houston to James Buchanan, Sept. 21, 1824, E.C.B. 2E250, Vol. II.
11. Houston to Margaret, Sept. 23, 1840, E.C.B. 3L249.
12. Braider, p. 82.
13. Kreneck, p. 11.
14. See Braider, p. 14. In later years Houston did his best to steer his own son, Sam, away from the classics toward more "practical" studies. See

Lenoir Hunt (ed.), *My Master: The Inside Story of Sam Houston and His Times, by His Former Slave, Jeff Hamilton* (Dallas, 1940), p. 46, and various letters of Houston to his son.

15. For example, see Houston to John Houston in 1826 and 1828, in Amelia W. Williams and Eugene C. Barker (eds.), *Writings of Sam Houston* (8 vols., Austin), II, pp. 7, 11, 12.

16. For Jackson, see Robert V. Remini, *Andrew Jackson and the Course of American Empire, 1767–1821* (3 vols., New York, 1977–1984).

17. Houston to son Sam, April 30, 1860, in *Writings*, VIII, p. 33.

18. See orders of Jackson, Oct. 4, 1806, and Jackson to Burr, Nov. 25, 1806, in Mary-Jo Kline (ed.), *Political Correspondence and Public Papers of Aaron Burr* (3 vols., Princeton, N.J., 1983), II, pp. 996, 1005n.

19. Martha Anne Turner, *Sam Houston and His Twelve Women: The Ladies Who Influenced the Life of Texas' Greatest Statesman* (Austin, 1966), p. 2.

20. Ibid., p. 1; Braider, p. 15; James, p. 11; Day and Ullom (eds.), p. 5.

21. See James, p. 11. He gives a suspiciously specific figure: $3,659.86. See also Braider, p. 15.

22. Robert V. Remini, *The Life of Andrew Jackson* (New York, 1988), p. 20n.

23. See John Ehle, *Trail of Tears: The Rise and Fall of the Cherokee Nation* (New York, 1988), pp. 2, 44.

24. Ibid., p. 106; Remini, *The Life*, pp. 13–14.

25. Remini, *The Life*, p. 16.

26. See James, p. 16.

27. See letters of Samuel D. Morgan and Willoughby Williams, in Josephus C. Guild, *Old Times in Tennessee, with Historical, Personal, and Political Scraps and Sketches* (Nashville, 1878), pp. 274, 283.

28. See Braider, p. 21; Llerena Friend, *Sam Houston: The Great Designer* (Austin, 1954), p. 5.

29. Day and Ullom (eds.), pp. 6–7.

30. James, p. 17.

31. Ibid., p. 19. This account does seem a bit cute.

32. See Ehle, pp. 3, 14; Cephas Washburn, "Mission Among the Cherokees of Arkansas," in Eugene L. Schwaab (ed.), *Travels in the Old South: Selected from Periodicals of the Times* (2 vols., Lexington, Ky., 1973), I, pp. 149–156.

33. See R. S. Cotterill, *The Southern Indians: The Story of the Civilized Tribes Before Removal* (Norman, Okla., 1954), pp. 60–67.

34. Ibid., p. 186.

35. Mary Whatley Clarke, *Chief Bowles and the Texas Cherokees* (Norman, Okla., 1971), pp. 4–8; Ehle, passim; A Traveler, "On the Condition of the Cherokees," in Schwaab (ed.), pp. 222–225.

36. Ehle, pp. 43, 84.

37. Cotterill, pp. 159–166; Ehle, pp. 95–97; Clarke, *Bowles*, p. 13.

38. James, pp. 20, 22.

39. Braider, p. 24.
40. See Samuel G. Heiskell, *Andrew Jackson and Early Tennessee History* (2 vols., Nashville, Tenn., 1920), I, p. 150.
41. Braider, p. 24; James, p. 20.
42. Quoted in Day and Ullom (eds.), p. 6.
43. Ibid.; James, p. 22.
44. Willoughby Williams to J. C. Guild, April 1, 1878, in Guild, p. 274.
45. Cotterill, pp. 4, 179; Braider, p. 26; Ehle, p. 97.
46. Cotterill, pp. 160, 170, 177.
47. Ehle, p. 105; Braider, p. 32.
48. Friend, p. 6; James, p. 24.
49. Friend, p. 6.
50. Day and Ullom (eds.), p. 8; Friend, p. 6.
51. M. A. Turner, p. 2.
52. Braider, pp. 27–29; Heiskell, p. 152; Friend, p. 6, claims it was the Union Academy.
53. Ehle, p. 105.
54. David Crockett, *A Narrative of the Life of David Crockett, of the State of Tennessee, Written by Himself* (Philadelphia, 1834), pp. 104–105.
55. Friend, p. 6; Samuel D. Morgan to Willoughby Williams, April 23, 1878, in Guild, p. 283; Braider, p. 29.
56. Day and Ullom (eds.), p. 9.
57. Ibid. The story of the musket is almost certainly apocryphal. The United States Army provided standardized arms to all recruits.
58. Willoughby Williams to J. C. Guild, April 1, 1878, and Samuel D. Morgan to Willoughby Williams, April 23, 1878, in Guild, pp. 275, 283.
59. Charles W. Crawford, *Governors of Tennessee, I, 1790–1835* (Memphis, 1979), p. 152. He incorrectly states the year as 1814.
60. Ibid.
61. James, p. 30.
62. Edward M. Coffman, *The Old Army: A Portrait of the American Army in Peacetime, 1784–1898* (New York, 1986), p. 17.
63. See Remini, *The Life*, p. 231.
64. Elbert B. Smith, *Magnificent Missourian: The Life of Thomas Hart Benton* (New York, 1958), p. 48.
65. Remini, *Andrew Jackson* (New York, 1966), pp. 62–64.
66. Crockett, p. 72; Remini, *Andrew Jackson*, p. 73; Cotterill, pp. 185–188.
67. Ehle, pp. 106–109; Cotterill, pp. 187–188.
68. Houston to Secretary of War William Crawford, Feb. 16, 1816, in *Writings*, I, p. 6; Remini, *Andrew Jackson*, pp. 71, 78–79.
69. Ehle, p. 116.
70. John K. Mahon, *The War of 1812* (Gainesville, Fla., 1972), p. 243.
71. Benson J. Lossing, *The Pictorial Field-Book of the War of 1812* (New York, 1868), p. 779; Mahon, pp. 243–244.

72. Day and Ullom (eds.), pp. 11–12.
73. See James, p. 33.
74. Ibid.
75. Lossing, pp. 779–780.
76. Day and Ullom (eds.), p. 14.
77. Ibid.
78. James, pp. 34–35; Braider, p. 33.
79. Francis S. Key, *Speech of Francis S. Key, Esq., Counsel for Gen. Samuel Houston, on His Trial Before the House of Representatives for a Breach of Privilege* (Washington, D.C., 1832), p. 4.
80. See Houston to John Houston, July 31, 1833: "My wound was sore, and some bones were working out of it when I came here." In *Writings*, V, p. 5.
81. Hunt (ed.), p. 103.
82. Ashbel Smith, "Opinions of Sam Houston," n.d., E.C.B. 2R50, Vol. XI.
83. Lossing, p. 780.
84. Remini, *Andrew Jackson*, p. 83; Remini, *Andrew Jackson and the Course*, I, p. 216.
85. Remini, *Andrew Jackson*, p. 83; Remini, *Andrew Jackson and the Course*, I, p. 216.
86. Remini, *Andrew Jackson and the Course*, I, p. 217.
87. Lossing, p. 782.
88. Remini, *Andrew Jackson*, p. 85; Ehle, p. 123. For an analysis of Jackson's consistent anti-Indian policies and sentiments, see James West Davidson and Mark Hamilton Lytle, *After the Fact: The Art of Historical Detection* (2d ed., New York, 1986), pp. 85–114.
89. Ehle, p. 121.
90. Day and Ullom (eds.), p. 15.
91. Willoughby Williams to J. C. Guild, April 1, 1878, in Guild, p. 275.
92. Quoted in Day and Ullom (eds.), p. 15.
93. Friend, p. 7.

2. SOME SAM HOUSTON CONTRETEMPS

1. Certificate of "waggon master Saml. Houston," July 6, 1814, E.C.B. 2E253.
2. Remini, *Andrew Jackson and the Course*, I, p. 321.
3. Houston to James Monroe, March 1, 1815, in *Writings*, I, p. 3.
4. Houston to John Rhea, March 1, 1815, ibid., p. 1.
5. Houston to Captain Alexander Campbell, April 25, 1815, ibid., p. 4.
6. Braider, p. 38.
7. See Day and Ullom (eds.), p. 17; James, p. 37.
8. Day and Ullom (eds.), p. 17.
9. Braider, p. 39; James, p. 39.

10. James, p. 37.
11. Remini, *Andrew Jackson and the Course,* I, p. 321.
12. Houston to William Crawford, Feb. 16, 1816, in *Writings,* I, p. 6.
13. Jackson to John C. Calhoun, Sept. 30, 1819, in Edwin W. Hemphill (ed.), *The Papers of John C. Calhoun* (18 vols., Columbia, S.C., 1961ff), IV, p. 355.
14. Braider, p. 39; Friend, p. 8.
15. Cotterill, p. 204.
16. Ehle, pp. 149–150, 154–155; Day and Ullom (eds.), p. 18.
17. Cotterill, p. 205.
18. Acting Secretary of War George Graham to Houston, Oct. 21, 1817, E.C.B. 2E250, Vol. III.
19. Ehle, pp. 133, 150.
20. Houston to John C. Calhoun, Dec. 14, 1817, in Hemphill (ed.), *Calhoun Papers,* II, p. 16.
21. Cherokee delegation note, Dec. 13, 1817, ibid., p. 15.
22. Governor McMinn to John C. Calhoun, Jan. 16, 1818, ibid., pp. 76–77.
23. John C. Calhoun to William G. Blount, Dec. 30, 1817, ibid., p. 45.
24. Braider, p. 44; James, p. 41.
25. Ehle, p. 179.
26. Day and Ullom (eds.), p. 19.
27. Houston to John C. Calhoun, Feb. 24, 1818, in Hemphill (ed.), *Calhoun Papers,* II, p. 158.
28. Braider, p. 45; Friend, p. 8.
29. Quoted in Day and Ullom (eds.), p. 19.
30. See Houston Senate speech, Sept. 9, 1850, in *Writings,* V, p. 245.
31. Quoted in M. A. Turner, p. 12.
32. Braider, p. 47.
33. John C. Calhoun to William Crawford, March 5, 1818, authorizing this disbursement, in Hemphill (ed.), *Calhoun Papers,* II, p. 174.
34. Braider, pp. 47–48; Friend, pp. 8–9. See also M. A. Turner, pp. 6–7.
35. James, p. 47; Day and Ullom (eds.), pp. 20–21.
36. Friend, p. 9; Braider, p. 48.
37. Remini, *The Life,* pp. 119–124.
38. Houston to John C. Calhoun, July 21, 1820, in Hemphill (ed.), *Calhoun Papers,* V, p. 275.
39. Houston to John C. Calhoun, March 11, 1822, ibid., VI, p. 737. In this letter, Houston recapitulated the matter.
40. Jackson to John C. Calhoun, May 2, 1822, ibid., VII, p. 90.
41. John C. Calhoun to Jackson, April 6, 1822, ibid., p. 14.
42. Houston to John C. Calhoun, July 5, 1822, ibid., p. 202.
43. Thomas S. Jesup, quartermaster general, to John C. Calhoun, April 20, 1824, ibid., IX, p. 41, for another such claim.
44. Braider, p. 49.

45. Jackson to John C. Calhoun, Sept. 30, 1819, in Hemphill (ed.), *Calhoun Papers*, IV, pp. 354–355.
46. James, p. 49. See also Houston Senate speech, Sept. 9, 1850, in *Writings*, V, pp. 241, 245.
47. Braider, p. 50.
48. Houston to Joseph McMinn, March 30, 1823, in *Writings*, I, p. 18.
49. James, p. 48; Day and Ullom (eds.), p. 22; Braider, p. 51.
50. Friend, p. 9.
51. Ibid.
52. Day and Ullom (eds.), p. 26; Friend, p. 10; James, p. 51; Crawford, p. 155.
53. Hugh Best (ed.), *Debrett's Texas Passage* (New York, 1983), p. 330.
54. See Melish, *Information and Advice to Emigrants to the United States* (1819), passim; Gordon Carruth, *The Encyclopedia of American Facts and Dates* (8th ed., New York, 1987), p. 146.
55. See Best (ed.), pp. 228–229, 334.
56. Gregory and Strickland, p. 144; Ehle, pp. 87, 142.
57. Smith, *Magnificent Missourian*, p. 160.
58. Ibid., pp. 144–145; Crawford, p. 162; certificate granting lot No. 463, Leftwich Grant, to Alex McClure, Oct. 15, 1825, signed by Secretary John Erwin, at Nashville. Lilly Library, Latin American MSS, Mexico.
59. Crawford, p. 162.
60. Petition of Haden Edwards to the Mexican Congress, Jan. 5, 1824, in Lilly Library, Latin American MSS, Mexico.
61. Crawford, p. 162; Braider, p. 51.
62. Friend, p. 10.
63. Braider, p. 54.
64. James, p. 53.
65. Ibid., p. 52.
66. See M. A. Turner, p. 9.
67. Friend, p. 10.
68. Ibid., p. 11.
69. See George Ticknor Curtis, *Life of James Buchanan* (2 vols., New York, 1883), I, p. 514n.
70. See James, p. 56.
71. M. A. Turner, p. 9.
72. Quoted in Day and Ullom (eds.), p. 29.
73. Braider, p. 57.
74. Quoted in Day and Ullom (eds.), pp. 32–33.
75. James K. Polk to Houston, Sept. 21, 1824, E.C.B. 2E250, Vol. III.
76. Eugene I. McCormac, *James K. Polk: A Political Biography* (Berkeley, Calif., 1922), p. 5.
77. See his speech on this issue in *Writings*, I, pp. 28–38.
78. Jackson to Houston, Feb. 15, 1826, E.C.B. 3N199.

79. Jackson to Houston, March 8, 1826, E.C.B. 3N197; Merrill D. Peterson, *The Great Triumvirate* (New York, 1987), p. 414.

80. Peterson, *The Great Triumvirate,* p. 414.

81. Houston to President Adams, March 18, 1826, E.C.B. 2E250.

82. See James F. Hopkins and Mary W. M. Hargreaves (eds.), *The Papers of Henry Clay* (5 vols., Lexington, Ky., 1959–1973), V, p. 699n; Friend, p. 14.

83. Colonel H. to Dr. Boyd McNairy, Sept. 21, 1826, E.C.B. 3N199.

84. See Friend, p. 14.

85. Braider, p. 68; Friend, p. 12.

86. Friend, p. 14.

87. Hopkins and Hargreaves (eds.), *The Papers of Henry Clay,* IV, p. 716.

88. James R. White to James K. Polk, Dec. 30, 1826, in Herbert Weaver (ed.), *Correspondence of James K. Polk* (4 vols., Nashville, 1969–1979), I, p. 67.

89. Braider, p. 66.

90. Charles Grier Sellers, *James K. Polk, Jacksonian, 1795–1843* (Princeton, N.J., 1957), pp. 136–137.

91. James, p. 69.

92. Julia Ann M. C. Conner, *Travel Journal, 1827,* in Conner Family Papers, South Carolina Historical Society.

3. SAM HOUSTON ON THE PENDULUM

1. Friend, p. 16.

2. W. J. Rorabaugh, *The Alcoholic Republic: An American Tradition* (New York, 1979), p. 25.

3. Ibid., p. 25.

4. Peterson, *The Great Triumvirate,* p. 394.

5. Remini, *The Life,* pp. 143, 180.

6. Ibid., p. 213.

7. Conner, *Travel Journal,* SCHS, Sept. 3, 1827.

8. Crawford, p. 162.

9. Weaver (ed.), *Correspondence of James K. Polk,* I, p. 48n.

10. See E.C.B. 3L249; Braider, p. 71.

11. See M. A. Turner, pp. 75–77.

12. A. Yell to James K. Polk, in Weaver (ed.), *Correspondence of James K. Polk,* I, p. 160.

13. Houston to John Houston, Nov. 10, 1828, E.C.B. 2E250, Vol. II.

14. Quoted in Braider, p. 73.

15. See Crawford, p. 161.

16. M.B.H. description of Eliza, Sept. 6, 1871, E.C.B. 3L249.

17. *Dallas News,* Oct. 27, 1934, ibid.

18. M.B.H. description of Eliza, Sept. 6, 1871, ibid.

19. See Paul I. Wellman, *The House Divides: The Age of Jackson and Lincoln, from the War of 1812 to the Civil War* (Garden City, N.Y., 1966), p. 122.
20. For example, James, p. 74.
21. M. A. Turner, p. 13.
22. Friend, p. 19.
23. Remini, *The Life,* p. 173.
24. *Dallas News,* Oct. 27, 1943, in E.C.B. 3L249; James, p. 74.
25. Anon., n.d., E.C.B. 3L249.
26. M. A. Turner, p. 13.
27. See Wellman, p. 121; M. A. Turner, p. 14.
28. James, p. 75.
29. Braider, p. 75; Day and Ullom (eds.), p. 45.
30. Crawford, p. 161.
31. Braider, p. 79.
32. Willoughby Williams to J. C. Guild, April 1, 1878, in Guild, p. 278.
33. Jackson to ?, April 2, 1829, in John Spencer Bassett (ed.), *Correspondence of Andrew Jackson* (6 vols., Washington, D.C., 1933), IV, p. 21.
34. Houston to John Allen, April 9, 1829, in *Writings,* I, p. 130.
35. Quoted in Crawford, p. 161; Braider, p. 80.
36. Willoughby Williams to J. C. Guild, April 1, 1878, in Guild, pp. 278–279; Braider, p. 83.
37. See M. A. Turner, p. 16; Braider, p. 79.
38. Friend, p. 21.
39. Willoughby Williams to J. C. Guild, April 1, 1878, in Guild, p. 278.
40. James, p. 81; Friend, p. 22.
41. Quoted in James, p. 78. See also Willoughby Williams to J. C. Guild, April 1, 1878, in Guild, p. 278.
42. Houston resignation, April 16, 1829, in *Writings,* I, pp. 131–132.
43. Braider, p. 87; Friend, p. 23.
44. Gregory and Strickland, p. 5.
45. Quoted in Wellman, p. 122.
46. Quoted in Guild, pp. 271–272. J. C. Guild was himself a member of this odd committee.
47. Ibid., p. 273.
48. See *Montgomery Advertiser,* Dec. 27, 1907, in E.C.B. 2R250, Vol. II; and M. A. Turner, p. 18.
49. Quoted in Crawford, p. 162.
50. Quoted in Braider, p. 89.
51. See Sellers, p. 139.
52. G. W. Featherstonhaugh, *Excursion Through the Slave States, from Washington on the Potomac to the Frontier of Mexico; with Sketches of Popular Manners and Geological Notices* (New York, 1844), p. 52.
53. "Cephas Washburn's Mission to Arkansas," in Schwaab (ed.), p. 151.
54. Quoted in James, p. 85.

55. Ibid., p. 90; Friend, p. 92; Gregory and Strickland, p. 6.
56. Friend, p. 92.
57. See Best (ed.), *Debrett's,* p. 228.
58. Lonnie J. White, *Politics on the Southwestern Frontier: Arkansas Territory, 1819–1836* (Memphis, 1964), pp. 34–35, 135, 203; *Writings,* VII, p. 3n.
59. Charles F. M. Noland to William Noland, from Little Rock, May 11, 1829, E.C.B. 2R49, Vol. II.
60. Houston to Jackson from Little Rock, May 11, 1829, in *Writings,* I, pp. 132–133.
61. Quoted in Friend, p. 51.
62. Daniel S. Donelson to Jackson, June (?) 1829, in "Documents," *Tennessee Historical Quarterly (THQ),* III, No. 4 (Dec., 1944), pp. 350–351.
63. Wellman, p. 123.
64. Thomas Hart Benton to Houston, Aug. 15, 1829, E.C.B. 3N197.
65. See Friend, p. 39.
66. Jackson to Secretary of War John Forsyth, Jan. 23, 1838, Bassett (ed.), V, pp. 530–531. In this letter, Jackson recapitulated the earlier affair.
67. Ibid., V, p. 529n.
68. Braider, p. 91.
69. Day and Ullom (eds.), p. 51.
70. Friend, pp. 24–25; James, p. 92.
71. Quoted in Kreneck, p. 106.
72. Gregory and Strickland, pp. 8–9; James, p. 99.
73. Houston to John Houston, June 24, 1829, E.C.B. 2E250, Vol. II.
74. James, p. 95.
75. Remini, *The Life,* pp. 212–215.
76. Quoted in Ehle, p. 220. See Davidson and Lytle, pp. 105–109.
77. Ehle, pp. 222–223.
78. Ibid., p. 237.

4. THE FRONTIER

1. Braider, p. 91; *Writings,* I, p. 151.
2. See Day and Ullom (eds.), p. 140.
3. James, p. 108.
4. George W. Pierson (ed.), *Tocqueville and Beaumont in America* (New York, 1938), p. 256.
5. James, pp. 105–106.
6. Friend, p. 9.
7. Gregory and Strickland, p. 158.
8. Friend, pp. 25–26.
9. James, p. 117.
10. Houston to Secretary of War John Eaton, June 24, 1829, in *Writings,* I, pp. 134–135.

11. Houston to Jackson from Cantonment Gibson, Sept. 19, 1829, ibid., pp. 141–143.
12. John Jolly, Walter Webber, Aaron Price and John Brown, certificate of citizenship for Sam Houston, Oct. 21, 1829, ibid., pp. 143–144.
13. Houston to John Overton, Dec. 28, 1829, ibid., pp. 144–145.
14. Wellman, p. 124.
15. Gregory and Strickland, pp. 159–160.
16. Day and Ullom (eds.), p. 58.
17. Braider, p. 97; James, p. 133.
18. See *Writings,* I, p. 205n; Braider, p. 99; Houston to James Prentiss, March 27, 1832, E.C.B. 2E250, Vol. II.
19. Houston to John Van Fossen, April 14, 1830, in *Writings,* I, p. 149.
20. Friend, p. 27; Braider, p. 98.
21. Houston to John Van Fossen, April 4, 1830, in *Writings,* I, pp. 147–149.
22. James, p. 135.
23. Day and Ullom (eds.), p. 66.
24. Friend, p. 51.
25. Robert Mayo, *Political Sketches of Eight Years in Washington* (Baltimore, 1839), p. 120.
26. Ibid., p. 119.
27. Ibid., pp. 120–129; Best (ed.), p. 363.
28. Jackson to William S. Fulton, Dec. 10, 1830, in Bassett (ed.), IV, pp. 212–213.
29. Jackson to Colonel Anthony Butler, Feb. 15, 1831, ibid., pp. 243–245. See also John M. Belohlavek, *"Let the Eagle Soar!" The Foreign Policy of Andrew Jackson* (Lincoln, Nebr., 1985), p. 223; John Niven, *Martin Van Buren* (New York, 1983), pp. 280–282.
30. Belohlavek, p. 223.
31. William S. Fulton testimony, 1837, in Bassett (ed.), V, p. 541n.
32. Mayo, p. 119; Allen Nevins (ed.), *The Diary of John Quincy Adams, 1794–1845* (New York, 1951), p. 488.
33. Mayo, p. 119, and Jackson to D. G. Goodlett, March 12, 1844, in Bassett (ed.), VI, pp. 273–275.
34. Nevins (ed.), *The Diary of John Quincy Adams,* entry for March 31, 1843, p. 548.
35. James, pp. 137–140.
36. Best (ed.), pp. 343–344.
37. Houston to Jackson, May 18, 1830, in *Writings,* I, pp. 149–150.
38. Gregory and Strickland, pp. 32–37; M. A. Turner, p. 21.
39. James, p. 150.
40. Lenoir Hunt (ed.), *My Master: The Inside Story of Sam Houston and His Times, by His Former Slave, Jeff Hamilton* (Dallas, 1940), p. 29.
41. Gregory and Strickland, pp. 99–101.
42. Ibid., p. 55.

43. Ibid., p. 56.
44. Ibid., pp. 59–60.
45. Houston to Colonel Matthew Arbuckle, July 21, 1830, E.C.B. 2E250, Vol. II.
46. Gregory and Strickland, p. 160.
47. Ibid. See also *Writings*, I, p. 205n.
48. Gregory and Strickland, pp. 70–71.
49. "A Traveler" (1830), in Schwaab (ed.), p. 223; Gregory and Strickland, pp. 75–77; Crawford, p. 163.
50. James, pp. 157–160.
51. Gregory and Strickland, p. 161.
52. Recollections of Matthew F. Maury, June 1831, E.C.B. 2E253.
53. Houston transfer of land to John C. McLemore and M. H. Howard, July 6, 1831, E.C.B. 2R49, Vol. I.
54. See James, p. 161; Braider, p. 109; Friend, p. 30. It should be noted that her grave has never been located. See Heiskell, p. 150.
55. Quoted in Braider, pp. 108–109.
56. Pierson (ed.), pp. 251–252, 256.
57. Braider, p. 110.
58. Sellers, p. 163.
59. See James, p. 163.
60. Braider, pp. 114–115.
61. Key, *Speech*, p. 15; James, p. 164.
62. Friend, p. 31.
63. See *Writings*, I, p. 202.
64. See Crawford, p. 165; James, p. 165. For Polk's ire, James K. Polk to Terry H. Cahal, May 4, 1832, in Weaver (ed.), *Correspondence of James K. Polk*, I, p. 473.
65. See *Writings*, I, p. 203.
66. See *Speech of Mr. Burges [Tristam] of Rhode Island in the Case of Samuel Houston, Delivered May 11, 1832* (Washington, D.C., 1832), pp. 6–9. This copy located in E.C.B.
67. Key, *Speech*, passim.
68. Quoted in Heiskell, p. 187.
69. James, p. 167.
70. Sellers, p. 164.
71. Ibid.
72. Quoted in Heiskell, p. 187. See also Day and Ullom (eds.), p. 68; Sellers, p. 164.
73. Quoted in Heiskell, p. 187. See also Day and Ullom (eds.), p. 68; Sellers, p. 164; James, pp. 168–169.
74. *Writings*, I, pp. 216–224.
75. See Wellman, p. 125.
76. Houston to James Prentiss, May 1, 1832, in *Writings*, I, p. 203.

77. Friend, p. 33; James, p. 171. See also Sellers, p. 164; *New York Times,* July 27, 1990, p. A8.
78. *Writings,* I, p. 225.
79. Friend, p. 34.
80. Houston to Jackson, April 20, 1834, in *Writings,* I, p. 239. Jackson's remission is dated July 3.
81. Quoted in Gregory and Strickland, p. 95.
82. Braider, p. 111.
83. See John Niven, *John C. Calhoun and the Price of Union: A Biography* (Baton Rouge, La., 1988), pp. 309–310.
84. Houston to Prentiss, May 1, 1832, E.C.B. 2E250.
85. James Prentiss to Houston, June 13, 1832, E.C.B. 2R49, Vol. I.
86. Houston to James Prentiss, June 1, 1832, E.C.B. 2E250.
87. Friend, p. 43, cites $8,502.90, but Prentiss to Houston, June 13, 1832, E.C.B. 2R49, Vol. I, notes the latter in debt to the former at this time for $5,000.
88. Houston to Prentiss, June 17, 1832, E.C.B. 2E250.
89. Houston to Prentiss, June 20, 1832, E.C.B. 2E250; Belohlavek, pp. 225, 228. By 1833, Jackson himself had lost faith in Butler, and become suspicious concerning not only his talents, but his honesty as well.
90. Houston to Charles F. M. Noland, June 10, 1832, in *Writings,* VII, pp. 2–3.
91. Houston to Daniel Jackson, July 12, 1832, E.C.B. 2E250.
92. Houston to Prentiss, July 10, 1832, E.C.B. 2E250.
93. Houston to Prentiss, Aug. 18, 1832, E.C.B. 2E250.
94. Houston to Prentiss, Sept. 11 and 15, 1832, E.C.B. 2E250; Kreneck, p. 95.
95. Houston to Prentiss, April 11, 1834, from City Hotel, New York, E.C.B. 2E250.
96. Gregory and Strickland, pp. 134–135; Day and Ullom (eds.), p. 77.
97. Anon., n.d., in E.C.B. 3L249.
98. James, p. 186.
99. Gregory and Strickland, pp. 49–52.
100. Two photographs of headstone, in E.C.B. 2R117.
101. Charles F. M. Noland to William Noland, Oct. 14, 1832, E.C.B. 2R49, Vol. I.
102. Houston to John Houston, Dec. 2, 1832, E.C.B. 2E250.

5. THE TEXAS CRUCIBLE

1. Donald W. Meinig, *Imperial Texas: An Interpretive Essay in Cultural Geography* (Austin, 1969), p. 23.
2. Joseph Milton Nance, *After San Jacinto: The Texas-Mexican Frontier, 1836–1841* (Austin, 1963), pp. 4–8.

3. Republished as *Journal of an Indian Trader: Anthony Glass and the Texas Trading Frontier, 1790–1810,* Dan L. Flores, ed. (College Station, Tex., 1983).

4. Best (ed.), pp. 27, 33–34.

5. See Best (ed.), p. 301.

6. See Gulick et al. (eds.), *Lamar,* III, pp. 280–281; Clarke, *Bowles,* p. 38n; Jacek Przygoda, *Texas Pioneers from Poland: A Study in the Ethnic History* (Waco, 1971), p. 6; David J. Weber, *The Mexican Frontier, 1821–1846: The American Southwest Under Mexico* (Albuquerque, 1982), p. 161; Francis R. Lubbock, *Six Decades in Texas: The Memoirs of Francis R. Lubbock, Confederate Governor of Texas* (Austin, 1968), p. 43; McMurtrie, pp. 5–11.

7. Lubbock, p. 43; *Texas Almanac (1861),* pp. 71–77.

8. See John Edward Weems, *Dream of Empire* (New York, 1971), pp. 27–28; Wellman, pp. 148–149.

9. Mark E. Nackman, "The Texas Experience, 1821–1861: The Emergence of Texas as a Separate Province and Texans as a Breed Apart." Ph.D. dissertation, Columbia University, 1973, pp. 22–23.

10. Weber, p. 162.

11. Meinig, p. 45.

12. Ibid., p. 33. See Haden Edwards, petition (in Spanish) for land grant, Jan. 5, 1824, in Lilly Library, Latin American MSS, Mexico.

13. Weber, p. 168; Kenneth William Wheeler, "Early Urban Development in Texas, 1836–1865." Ph.D. dissertation, University of Rochester, New York, 1964, pp. 21, 23.

14. Alexander Horton, "Recollections of Alexander Horton," *Texana,* VII, No. 3 (1967), pp. 275–276. Horton fought against the Edwards brothers, although he had settled in their colony.

15. Ibid., pp. 276–278.

16. Weber, pp. 167–169.

17. Ibid., p. 174; Best (ed.), p. 306.

18. See scrip of the Galveston Bay and Texas Land Company, dated Oct. 16, 1830, for *labor* No. 6292, in Mendel Collection, Lilly Library.

19. Weber, pp. 172–173.

20. Ibid., p. 230; Wheeler, dissertation, p. 99; McMurtrie, p. 5.

21. An Emigrant, *Texas in 1840, or the Emigrant's Guide to the New Republic* (New York, 1840), p. 231.

22. Frederick Law Olmsted, *A Journey Through Texas, or, a Saddle-Trip on the Southwestern Frontier* (New York, 1860), p. 111.

23. Weber, p. 171.

24. John H. Jenkins, *Audubon and Other Capers: Confessions of a Texas Bookmaker* (Austin, 1976), p. 52.

25. Anon., *A Visit to Texas: Being the Journal of a Traveler Through Those Parts Most Interesting to American Settlers* (New York, 1834), p. 214.

26. Weber, p. 97.

27. Ibid., p. 89.

28. Geoffrey Perrett, A *Country Made by War: From the Revolution to Vietnam —the Story of America's Rise to Power* (New York, 1989), p. 138.

29. Fanny Calderón de la Barca, *Life in Mexico: The Letters of Fanny Calderón de la Barca* (Garden City, N.Y., 1966), p. 509; Weber, pp. 98, 119–122.

30. Ralph Moody, *Old Trails West* (Salt Lake City, 1963), p. 80; Odie B. Faulk, *The Crimson Desert: Indian Wars of the American Southwest* (New York, 1974), see Chapter 4, "The Comanche Barrier."

31. Weber, p. 246.

32 Jan Bazant, A *Concise History of Mexico* (London, 1977), pp. 39–42.

33. Horton, "Recollections," pp. 280–284; Weber, p. 155.

34. Anon., A *Visit*, p. 102.

35. Houston to Guy M. Bryan, Nov. 15, 1852, E.C.B., SN 199.

36. Friend, p. 58.

37. James, p. 192.

38. Houston to Jackson, Feb. 13, 1833, in *Writings*, I, pp. 274–276.

39. David G. Burnet, William Wharton, et al., *Memorial al Congreso General de los Estados Unidos Mexicanos*, April 13, 1833, in Lilly Library, Latin American MSS, Mexico, II.

40. Weber, p. 246; Braider, p. 126.

41. Quoted in Day and Ullom (eds.), p. 80, and dated July 31, 1833.

42. Houston to Lewis Cass, July 30, 1833, in *Writings*, II, p. 16.

43. Day and Ullom (eds.), p. 82.

44. Houston petition, April 21, 1835, E.C.B. 2E53.

45. See Archie P. McDonald (ed.), *Hurrah for Texas! The Diary of Adolphus Sterne, 1838–1851* (Waco, Tex., 1969), pp. ix–xi; M. A. Turner, p. 26; Crawford, pp. 166–167.

46. Wellman, p. 149.

47. For example, see various documents, E.C.B. 2E250, 2E253. See also Friend, p. 59.

48. Anon., A *Visit*, p. 262; Weber, p. 237.

49. See Braider, p. 129; Friend, p. 59; The latter notes the date as Nov. 30.

50. Robert McElroy, *Jefferson Davis: The Unreal and the Real* (2 vols., New York, 1937), I, pp. 32, 147.

51. See Braider, p. 131; Perrett, p. 167. This term refers to Chapultepec Palace in Mexico City (a phrase added to the Marine Corps Hymn to commemorate the actual assault on the palace in 1847). He would never revel in its halls, but thousands of United States troops did, following the last battle of the Mexican War.

52. Featherstonhaugh, p. 119.

53. Best (ed.), p. 249.

54. Juan Nepomuceno Almonte, *Noticia estadística sobre Tejas* (Mexico City, 1835), Lilly Library.

55. Featherstonhaugh, pp. 123–124.
56. See Houston to Anna Raguet, Feb. 14, 1839, in Shannon Irion and Garrett Jenkins (eds.), *Ever Thine Truly: Love Letters from Sam Houston to Anna Raguet* (Austin, 1975), pp. 111–112.
57. Remini, *The Life,* p. 273.
58. See Braider, p. 133.
59. Gulick et al. (eds.), *Lamar,* I, p. 201.
60. See Nacogdoches Archives, E.C.B. 2Q309, 2Q310, etc., for legal papers, many with Houston as witness.
61. Irion and Jenkins (eds.), *Ever Thine Truly,* introduction (not paginated). Note from the title that there are no letters from Anna to Houston.
62. Nacogdoches Archives, E.C.B. 2Q310, Vol. 85, p. 204, n.d. This document bears Houston's signature as witness.
63. Ibid., Vol. 77, p. 43, April 21, 1835. His character was vouched for by "Juan" M. Dor, his occasional Nacogdoches law partner. See also William Bollaert, *William Bollaert's Texas* (Norman, Okla., 1956), p. 107.
64. Nacogdoches Archives, E.C.B. 2Q310, Vol. 77, p. 42, May 2, 1835.
65. Gordon Carruth (ed.), *The Encyclopedia of American Facts and Dates* (9th ed., New York, 1989), pp. 400–401.
66. See Best (ed.), p. 230.
67. Weber, pp. 248–249.
68. Weems, pp. 39–40.
69. Weber, p. 249.
70. Houston to Isaac Parker, Oct. 5, 1835, in *Writings,* I, p. 302.
71. Cotterill, p. 239.

6. TEXAS IN THE FIRE

1. No date, E.C.B. 3H90. Brooks was a remarkably literate, observant and sensitive man, as his many letters of 1835 and 1836 to family members attest.
2. Mary Austin Holly, *Texas: Observations Historical, Geographical, and Descriptive* (Baltimore, 1833), p. 15.
3. Nance, *After San Jacinto,* pp. 5–9.
4. Estevan F. Austin, *Exposición al Público Sobre los Asuntos de Tejas* (Mexico City, 1835), pp. 3, 7, 13–14, Lilly Library.
5. Weber, p. 288; Burnet, Wharton, et al., *Memorial.*
6. Herman Ehrenberg, *With Milam and Fannin: Adventures of a German Boy in Texas' Revolution* (Austin, 1968), p. vii.
7. Ibid., p. viii.
8. See Louis E. Brister, "Colonel Eduard Harkort: A German Soldier of Fortune in Mexico and Texas, 1832–1836," *Southwest Historical Quarterly,* 88, No. 3 (1985), pp. 230, 243.
9. Ben Milam to Richard Pryor, Jan. 6, 1835, E.C.B. 2R117.

10. Nackman, p. 26; Anon., *A Visit*, p. 102.
11. Weber, pp. 276, 177.
12. Gulick et al. (eds.), *Lamar*, I, p. 213.
13. Weber, p. 243.
14. Letter of Sherwood Y. Reams to ?, n.d. (1836), E.C.B. 2G23. See also Friend, p. 61.
15. Nicholas Clopper, "The Clopper Correspondence, 1834–1838," *The Quarterly of the Texas State Historical Association,* XIII, No. 2 (Oct. 1909), p. 130.
16. Reams letter, E.C.B. 2G23.
17. Weber, p. 149.
18. Vigilance Committee documents, Nacogdoches Archives, Sept. 1835, E.C.B. 2R49, Vol. I. See also Friend, p. 62.
19. Houston broadside, Oct. 8, 1835, E.C.B. 3L249.
20. Weber, p. 250.
21. See Reams letter, in E.C.B. 2G23, and Day and Ullom (eds.), p. 84; Guy M. Bryan to Houston, April 21, 1853, E.C.B., SN 199.
22. Friend, pp. 62–63.
23. Ibid., p. 209.
24. See various documents, E.C.B. 2R49, Vol. I.
25. Houston to A. Hitchinson, Nov. 30, 1835, in *Writings*, I, p. 309.
26. Ibid.; Friend, pp. 63–64.
27. See Amasa Turner, "Reminiscences," p. 1, E.C.B. 2R275; Moseley Baker to Houston, October 11, 1844, E.C.B. 2Q444; Robert Morris Coleman Papers, n.p., E.C.B. 2Q484. Coleman was an officer on Houston's staff throughout the revolution, and later a bitter enemy.
28. Houston to Guy M. Bryan, Oct. 21, 1853, E.C.B., SN 199.
29. Sherwood Y. Reams to ? (1836), E.C.B. 2G23. Reams served one of those few light cannon.
30. Mary W. Clarke, *Thomas J. Rusk: Soldier, Statesman, Jurist* (Austin, Tex., 1971), p. 9.
31. Houston to Guy M. Bryan, Nov. 15, 1852, E.C.B., SN 199.
32. This account is drawn largely from the very detailed letter of Sherwood Y. Reams to ? (1836), E.C.B. 2G23.
33. Ibid.
34. Edward Burleson to Stephen Austin, Dec. 10, 1835, E.C.B. 2B158.
35. "Clopper Correspondence," p. 129.
36. Letter of Sherwood Y. Reams to ? (1836), E.C.B. 2G23. See also A. J. Yates to ?, Jan. 9, 1836, E.C.B. 2J141; Kreneck, p. 124; John S. Ford, *Rip Ford's Texas* (Austin, Tex., 1962), p. 206.
37. A. J. Yates to ?, Jan. 9, 1836, E.C.B. 2J141; Day and Ullom (eds.), p. 85.
38. Friend, p. 64; Houston to Almanzon Huston, Dec. 8, 1835, in *Writings*, IV, p. 13.

39. Houston order, Dec. 12, 1835, E.C.B. 2R49, Vol. I; Day and Ullom (eds.), pp. 86–89; James, p. 218.

40. See *Writings,* I, p. 478n; Gulick et al. (eds.), *Lamar,* I, p. 260; Ehrenberg, p. 126; John Sowers Brooks Papers, E.C.B. 3H90. Sterne, years later, was to receive nine hundred dollars on his claims from the Texas government.

41. Henry Smith to Houston, Dec. 17, 1835, E.C.B. 2R49, Vol. I.

42. See James, p. 219.

43. Houston speech to Senate, Feb. 28, 1859, in *Writings,* VII, p. 309.

44. Ehrenberg, p. 126.

45. John S. Brooks to father, Jan. 20, 1836, E.C.B. 3H90.

46. Houston to D. C. Barrett, Jan. 2, 1836, E.C.B. 2R44, B14/18.

47. Henry Millard to D. C. Barrett, Dec. 29, 1835, ibid.

48. Clarke, *Bowles,* pp. 62–63.

49. Orders, Dec. 26, 1835, E.C.B. 2R49, Vol. I; Kreneck, p. 154.

50. Houston to Fannin, Dec. 30, 1835, E.C.B. 2R49, Vol. I.

51. Houston to D. C. Barrett, Jan. 2, 1836, E.C.B. 2R44, B14/18.

52. Quoted in Day and Ullom (eds.), p. 91.

53. See *Writings,* VII, p. 309.

54. Friend, p. 66; Houston to Henry Smith from Goliad, Jan. 17, 1836, in *Writings,* I, p. 339.

55. Day and Ullom (eds.), p. 92; John M. Niles, *History of South America and Mexico: Comprising Their Discovery, Geography, Politics, Commerce and Revolutions, to Which Is Annexed, a Geographical and Historical View of Texas* (Hartford, 1839), p. 326.

56. Gulick et al. (eds.), *Lamar,* I, p. 324. He was deposed Jan. 11, but it was officially announced only on Feb. 12.

57. Day and Ullom (eds.), pp. 93–94.

58. Quoted in Nackman, p. 356.

59. Day and Ullom (eds.), p. 97.

60. Ehrenberg, pp. 147–149.

61. Austin to Houston, Jan. 16, 1836, E.C.B. 2R49, Vol. I.

62. Friend, p. 66.

63. Day and Ullom (eds.), p. 97; Henry Smith to Houston, Feb. 1, 1836, E.C.B. 2R49, Vol. I.

64. Friend, p. 66.

65. Clarke, *Bowles,* p. 53; John H. Reagan, "Expulsion of the Cherokees from East Texas," *The Quarterly of the Texas State Historical Association,* I, No. 1 (July 1897), pp. 38–39.

66. Quoted in Day and Ullom (eds.), p. 100; Friend, p. 67; Kreneck, p. 154.

67. Moseley Baker to Houston, Oct. 1844, in *Houston Displayed,* p. 14, E.C.B. 2Q444.

68. Quoted in Day and Ullom (eds.), p. 101.

69. Niles, p. 256.

70. Ehrenberg, pp. 160–164.
71. Ibid., p. 153; Niles, p. 326.
72. Quoted in Weems, p. 88.
73. John S. Brooks to sister, n.d., E.C.B. 3H90.
74. Most of this account is drawn from Ehrenberg, pp. 175–204, and the John S. Brooks letters, E.C.B. 3H90.
75. Ehrenberg, p. 204.
76. Rosa Kleberg, "Some of My Early Experiences in Texas," *The Quarterly of the Texas State Historical Association,* II, No. 2 (Oct. 1898), p. 173.
77. Corner, "John Crittenden Duval," p. 53; Weems, pp. 96–97; Andrew A. Boyle, "Reminiscences of the Texas Revolution," *The Quarterly of the Texas State Historical Association,* XIII, No. 4 (April 1910), p. 289.
78. Corner, p. 53.
79. *Biographical Souvenir,* p. 289.
80. Joseph E. Field to N. C. Brooks, n.d., E.C.B. 3H90; Weems, p. 97.
81. Boyle, "Reminiscences," p. 289; Weems, p. 110.
82. Sam Houston, *A Lecture on the Trials and Dangers of Frontier Life as Exemplified in the History of Texas, by the Hon. Sam Houston, of Texas* (Philadelphia, 1851), n.p.
83. Senate speech, Feb. 28, 1859, in *Writings,* VII, p. 311.

7. THE SAN JACINTO CONTROVERSY

1. John S. D. Eisenhower, *So Far from God: The U.S. War with Mexico, 1846–1848* (New York, 1989), p. 13.
2. Day and Ullom (eds.), p. 114.
3. Houston, *A Lecture,* n.p.
4. Calderón de la Barca, pp. 65–66.
5. James, p. 226.
6. Ibid.
7. David G. Burnet, *Review of the Life of Gen. Sam Houston* (New York, 1850?), p. 5.
8. Convention President Richard Ellis to Houston, March 5, 1836, enclosing the resolution of the preceding day, E.C.B. 3N199.
9. Richard Ellis, convention president, to Houston, March 5, 1836, E.C.B., SN 199.
10. Houston, *A Lecture,* n.p.; Day and Ullom (eds.), p. 102; Houston to Fannin, March 11, 1836, in *Writings,* I, p. 365.
11. Houston to Captain Philip Dimmit, March 12, 1836, in *Writings,* II, p. 22.
12. James Collinsworth to Houston, March 6, 1836, E.C.B. 3N199.
13. Burnet, *Review,* p. 6.
14. *Biographical Souvenir,* p. 288.
15. Houston, *A Lecture,* n.p.; Day and Ullom (eds.), p. 105.

16. Virgil E. Baugh, *Rendezvous at the Alamo* (New York, 1960), p. 206.

17. Mary A. Baylor, "Reminiscences," p. 8, E.C.B. 2Q430.

18. John M. Swisher, *Remembrances of Texas and Texas People* (1879), p. 47, E.C.B. 2R204. See also Kleberg, p. 300.

19. Coleman, *Houston Displayed*, p. 20, E.C.B. 2Q484.

20. See Day and Ullom (eds.), pp. 107–110.

21. George Hockley to Thomas J. Rusk, March 21, 1836, E.C.B. 3N197.

22. Quoted in Day and Ullom (eds.), pp. 109–110.

23. James, p. 235, claims Houston retreated only after Sesma was reinforced, but admits that the general was dangerously indecisive.

24. Swisher, *Remembrances*, p. 46, E.C.B. 2R204.

25. Moseley Baker to Houston, Oct. 1844, pp. 18–24, E.C.B. 2Q444. Baker erroneously gives Texian strength as seventeen hundred.

26. Gulick et al. (eds.), *Lamar*, I, p. 377.

27. Frederic Gaillardet, *Sketches of Early Texas and Louisiana* (1839; facsimile edition, Austin, Tex., 1966), p. 67.

28. Quoted in Kleberg, p. 301; Houston Senate speech, Feb. 28, 1859, in *Writings*, VII, p. 316.

29. David Lavender, *The Great West* (New York, 1985), p. 212.

30. Quoted in Day and Ullom (eds.), pp. 111–112.

31. Gaillardet, pp. 69, 71.

32. Swisher, *Remembrances*, p. 48, E.C.B. 2R204; Sherwood Y. Reams to ? (1836), E.C.B. 2G23.

33. Quoted in Friend, p. 68.

34. Baker, *Houston Displayed*, p. 32, E.C.B. 2Q444, and various documents, E.C.B. 2R49, Vol. I.

35. Day and Ullom (eds.), pp. 114–115.

36. Ibid., p. 115.

37. David G. Burnet to Houston, April 1, 1836, in *Writings*, I, p. 412.

38. Clarke, *Rusk*, p. 51.

39. Diary of Robert Hancock Hunter, p. 14. E.C.B. 2R56; Coleman, *Houston Displayed*, p. 22, E.C.B. 2Q484. Oddly, he charged that in March he had once found Houston "lying in a tent with his head upon a certain woman's lap," identifying that "certain" woman as Mrs. Mann.

40. Houston to Burnet, April 25, 1836, report on the battle, in *Documents of Major Gen. Sam Houston, Commander in Chief of the Texian Army, to His Excellency David G. Burnet, President of the Republic of Texas, Containing a Detailed Account of the Battle of San Jacinto* (Gonzales, Tex., 1874), p. 1.

41. Ibid.

42. Day and Ullom (eds.), p. 114.

43. Houston to Henry Raguet, April 19, 1836, in *Writings*, I, p. 413.

44. Drawn from Houston's report to Burnet, April 25, 1836, in *Documents*, pp. 1–2.

45. Amasa Turner, *Reminiscences*, p. 8, E.C.B. 2R275.
46. W. N. Bate, *General Sidney Sherman: Texas Soldier, Statesman and Builder* (Waco, Tex., 1974), pp. 65–67.
47. Baker, *Houston Displayed*, pp. 39–40, E.C.B. 2Q444; Swisher, *Remembrances*, pp. 57–59, E.C.B. 2R204; Lavender, p. 213; Houston, *Documents*, p. 2.
48. Weems, pp. 105–106.
49. Houston, *Documents*, p. 3.
50. Lavender, p. 213.
51. Swisher, *Remembrances*, p. 59, E.C.B. 2R204; Houston, *Documents*, p. 2; Houston Senate speech, Feb. 28, 1859, in *Writings*, VIII, p. 319.
52. Houston, *Documents*, p. 2.
53. Gustav Dresel, *Gustav Dresel's Houston Journal: Adventures in North America and Texas, 1837–1841* (Austin, 1954), p. 133n; Houston, *Documents*, pp. 2–3; James, p. 246.
54. Swisher, *Remembrances*, p. 59, E.C.B. 2R204.
55. In his Feb. 28, 1859, Senate speech, in *Writings*, VIII, pp. 319–320, Houston admitted that the council was not his idea, but that he was "asked" to convene it.
56. Bate, p. 68.
57. James, p. 249; Bate, p. 67.
58. Houston Senate speech, Feb. 28, 1859, in *Writings*, VIII, p. 319; Jesse Billingsly Papers, n.d., E.C.B. 3H52.
59. Burnet, *Review*, p. 333; Houston Senate speech, Feb. 28, 1859, in *Writings*, VIII, p. 320.
60. Coleman, *Houston Displayed*, pp. 49–50, E.C.B. 2Q484; Amasa Turner, *Reminiscences*, p. 8, E.C.B. 2R275. The latter claimed that he personally heard Houston tell William Wharton at that time that he could not order an attack because "the officers will not fight."
61. Bate, p. 68.
62. Swisher, *Remembrances*, p. 59, E.C.B. 2R204; Lavender, p. 213.
63. Clarke, *Rusk*, p. 60; Bate, p. 68; Crawford, p. 168.
64. Swisher, *Remembrances*, pp. 60–62, E.C.B. 2R204.
65. Ibid.
66. Bate, p. 68.
67. Burnet, *Review*, p. 11. He claimed that Houston "chewed opium in these days," which may have clouded his vision. See Amasa Turner, *Reminiscences*, pp. 10–11, E.C.B. 2R275.
68. Swisher, *Remembrances*, p. 52, E.C.B. 2R204.
69. Ibid., p. 61.
70. Diary of Robert Hancock Hunter, p. 16, E.C.B. 2R56.
71. Clarke, *Rusk*, p. 60; Houston, *Documents*, pp. 3–4.
72. James, p. 251; Clarke, *Rusk*, pp. 62–63; Anon., *Texas in 1837*, p. 184n.
73. Hunter, *Diary*, p. 17, E.C.B. 2R56.

74. Ibid.
75. Houston, *Documents*, pp. 3–4; Clarke, *Rusk*, p. 67.
76. Houston, *Documents*, pp. 3–4; Clarke, *Rusk*, p. 67.
77. Houston, *Documents*, p. 3; Swisher, *Remembrances*, p. 62, E.C.B. 2R204.
78. Burnet to Lamar, Oct. 6, 1855, Gulick et al. (eds.), *Lamar*, IV, Part 2, p. 27.
79. Clarke, *Rusk*, p. 63; Bate, p. 68.
80. Clarke, *Rusk*, p. 63; James, p. 253.
81. Anon., *Texas in 1837*, p. 184n.
82. Hunter, *Diary*, p. 17, E.C.B. 2R56.
83. Dresel, p. 31.
84. James, p. 252.
85. Lavender, p. 213.
86. Houston, *A Lecture*, n.p.
87. Quoted in James, p. 253.
88. Bassett (ed.), *Correspondence of Andrew Jackson*, V, p. 402.
89. Anon., *Texas in 1837*, p. 197n.
90. James, p. 247.
91. Houston, *Documents*, p. 12: Houston lists Sherman as regimental commander, with no derogatory comments.
92. Houston Senate speech, Feb. 28, 1859, in *Writings*, VII, p. 322.
93. In 1837, President Houston had peremptorily and angrily recalled Sherman from a government recruiting post in Cincinnati, deepening their mutual antipathy. See Bate, p. 146.
94. "Court of Inquiry" report, April 28, 1836, E.C.B. 2R49, Vol. VI.
95. Coleman, *Houston Displayed*, pp. 9, 11, 34, 41, 51, E.C.B. 2Q484.
96. See biographical note, ibid.
97. Burnet, *Review*, p. 14.
98. John S. Ford, *Memoirs*, p. 138, E.C.B. 2D154; Houston Senate speech, Feb. 28, 1859, in *Writings*, VII, pp. 322–326.
99. John Campbell to Houston, October 6, 1837, E.C.B. 3N199.

8. PRESIDENT SAM HOUSTON AND THE REPUBLIC OF TEXAS

1. See Braider, p. 153.
2. Clarke, *Rusk*, pp. 63–64.
3. Ruffin, *Diary*, II, p. 33, Feb. 14, 1857.
4. Ehrenberg, pp. 124–125.
5. Ibid., pp. 1–4, 60–61.
6. Houston Senate speech, Feb. 28, 1859, in *Writings*, VII, p. 330.
7. Petition to Houston and Rusk, May 3, 1836, E.C.B. 2R49, Vol. I.
8. Rusk to ?, April 23, 1836, ibid.
9. Rusk report, April 26, 1836, ibid. It is endorsed by Houston.

10. Clarke, *Rusk*, p. 63.
11. Swisher, *Remembrances*, p. 65, E.C.B. 2R204.
12. Friend, p. 71.
13. Houston to Lewis C. Fergusen, April 3, 1836, in *Writings*, VII, pp. 3–4.
14. Day and Ullom (eds.), p. 125; Friend, p. 72; Burnet, *Review*, p. 13.
15. Quoted in Day and Ullom (eds.), p. 123.
16. Michael T. Kingston, *The Texas Almanac, 1984–1985* (Dallas, 1983), p. 538.
17. Hay, p. 238.
18. Day and Ullom (eds.), p. 126; Houston's grandson, Temple Houston Morrow, claimed this, and it has been often repeated, E.C.B. 2E253.
19. In E.C.B. 2E253, n.d.
20. Quoted in Day and Ullom (eds.), p. 126.
21. In E.C.B. 2E253, n.d.
22. Friend, p. 73.
23. Houston to Guy M. Bryan, Nov. 15, 1852, E.C.B., SN 199.
24. Braider, pp. 165–166; Friend, pp. 72–73.
25. M. A. Turner, pp. 31–32.
26. Ford, p. 14; Friend, p. 166.
27. Gulick et al. (eds.), *Lamar*, V, p. 102.
28. Rusk to Houston, July 2, 1836, E.C.B. 3N197.
29. *Writings*, I, p. 424n.
30. W. P. Zuber to Edgar Hull, April 3, 1905, E.C.B. 3L249.
31. Houston, *A Lecture*, n.p.
32. Sam Carson, Texas Department of State, to T. J. Green, March 20, 1836, E.C.B. 2D222; David G. Burnet to Green, March 19, 1836, ibid.
33. Houston to Thomas J. Green, Dec. 27, 1836, in *Writings*, V, p. 8.
34. *Writings*, I, pp. 516n, 517n.
35. Lamar to Burnet, July 17, 1836, in Gulick et al. (eds.), *Lamar*, I, p. 417.
36. Austin to Lamar, June 27, 1836, ibid., V, pp. 102–103.
37. Santa Anna (in Spanish) to Houston, July 22, 1836, E.C.B. 3N197; Santa Anna to Houston, July 4, 1836, in Oakah L. Jones, Jr., *Santa Anna* (New York, 1968), pp. 161–162.
38. Houston to Rusk, July 26, 1836, E.C.B. 3N199.
39. Remini, *The Life*, p. 311. This was one of the first, if not the first, American uses of "gunboat diplomacy."
40. Hunter, *Diary*, p. 29, E.C.B. 2R56.
41. Day and Ullom (eds.), p. 130.
42. Rusk to Houston, Aug. 9, 1836, E.C.B. 2R49, Vol. I.
43. William Physick Zuber, *My Eighty Years in Texas* (Austin, 1971), p. 64.
44. Houston to Robert Houston, Sept. 7, 1836, E.C.B. 2E253.
45. Houston to various chiefs, n.d. (Aug. 1836), E.C.B., SN 199.
46. Houston to Guy M. Bryan, Nov. 15, 1852, E.C.B., SN199.

47. Quoted in Friend, p. 75; Thomas North, *Five Years in Texas, or What You Did Not Hear During the War from January 1861 to January 1866: A Narrative of His Travels, Experiences, and Observations in Texas and Mexico* (Cincinnati, 1871), p. 91. See also John Henry Brown, *The Life and Times of Henry Smith, the First American Governor of Texas* (Dallas, 1887), pp. 57–59.

48. Ibid. See also Edwin Meyrick, *The Texian Grand March for the Piano Forte; Respectfully Dedicated to Genl. Houston and His Brave Companions in Arms* (New York, 1836). While not written as a campaign ditty, Meyrick's little hymn to Houston did serve as one.

49. Day and Ullom (eds.), p. 132; James, p. 266.

50. James, pp. 268–271.

51. Christian, *Lamar,* p. 14.

52. James, p. 266.

53. Braider, p. 174.

54. See Houston to Colonel James Smith, Sept. 18, 1836, E.C.B. 3N199; Brister, p. 243; Houston to Texian Congress, Nov. 22, 1836, in *Writings,* I, p. 489; Houston to Thomas Toby, Oct. 25, 1836, ibid., p. 455; Houston to Texas Senate, Dec. 9, 1836, ibid., p. 499; Houston proclamation, Dec. 16, 1836, ibid., p. 508; Houston to Texas Senate, Dec. 20, 1836, E.C.B. 2R49, Vol. I.

55. Houston approval of resolution, Dec. 22, 1836, E.C.B. 2R49, Vol. I; Marilyn M. Sibley (ed.), "Letters from Sam Houston to Albert Sidney Johnston, 1836–1837," *Southwestern Historical Quarterly,* 66, No. 2 (1962–1963), pp. 165, 170, 173.

56. Santa Anna to Houston, Nov. 5, 1836, from Dr. Phelps's plantation, E.C.B. 2R49, Vol. I.

57. Gulick et al. (eds.), *Lamar,* I, p. 501; Braider, p. 174.

58. John Campbell to Houston, Oct. 6, 1836, E.C.B. 3N199.

59. Braider, p. 175.

60. Irion and Jenkins, intro., n.p.

61. M. A. Turner, pp. 35, 28.

62. Thomas J. Rusk to the "People of Texas," from army headquarters at Victoria, June 27, 1836, E.C.B. 3N197.

63. James, p. 276.

64. Weber, pp. 255, 261.

65. Holly, *Texas,* p. 38; Houston to Guy M. Bryan, Nov. 15, 1852, E.C.B., SN 199; Houston general orders concerning Austin's death, Dec. 27, 1836, in *Writings,* II, p. 28.

66. Houston to Henry Raguet, Nov. 1, 1836, in *Writings,* I, p. 465.

67. Houston to John Houston, Nov. 20, 1836, ibid., II, p. 27.

68. Holly, *Texas,* p. 43.

69. *Writings,* II, p. 42n; Lubbock, p. 35.

70. James, pp. 272–273.

71. Ibid., p. 274; Day and Ullom (eds.), p. 139.

72. Quoted in Ehle, p. 302.

73. John Niven, *Martin Van Buren: The Romantic Age of American Politics* (New York, 1983), p. 445.

74. Quoted in Day and Ullom (eds.), p. 139.

75. James, p. 279; Nance, *After San Jacinto,* pp. 11–17.

76. Day and Ullom (eds.), pp. 144–145.

77. Christian, p. 66.

78. Quoted in Day and Ullom (eds.), p. 144; Houston to A. S. Thurston, March 17, 1837, in *Writings,* II, p. 71.

79. Holly, *Texas,* p. 22.

80. Wheeler, dissertation, p. 2; Day and Ullom (eds.), p. 140; "Houston at a Glance," *New York Times,* July 5, 1990, p. A9.

81. Wheeler, dissertation, p. 44.

82. Houston to Robert Irion, Feb. 2, 1837, E.C.B. 3L249.

83. Houston to Robert Irion, April 28, 1837, in *Writings,* IV, pp. 29–30.

84. Holly, *Texas,* p. 51.

85. Quoted in James, p. 289; Lubbock, p. 51.

86. Lubbock, pp. 66–67.

87. James, p. 291.

88. Lubbock, p. 46; Dresel, p. 32.

89. John Hunter Herndon, *Diary,* n.p. (1838), E.C.B. 2E239.

90. Weems, pp. 129, 137. See also the charming Z. N. Morrell, *Flowers and Fruits in the Wilderness; or Forty-six Years in Texas and Two Winters in Honduras* (4th ed., Dallas, 1886). Morrell certainly suffered for his faith!

91. For prices, see Holly, *Texas,* p. 36; Lubbock, p. 48; Wheeler, dissertation, p. 104.

92. James, p. 281.

93. Quoted in Kreneck, p. 179.

94. Harry Hunt Ransom, *The Other Texas Frontier* (Austin, 1984), pp. 40–42.

95. Houston to Jackson, Jan. 4, 1838, in *Writings,* II, p. 178.

96. Jesse D. Lunn to J. E. Hollingsworth, Sept. 9, 1891, E.C.B. 2J142. This drunk took place in 1838.

97. Lavender, p. 214.

98. James, pp. 286–288.

99. Nance, *After San Jacinto,* pp. 74–77.

100. Houston proclamation, Dec. 19, 1836, in *Writings,* I, p. 510.

101. Houston bill of sale, June 23, 1837, E.C.B. 2R49, Vol. II.

102. J. P. Henderson to Houston, n.d. (1837), E.C.B. 2D274.

103. Lubbock, p. 42; Weems, p. 101.

104. Weems, p. 101; Gulick et al. (eds.), *Lamar,* IV, p. 26.

105. Houston to Thomas Toby, Feb. 1, 1837, in *Writings,* II, p. 47.

106. Frances Harwood, "Colonel Amasa Turner's Reminiscences of Galves-

ton," *The Quarterly of the Texas State Historical Association,* III, No. 1 (July 1899), p. 47.

107. James, p. 288.
108. Houston address to army, May 20, 1837, E.C.B. 3L249.
109. Weems, pp. 255, 257, 261.
110. Nance, *After San Jacinto,* pp. 111–114.
111. Christian, pp. 66, 88–91.
112. James, pp. 294, 302.
113. Irion and Jenkins (eds.), introduction, n.p.; Anon., n.d. (1837), concerning Eliza, E.C.B. 3L249.
114. Houston to Robert Irion, Jan. 23, 1837, in *Writings,* II, p. 36.
115. Houston to Robert Irion, Feb. 2, 1837; ibid., p. 48.
116. Houston to Anna, May 20, 1837, ibid., p. 99.
117. Jacob Snively to Houston, Nov. 22, 1837, E.C.B. 3N197.
118. Ford, p. 14.
119. Lubbock, p. 73.
120. An Emigrant, p. 87.

9. TEXAS ON THE BRINK

1. Agreement between Houston and A. C. Allen, Jan. 7, 1838, in *Writings,* II, p. 180.
2. W. M. Pierpont to D. C. Barrett, Dec. 11, 1837, E.C.B. 2Q430.
3. Day and Ullom (eds.), p. 151.
4. Houston to Anna Raguet, Feb. 1, 1838, in *Writings,* II, p. 189.
5. John Hunter Herndon, *Diary,* Feb. 17, 1838, E.C.B. 2E239.
6. M. A. Turner, p. 56.
7. Anon., *Texas in 1837,* p. 197n.
8. Ben Fort Smith bills, April 20, 22, and 25, 1838, E.C.B. 2E253; Anon., *Texas in 1837,* p. 197n.
9. Houston to Ben Fort Smith, April 23, 1838, E.C.B. 2E253.
10. John Hunter Herndon, *Diary,* April 14, 1838, E.C.B. 2E239.
11. Houston to Anna Raguet, May 15, 1838, in *Writings,* II, p. 277.
12. James, p. 290; *Writings,* III, p. 11n.
13. Quoted in Irion and Jenkins (eds.), p. 91. This was in a letter of June 4.
14. Walter Prescott Webb, *The Texas Rangers: A Century of Frontier Defense* (New York, 1935), p. 204.
15. Reagan, "The Expulsion," p. 38.
16. Weber, p. 266.
17. Nance, *After San Jacinto,* pp. 113–114; Weems, pp. 150–151.
18. Houston to Bowl, July 3, 1837, in Gulick et al. (eds.), *Lamar,* I, p. 559.
19. James, p. 302; Braider, p. 187.
20. *Writings,* II, p. 294n.
21. Nance, *After San Jacinto,* pp. 114–115; Braider, p. 186; Weems, p. 151.

22. Christian, pp. 68–70; Clarke, *Bowles,* pp. 86–87; Nance, *After San Jacinto,* pp. 113–135; Faulk, *Crimson Desert,* p. 97.
23. Houston to Big Mush, Aug. 10, 1838, in *Writings,* II, p. 269.
24. Houston to Rusk, Aug. 13, 1838, ibid., p. 276.
25. Houston to Bowl, Aug. 14, 1838, ibid., p. 277.
26. Houston to Liney, Sept. 28, 1838, ibid., p. 284.
27. Houston to C. H. Sims, Sept. 30, 1838, E.C.B. 3L249.
28. Clarke, *Bowles,* pp. 86–87.
29. *Writings,* II, p. 294n.
30. Clarke, *Bowles,* p. 89.
31. Anson Jones to Secretary of War Forsyth, Nov. 26, 1838, E.C.B. 2E272.
32. Houston to Rusk, March 25, 1837, in *Writings,* II, p. 75.
33. Proclamation, Nov. 6, 1838, E.C.B. 2R49, Vol. II; Proclamation, Dec. 8, 1838, ibid.
34. Gulick et al. (eds.), *Lamar,* V, p. 215.
35. Harwood, p. 46.
36. A. T. Burnley to Anson Jones, Oct. 11, 1838, E.C.B. 2E272.
37. Gaillardet, p. 58.
38. Weems, pp. 149–150.
39. Best (ed.), pp. 243, 313. See also Christian, p. 18.
40. Gulick et al. (eds.), *Lamar,* II, pp. 316–319.
41. Anson Jones speech at public dinner, Galveston, June 29, 1939, E.C.B. 2E272.
42. Statement concerning Houston's salary, Feb. 23, 1838, in *Writings,* II, p. 198; Weems, pp. 145, 151, 189.
43. Quoted in Gulick et al. (eds.), *Lamar,* II, p. 309.
44. Ibid., p. 308.
45. Ibid., p. 381.
46. Hugh McLeod to Lamar, Jan. 9, 1839, in Gulick et al. (eds.), *Lamar,* II, p. 406.
47. T. J. Green to Lamar, Feb. 10, 1839, ibid., pp. 444–446.
48. Ibid., III, pp. 84–85.
49. Clarke, *Bowles,* p. 89; Weems, p. 156; Lubbock, p. 105.
50. Colonel Richard Pease to George Hockley, Feb. 23, 1839, E.C.B. 3N197.
51. George Hockley to Albert S. Johnston, March 28, 1839, in Gulick et al. (eds.), *Lamar,* II, pp. 503–504.
52. Memucan Hunt to Lamar, April 27, 1839, ibid., p. 546.
53. Albert S. Johnston to Bowl, April 10, 1839, ibid., p. 522.
54. Lamar to Bowl, May 26, 1839, ibid., p. 590.
55. Lamar to Linee, June 3, 1839, ibid., III, pp. 11–12.
56. Christian, pp. 98–99.
57. Ford, pp. 29–30.
58. Quoted in Kreneck, p. 159.

59. Clarke, *Bowles,* pp. 108–116, 124.
60. Ralph K. Andrist, *The Long Death: The Last Days of the Plains Indian* (New York, 1964), p. 15.
61. Christian, pp. 99–101; Clarke, *Bowles,* p. 124.
62. Houston speech, Nov. 8, 1843, in *Writings,* III, p. 451.
63. Faulk, *Crimson Desert,* pp. 93–94; Weems, pp. 172–173.
64. Hugh McLeod to Lamar, Aug. 28, 1840, in Gulick et al. (eds.), III, p. 439.
65. See Gulick et al. (eds.), *Lamar,* III, p. 428; Faulk, *Crimson Desert,* p. 95.
66. Faulk, *Crimson Desert,* p. 96; Christian, p. 78.
67. See document of Nov. 29, 1839, E.C.B. 2E272.
68. Houston to Anson Jones, June 12, 1838, in *Writings,* II, p. 246.
69. Houston to Anna Raguet, Feb. 8, 1839, E.C.B. 3L249.
70. Houston to Anna Raguet, Feb. 14, 1839, quoted in Irion and Jenkins (eds.), pp. 111–112.
71. Related in Friend, p. 93.
72. Memucan Hunt to Lamar, July 13, 1839, in Gulick et al. (eds.), *Lamar,* III, p. 42.
73. Seale, pp. vii, 8–12; Crawford, p. 170.
74. Report of Dr. William B. Powell, certified by W. W. Humphries, March 21, 1839, E.C.B. 2R49, Vol. II.
75. Kreneck, p. 199; Seale, pp. 4, 8.
76. Seale, pp. 6, 10; Mrs. Sam W. Jackson to Emma Burleson, May 24, 1836, about Margaret, E.C.B. 3L249.
77. Ibid. See also virtually *all* of her correspondence with her children over the years.
78. Mary Lea Hume to Mrs. Underwood, n.d., describing Aunt Margaret, E.C.B. 2R50, Vol. XI.
79. Houston to Margaret, March 2, 1839, E.C.B. 2R49, Vol. II.
80. Margaret's poem, May 31, 1839, written at Somerville, Ala., ibid.
81. Margaret to Houston, July 17, 1839, E.C.B. 2R44, B14/18.
82. Contract between Houston and Hickman Lewis, Aug. 30, 1839, in *Writings,* II, p. 313; Seale, pp. 13–15; Crawford, p. 170.
83. Houston to William G. Harding, July 17, 1841, in *Writings,* III, p. 10.
84. See Gulick et al. (eds.), *Lamar,* III, pp. 193–195; Braider, pp. 192–193; Seale, p. 17.
85. Margaret, poem, April 15, 1840, E.C.B. 2R49, Vol. II.
86. Margaret to Nancy Lea, April 25, 1840, E.C.B. 2R44, B 14/18.
87. Mrs. Sam W. Jackson to Emma Burleson, May 24, 1936, E.C.B. 3L249; Crawford, p. 170; Seale, p. 17.
88. Hunt (ed.), p. 28.
89. Quoted in Crawford, p. 171.
90. Ephraim Adams (ed.), "British Correspondence," I, p. 220.

91. M. A. Turner, p. 67; Hunt (ed.), p. 29.
92. Seale, p. 29; Irion and Jenkins (eds.), n.p.
93. Wheeler, dissertation, pp. 180–187.
94. Ibid., p. 4.
95. An Emigrant, p. 69.
96. Wheeler, dissertation, p. 52.
97. Faulk, *Crimson Desert*, p. 102.
98. Houston to Anna Raguet, Dec. 10, 1839, in *Writings*, II, p. 322.
99. Weems, pp. 167–168.
100. *Texas Almanac*, p. 538; Nance, *After San Jacinto*, pp. 338–339.
101. James, pp. 303, 305.
102. Charter, dated Feb. 27, 1840, in Gulick et al. (eds.), *Lamar*, III, p. 336.
103. Christian, pp. 133–134; Leslie B. Simpson, *Many Mexicos* (3d ed., Berkeley, Calif., 1962), pp. 215–217. Mexico was in such a shambles that in their comprehensive 1988 history of nineteenth-century Latin America, *The Emergence of Latin America in the Nineteenth Century* (Cambridge, Mass., 1988), David Bushnell and Neill Macaulay include a chapter simply entitled "Mexico in Decline (1821–1855)," pp. 55–82. See also D. C. M. Platt, *Latin America and British Trade, 1806–1914* (New York, 1973), p. 57.
104. Quoted in Weems, p. 162. See also Christian, pp. 135–143; Nance, *After San Jacinto*, p. 181.
105. Rusk resignation, May 15, 1840, in Gulick et al. (eds.), *Lamar*, III, p. 391.
106. Christian, pp. 154–155; Nelson Reed, *The Caste War of Yucatan* (Palo Alto, Calif., 1964), pp. 12–38.
107. Christian, p. 156.
108. Ibid. See also Nance, *After San Jacinto*, pp. 252–263.
109. Christian, pp. 154–159; John L. Stephens, *Incidents of Travel in Yucatan* (2 vols., New York, 1843), I, pp. 42–43. Stephens was in Mérida, Yucatan, when news of the agreement reached the peninsula.
110. Stephens, I, pp. 44–45; II, p. 247.
111. Quoted in Gulick et al. (eds.), *Lamar*, III, p. 307.
112. PRO, FO 75, I, p. 23, James Hamilton to Lord Palmerston, Oct. 20, 1840.
113. Lubbock, p. 97.
114. Braider, p. 201. See also Lamar's ideas about recruiting Irish colonists to settle near the Rio Grande, in Gulick et al. (eds.), *Lamar*, III, p. 33.
115. James, p. 311.
116. Wheeler, dissertation, p. 56.
117. Christian, p. 30.
118. See Gulick et al. (eds.), *Lamar*, III, pp. 202–203.
119. PRO, FO 75, I, p. 35, James Hamilton to Lord Palmerston, Nov. 4, 1840.

120. K. C. Tessendorf, "The Texas Navy's Last Hurrah," *United States Naval Institute Proceedings* (June 1988), p. 68. See also Senate annals of secret sessions, Nov. 1839, E.C.B. 2E272.
121. Christian, pp. 47–49.
122. Ibid., pp. 32–33.
123. PRO, FO 75, I, pp. 62–77, Francis C. Sheridan to Lord Palmerston, July 12, 1840.
124. M. A. Turner, p. 66.
125. Seale, p. 55.
126. Houston to Margaret, Sept. 23, 1840, in *Writings,* II, pp. 352–353; Houston speech, Dec. 22, 1839, ibid., pp. 323–347.
127. In Gulick et al. (eds.), *Lamar,* III, p. 349.
128. Margaret Houston, poem, June 1, 1841, E.C.B. 2R49, Vol. II.
129. Houston to William G. Harding, July 17, 1841, E.C.B. 2R49, Vol. II.
130. Kreneck, p. 160.

10. TEXAS IN FLAMES AND INFLAMED

1. James, p. 317.
2. In Gulick et al. (eds.), *Lamar,* II, pp. 438–439.
3. Christian, pp. 110–111; Gulick et al. (eds.), *Lamar,* III, p. 370.
4. Lubbock, p. 105.
5. Best (ed.), p. 279.
6. George W. Kendall, *Narrative of an Expedition Across the Great South-Western Prairies, from Texas to Santa Fe* (2 vols., London, 1845), I, pp. 334–335.
7. Ibid., pp. 69, 335.
8. Quoted in Christian, p. 130.
9. Calderón de la Barca, p. 602; Kendall, pp. 314–315.
10. James, pp. 317–318.
11. Lubbock, p. 141.
12. Braider, p. 209; Paul Horgan, *Great River: The Rio Grande in North American History* (2 vols., New York, 1954), II, p. 587.
13. Braider, pp. 209–210.
14. Seale, p. 76.
15. Houston to Ashbel Smith, Aug. 25, 1841, in *Writings,* II, p. 374, as one example among many.
16. Houston to Samuel M. Williams, July 28, 1841, ibid., p. 369.
17. Lubbock, p. 144.
18. See Day and Ullom (eds.), p. 73.
19. Houston to Congress, Dec. 20, 1841, in *Writings,* II, pp. 402–403.
20. Houston to Todd Robinson, chairman of the Senate Finance Committee, Jan. 5, 1842, ibid., p. 421.
21. Houston to Congress, Dec. 30, 1841, ibid., pp. 415–416.
22. James, p. 321.

23. Houston to Texas Congress, Feb. 1, 1842, in PRO, FO 75, XVI, p. 286.

24. Day and Ullom (eds.), pp. 174–175.

25. Houston proclamation, Feb. 5, 1842, in *Writings*, II, pp. 476–477.

26. Washington D. Miller to Houston, Feb. 16, 1842, in John D. P. Fuller, *The Movement for the Acquisition of All Mexico, 1846–1848* (Baltimore, 1936), p. 18.

27. Houston, General Call to Arms, March 10, 1842, in *Writings*, II, p. 490; Houston to General Edwin Morehouse, March 10, 1842, ibid., p. 491.

28. Houston to General Leslie Combs, March 16, 1842, ibid., pp. 504–505; Peterson, *Triumvirate*, pp. 353, 484.

29. BM, Add. Ms. 43,184, p. 3, Lord Aberdeen to Charles Elliot, July 1, 1842.

30. Houston to Santa Anna, March 21, 1842, in *Writings*, II, pp. 513–527.

31. Bollaert, p. 55.

32. Burleson to "Citizen Volunteer Soldiers," April 2, 1842, E.C.B. 2R49, Vol. III; Burleson, "Commanding," to Alex Somerville, March 31, 1842, ibid. At the latter date, it was Somerville who was legally "Commanding."

33. Burleson to Houston, April 6, 1842, ibid.

34. Houston to Messrs. Black, Ruthven, Hadley et al., Aug. 5, 1844, in *Writings*, IV, p. 356.

35. Houston to Alex Somerville, March 22, 1842, ibid., II, pp. 530–531.

36. Houston to William Henry Daingerfield, March 25, 1842, ibid., p. 536; Houston to Daingerfield, April 1, 1842, in Day and Ullom (eds.), p. 179.

37. Houston to General Pickens, May 1, 1842, in *Writings*, IV, p. 92.

38. Houston to James Davis, May 31, 1842, ibid., p. 115.

39. Marilyn M. Sibley, "James Hamilton, Jr. vs. Sam Houston: Repercussions of the Nullification Controversy," *Southwestern Historical Quarterly*, 89, No. 2 (1985), p. 177.

40. Washington D. Miller to William H. Daingerfield, April 13, 1842, E.C.B. 2R49, Vol. III.

41. Houston to Timothy Pilsbury, May 18, 1842, in *Writings*, IV, p. 110.

42. Quoted in Day and Ullom (eds.), p. 180; Houston to Ben McCulloch, June 18, 1842, *Writings*, III, p. 72; Lubbock, p. 91.

43. Bollaert, p. 122n.

44. Houston to Texas House, July 22, 1842, *Writings*, III, pp. 116–123.

45. Houston to James Davis (acting adjutant), June 15, 1842, *Writings*, IV, p. 119; Houston to Treasurer Asa Brigham, Jan. 2, 1843, E.C.B. 2R49, Vol. IV.

46. Jackson to Houston, Aug. 17, 1842, E.C.B. 2R49, Vol. III.

47. Memucan Hunt to Houston, July 30, 1842, E.C.B. 3N197.

48. See various letters of Kennedy and Elliot, June–Aug. 1842, in Ephraim D. Adams, "British Correspondence Concerning Texas," Parts I, II, pp. 300, 317, 327–338.

49. Houston to William Christy, Aug. 15, 1842, in *Writings*, IV, p. 103.

50. See *Writings*, III, p. 166n.

51. Burleson to Houston, Oct. 3, 1842, E.C.B. 2R49, Vol. III.

52. Quoted in Day and Ullom (eds.), p. 178.

53. Ford, p. 25.

54. Marilyn McAdams Sibley (ed.), *Samuel H. Walker's Account of the Mier Expedition* (Waco, Tex., 1978), p. 8.

55. Ibid., p. 9; Weems, p. 239.

56. PRO, FO 75, XIX, pp. 33–36, Chargé Packenham to Lord Aberdeen, Jan. 24, 1843.

57. William Kennedy to Lord Aberdeen, Oct. 17, 1842, in Ephraim D. Adams, "British Correspondence Concerning Texas," Part II, p. 344.

58. Weems, pp. 240–241.

59. Braider, p. 201.

60. PRO, FO 75, XVII, pp. 33–36, Chargé Packenham to Lord Aberdeen, Jan. 24, 1843.

61. Horgan, *Great River*, II, p. 599; Weems, pp. 255–268; Joseph M. Nance, *Attack and Counter-Attack: The Texas-Mexican Frontier, 1842* (Austin, 1964), pp. 202–211, 412.

62. James, p. 328; Weems, pp. 271, 286, 304–305; Horgan, *Great River*, II, p. 599.

63. Houston annual message to Congress, Dec. 1, 1842, in *Writings*, III, pp. 202–205.

64. Speech, Dec. 17, 1845, ibid., IV, p. 435.

65. Houston to James Hamilton, Dec. 21, 1845, ibid., p. 441.

66. Houston Senate speech, Aug. 1, 1859, ibid., IV, p. 435. See also Houston Senate speech, Aug. 1, 1854, ibid., VI, p. 86; Thomas Jefferson Green, *Journal of the Texian Expedition Against Mier; Subsequent Imprisonment of the Author; His Sufferings; and Final Escape from the Castle of Perote* (New York, 1845), passim.

67. Gulick et al. (eds.), *Lamar*, IV, p. 26.

68. Ibid.; Tessendorf, p. 68.

69. Tessendorf, p. 68.

70. Ashbel Smith, *Reminiscences of the Texas Republic* (Galveston, Tex., 1876), pp. 35–36; PRO, FO 75, XIX, pp. 3–11, Ashbel Smith to ?, Oct. 10, 1842, for an example of his protests; BM, Add. Ms. 43,184, pp. 4–5, Lord Aberdeen to Chargé Elliot, July 16, 1842.

71. Quoted in Ashbel Smith, *Reminiscences*, pp. 40–41.

72. Reed, pp. 84–87, 103; Tom H. Wells, *Commodore Moore and the Texas Navy* (Austin, 1988), p. 128.

73. Houston to James W. Morgan and William Bryan, March 23, 1843, in *Writings*, III, pp. 336–338.

74. Wells, p. 132; Bollaert, pp. 170–171.

75. Wells, pp. 138–139; Weems, p. 273.

76. Wells, pp. 142–143. See also Alexander Dienst, "The Navy of the Re-

public of Texas," *The Quarterly of the Texas State Historical Association,* XIII, No. 2 (Oct. 1909), pp. 91–97.

77. Ibid., p. 145.
78. Quoted in Wells, pp. 159–160.
79. Tessendorf, p. 69; Bollaert, pp. 170–171.
80. Wells, pp. 168–170.
81. Act to sell the navy, Feb. 24, 1844, E.C.B. 2F49, Vol. IV. See also Dienst, pp. 123–125.
82. Houston to Thomas Bagby, May 13, 1843, in *Writings,* III, p. 382.
83. George Hockley to Houston, March 6 and 7, 1842, E.C.B. 2R49, Vol. III. See also Ford, pp. xxi, 213.
84. S. Whiting to Lamar, April 12, 1842, in Gulick et al. (eds.), *Lamar,* IV, p. 5.
85. James Webb to Lamar, May 4, 1842, ibid., p. 20; Wheeler, dissertation, p. 48.
86. James Webb to Houston, July 6, 1842, E.C.B. 3N197.
87. See Wheeler, dissertation, p. 47.
88. Houston proclamation, Dec. 10, 1842, in *Writings,* III, p. 227; M. A. Turner, p. 59.
89. Braider, p. 221; M. A. Turner, p. 59; *Writings,* III, p. 230n.
90. Quoted in Jenkins, *Audubon,* p. 58.
91. Houston to House of Representatives (Texas), Jan. 18, 1844, in *Writings,* III, p. 516.
92. Kreneck, p. 252; Weems, p. 221.
93. Houston to "Chief of the Apaches," Sept. 1, 1842, in *Writings,* III, p. 151; Houston, "A Talk with Various Border Chiefs," March 20, 1843, ibid., pp. 333–334.
94. Houston, poem, March 28, 1843, in *Writings,* III, pp. 341–342.
95. Houston to Indian Agent Ben Bryant, March 23, 1843, ibid., p. 344.
96. For example, Nov. 18, 1842, contract with Victor Pirsum and associates (Belgium), E.C.B. 2R49, Vol. III; contracts with Alexander Bourgeois d'Orvanne, dated June 3 and June 10, 1842, ibid.; Terry G. Jordan, *German Seed in Texas Soil: Immigrant Farmers in Nineteenth-Century Texas* (Austin, 1966).
97. An Emigrant, p. 228.
98. Holly, p. 50.
99. An Emigrant, p. 76.
100. Houston to Thomas Bagby, Dec. 18, 1842, in *Writings,* III, p. 236; Seale, pp. 74–75.
101. Houston to William H. Daingerfield, April 27, 1842, *Writings,* III, p. 38.
102. M. A. Turner, pp. 68–69; Seale, p. 80.
103. Ashbel Smith, p. 30.
104. Moseley Baker to Houston, n.d. (1842), E.C.B. 2Q444.
105. Houston to Washington D. Miller, Jan. 8, 1843, E.C.B. 2E250.

106. Houston to Chargé Elliot, July 15, 1843, in *Writings,* IV, p. 220.

107. Kreneck, p. 247.

108. Seale, p. 85.

109. Quoted in Day and Ullom (eds.), p. 190.

110. Quoted in James, p. 341; Houston to Thomas Bagby, Dec. 18, 1842, in *Writings,* III, p. 236.

111. BM, Add. Ms. 40,507, pp. 121–124, Chargé Elliot to Lord Aberdeen, April 26, 1842.

112. BM, Add. Ms. 43,184, pp. 4–5, Aberdeen to Elliot, July 1 and July 15, 1842; Ephraim D. Adams, *British Interests and Activities in Texas, 1838–1846* (Gloucester, Mass., 1963), pp. 44–49. See also PRO, FO 75, XVIII, p. 36, protest of the Liverpool "Mexican and South American Association," June 28, 1842.

113. BM, Add. Ms. 43,184, p. 5, Lord Aberdeen to Chargé Elliot, July 15, 1842.

114. PRO, FO 75, XI, pp. 74–80, Anon., "Memorandum Relative to Texas," n.d. See also BM, Add. Ms. 43,126, pp. 91–92, William Kennedy to Lord Aberdeen, May 13, 1842.

115. BM, Add. Ms. 43,184, p. 6, Lord Aberdeen to Chargé Elliot, Oct. 3, 1842.

116. Weems, p. 250; Nance, *Attacks,* p. 311.

117. Lubbock, p. 153.

118. BM, Add. Ms. 43,184, pp. 7–8, Lord Aberdeen to Chargé Elliot, May 18, 1843. See also Houston defense against charges of selling out Texas, in speech of Nov. 18, 1843, in *Writings,* III, pp. 443–470.

119. Ashbel Smith, p. 32; *Writings,* III, p. 377n.

120. George S. McIntosh to Houston, June 15, 1842, E.C.B. 2R49, Vol. III.

121. Seale, p. 64.

122. PRO, FO 75, XVIII, p. 177, Ashbel Smith to Guizot, Aug. 15, 1842.

123. Houston to Chargé Elliot, May 13, 1843, in *Writings,* III, p. 388.

124. Lubbock, p. 148.

125. Houston speech, Nov. 8, 1843, in *Writings,* III, p. 465.

11. THE END OF THE REPUBLIC

1. Houston valedictory speech to Congress, Dec. 9, 1844, in *Writings,* IV, p. 403.

2. In Gulick et al. (eds.), *Lamar,* V, p. 112.

3. Lamar address, Nov. 10, 1838, ibid., II, p. 319.

4. Robert Irion to Anson Jones, March 21, 1838, E.C.B. 2E272.

5. See Schwaab (ed.), p. 431n.

6. Houston to Chargé Elliot, May 13, 1843, in *Writings,* III, p. 388.

7. Washington D. Miller to President John Tyler, Jan. 30, 1843, E.C.B. 2R117.

8. See Peterson, *Great Triumvirate,* p. 312; Robert Seager II, *And Tyler*

Too: A Biography of John and Julia Gardiner Tyler (New York, 1963), pp. 210–213.

9. Ashbel Smith to Houston, Nov. 29, 1843, E.C.B. 3N197.

10. Frederick Merk, *Slavery and the Annexation of Texas* (New York, 1972), pp. 39–42.

11. Houston to Jackson, Feb. 16, 1844, in *Writings*, IV, p. 261.

12. Jackson to Houston, Feb. 20 (?), 1844, ibid., p. 266n.

13. Houston to Jackson, Feb. 16, 1844, E.C.B. 2E272.

14. Houston to Washington D. Miller, April 16, 1844, in *Writings*, IV, p. 302; Miller's appointment to "a special secret mission," Feb. 14, 1844, ibid., p. 256.

15. Quoted in Merk, pp. 36–38.

16. Braider, p. 233.

17. Quoted in Day and Ullom (eds.), p. 201.

18. Quoted in Friend, p. 131.

19. Friend, p. 134; Walter Millis, *Arms and Men: America's Military History and Military Policy from the Revolution to the Present* (New York, 1956), pp. 90–91.

20. John Niven, *John C. Calhoun and the Price of Union: A Biography* (Baton Rouge, La., 1988), p. 272.

21. Oliver Perry Chitwood, *John Tyler: Champion of the Old South* (New York, 1939), p. 350.

22. Nevins (ed.), *The Diary of John Quincy Adams, 1794–1845* (New York, 1951), pp. 550–551, June 17, 1843.

23. Calhoun to Van Zandt, April 11, 1844, E.C.B. 2R49, Vol. IV.

24. Quoted in Merk, p. 168.

25. Quoted in Frantz, p. 20. This was written to Henderson and Van Zandt on April 16, 1844. See also "Notes," a translation from the Spanish, n.d., in BM, Add. Ms. 43,126, p. 13.

26. Houston to William Murphy, May 6, 1844, as quoted in Frantz, pp. 24–26.

27. Lubbock, p. 155.

28. BM, Add. Ms. 43,126, William Kennedy to Lord Aberdeen, July 30, 1844.

29. Zachary Taylor to Houston from Fort Jessup, Louisiana, Aug. 13, 1844, E.C.B. 2R49, Vol. IV.

30. Jackson to Andrew Jackson Donelson, Dec. 2, 1844, E.C.B. 2R49, Vol. IV.

31. PRO, FO 75, XI, p. 63, Ashbel Smith to Mr. Rate, from Paris, Sept. 23, 1844.

32. Quoted in Fuller, p. 18.

33. BM, Add. Ms. 43,184, p. 10, Lord Aberdeen to Chargé Elliot, Dec. 31, 1844.

34. PRO, FO 75, XX, pp. 82–83, Charles Bankhead to Lord Aberdeen, July

31, 1844; same to same, Nov. 19, 1844, ibid., XXI, pp. 8–12. The former gives details of the projected expedition against Texas, as does General Juan Alcorta, *Reglamento del Estado Mayor del Ejército que Debe Operar Sobre Tejas* (Mexico City, 1844), passim.

35. Anson Jones, "Description of Presidency," n.d., E.C.B. 2E272.
36. Ashbel Smith, pp. 63, 69–70.
37. Ashbel Smith, "Opinions of Sam Houston," E.C.B. 2R50, XI.
38. Ashbel Smith, pp. 76–79.
39. See Dresel, p. 129n; Weems, p. 319.
40. BM, Add. Ms. 43,184, pp. 10–11, Lord Aberdeen to Chargé Elliot, Jan. 23, 1845; same to same, PRO, FO 75, XXI, pp. 1–6, Jan. 23, 1845.
41. PRO, FO 75, XVI, p. 64, Chargé Elliot to Lord Aberdeen, Jan. 26, 1846.
42. Remini, *The Life*, p. 352.
43. BM, Add. Ms. 43,126, pp. 68–69, Chargé Elliot to Lord Aberdeen, March 24, 1845.
44. BM, Add. Ms. 43,184, p. 11, Lord Aberdeen to Chargé Elliot, May 3, 1845.
45. BM, Add. Ms. 43,126, p. 132, Lord Aberdeen to G. W. Terrell, June 3, 1845, concerning those orders.
46. BM, Add. Ms. 43,184, p. 12, Lord Aberdeen to Chargé Elliot, July 3, 1845.
47. Chitwood, p. 360; Merk, p. 169.
48. Houston to Margaret, July 27, 1845, E.C.B. 2-325/V8.
49. BM, Add. Ms. 43,184, p. 11, Lord Aberdeen to Chargé Elliot, May 3, 1845.
50. Houston to Polk, Sept. 29, 1845, E.C.B. 3N199.
51. Quoted in Day and Ullom (eds.), p. 211.
52. Braider, p. 244; Friend, p. 148.
53. Thomas P. Anderson to Lamar, Nov. 15, 1845, in Gulick et al. (eds.), *Lamar*, VI, p. 12.
54. Lamar to citizens of Galveston, Nov. 18, 1845, ibid., IV, p. 115.
55. BM, Add. Ms. 43,184, p. 13, Lord Aberdeen to Chargé Elliot, Dec. 3, 1845.
56. Houston to Robert Irion, May 12, 1843, in *Writings*, IV, p. 203.
57. Houston to Jones, May 17, 1844, ibid., p. 328.
58. Houston to Jones, Sept. 19, 1842, ibid., III, p. 161, Jones addendum.
59. Houston to Jones, June 11, 1844, ibid., IV, p. 332, Jones addendum.
60. Houston to Jones, Sept. 15, 1843, ibid., III, p. 430.
61. See various salary withdrawals, in *Writings*, IV, pp. 177, 179, 180, 208, 209, 212, 213, 216, 220, 222, 223, 224, ad infinitum. Some withdrawals note the discount rate of the Exchequer.
62. Seale, p. 121; Houston receipt, Oct. 27, 1845, in *Writings*, IV, p. 428; J. Shackleford to Houston, April 11, 1844, E.C.B. 2R49, Vol. IV.

63. Bill of sale, n.d., in E.C.B. 2R49, Vol. II; Houston to Thomas Bagby, Dec. 18, 1842, in *Writings,* III, p. 236; land note, April 21, 1835, and deposition, E.C.B. 2E253.

64. Seale, p. 54.

65. Poem, dated April 15, 1841, E.C.B. 2R49, Vol. II.

66. Margaret, poem, "To My Husband," Dec. 20, 1844, E.C.B. 2R49, Vol. IV.

67. Seale, p. 89.

68. Houston to Polk, June 8, 1845, from the Hermitage, in *Writings,* IV, p. 424; Seale, p. 101; Friend, p. 157.

69. Friend, p. 157.

70. Thomas Hart Benton to Houston, Oct. 1, 1845, E.C.B. 2R49, Vol. 5.

71. Friend, p. 166.

72. Harriet Virginia Scott to Cousin B. Slade, Jan. 13, 1846, E.C.B. 2G180. See also Braider, p. 245.

73. PRO, FO 75, I, p. 6, James Hamilton to Lord Palmerston, Oct. 14, 1840.

74. Kingston (ed.), *Texas Almanac,* p. 338; BM, Add. Ms. 30,141, pp. 40–41, anonymous report to Lord Aberdeen, n.d. (1844).

75. BM, Add. Ms. 43,126, pp. 31–32, Chargé Elliot to Lord Aberdeen, Sept. 15, 1842; Wheeler, dissertation, p. 180.

76. PRO, FO 75, XVI, pp. 41–42, Chargé Elliot to Lord Aberdeen, Jan. 18, 1846.

77. Bollaert, p. 326.

78. Houston to George T. Howard, Jan. 24, 1842, about Castro's colony, in *Writings,* II, pp. 440–442.

79. Ibid.; Meinig, p. 51.

80. Jordan, pp. 48–50.

81. Ibid., p. 52.

82. Olmsted, pp. 178, 142.

83. Ibid., pp. 133, 311, 178; Jordan, p. 54.

84. Meinig, p. 34. See also Melinda Rankin, *Texas in 1850* (Waco, Tex., 1966).

85. Meinig, pp. 34–36, 52, 56; Robert L. Skrabanek, *We're Czechs* (College Station, Tex., 1988); John L. Davis, *The Danish Texans* (Austin, 1979).

86. Andrist, p. 21.

87. Hunt (ed.), pp. 111–113.

88. Wheeler, dissertation, pp. 92, 112.

89. Ibid., p. 112.

90. Dillon, p. 37.

91. Ibid., p. 29; Wheeler, dissertation, p. 59.

12. SENATOR SAM HOUSTON OF TEXAS

1. Eisenhower, pp. 48–51.
2. Perret, pp. 149–150; Bazant, p. 85.
3. Quoted in Day and Ullom (eds.), p. 212.
4. Hudson Strode, *Jefferson Davis: American Patriot, 1808–1861* (3 vols., New York, 1955–1964), I, p. 147.
5. Peterson, *Great Triumvirate*, pp. 14, 59, 375.
6. Ibid., pp. 35, 96, 401, 394.
7. Smith, *Magnificent Missourian*, pp. 184–186.
8. Ibid., p. 416; Niven, *Calhoun*, pp. 262, 173, 248.
9. Strode, pp. 147–151; James, p. 378.
10. Milo M. Quaife (ed.), *The Diary of James K. Polk, During His Presidency, 1845 to 1849* (4 vols., Chicago, 1910), I, p. 309, March 29, 1846.
11. In Day and Ullom (eds.), p. 214.
12. Braider, p. 246; James, p. 361.
13. Margaret to Houston, June 20, 1846, E.C.B. 2R49, Vol. V.
14. Quaife (ed.), II, p. 364, Feb. 1, 1847.
15. Quoted in Friend, p. 32.
16. Eisenhower, pp. 63–68; Perret, p. 150.
17. Houston Senate speech, April 15, 1846, in *Writings,* IV, p. 469.
18. Perret, p. 165.
19. Seale, p. 109; James, p. 362.
20. Fuller, pp. 114–115; Bernard DeVoto, *The Year of Decision, 1846* (Boston, 1943), pp. 69–72.
21. Eisenhower, pp. 208–210; Perret, p. 159; DeVoto, pp. 406–408.
22. Braider, pp. 247, 253; DeVoto, pp. 491–492.
23. Margaret to Houston, May 16, 1846, E.C.B. 2R44.
24. Margaret to Houston, June 20, 1846, ibid.
25. James, p. 365.
26. Rankin, p. 35.
27. Eisenhower, pp. 102–103; Perret, pp. 153, 155, 165; DeVoto, pp. 290–294.
28. Friend, p. 174.
29. Houston to James Gadsden, Sept. 20, 1849, in *Writings,* V, p. 105.
30. New York, 1850; James, p. 362.
31. Seale, pp. 121–124.
32. Margaret to Houston, Dec. 5, 1846, E.C.B. 2R49, Vol. V.
33. Lavender, pp. 253–256; DeVoto, pp. 452–458.
34. Niven, *Calhoun*, pp. 306–310, 313–316; James, p. 370; DeVoto, pp. 296–300.
35. Houston Senate speech, Feb. 1, 1847, in *Writings,* IV, p. 517.
36. Niven, *Calhoun*, p. 312.
37. Houston Senate speech, Feb. 19, 1847, in *Writings,* IV, p. 539.

38. Seale, pp. 122–126.

39. Margaret to Houston, March 4, 1847, E.C.B. 2R44, B14/18.

40. Hunt (ed.), p. 39.

41. Houston to Ashbel Smith, April 27, 1847, in *Writings*, V, p. 11.

42. Friend, pp. 185–187.

43. Eisenhower, pp. 166–191.

44. Braider, p. 253.

45. Quoted in Friend, p. 108.

46. Quoted in Day and Ullom (eds.), p. 218.

47. Fuller, p. 153.

48. Houston Senate speech, May 8, 1848, in *Writings*, V, pp. 37–40.

49. Fuller, p. 158.

50. Eisenhower, p. 367; Fuller, p. 155.

51. Fuller, p. 109.

52. Houston to Margaret, Feb. 19, 1848, E.C.B. 3N199.

53. Kreneck, p. 207.

54. Niven, *Calhoun*, p. 316.

55. Remini, *The Life*, p. 239; Friend, p. 193. See also Peterson, *Great Triumvirate*, p. 496.

56. Houston Senate speech, Aug. 12 and 14, 1848, in *Writings*, V, p. 60.

57. Ashbel Smith, p. 69.

58. Smith, *Magnificent Missourian*, p. 245.

59. Niven, *Calhoun*, pp. 323–324.

60. Ibid., pp. 324–325.

61. Quoted in Day and Ullom (eds.), p. 221.

62. Quoted ibid., pp. 221–222. The date of the speech was March 2, 1849.

63. Houston Senate speech, Jan. 8, 1849, in *Writings*, V, p. 65; John Hoyt Williams, *A Great and Shining Road: The Epic Story of the Transcontinental Railroad* (New York, 1988), pp. 7–10.

64. Houston to Margaret, March 11, 1849, in *Writings*, V, p. 65.

65. Houston to Ashbel Smith, May 31, 1849, in *Writings*, V, p. 94.

66. Houston to James Gadsden, Sept. 20, 1849, ibid., pp. 98–99.

13. SAM HOUSTON AND THE UNION

1. Niven, *Calhoun*, p. 341. See Calhoun's *A Disquisition on Government, and Selections from the Discourse* (New York, 1953).

2. Niven, *Calhoun*, p. 344. Gone too was Benton, ejected from the Senate by Missourians for failing to defend slavery; Smith, *Magnificent Missourian*, p. 237.

3. Niven, *Calhoun*, p. 338; Kreneck, p. 302.

4. Friend, p. 210.

5. Smith, *Magnificent Missourian*, p. 237.

6. Lavender, p. 310.

7. Kingston (ed.), *Texas Almanac,* p. 541.
8. Peterson, *Great Triumvirate,* p. 472; Ford, p. 129.
9. Lavender, p. 310.
10. Houston Senate speech, Feb. 8, 1850, in *Writings,* V, pp. 142–144.
11. Houston to Henderson Yoakum, May 14, 1850, ibid., p. 153.
12. Braider, p. 260; Friend, p. 203; Seale, p. 141.
13. Margaret to Houston, Jan. 28, 1850, E.C.B. 2R49, Vol. V.
14. Seale, pp. 151–153.
15. Quoted in Day and Ullom (eds.), p. 227.
16. Houston to son Sam, July 29, 1850, in *Writings,* V, p. 204.
17. Houston to Thomas Bagby, Aug. 6, 1850, ibid., p. 211.
18. Friend, p. 205.
19. Houston Senate speech, July 3, 1850, in *Writings,* V, p. 191.
20. Houston Senate speech, Aug. 13, 1850, ibid., pp. 214–221.
21. Houston Senate speech, Aug. 15, 1850, ibid., pp. 234–235.
22. Leroy P. Graf and Ralph W. Haskins (eds.), *The Papers of Andrew Johnson* (4 vols., Memphis, Tenn., 1967–1976), I, p. 595.
23. Niven, *Van Buren,* p. 594.
24. Printed in Gulick et al. (eds.), *Lamar,* VI, p. 312. Apparently Johnson had sent him the book.
25. T. J. Green to Mr. Howell, March 16, 1857, ibid., p. 342.
26. Ibid., IV, p. 291.
27. Quoted in Friend, p. 209.
28. Houston Senate speech, Sept. 9, 1850, in *Writings,* V, pp. 250–251.
29. Houston to son Sam, Aug. 23, 1850, ibid., p. 237.
30. Houston to son Sam, Sept. 23, 1850, ibid., p. 258.
31. Day and Ullom (eds.), p. 233.
32. Ibid., p. 238.
33. Gaillardet, p. 59.
34. Strode, I, p. 147.
35. James, p. 401.
36. Braider, p. 65.
37. Margaret to Houston, Jan. 28, 1850, E.C.B. 2R49, Vol. V.
38. Seale, p. 147.
39. Hunt (ed.), p. 45.
40. Seale, p. 160.
41. Ibid., pp. 163–164.
42. Margaret to Houston, Jan. 28, 1850, E.C.B. 2R49, Vol. V; same to same, Feb. 8, 1851, E.C.B. 2R44, B14/18; same to same, June 14, 1854, E.C.B. 3N199.
43. Seale, p. 160.
44. Margaret to Houston, Feb. 8, 1851, E.C.B. 2R44, B14/18.
45. Quoted in Day and Ullom (eds.), p. 233.
46. Hunt, p. 19.

47. Christian F. Eckloff, *Memoirs of a Senate Page (1855–1859)* (New York, 1881?), pp. 43–44.
48. Temple Houston Morrow notes, n.d., E.C.B. 2E253; Hunt, p. 19.
49. Hunt, p. 19.
50. Margaret to Houston, Feb. 8, 1851, E.C.B. 2R44, B14/18.
51. Carruth (ed.), *Encyclopedia*, p. 244.
52. Quoted in Day and Ullom (eds.), p. 234.
53. Friend, p. 298.
54. Charles H. Brown, *Agents of Manifest Destiny: The Lives and Times of the Filibusters* (Chapel Hill, N.C., 1980), p. 446.
55. James Pike, *Scout and Ranger: Being the Personal Adventures of James Pike, of the Texas Rangers in 1859–1860* (Cincinnati, Ohio, 1865), p. 125n.
56. John S. Ford, *Memoirs*, p. 650, E.C.B. 2Q511. See also Best (ed.), *Debrett's*, p. 343.
57. Houston, *A Lecture*, n.p.
58. Braider, p. 268.
59. Ruffin, *Diary*, p. 34, Feb. 14, 1857.
60. Houston to John Letcher, Jan. 24, 1851, in *Writings*, V, p. 263.
61. Houston Senate speeches, March 10, 1851, and Dec. 22, 1851, ibid., pp. 293–294, 330.
62. In Graf and Haskins (eds.), *Johnson*, I, p. 629.
63. Ibid., II, p. 61.
64. Guy M. Bryan to Houston, March 11, 1852, E.C.B. 3N199.
65. Ibid., p. 68.
66. Friend, pp. 217–218; Houston to Lewis Coryell, Aug. 28, 1852, in *Writings*, V, p. 361.
67. Wheeler, dissertation, p. 211.
68. George Johnson, "A Menace or Just a Crank?" *New York Times Book Review*, June 18, 1989, p. 7.
69. Houston to son Sam, Jan. 15, 1853, E.C.B. 3N199.
70. Houston to Nannie, Feb. 2, 1853, in *Writings*, V, p. 374.
71. Houston to Nannie, Feb. 17, 1853, ibid., p. 397.
72. Houston to Franklin Pierce, Jan. 28, 1853, ibid., p. 373.
73. Houston to Washington D. Miller, Oct. 7, 1853, ibid., p. 458.
74. Houston to Washington D. Miller, June 10, 1853, ibid., p. 451.
75. Quoted in Day and Ullom (eds.), p. 240.
76. Moody, pp. 80–81.
77. Williams, *Great and Shining Road*, p. 24.
78. Friend, pp. 222, 255.
79. Eisenhower, p. 373; Williams, *Great and Shining Road*, p. 23.
80. James R. Hine receipt, Nov. 6, 1853, E.C.B. 2R49, Vol. VI.
81. Seale, p. 161.
82. Ibid.
83. Braider, p. 273.
84. Ibid., p. 272.

14. SAM HOUSTON, PRESIDENT?

1. Quoted in Day and Ullom (eds.), p. 244.
2. Houston Senate speech, Feb. 14–15, 1854, in *Writings*, V, pp. 469–504.
3. Crawford, p. 172.
4. Houston Senate speech, March 3, 1854, in *Writings*, V, pp. 508–522.
5. Frank L. Burr to Gideon Welles, March 6, 1854, E.C.B. 2E253.
6. William J. Cooper, Jr., *The South and the Politics of Slavery, 1828–1856* (Baton Rouge, La., 1978), pp. 356–357.
7. Friend, pp. 228–230.
8. Quoted in Braider, p. 277.
9. See Lavender, pp. 329–331.
10. Houston speech, Dec. 21, 1855, in *Writings*, VI, p. 237.
11. Lavender, pp. 332–334.
12. Braider, p. 277.
13. Friend, p. 235.
14. C. Edwards Lester, *Life of Sam Houston (The Only Authentic Memoir of Him Ever Published)* (New York, 1855); Lester to Houston, March 28, 1855, E.C.B. 2R49, Vol. VI.
15. Houston to ?, 1856, in *Writings*, VI, p. 227.
16. Kreneck, p. 341.
17. Margaret to Houston, June 14, 1854, E.C.B. 3N199.
18. Quoted in Friend, p. 290.
19. Houston Senate speech, July 15, 1854, in *Writings*, VI, p. 57.
20. Seale, p. 168.
21. Ibid., pp. 170–171.
22. Hunt (ed.), p. 30; Seale, p. 171.
23. Friend, p. 224.
24. Kreneck, p. 337.
25. Houston speech, March 3, 1855, in *Writings*, VI, p. 226.
26. C. Edwards Lester to Houston, March 28, 1855, E.C.B. 2R49, Vol. VI.
27. Houston speech, Nov. 23, 1855, in *Writings*, VI, pp. 209–234.
28. Houston to John Hancock, July 21, 1856, E.C.B., SN 199.
29. Houston to Margaret, n.d. (Feb. 1856), fragment, E.C.B. 3N199.
30. Baggett, "The Constitutional Union," pp. 234–236; James, p. 387; Friend, p. 246.
31. Houston to John Hancock, July 21, 1856, E.C.B. 3N199.
32. Lubbock, p. 207.
33. Braider, p. 284.
34. Margaret, poem, "Farewell to Independence," Nov. 10, 1855, E.C.B. 2R49, Vol. VI.
35. Houston to Margaret, n.d. (Feb. 1856), fragment, E.C.B. 3N199.
36. Houston to Margaret, April 14, 1856, ibid.
37. Quoted in Seale, p. 176. See also p. 172.
38. Quoted in James, p. 386.

39. Houston to Ana S. Stephens, Feb. 9, 1856, in *Writings*, VI, p. 300.
40. Margaret to Houston, March 11, 1856, E.C.B. 2R49, Vol. VI.
41. Houston to Margaret, Aug. 8, 1856, E.C.B. 3N199; Seale, p. 174.
42. Houston to John Hancock, July 21, 1856, in *Writings*, VI, pp. 358–362.
43. Houston to John Hancock, Aug. 16, 1856, ibid., pp. 374–377; Houston to John Hancock, April 7, 1856, ibid., p. 305.
44. Seale, p. 185.
45. *Dictionary of American Biography*, Vol. 16, pp. 336–337.
46. Ford, p. 18.
47. Lubbock, p. 224.
48. Ford, p. 217.
49. Quoted in Brown, *Agents*, p. 447.
50. William Kyle to Edward Burleson, Jr., Oct. 7, 1855, E.C.B. 2B158.
51. Rip Ford to Edward Burleson, Jr., Feb. 15, 1856, E.C.B. 2B158.

15. HOUSTON, TEXAS AND THE COMING OF THE CIVIL WAR

1. Quoted in Hunt (ed.), p. 42.
2. Report on July 25, 1857, speech at Austin, in Austin newspaper, *The State Gazette*, same day, in *Writings*, VII, pp. 28–32.
3. James, p. 390; Friend, p. 252.
4. Friend, p. 246.
5. Houston to Maggie, Dec. 26, 1858, E.C.B., SN 199.
6. Carruth (ed.), *Encyclopedia*, p. 262. See also John Hoyt Williams, *The Rise and Fall of the Paraguayan Republic, 1800–1870* (Austin, 1979), pp. 221–222, 225.
7. See Calhoun, *Disquisition*, Introduction, p. x.
8. Hubert Howe Bancroft, *History of Utah* (San Francisco, 1890), pp. 512–538.
9. Williams, *Great and Shining Road*, pp. 26–28; Bancroft, pp. 557, 512–542; letter to the editor of *Civilian and Galveston Gazette*, Aug. 25, 1857, in *Writings*, VI, pp. 448–461.
10. Quoted in Seale, p. 187.
11. Senate resolution, Feb. 16, 1858, in *Writings*, VII, pp. 33–34.
12. Houston remarks to the Senate, Feb. 16, 1858, ibid., VI, pp. 508–509.
13. Samuel F. Bemis, *The Latin American Policy of the United States: An Historical Interpretation* (New York, 1943), p. 109.
14. W. P. Zuber to Edgar Hull, Nov. 7, 1906, E.C.B. 3L249.
15. Senate Bill No. 178, March 1, 1858, E.C.B. 2R49, Vol. VI.
16. Braider, p. 290.
17. Joint resolution of the Texas Legislature, March 9, 1858, E.C.B. 2R49, Vol. VI.
18. Houston Senate speech, April 1, 1858, in *Writings*, VII, pp. 54–60.
19. Weigley, p. 155; Perrett, p. 172.

20. Houston Senate speech, April 20, 1858, in *Writings,* VII, pp. 84–89.
21. Friend, pp. 299–300; Day and Ullom (eds.), p. 253.
22. Houston to Margaret, April 22, 1858, in *Writings,* VII, p. 100.
23. Hunt (ed.), p. 46.
24. Houston to Maggie and Nannie, Jan. 17, 1858, E.C.B. 2N199.
25. Hunt (ed.), p. 116.
26. Nannie Houston to Houston, April 6, 1858, E.C.B. 2R49, Vol. VI.
27. Quoted in Day and Ullom (eds.), pp. 254–255.
28. Quoted in Seale, p. 187.
29. Ibid., pp. 188–191.
30. See *Writings,* VII, pp. 104, 127, 130–132.
31. Braider, p. 290.
32. Gulick et al. (eds.), *Lamar,* IV, Part Two, p. 162, July 26, 1858, "Protest."
33. Houston speech, Aug. 17, 1858, in *Writings,* VII, pp. 181–182.
34. Carruth (ed.), *Encyclopedia,* p. 264.
35. Houston to Maggie, Dec. 23, 1858, E.C.B. 3N199.
36. Braider, pp. 291–292.
37. Houston Senate speech, Jan. 27, 1859, in *Writings,* VII, p. 223.
38. Quoted in Bemis, p. 110. See also Bazant, pp. 78–84.
39. Eckloff, p. 27.
40. Olmsted, p. 113.
41. Friend, pp. 263–264.
42. Houston to Maggie, Jan. 10, 1859; same to same, July 10, 1859, E.C.B. 3N199.
43. Houston to Margaret, Jan. 20, 1859, in *Writings,* VII, p. 219.
44. Quoted in Friend, p. 268.
45. Eckloff, p. 43.
46. Houston to Maggie, from the Senate Chamber, July 10, 1859, E.C.B. 3N199.
47. Houston to Maggie, July 24, 1859, E.C.B. 3N199.
48. Houston speech, July 9, 1859, in *Writings,* VII, pp. 343–367.
49. Walter L. Buenger, "Secession and the Texas German Community: Editor Lindheimer vs. Editor Flake," *Southwestern Historical Quarterly,* LXXXII, No. 4 (April 1979), p. 384; Baggett, p. 236.
50. Houston to Simon Mussina, Aug. 6, 1859, in *Writings,* VII, p. 370.
51. James, p. 393.
52. Buenger, p. 386.
53. John S. Ford, *Memoirs,* p. 785, E.C.B. 2Q511.
54. Ford, *Rip Ford's Texas,* p. 262.
55. Ibid., p. 264.
56. John S. Campbell to his brother, Nov. 16, 1859, E.C.B. 2J143.
57. Ford, *Rip Ford's Texas,* p. 265.
58. Juan N. Cortina, "Proclamation," Nov. 23, 1859, E.C.B. 2R49, Vol. V.

59. John S. Ford, *Memoirs*, pp. 793–794, E.C.B. 2Q511. See also *Writings*, VII, p. 393n.
60. John S. Ford, *Memoirs*, pp. 793–794, E.C.B. 2Q511; Ford, *Rip Ford's Texas*, pp. 270–275.
61. Ford, *Rip Ford's Texas*, p. 276.
62. John S. Campbell to his brother, Aug. 26, 1859, E.C.B. 2J143.
63. Houston inaugural address, Dec. 21, 1859, in *Writings*, VII, pp. 379–383.
64. Friend, p. 302.
65. Webb, *Rangers*, p. 203.

16. HOUSTON AND THE GRAND PLAN (OR TWO)

1. Ford, *Rip Ford's Texas*, pp. 271, xviii, xxx.
2. Ben McCulloch to his mother, July 28, 1859, E.C.B. 2.325, Vol. 21.
3. Houston message to legislature, Jan. 13, 1860, in *Writings*, VII, p. 415.
4. Houston to Cyrus Randolph, state treasurer, Feb. 29, 1860, ibid., p. 495.
5. Houston to Captain W. C. Dalyrymple, "Ranging Company Orders," Jan. 20, 1860, ibid., p. 424.
6. Houston to Lewis Cass, Jan. 23, 1860, ibid., p. 441; Ford, *Rip Ford's Texas*, p. 204.
7. Friend, p. 306.
8. Houston to John B. Floyd, Feb. 15, 1860, in *Writings*, VII, pp. 478–479.
9. Houston telegram to John B. Floyd, Feb. 20, 1860, E.C.B. 2R50, Vol. 7.
10. Braider, pp. 303–304. See also the *Richmond Enquirer*, April 20, 1860, p. 2.
11. Houston to Elkanah Greer, Feb. 29, 1860, in *Writings*, VII, p. 495.
12. Brown, *Agents*, pp. 446–447.
13. Pike, *Scout and Ranger*, pp. 124–125.
14. Friend, p. 307.
15. Ben McCulloch to his mother, Feb. 26, 1860, E.C.B. 3G37.
16. Edward Burleson, Jr., to Houston, March 15, 1860, E.C.B. 2B158.
17. Houston to Edward Burleson, Jr., June 26, 1860, ibid.
18. Major Heintzelman to John B. Floyd, Feb. 29, 1860, E.C.B. 2R50, Vol. 7.
19. Ben McCulloch to Houston, April 6, 1860, E.C.B. 2R50, Vol. 7.
20. Webb, *Rangers*, p. 201.
21. Anon., "The United States Army in Texas, 1845–1860," typescript, E.C.B. 2R275.
22. *Writings*, VII, p. 522n.
23. Webb, *Rangers*, p. 212; Katherine Elliott, "The Frontier Regiment," typescript (1921), pp. 3–4, E.C.B. 2Q503.

24. Houston to John B. Floyd, March 8, 1860, two letters of that date, *Writings*, VII, pp. 502, 506; Kreneck, pp. 372–373.
25. W. R. Dunkard to Houston, March 14, 1860, E.C.B. 2R250, Vol. 7; Elliott, "Frontier Regiment," pp. 6–7.
26. Houston to John B. Floyd, March 12, 1860, in *Writings*, VII, p. 520.
27. E. W. Cave to E. W. Whitney, March 12, 1860, ibid., p. 518.
28. Houston proclamation, March 12, 1860, ibid., p. 534.
29. Houston to John W. Harris et al., March 25, 1860, ibid., p. 552.
30. Anon., "The United States Army," p. 28, E.C.B. 2R275.
31. Houston to John B. Floyd, April 14, 1860, in *Writings*, VIII, pp. 14–20; Webb, *Rangers*, p. 203.
32. Houston to Middleton T. Johnson, May 7, 1860, in *Writings*, VIII, p. 49.
33. Sam D. Carothers to his brother John, May 23, 1860, E.C.B. 2K262.
34. Middleton T. Johnson to Houston, May 16, 1860, E.C.B. 2R50, Vol. 8; Webb, *Rangers*, pp. 203, 212.
35. Seale, p. 192.
36. Houston to Reverend George W. Baines, Jan. 6, 1860, E.C.B. 2R50, Vol. 7.
37. Seale, p. 196.
38. Houston to son Sam, Jan. 27, 1860, E.C.B. 3N199.
39. Houston to son Sam, April 23, 1860, ibid.
40. Houston receipt signed by F. D. Elberfield, April 27, 1860, E.C.B. 2R50, Vol. 7.
41. Houston to son Sam, April 18, 1860, E.C.B. 3N199.
42. Houston to Maggie, Jan. 18, 1859, E.C.B. 3N199: "Take care of Willie and Andrew as they are the least of the family"; Houston to Sam, April 25, 1860, ibid.
43. Baggett, p. 238.
44. Ben McCulloch to his mother, Dec. 4, 1859, E.C.B. 2.325, Vol. 21.
45. Baggett, p. 238.
46. Houston to John W. Harris et al., March 25, 1860, in *Writings*, VII, pp. 546–554.
47. James, p. 396; Buenger, p. 387.
48. Baggett, p. 240; James, p. 397.
49. Buenger, p. 392; Baggett, p. 239; Wheeler, dissertation, p. 196.
50. Quoted in Hesseltine (ed.), p. 127.
51. Ibid., pp. 126, 291.
52. John S. Ford, *Memoirs*, p. 660, E.C.B. 2Q511.
53. Olmsted, p. 104.
54. Sam D. Carothers to his brother John, June 27, 1860, E.C.B. 2K262. Their brother Thomas was the campaign manager.
55. Houston to son Sam, May 2, 1860, E.C.B. 3N199.
56. Baggett, pp. 241–242.

57. Ibid., p. 242.
58. Houston to son Sam, May 17, 1860, E.C.B., SN 199.
59. James, p. 397.
60. Houston to son Sam, May 17, 1860, E.C.B. 3N199.
61. Houston to John H. Manly, May 17, 1860, in *Writings*, VIII, p. 126.
62. *Writings*, VIII, p. 60n.
63. Quoted in Friend, p. 319.
64. Houston to Messrs. D. D. Atchinson and J. W. Harris, May 24, 1860, *Writings*, VIII, p. 66.
65. Houston to W. S. Hotchkiss, application, June 4, 1860, *Writings*, VIII, p. 76.
66. Houston to Ashbel Smith, July 25, 1860, *Writings*, VIII, p. 109.
67. Baggett, p. 243.
68. Houston to A. Daly, Aug. 14, 1860, in *Writings*, VIII, p. 119.
69. Houston letter, August 18, 1860, ibid., p. 121.
70. Houston to Charles L. Mann, Aug. 27, 1860, ibid., pp. 126–127.
71. Houston to Ben McCulloch, Aug. 28, 1860, ibid., p. 128; Seale, p. 199.
72. Houston to Middleton T. Johnson, Aug. 6, 1860, E.C.B. 2R50, Vol. 7.
73. Ibid. See various letters, Aug. to Oct., to Colonel Johnson, Captains Burleson, Dalyrymple, Francis Duffan and other Ranger officers.
74. Ibid.
75. Ralph A. Wooster, *The Secession Conventions of the South* (Princeton, N.J., 1962), p. 123; Baggett, p. 248.
76. Sam D. Carothers to his brother John, Sept. 15, 1860, E.C.B. 2K262.
77. Allen Nevins and M. H. Thomas (eds.), *The Diary of George Templeton Strong: The Civil War, 1860–1865* (New York, 1952), p. 42.
78. Houston speech, Sept. 22, 1860, in *Writings*, VIII, pp. 145–160.
79. Houston to G. W. Crawford, Sept. 29, 1860, ibid., p. 135.
80. Baggett, pp. 248–252.
81. Ford, *Rip Ford's Texas*, p. 315n.
82. Friend, p. 329.
83. Ruffin, *Diary*, Nov. 12, 1860, p. 493.
84. Wooster, p. 123.
85. Ford, *Rip Ford's Texas*, p. 315; Ollinger Crenshaw, *The Slave States in the Presidential Election of 1860* (Baltimore, Md., 1945), p. 293; Houston circular to Southern governors, No. 28, 1860, in *Writings*, VIII, pp. 197–198.
86. Ford, *Rip Ford's Texas*, p. 315; James, p. 405; Braider, p. 305.
87. Houston to John B. Floyd, Nov. 17, 1860, E.C.B. 2R50, Vol. 8.
88. Houston to Edward Burleson, Jr., Nov. 9, 1860, E.C.B. 2B158.
89. A. B. Burleson to Edward Burleson, Jr., Nov. 19, 1860, ibid.
90. Houston to H. M. Watkins, Nov. 20, 1860, in *Writings*, VIII, pp. 194–195.
91. Houston to the people of Texas, Dec. 3, 1860, ibid., pp. 206–207.

92. Proclamations of Dec. 17 and Dec. 27, 1860, ibid., pp. 221, 225–226.
93. Braider, p. 305.
94. Katherine Elliott, "The Frontier Regiment," p. 11.
95. Ibid., p. 12.
96. Houston to son Sam, July 10, 1860, E.C.B. 3N199.
97. Hunt (ed.), p. 69.
98. Seale, pp. 193–194.
99. Wooster, p. 123.

17. SAM HOUSTON FACES CIVIL WAR

1. Friend, p. 334.
2. Houston to R. M. Calhoun, Jan. 7, 1861, in *Writings*, VIII, pp. 228–231.
3. Katherine Elliott, "The Frontier Regiment," p. 15.
4. Houston executive orders, Jan. 25, 1861, E.C.B. 2R50, Vol. 10.
5. Houston to General D. E. Twiggs, Jan. 20, 1861, in *Writings*, VIII, pp. 234–235.
6. Margaret to Nancy Lea, Jan. 21, 1861, E.C.B. 2R50, Vol. 10.
7. Houston to legislature, Jan. 21, 1861, in *Writings*, VIII, pp. 236–252.
8. Philip Rutherford, "Texas Leaves the Union," *Civil War Times Illustrated*, 20, No. 3 (1981), pp. 14–17; Avery O. Craven, *The Growth of Southern Nationalism, 1848–1861* (Baton Rouge, La., 1953), pp. 230–234; Howard Cecil Perkins (ed.), *Northern Editorials on Secession* (New York, 1942), p. 177.
9. Rutherford, pp. 19–20.
10. Houston to committee of the Secession Convention, Jan. 31, 1861, in *Writings*, VIII, pp. 253–254.
11. Wooster, pp. 126–130.
12. Ibid., p. 132.
13. Katherine Elliott, "The Frontier Regiment," p. 15.
14. Quoted in James, p. 409.
15. Friend, p. 337; Wooster, pp. 134–135.
16. Houston to ?, Feb. 20, 1861, in *Writings*, VIII, pp. 263–264.
17. Wooster, pp. 135–136.
18. North, p. 131; Wooster, p. 132n.
19. North, p. 132.
20. Jim McCord to Edward Burleson, Jr., Feb. 18, 1861, E.C.B. 2B158.
21. Houston proclamation, March 4, 1861, E.C.B. 2R50, Vol. 10.
22. North, p. 132.
23. In Day and Ullom (eds.), p. 270.
24. Davis M. Potter, *Lincoln and His Party in the Secession Crisis* (New Haven, Conn., 1942), p. 350.
25. David R. Barbee, "The Line of Blood: Lincoln and the Coming of the

War," *Tennessee Historical Quarterly*, XVI, No. 1 (March 1957), pp. 46–54.

26. Potter, p. 350; Howard C. Westwood, "President Lincoln's Overture to Sam Houston," *Southwestern Historical Quarterly*, 88, No. 2 (1984), pp. 134–135.

27. E. W. Cave to Leroy Pope Walker, March 13, 1861, in *Writings*, VIII, pp. 268–271.

28. Quoted in Braider, p. 309, according to Nannie's recollection.

29. Hunt (ed.), p. 71.

30. See Frantz, p. 28; Seale, p. 207.

31. Houston proclamation, March 16, 1861, in *Writings*, VIII, pp. 271–278.

32. Westwood, p. 129; Potter, pp. 350–351.

33. Hunt (ed.), pp. xi, 74.

34. Nevins (ed.), *Diary*, p. 115, April 6, 1861.

35. Hunt (ed.), pp. 74–76; Potter, p. 351; Westwood, pp. 138–140.

36. Potter, p. 350.

37. Quoted in Day and Ullom (eds.), p. 271. See also Westwood, p. 129.

38. *Texas Republican*, March 23, 1861, p. 1.

39. Houston to Colonel Charles A. Waite, March 29, 1861, in *Writings*, VIII, p. 294; Westwood, pp. 134–135.

40. Ford, *Rip Ford's Texas*, p. 321.

41. Ibid., p. 322.

42. Katherine Elliott, "The Frontier Regiment," pp. 17, 22.

43. Anon., to Edward Burleson, Jr., Aug. 1, 1861, E.C.B. 2B158.

44. Houston speech, March 31, 1861, in *Writings*, VIII, pp. 295–299.

45. Seale, pp. 211, 213, 237.

46. Ibid., pp. 203, 215; Friend, p. 349.

47. Seale, p. 195.

48. Margaret to Nancy Lea, Jan. 21, 1861, E.C.B. 2R50, Vol. 10.

49. Charles Power to Houston, April 16, 1861, ibid.

50. Houston speech, May 10, 1861, in *Writings*, VIII, pp. 301–304.

51. Houston to son Sam, May 22, 1861, ibid., pp. 306–307.

52. Unpaginated notes, E.C.B. 2G37 (Ben McCulloch Papers).

53. North, pp. 89, 95–97.

54. Seale, p. 215.

55. Quoted in North, pp. 90–93.

56. Houston to Maggie, April 10, 1862, E.C.B. 3N199.

57. Friend, p. 351.

58. Perkins, p. 664; Westwood, p. 126.

59. Lubbock, p. 314; Wheeler, dissertation, pp. 196–198; Buenger, p. 392; Ford, *Rip Ford's Texas*, p. 315.

60. Westwood, p. 127.

61. *Texas Republican*, Oct. 12, 1861, p. 2.

62. Houston to S. M. Swenson, Aug. 14, 1862, in *Writings*, VIII, p. 321.

63. See Harold B. Simpson, *Hood's Texas Brigade: A Compendium* (Hillsboro, Tex., 1977), *passim*; Wiley Sword, *Shiloh: Bloody April* (Dayton, Ohio, 1983), p. 166.

64. Ford, *Rip Ford's Texas*, p. 323.

65. Ibid., p. 329.

66. Wheeler, dissertation, pp. 273–274.

67. James McPherson, *Ordeal by Fire* (2 vols., New York, 1982), II, p. 229.

68. Cousin C.W.K.E. to Margaret, April 2, 1862, E.C.B. 2R44, B14/18.

69. Houston to Williamson S. Oldham, April 5, 1862, in *Writings*, VIII, p. 315.

70. McPherson, II, p. 229.

71. Quoted in David P. Smith, "Civil War Letters of Sam Houston," *Southwestern Historical Quarterly*, 81, No. 4 (1978), p. 421.

72. McPherson, II, p. 229; Sword, p. 460.

73. Houston to Maggie, April 10, 1862, E.C.B. 3N199.

74. Sword, p. 230.

75. Margaret to Maggie, May 10, 1862, E.C.B. 3N199; Ashbel Smith to Houston, April 16, 1862, E.C.B. 2R50, Vol. 11.

76. Hunt (ed.), pp. 95–97; Temple Lea Houston notes, E.C.B. 3L249.

77. Hunt (ed.), p. 108; Seale, p. 221.

78. Hunt (ed.), p. 108; Seale, p. 221.

79. Sam Houston, Jr., *Shiloh Shadows*, Part Two, and various notes, E.C.B. 3L249.

80. Seale, p. 225.

81. Margaret to Nannie, May 10, 1862, E.C.B. 3N198.

82. Seale, p. 224.

83. Ford, *Rip Ford's Texas*, p. 334.

84. Hunt (ed.), pp. 83, 85–88, 90.

85. Ehle, pp. 388–389.

86. Quoted in Hunt (ed.), p. 95.

87. Ford, *Rip Ford's Texas*, pp. 338–340n.

18. QUOTH THE RAVEN NEVERMORE

1. John H. Reagan, "A Conversation with Governor Houston," *The Quarterly of the Texas State Historical Association*, III, No. 4 (April 1900), p. 280.

2. Seale, p. 227.

3. Charles Power to Houston, April 14, 1863, E.C.B. 2R50, Vol. 11.

4. Houston to G. Robinson, May 27, 1863, in *Writings*, VIII, p. 346.

5. Quoted in Smith, "Civil War Letters," p. 423.

6. Houston to Nannie, April 14, 1863, in *Writings*, VIII, p. 345.

7. Charles Power to Houston, April 14, 1863, E.C.B. 2R50, Vol. 11.

8. Quoted in Smith, "Civil War Letters," p. 420.

9. Houston to Nannie, April 14, 1863, in *Writings*, VIII, p. 345.

10. Quoted in Smith, "Civil War Letters," p. 424.

11. Houston speech, March 18, 1863, in *Writings*, VIII, pp. 327–328.

12. Hunt (ed.), pp. 114–115.

13. Quoted in Ford, *Rip Ford's Texas*, p. 316n. See also Arthur James L. Fremantle, *The Fremantle Diary* (Boston, 1954), passim.

14. Margaret to Houston, June 8, 1863, E.C.B. 2R50, Vol. 11; Hunt (ed.), p. 117.

15. W. H. Kittrell, Notes, Nov. 30, 1926, E.C.B. 3L249; Seale, p. 231; Day and Ullom (eds.), p. 281.

16. Hunt (ed.), pp. 118–119.

17. Quoted in Seale, p. 233.

18. Ibid., pp. 232, 235.

19. *Tri-Weekly Telegraph* (Houston), July 29, 1863, in *Writings*, VIII, pp. 348–349.

20. See Hunt (ed.), pp. 122–123.

21. Inventory of Houston estate, Aug. 17, 1863, in *Writings*, VIII, pp. 341–343.

22. Hunt (ed.), p. 123.

23. Seale, p. 247.

24. Ibid, p. 239.

25. Margaret to son Sam, Nov. 24, 1863, E.C.B. 2R44, B14/18.

26. Seale, p. 238.

27. Margaret to Sam, Jan. 18, 1864, E.C.B. 3N198.

28. Margaret to Sam, Feb. 16, 1864, ibid.

29. Maggie to Sam, Feb. 16, 1864, ibid.

30. Maggie to Sam, Feb. 18, 1864, ibid.

31. Margaret to Sam, Feb. 18, 1864, ibid.; Sam to Margaret, from Mansfield, La., April 11, 1864, E.C.B. 2R44, B14/18.

32. William Alexander to Margaret, April 20, 1866, E.C.B. 2R50, Vol. 11.

33. William Carey Crane, *Life and Select Literary Remains of Sam Houston of Texas* (2 vols., New York, 1884), p. 3.

34. Margaret to Andrew, Sept. 3, 1867, E.C.B. 2R44, B14/18.

35. Margaret to Nannie, Oct. 25, 1867, E.C.B. 2R50, Vol. 11.

36. Hunt (ed.), p. 127; Seale, 257.

37. Seale, p. 263; Temple Houston Morrow, Notes, E.C.B. 2E253.

38. John Henry Brown to Commissioner J. J. Gross, Oct. 8, 1875, E.C.B. 2R50, Vol. 11.

BIBLIOGRAPHY

PRIMARY SOURCES: DOCUMENTS

Documents used in the writing of this book were drawn from a variety of archival sources, in addition to those found in edited, published works. The principal source of archival documents relating to Sam Houston, the people around him and Texas is the superbly organized Eugene C. Barker (E.C.B.) Texas History Collection at the University of Texas, Austin. There, I had the opportunity to draw from not only the papers and letters of Houston himself, but the papers of dozens of others whose lives touched his, such as Ben McCulloch, Anson Jones, Ashbel Smith, Edward Burleson, Jr., and David G. Burnet. Below, I list the important collections-within-collections, with their archival call numbers.

E.C.B. Number

2R275	Anon., "The United States Army in Texas, 1845–1860."
2Q444	Baker, Moseley, Letters.
2Q430	Barrett, D. C., Letters.
2R44, B14/18	Barrett, D. C., Letters.
2Q430	Baylor, Mary A., "Reminiscences."
3H52	Billingsly, Jesse, Papers.
3H90	Brooks, John Sowers, Papers.
2B158	Burleson, Edward (Sr. and Jr.), Papers.
2D222	Burnet, David G., Papers.
2J143	Campbell, John E., Letters.
2K262	Carrothers, Sam D., Family Papers.

2Q460	Cartwright, Robert L., typescript of *The Earliest American History of Texas* (1836).
2Q484	Coleman, Robert Morris, Papers, including *Houston Displayed: Or, Who Won the Battle of San Jacinto,* Velasco, 1837.
2Q503	Elliott, Katherine, typescript of "The Frontier Regiment, 1857–1861" (1921).
2D154	Ford, John Salmon, Papers.
2Q511	Ford, John Salmon, Memoirs (differs in many ways from the published version, *Rip Ford's Texas*).
2D222	Green, Thomas Jefferson, Papers.
3N197	Hearne (Madge Williams) Collection.
3N198	Hearne (Sam Houston) Collection.
3N199	Hearne (Sam Houston) Collection.
2D274	Henderson, James Pinckney, Family Papers.
2E239	Herndon, John Hunter, *Diary* (1837–1838).
2R44 B14/18	Houston, Margaret Lea, Letters.
2R49	Houston, Sam, Unpublished Correspondence (6 vols.).
2R50	Houston, Sam, Unpublished Correspondence (5 vols.).
2E250	Houston, Sam, Papers.
2E253	Houston, Sam, Papers.
2J142	Houston, Sam, Scrapbook.
3L249	Houston, Sam, Scrapbook.
2R56	Hunter, Robert Hancock, *Diary.*
2E265	Jackson, Andrew, Papers
2E272	Jones, Anson, Papers.
2E356	Lee, Robert E., Letters.
2J142	Lunn, Jesse D., Letter.
2J141	McClure, Alex, Land Grant, 1825.
3G37	McCulloch, Ben, Papers.
2.325/V21	McCulloch, Family Papers.
2R117	Miller, Washington D., Letter.
2Q309	Nacogdoches Archives.
2Q310	Nacogdoches Archives.
2G23	Reams, Sherwood Y., Letter.
2G180	Scott, Harriet Virginia, Letters.
A14/163	Smith, Ashbel, Papers.
2R204	Swisher, John M., *Remembrances of Texas and Texas People.*
2R275	Turner, Amasa, *Reminiscences.*
2.325/V8	Van Zandt, Isaac, Letters.
2J141	Yates, A. J., Letter.

Other documentary repositories consulted included the South Carolina Historical Society (SCHS), in Charleston, whose collection of scarce Texas and Tennessee state historical journals was of great value, as was the unpublished travel journal (1827) of Miss Julia Ann M. C. Conner. The Lilly Library, of

Indiana University, Bloomington, was also of considerable help, especially for its various scarce and rare pamphlets, and its (mainly Spanish-language) individual documents, which the reader will find cited in the text. In London, documents were consulted in the Foreign Office Files of the Public Record Office (PRO, FO), and cited according to volume and page numbers, and in the Additional Manuscripts Section of the British Museum (BM, Add. Ms.), cited in the same manner.

PRIMARY ACCOUNTS AND PRINTED SOURCES

Adams, Ephraim D., "British Correspondence Concerning Texas," *The Quarterly of the Texas State Historical Association*, XV, No. 3 (January 1912), pp. 118–131, and No. 4 (April 1912), pp. 295–355.

Alcorta, General Lino J., *Reglamento del Estado Mayor del Ejército que Debe Operar Sobre Tejas*, Mexico City, 1844.

Almonte, Juan Nepomuceno, *Noticia Estadística Sobre Tejas*, Mexico City, 1835.

Anon., *A Visit to Texas: Being the Journal of a Traveller Through Those Parts Most Interesting to American Settlers*, New York, 1834.

Austin, Estevan (Stephen) F., *Exposición al Público Sobre los Asuntos de Tejas*, Mexico City, 1835.

Austin, William T., "Account of the Campaign of 1835 by William T. Austin, Aide to General Stephen F. Austin and General Edward Burleson," *Texana*, IV, No. 4 (1966), pp. 287–322.

Bassett, John Spencer (ed.), *Correspondence of Andrew Jackson*, 6 vols., Washington, D.C., 1933.

Biographical Souvenir of the State of Texas, Chicago, 1889. Reprinted at Easly, S.C., 1978.

Bollaert, William, *William Bollaert's Texas*, Norman, Okla., 1956.

Boyle, Andrew A., "Reminiscences of the Texas Revolution," *The Quarterly of the Texas State Historical Association*, XIII, No. 4 (April 1910), pp. 285–292.

Burges, Tristam, *Speech of Mr. Burges of Rhode Island on the Case of Samuel Houston, Delivered May 11, 1832*, Washington, D.C., 1832.

Burnet, David G., *Memorial al Congreso General de los Estados Unidos Mexicanos*, April 13, 1833. Lilly Library.

————, "Burnet's Narrative of the Campaign," *The Quarterly of the Texas State Historical Association*, IV, No. 4 (April 1901), pp. 325–334.

————, *Review of the Life of Gen. Sam Houston*, New York, 1855. Pamphlet, E.C.B.

Calder, R. J., "R. J. Calder's Recollections of the Campaign," *The Quarterly of the Texas State Historical Association*, IV, No. 4 (April 1901), pp. 334–338.

Calderón de la Barca, Fanny, *Life in Mexico: The Letters of Fanny Calderón de la Barca*, Garden City, N.Y., 1966.

Calhoun, John C., *A Disquisition on Government, and Selections from the Discourse*, New York, 1953.

"The Clopper Correspondence, 1834–1838," *The Quarterly of the Texas State Historical Association*, XIII, No. 2 (October 1909), pp. 128–144.

Conner, Julia M. C., *Travel Journal, 1827*, Ms. in the Conner Family Papers, SCHS.

Correspondence Between Col. Anthony Butler and Gen. Sam Houston, New York, n.d. Pamphlet in Lilly Library.

Crane, William Carey, *Life and Select Literary Remains of Sam Houston of Texas*, 2 vols., Philadelphia, 1884.

Crockett, David, *A Narrative of the Life of David Crockett, of the State of Tennessee, Written by Himself*, Philadelphia, 1834.

Documents of Major Gen. Sam Houston, Commander in Chief of the Texian Army, to His Excellency David G. Burnet, President of the Republic of Texas, Containing a Detailed Account of the Battle of San Jacinto, Gonzales, Tex., 1874. Pamphlet in E.C.B.

Dresel, Gustav, *Gustav Dresel's Houston Journal: Adventures in North America and Texas, 1837–1841*, Austin, 1954.

Eckloff, Christian F., *Memoirs of a Senate Page (1855–1859)*, New York, n.d.

Edwards, Haden, Document petitioning for right to immigrate to Texas, January 5, 1824. Document in Lilly Library.

Emigrant, An, *Texas in 1840, or the Emigrant's Guide to the New Republic*, New York, 1840.

Falconer, Thomas, *On the Discovery of the Mississippi, and on the South-Western, Oregon, and North-Western Boundary of the United States*, London, 1844.

Featherstonhaugh, G. W., *Excursion Through the Slave States, from Washington on the Potomac to the Frontier of Mexico; with Sketches of Popular Manners and Geological Notices*, New York, 1844.

Filísola, Vicente, *Memorias para la Historia de la Guerra de Tejas, por el Sr. General de División . . . Don Vicente Filísola*, 2 vols., Mexico City, 1848–1849.

Flores, Dan L. (ed.), *Journal of an Indian Trader: Anthony Glass and the Texas Trading Frontier, 1790–1810*, College Station, Tex., 1983.

Ford, John Salmon, *Rip Ford's Texas*, Austin, 1962.

Frantz, Joe B., "The Sam Houston Letters: A Corner of Texas in Princeton," *Princeton University Library Chronicle*, XXXIII, No. 1 (1971), pp. 18–29.

Fremantle, Arthur James L., *The Fremantle Diary*, Boston, 1954.

Gaillardet, Frederic, *Sketches of Early Texas*, Austin, 1966.

Galveston Bay and Texas Land Company, Scrip No. 6292, Oct. 16, 1830. Document in Lilly Library.

Gorman, William A., *Speech in the House, Aug. 30, 1850*, Washington, D.C., 1850. Pamphlet in Lilly Library.

Graf, Leroy P., and Ralph W. Haskins, *The Papers of Andrew Johnson,* 4 vols., Memphis, Tenn., 1967–1976.

Green, Thomas Jefferson, *Journal of the Texian Expedition Against Mier; Subsequent Imprisonment of the Author; His Sufferings; and Final Escape from the Castle of Perote,* New York, 1845.

Guild, Josephus C., *Old Times in Tennessee, with Historical, Personal, and Political Scraps and Sketches,* Nashville, Tenn., 1878.

Gulick, C. A., et al. (eds.), *The Papers of Mirabeau Buonaparte Lamar,* 6 vols., Austin, 1921–1927.

Harwood, Frances, "Colonel Amasa Turner's Reminiscences of Galveston," *The Quarterly of the Texas State Historical Association,* III, No. 1 (July 1899), pp. 44–67.

Hemphill, W. Edwin (ed.), *The Papers of John C. Calhoun.* 18 vols., Columbia, S.C., 1961ff.

Holly, Mary Austin, *Texas: Observations, Historical, Geographical, and Descriptive,* Baltimore, 1833.

Hopkins, James F., and Mary W. M. Hargreaves (eds.), *The Papers of Henry Clay,* 5 vols., Lexington, Ky., 1959–1973.

Horton, Alexander, "Recollections of Alexander Horton," *Texana,* VII, No. 3 (1967), pp. 253–288.

Houston, Sam, *A Lecture on the Trials and Dangers of Frontier Life, as Exemplified in the History of Texas, by the Hon. Sam Houston, of Texas,* Philadelphia, 1851. Pamphlet in E.C.B.

Hunt, Lenoir (ed.), *My Master: The Inside Story of Sam Houston and His Times, by His Former Slave, Jeff Hamilton,* Dallas, 1940.

Irion, Shannon, and Garrett Jenkins (eds.), *Ever Thine Truly: Letters from Sam Houston to Anna Raguet,* Austin, 1975.

Jenkins, John H. (ed.), *Recollections of Early Texas: The Memoirs of John Holland Jenkins,* Austin, 1958.

Journals of the Convention, Assembled at the City of Austin on the Fourth of July, 1845, for the Purpose of Framing a Constitution for the State of Texas, Austin, 1845. Pamphlet in PRO, FO 75, XVI.

Kendall, George W., *Narrative of an Expedition Across the Great South-Western Prairies, from Texas to Santa Fe,* 2 vols., London, 1845.

Key, Francis S., *Speech of Francis S. Key, Esq., Counsel for Gen. Samuel Houston, on His Trial Before the House of Representatives for a Breach of Privilege,* Washington, D.C., 1832. Pamphlet in E.C.B.

Kleberg, Rosa, "Some of My Early Experiences in Texas," *The Quarterly of the Texas State Historical Association,* I, No. 4 (April 1898), pp. 297–302, and II, No. 2 (October 1898), pp. 170–173.

Kline, Mary-Jo (ed.), *Political Correspondence and Public Papers of Aaron Burr,* 3 vols., Princeton, N.J., 1983.

Lester, Charles Edwards, *The Life of Sam Houston (the Only Authentic Memoir of Him Ever Published),* New York, 1855.

———, *Sam Houston and His Republic,* New York, 1850.

Lubbock, Francis R., *Six Decades in Texas: The Memoirs of Francis R. Lubbock, Confederate Governor of Texas*, Austin, 1968.

Mayo, Robert, *Political Sketches of Eight Years in Washington*, Baltimore, 1839.

McDonald, Archie P. (ed.), *Hurrah for Texas! The Diary of Adolphus Sterne, 1838–1851*, Waco, Tex., 1969.

Melish, John, *Information and Advice to Emigrants to the United States*, 1819.

Meyrick, Edwin, *The Texian Grand March for the Piano Forte; Respectfully Dedicated to Genl. Houston and His Brave Companions in Arms*, New York, 1836. Musical score, in Lilly Library.

Molinos del Campo, Francisco, *El Sistema de Compañías Presidiales Para la Defensa de los Estados Interiores*, April 27, 1826. Document in Lilly Library.

Morrell, Z. N., *Flowers and Fruits in the Wilderness: or, Forty-six Years in Texas and Two Winters in Honduras*, 4th ed., Dallas, 1886.

Muir, Andrew F. (ed.), *Texas in 1837: An Anonymous, Contemporary Narrative*, Austin, 1958.

Nevins, Allan, and Milton Halsey Thomas (eds.), *The Diary of George Templeton Strong: The Civil War, 1860–1865*, New York, 1952.

Nevins, Allan (ed.), *The Diary of John Quincy Adams, 1794–1845*, New York, 1951.

Niles, John M., *History of South America and Mexico, Comprising Their Discovery, Geography, Politics, Commerce and Revolutions, to Which Is Annexed, a Geographical and Historical View of Texas*, Hartford, Conn., 1839. In Lilly Library.

North, Thomas, *Five Years in Texas, or, What You Did Not Hear During the War from January 1861 to January 1866: A Narrative of His Travels, Experiences, and Observations in Texas and Mexico*, Cincinnati, Ohio, 1871.

Olmsted, Frederick Law, *A Journey Through Texas, or, a Saddle-Trip on the Southwestern Frontier*, New York, 1860.

Pike, James, *Scout and Ranger: Being the Personal Adventures of James Pike, of the Texas Rangers in 1859–1860*, Cincinnati, Ohio, 1865.

Quaife, Milo Milton (ed.), *The Diary of James K. Polk, During His Presidency, 1845 to 1849*, 4 vols., Chicago, 1910.

Rankin, Melinda, *Texas in 1850*, Waco, Tex., 1966.

Ruffin, Edmund, *The Diary of Edmund Ruffin*, 2 vols., Baton Rouge, La., 1972–1976.

Santa Anna, Antonio López de, et al., *The Mexican Side of the Texan Revolution, 1836, by the Chief Mexican Participants*, Dallas, 1956.

Schwaab, Eugene L. (ed.), *Travels in the Old South: Selected from Periodicals of the Times*, 2 vols., Lexington, Ky., 1973.

Sibley, Marilyn M. (ed.), "Letters from Sam Houston to Albert Sidney Johnston, 1836–1837," *Southwestern Historical Quarterly*, LXVI, No. 2 (1962–1963), pp. 252–261.

———, *Samuel H. Walker's Account of the Mier Expedition*, Waco, Tex., 1978.

Smith, Ashbel, *Reminiscences of the Texas Republic*, Galveston, Tex., 1876. Pamphlet in E.C.B.

Smith, David, "Civil War Letters of Sam Houston," *Southwestern Historical Quarterly*, LXXXI, No. 4 (1978), pp. 417–426.

Smith, Henry (ed.), *With Milam and Fannin: Adventures of a German Boy [Herman Ehrenberg] in Texas' Revolution*, Austin, 1968.

Smither, Harriet, "Diary of Adolphus Sterne," *Southwestern Historical Quarterly*, XXXI, No. 2 (1927–1928), pp. 181–187.

Stephens, John L., *Incidents of Travel in Yucatan*, 2 vols., New York, 1843.

The Texas Almanac for 1861, Galveston, 1860.

Urrea, José, *Diario de las Operaciónes Militares de la División Que al Mando del General José Urrea Hizo la Campaña de Tejas*, Durango, Mexico, 1838.

Weaver, Herbert (ed.), *Correspondence of James K. Polk*, 4 vols., Nashville, Tenn., 1969–1979.

Williams, Amelia W., and Eugene C. Barker (eds.), *The Writings of Sam Houston*, 8 vols., Austin, 1938–1943.

Yoakum, Henderson, *History of Texas from Its First Settlement in 1685 to Its Annexation to the United States in 1846*, 2 vols., New York, 1855.

Zuber, William Physick, *My Eighty Years in Texas*, Austin, 1971.

SECONDARY SOURCES: BOOKS

Adams, Ephraim D., *British Interests and Activities in Texas, 1838–1846*, Gloucester, Mass., 1963.

Agnew, Brad, *Fort Gibson: Terminal on the Trail of Tears*, Norman, Okla., 1980.

Andrist, Ralph K., *The Long Death: The Last Days of the Plains Indian*, New York, 1964.

Bancroft, Hubert Howe, *History of Utah*, San Francisco, 1890.

Barnum, Phineas T., *The Life of P. T. Barnum, Written by Himself*, New York, 1855.

Bate, W. N., *General Sidney Sherman: Texas Soldier, Statesman and Builder*, Waco, Tex., 1974.

Baugh, Virgil E., *Rendezvouz at the Alamo*, New York, 1960.

Bazant, Jan, *A Concise History of Mexico*, London, 1977.

Bearss, Edwin C., and Arrell M. Gibson, *Fort Smith: Little Gibraltar on the Arkansas*, Norman, Okla., 1969.

Belohlavek, John M., *"Let the Eagle Soar!" The Foreign Policy of Andrew Jackson*, Lincoln, Nebr., 1985.

Bemis, Samuel F., *The Latin American Policy of the United States: An Historical Interpretation*, New York, 1943.

Best, Hugh (ed.), *Debrett's Texas Peerage*, New York, 1983.

Braider, Donald, *Solitary Star: A Biography of Sam Houston*, New York, 1974.

Brown, Charles H., *Agents of Manifest Destiny: The Lives and Times of the Filibusters*, Chapel Hill, N.C., 1980.

Brown, John Henry, *Life and Times of Henry Smith, the First American Governor of Texas*, Dallas, 1887.

Bushnell, David, and Neill Macaulay, *The Emergence of Latin America in the Nineteenth Century*, Cambridge, Mass., 1988.

Carruth, Gordon (ed.), *The Encyclopedia of American Facts and Dates*, 9th ed., New York, 1989.

Chitwood, Oliver Perry, *John Tyler: Champion of the Old South*, New York, 1939.

Christian, Asa Kyrus, *Mirabeau Buonaparte Lamar*, Austin, 1922.

Clarke, Mary W., *Chief Bowles and the Texas Cherokees*, Norman, Okla., 1971.

———, *Thomas J. Rusk, Soldier, Statesman, Jurist*, Austin, 1971.

Coffman, Edward M., *The Old Army: A Portrait of the American Army in Peacetime, 1784–1898*, New York, 1986.

Cooper, William J., Jr., *The South and the Politics of Slavery, 1828–1856*, Baton Rouge, La., 1978.

Cotterill, R. S., *The Southern Indians: The Story of the Civilized Tribes Before Removal*, Norman, Okla., 1954.

Craven, Avery O., *The Growth of Southern Nationalism, 1848–1861*, Baton Rouge, La., 1953.

Crawford, Charles W., *Governors of Tennessee*, 2 vols., Memphis, Tenn., 1979.

Crenshaw, Ollinger, *The Slave States in the Presidential Election of 1860*, Baltimore, 1945.

Curtis, George Ticknor, *The Life of James Buchanan*, 2 vols., New York, 1883.

Daddysman, James W., "The Matamoros Trade, 1861–1865." Ph.D. dissertation, University of West Virginia, 1967.

Davidson, James West, and Mark Hamilton Lytle, *After the Fact: The Art of Historical Detection*, 2d ed., New York, 1986.

Davis, John L., *The Danish Texans*, Austin, 1979.

Day, Donald, and Harry H. Ullom (eds.), *The Autobiography of Sam Houston*, Norman, Okla., 1954.

DeVoto, Bernard, *The Year of Decision, 1846*, Boston, 1943.

Dictionary of American Biography. 21 vols., New York, 1928–1944.

Dillon, Richard H., *J. Ross Browne: Confidential Agent in Old California*, Norman, Okla., 1965.

Ehle, John, *Trail of Tears: The Rise and Fall of the Cherokee Nation*, New York, 1988.

Eisenhower, John S. D., *So Far from God: The U.S. War with Mexico, 1846–1848*, New York, 1989.

Faulk, Odie B., *The Crimson Desert: Indian Wars of the American Southwest*, New York, 1974.

———, *The Last Years of Spanish Texas, 1778–1821*, London, 1964.

Friend, Llerena, *Sam Houston: The Great Designer*, Austin, 1954.

Fuller, John D. P., *The Movement for the Acquisition of All Mexico, 1846–1848*, Baltimore, 1936.

Gambrell, Herbert, *Anson Jones: The Last President of Texas*, Garden City, N.Y., 1948.

Garrett, Jill L. (ed.), *Obituaries from Tennessee Newspapers*, Easley, S.C., 1950 (?).

Hayes, Melvin L., *Mr. Lincoln Runs for President*, New York, 1960.

Heiskell, Samuel G., *Andrew Jackson and Early Tennessee History*, 2d ed., 2 vols., Nashville, Tenn., 1920.

Hesseltine, William B. (ed.), *Three Against Lincoln: Murat Halstead Reports the Caucuses of 1860*, Baton Rouge, La., 1960.

Horgan, Paul, *The Great River: The Rio Grande in North American History*, 2 vols., New York, 1954.

James, Marquis, *The Raven: A Biography of Sam Houston*, New York, 1929.

Jenkins, John H., *Audubon and Other Capers: Confessions of a Texas Bookmaker*, Austin, 1976.

Jones, Oakah, Jr., *Santa Anna*, New York, 1968.

Jordan, Terry G., *German Seed in Texas Soil: Immigrant Farmers in Nineteenth Century Texas*, Austin, 1966.

Keegan, John, *The Face of Battle*, New York, 1976.

Kingston, Michael T. (ed.), *The Texas Almanac, 1984–1985*, Dallas, 1983.

Kiple, Kenneth F., *Blacks in Colonial Cuba, 1774–1899*, Gainesville, Fla., 1976.

Kreneck, Thomas H., "Sam Houston's Quest for Personal Harmony: An Interpretation." Ph.D. dissertation, Bowling Green State University, 1981.

Lavender, David, *The Great West*, Boston, 1985.

Lossing, Benson J., *The Pictorial Field-Book of the War of 1812*, New York, 1868.

Lucas, Silas Emmett, Jr., *Marriages from Early Tennessee Newspapers, 1794–1851*, Easley, S.C., 1920 (?).

Mahon, John K., *The War of 1812*, Gainesville, Fla., 1972.

Maynaghi, Russell, "The Indian Slave Trade: The Comanche, a Case Study." Ph.D. dissertation, St. Louis University, 1970.

McCormac, Eugene I., *James K. Polk: A Political Biography*, Berkeley, Calif., 1922.

McElroy, Robert, *Jefferson Davis: The Unreal and the Real*, 2 vols., New York, 1937.

McGrath, Sister Paul of the Cross, *Political Nativism in Texas, 1825–1860*, Washington, D.C., 1957.

McMurtrie, Douglas C., *The Establishment of the First Texas Newspaper*, El Paso, Tex., 1971.

McPherson, James, M., *Ordeal by Fire*, 2 vols., New York, 1982.

Meinig, Donald W., *Imperial Texas: An Interpretative Essay in Cultural Geography*, Austin, 1969.

Merk, Frederick, *Slavery and the Annexation of Texas*, New York, 1972.

Millis, Walter, *Arms and Men: America's Military History and Military Policy from the Revolution to the Present*, New York, 1956.

Moody, Ralph, *Old Trails West*, Salt Lake City, Utah, 1963.

Nackman, Mark Edward, "The Texas Experience, 1821–1861: The Emergence of Texas as a Separate Province and Texans as a Breed Apart." Ph.D. dissertation, Columbia University, 1973.

Nance, Joseph Milton, *After San Jacinto: The Texas-Mexican Frontier, 1836–1841*, Austin, 1963.

———, *Attack and Counter-Attack: The Texas-Mexican Frontier, 1842*, Austin, 1964.

Niven, John, *John C. Calhoun and the Price of Union: A Biography*, Baton Rouge, La., 1988.

———, *Martin Van Buren: The Romantic Age of American Politics*, New York, 1983.

Perkins, Howard Cecil (ed.), *Northern Editorials on Secession*, New York, 1942.

Perrett, Geoffrey, *A Country Made by War: From the Revolution to Vietnam —the Story of America's Rise to Power*, New York, 1989.

Peterson, Merrill D., *The Great Triumvirate: Webster, Clay, and Calhoun*, New York, 1987.

Pierson, George W. (ed.), *Tocqueville and Beaumont in America*, New York, 1938.

Platt, D. C. M., *Latin America and British Trade, 1806–1914*, New York, 1973.

Potter, David M., *Lincoln and His Party in the Secession Crisis*, New Haven, Conn., 1942.

Przygoda, Jacek, *Texas Pioneers from Poland: A Study in the Ethnic History*, Waco, Tex., 1971.

Ransom, Harry Hunt, *The Other Texas Frontier*, Austin, 1984.

Reed, Nelson, *The Caste War of Yucatan*, Stanford, Calif., 1964.

Remini, Robert V., *Andrew Jackson and the Course of American Empire, 1767–1821*, 3 vols., New York, 1977–1984.

———, *The Life of Andrew Jackson*, New York, 1988.

Rorabaugh, W. J., *The Alcoholic Republic: An American Tradition*, New York, 1979.

Seager, Robert, Jr., *And Tyler Too: A Biography of John and Julia Gardiner Tyler*, New York, 1963.

Seale, William, *Sam Houston's Wife: A Biography of Margaret Lea Houston*, Norman, Okla., 1970.

Sellers, Charles Grier, *James K. Polk, Jacksonian, 1795–1843*, Princeton, N.J., 1957.

Siegel, Stanley, *A Political History of the Texas Republic, 1836–1845*, Austin, 1956.

Simpson, Harold B., *Hood's Texas Brigade: A Compendium*, Hillsboro, Tex., 1977.

Simpson, Leslie B., *Many Mexicos*, 3d ed., Berkeley, Calif., 1962.

Skrabanek, Robert L., *We're Czechs*, College Station, Tex., 1988.

Smith, Elbert B., *Magnificent Missourian: The Life of Thomas Hart Benton*, New York, 1958.

Sobel, Robert, and John Raimo (eds.), *Biographical Directory of the Governors of the United States, 1789–1978*, 4 vols., Westport, Conn., 1978.

Strode, Hudson, *Jefferson Davis: American Patriot, 1808–1861*, 3 vols., New York, 1955–1964.

Sword, Wiley, *Shiloh: Bloody April*, Dayton, Ohio, 1983.

Turner, Martha Anne, *Sam Houston and His Twelve Women: The Ladies Who Influenced the Live of Texas' Greatest Statesman*, Austin, 1966.

Van Deusen, Glyndon G., *William Henry Seward*, New York, 1967.

Van Every, Dale, *The Final Challenge: The American Frontier, 1804–1845*, New York, 1964.

Webb, Walter Prescott, *The Texas Rangers: A Century of Frontier Defense*, New York, 1935.

Weber, David J., *The Mexican Frontier, 1821–1846: The American Southwest Under Mexico*, Albuquerque, N. Mex., 1982.

Weems, John Edward, *Dream of Empire: A Human History of the Republic of Texas, 1836–1846*, New York, 1971.

Weigley, Russel, *The American Way of War*, Bloomington, Ind., 1976.

Wellman, Paul I., *The House Divides: The Age of Jackson and Lincoln, from the War of 1812 to the Civil War*, New York, 1966.

Wells, Tom H., *Commodore Moore and the Texas Navy*, Austin, 1988.

Wheeler, Kenneth William, "Early Urban Development in Texas, 1836–1865." Ph.D. dissertation, University of Rochester (N.Y.), 1964.

White, Lonnie J., *Politics on the Southwestern Frontier: Arkansas Territory, 1819–1836*, Memphis, Tenn., 1964.

Wilhelm, Hubert G. H., "Organized German Settlement and Its Effect on the Frontier of South-Central Texas." Ph.D. dissertation, Louisiana State University, 1960(?).

Williams, John Hoyt, *A Great and Shining Road: The Story of the Transcontinental Railroad*, New York, 1988.

———, *The Rise and Fall of the Paraguayan Republic, 1800–1870*. Austin, 1979.

Wisehart, M. K., *Sam Houston: American Giant*, Washington, D.C., 1962.

Wooster, Ralph A., *The Secession Conventions of the South*, Princeton, N.J., 1962.

Wyatt-Brown, Bertram, *Honor and Violence in the Old South*, New York, 1986.

SECONDARY SOURCES: ARTICLES

Baggett, James Alex, "The Constitutional Union Party in Texas," *Southwestern Historical Quarterly*, LXXXII, No. 3 (Jan. 1979), pp. 233–264.

Barbee, David Rankin, "The Line of Blood: Lincoln and the Coming of the War," *Tennessee Historical Quarterly*, XVI, No. 1 (March 1957), pp. 3–54.

———, "Sam Houston—the Last Phase," *Tennessee Historical Quarterly*, XIII, No. 1 (March 1954), pp. 12–64.

Barker, Eugene C., "The San Jacinto Campaign," *The Quarterly of the Texas State Historical Association*, IV, No. 4 (April 1901), pp. 260–344.

Brister, Louis E., "Colonel Eduard Harkort: A German Soldier of Fortune in Mexico and Texas, 1832–1836," *Southwestern Historical Quarterly*, LXXXVIII, No. 3 (Jan. 1985), pp. 229–246.

Buenger, Walter L., "Secession and the Texas German Community: Editor Lindheimer vs. Editor Flake," *Southwestern Historical Quarterly*, LXXXII, No. 4 (April 1979), pp. 379–402.

Campbell, Randolph, "Texas and the Nashville Convention of 1850," *Southwestern Historical Quarterly*, LXXVI, No. 1 (Sept. 1972), pp. 1–14.

Corn, James F., "Sam Houston: The Raven," *Journal of Cherokee Studies*, VI, No. 1 (Feb. 1981), pp. 34–49.

Corner, William, "John Crittenden Duval: The Last Survivor of the Goliad Massacre," *The Quarterly of the Texas State Historical Association*, I, No. 1 (July 1897), pp. 47–67.

Dienst, Alexander, "The Navy of the Republic of Texas," *The Quarterly of the Texas State Historical Association*, XIII, No. 2 (Oct. 1909), pp. 85–127.

Dunn, William Edward, "Apache Relations in Texas, 1718–1750," *The Quarterly of the Texas State Historical Association*, XIV, No. 3 (Jan. 1911), pp. 198–269.

Hay, Thomas Robson, "Who Is James K. Polk?" *Tennessee Historical Magazine*, VII, No. 4 (Jan. 1922), pp. 235–242.

"Houston at a Glance," *New York Times*, July 5, 1990, p. A9.

Johnson, George, "A Menace or Just a Crank?" *New York Times Book Review*, June 18, 1989, p. 7.

Jones, Robert L., and Pauline H. Jones, "Memucan Hunt: His Private Life," *Texana*, IV, No. 3 (1966), pp. 213–232.

Oates, Stephen B., "Hugh F. Young's Account of the Snively Expedition as Told to John S. Ford," *Southwestern Historical Quarterly*, LXX, No. 1 (Sept. 1966), pp. 71–92.

Parks, Norman L., "The Career of John Bell as Congressman from Tennessee, 1827–1841," *Tennessee Historical Quarterly*, I, No. 3 (Sept. 1943), pp. 229–249.

Reagan, John H., "A Conversation with Governor Houston," *The Quarterly of the Texas State Historical Association*, III, No. 4 (April 1900), pp. 279–281.

———, "Expulsion of the Cherokees from East Texas," *The Quarterly of the Texas State Historical Association*, I, No. 1 (July 1897), pp. 38–46.

Rutherford, Philip, "Texas Leaves the Union," *Civil War Times Illustrated,* XX, No. 3 (1981), pp. 12–23.

Seale, William, "The House That Sam Houston Never Built," *Southwestern Historical Quarterly,* LXXXVII, No. 4 (April 1984), pp. 393–400.

Sibley, Marilyn M., "James Hamilton, Jr., vs. Sam Houston: Repercussions of the Nullification Controversy," *Southwestern Historical Quarterly,* LXXXIX, No. 2 (Oct. 1985), pp. 165–180.

Smith, Culver H., "Andrew Jackson, Post Obitum," *Tennessee Historical Quarterly,* IV, No. 3 (Sept. 1945), pp. 195–221.

Stenberg, Richard R., "The Texas Schemes of Jackson and Houston, 1829–1836," *Social Science Quarterly,* L, No. 4 (1970), pp. 944–965.

Tessendorf, K. C., "The Texas Navy's Last Hurrah," *United States Naval Institute Proceedings,* June 1988, pp. 68–71.

Westwood, Howard C., "President Lincoln's Overture to Sam Houston," *Southwestern Historical Quarterly,* LXXXVIII, No. 2 (April 1984), pp. 125–144.

Wooster, Ralph A., "Texas Military Operations Against Mexico, 1842–1843," *Southwestern Historical Quarterly,* LXVII, No. 4 (July 1966), pp. 465–484.

INDEX